Land Records
Of
King George County
Virginia
1721—1743

Sue Ann Damron

Willow Bend Books
Westminster, Maryland
1999

Willow Bend Books

65 East Main Street
Westminster, Maryland 21157-5036
1-800-876-6103

Source books, early maps, CD's—Worldwide

For our listing of thousands of titles offered
by hundreds of publishers
see our website
<www.WillowBend.net>

Visit our retail store

International Standard Book Number: 1-58549-052-0

Printed in the United States of America

Table of Contents

Preface

King George County, Virginia was formed from Richmond County in 1721 This work is based on a microfilm copy of Deed Books 1 and 2. Except for a few missing pages the records are complete for this period 1721 to 1743.

The Publisher
Westminster, Maryland
1999

Preface

King George County, Virginia, was formed from Stafford County in 1721. This is the transcription of the Deed Books and tax records.

Clan Publishers

Westminster, Maryland

KING GEORGE COUNTY, VIRGINIA, DEED BOOK 1

Pages 1:1 and 2 are missing.

1:3 - DEED OF RELEASE - 30 June 1721 - Cornelius Edmonds of Sittenburn Parish to William Grant. 50 pounds sterling for 185A formerly belonging to Nebichodnizor Jones who bequeathed to his son John Jones who bequeathed to his sister Ann Dean who with her husband Charles Dean sold it to Cornelius Edmonds. Bounded by land of David Brenough. Power of Attorney to William Brooks to release right of dower, signed by Anne Edmonds wife of Cornelius Edmonds; acknowledged in presence of Charles Dean and Joseph Wing. Signed Cornelius Edmonds. Delivered in presence of Joseph Wing and Alexander Carson. Recorded 7 July 1721 E. Turbervile.

1:5 - BOND - 30 June 1721 - Cornelius Edmonds bound to William Grant in the sum of 100 pounds sterling. Condition such that if Cornelius Edmonds observes true intent and meaning of a certain deed bearing same date, obligation is void. Delivered in presence of Joseph Winge and Alexander Carson. Recorded 7 July 1721 E. Turbervile.

1:5 - POWER OF ATTORNEY - 10 February 1720 - Sir Abraham Elton, Baron; Peter Day, Esq.; Lewis Casamajor, merchant; and John Thomas, merchant, all of the city of Bristol and executors of the last will and testament of Isaac Elton, late of the city of Bristol merchant; and also John Beecher and Thomas Longman, merchants of same city appoint George Mason of Potomack River in Virginia Esquire and William Stratton of the city of Bristol marrinor their true and lawful attorneys to recover from Henry Connyers of Potomack River in Virginia and from all and every person all such that was contracted by and due and owing to Arthur Jackson their factor and agent. Signed Abra. Elton, Pr. Day, L. Cassamajor, John Beecher, Thomas Longman. Delivered in presence of Edward James, John Evans, James Adams. Recorded 7 July 1721 E. Turbervile.

1:6 - WILL - 24 October 1717 - Francis James of Sittonburn Parish in the county of Richmond bequeathed to son Sherwood James all that plantation whereon Francis now lives being 50A; that 50A he bought of sister-in-law Martha Marshall adjoining upon the above 50A and also upon the branches of Thatchers dam; and one young bay mare branded IF on near buttock when he shall arrive and come to the age of 21 years. All the rest of personal estate to be equally divided between daughter Jane James and wife Margaret James who is appointed sole Executrix. Signed Francis James. Delivered in presence of John Gilbert, Peter Jett, Mary Hasell. Recorded 7 July 1721E.Turbervile.

1:7 - POWER OF ATTORNEY - 13 January 1720 - Cornelius Sarjant, the

Elder; Caleb Lloyc; Cornelius Sarjant, the Younger; Samuel Wyatt; Thomas Smith; and John Pollard, assignee of George Bridges, all of the city of Bristol and owners of the ship called Crown Frigate of Bristol, appoint William Sarjant, merchant of the city of Bristol, their true and lawful attorney to remove such belonging to said owners now in the custody and possession of William Skrine. Signed Cornelius Sarjant, the Elder; Caleb Lloyd; Cornelius Sarjant, the Younger; Samuel Wyatt; Thos. Smith, John Pollard. Delivered in presence of William Lloyd, John Eagelston, John Bengall. Recorded 4 August 1721 E. Turbervile.

1:8 - POWER OF ATTORNEY - 14 January 1720 - Cornelius Sarjant, the Elder; Caleb Lloyd; John Walker; Samuel Wyatt; and Aquilas Bevan, all of the city of Bristol, merchants and owners of the ship George Gally of Bristol, appoint William Sarjant of the city of Bristol to demand and receive from William Skrine all such belonging to said owners. Signed Cornelius Sarjant, the Elder; Caleb Lloyd; John Walker; Saml. Wyatt; Aquilas Bevan. Delivered in presence of William Lloyd, John Eagelstone, John Bengall. Recorded 4 August 1721 E. Turbervile.

1:9 - POWER OF ATTORNEY - 16 January 1720 - William Reeve, John Reeve, Caleb Lloyd, Edward Lowe and John Parkin, all of the city of Bristol merchants appoint Major Nicholas Smith of Rappahanock River in Virginia merchant our lawful attorney to demand and recover from William Skrine all that is due upon accounts of the ship Bensworth, Nicholas Gardner master of said ship. Signed Wm. Reeve, John Reeve, Caleb Lloyd, Edwd. Lowe, Jno. Parkin. Delivered in presence of William Lloyd, John Bengall. Recorded 4 August 1721 E. Turbervile.

1:10 - INDENTURE - 10 August 1721 - Michael Neal of Hanover Parish, planter in consideration of 2500 pounds of tobacco binds himself a servant to William Rowly from the day of the date hereof for and during the term of 2 years 4 mos. 15 days. In consideration of which the said William Rowly agrees to find and allow him good and sufficient meat, drink, washing, and lodging according to the custom of servants in such cases. Signed Michael Neal. Delivered in presence of Joseph Rainolds, John Mardos, E. Turbervile. Recorded 1 September 1721 E. Turbervile.

1:11 - DEED OF SALE - 30 August 1721 - Nicholas Smith of Sittenburn Parish, gentleman to John Spicer, gentleman. 5 pounds sterling for 1A purchased by Smith from John Paine. Bounded by Paine and a run called Bever Dam run. Signed Nicholas Smith. Memorandum dated 31 August 1721 signed by Cornelius Edmonds and Thomas Brock. Delivered in presence of Cornelius Edmonds, Charles Steward. Recorded 1 September 1721 E. Turbervile.

1:12 - DEED OF LEASE - 11 August 1721 - John Motlen of St. Anne's Parish in Essex County, planter to Merriday Price of Sittenburn Parish, planter. 5 shillings sterling to lease 130A bought by Major Nicholas Smith of William Stone and Catherine his wife and sold by Major Smith to John Motlen. Bounded by Silvester Thatcher, Samuel Nicholls, a swamp which empties itself into Thatchers Creek. Signed John Motlen. Delivered in the presence of John Gilbert, John Paine. Recorded 1 September 1721 E. Turbervile.

1:13 - DEED OF RELEASE - 12 August 1721 - John Motlen of St. Anne's Parish in Essex County, planter to Meriday Price of Sittenburn Parish, planter. 32 pounds sterling and 2000 pounds of tobacco for 130A described in deed of lease. Elizabeth, wife of John Motlen, authorizes John Gilbert power of attorney to relinquish her right of dower, acknowledged by John Paine, Thomas Monroe. Signed John Motlen. Delivered in presence of John Gilbert, John Paine. Recorded 1 September 1721 E. Turbervile.

1:14 - DEED OF LEASE - 10 July 1721 - Richard Tutt of Sittenbourne Parish, planter to John King, Esquire and Company, merchants in Bristol and setlers of the Iron Works in the aforesaid parish. 100 pounds sterling to lease 50A and Grist Mill for remaining 48 years of a 99 year lease. Whereas Major William Underwood,dec'd, did by deed dated 4 July 1680 sell mill and 50A to John Foxhall, late of Popes Creek in Westmoreland county, to hold said mill and 50A for 99 years; and John Foxhall, by his will bequeathed unto John Elliott and James Vaulx, both of Westmoreland county, his right and title to mill for remainder of original 99 years; and upon their deaths said lease went to Francis Gouldman and Paul Mason of St. Anne's Parish in Essex County; and thence to Richard Tutt. Signed Richard Tutt. Delivered in presence of Phillip Ellway, George Mullins, Thomas Baker. Recorded 3 November 1721 E. Turbervile.

1:18 - DEED - 10 July 1721 - John Underwood of Sittenbourne Parish, planter and son of William Underwood, dec'd, makes over his right of reversion and inheritance of that grist mill commonly called and known by the name of Major Underwood's Mill to John King and Company, merchants in Bristol and setlers of the Iron Works, for 20 pounds sterling for 50A and Grist Mill. Signed John Underwood who personally acknowledged this deed to John Lomax, gentleman, to the use of John King,Esquire, and Company. Delivered in presence of Phillip Ellway, Geo. Mullins, Thos. Baker. Recorded 3 Novemer 1721 E. Turbervile.

1:20 - DEED OF LEASE - 5 October 1721 - Henry Fewell of Stafford County to Margaret Heaberd of same. 500 pounds of tobacco to lease 50A formerly belonging to John Owens of Richmond County who deeded it to Stephen Fewell 20 February 1694 from whom Henry inherited it. Bounded by the south side of a branch of Poplar Swamp, land of James Lamb. Signed Henry Fewell.

Delivered in presence of David Waugh, Grace Waugh. Recorded 6 October 1721 E. Turberville.

1:21- DEED OF RELEASE - 6 October 1721 - Henry Fewell of Stafford County to Margaret Heaberd, widow, 3000 pounds of tobacco for 50A described in deed of lease. Catherine Fewell relinquishes all her right of dower and thirds. Signed Henry Fewell. Delivered in presence of David Waugh, Grace Waugh. Recorded 6 October 1721 E. Turbervile.

1:22 - INDENTURE - 16 September 1721 - Thomas Riddle of Hanover Parish, planter in consideration of 1590 pounds of good tobacco, binds himself to Benjamin Rush, planter of same for a term of 3 years 3 months 14 days for good and sufficient meat and drink, washing, lodging, and clothes according to custom. Signed Thos. Riddle. Delivered in presence of John Skinner, Thomas Steward, Richard Elkins. Recorded 6 October 1721 E. Turbervile.

1:23 - DEED OF LEASE - 2 November 1721 - John Grason of Spotsylvania County, planter to William Pattishall of Christ Church Parish in Middlesex County. 5 shillings current Virginia money to lease 908A on Gravelly Run. Being part of a tract granted 2 June 1704 to Andrew Jackson of Lancaster County by the honorable Robert Carter,Esquire, agent and attorney of Margueritte, Lady Culpepper, Thomas Lord Fairfax and Catherine his wife, Proprietors of the Northern Neck of Virginia. Surveyed, marked, and bounded by Edwin Conway. Signed John Grayson. Delivered in presence of John Grimsly, John James, John Cooke. Recorded 3 November 1721 E. Turbervile.

1:24 - DEED OF RELEASE - 3 November 1721 - John Grayson, planter to William Pattishall of Christ Church Parish in Middlesex County. 110 pounds sterling for 908A described in lease. Now bounded by James Jones, John Waugh. Susanna Grayson, wife of John Grayson, authorized Mr. John Grimsly to acknowledge her release of dower and thirds, acknowledged by Waugh Darnall, John Cooke, John James. Signed John Grayson. Delivered in presence of John Cooke, John Grimsly, John James. Recorded 3 November 1721 E. Turbervile.

1:26 - BOND - 3 November 1721 - John Grason of Spotsylvania County binds himself in the amount of 500 pounds sterling to William Pattishall of Middlesex County. Condition such that if terms of indentures of lease and release are observed, obligation is void. Signed John Grayson. Delivered in presence of Waugh Darnall, John Cooke. Recorded 3 November 1721 E. Turberville.

1:26 - DEED OF LEASE - 2 November 1721 - Nicholas Smith of Sittenbourn Parish, gentleman, to Richarad Tutt, planter. 5 shillings sterling to lease 227A being the uppermost part of a tract of land commonly called Moyakin between Nicholas Smith and Nathaniel Pope,dec'd, late practioner at law of Westmoreland County. Part of 580A patent to William Yarrel and Francis Whitington dated 29 July 1650 which by means of conveyance became the right of John Tankard of Northampton who by deed dated 11 February 1708 sold it to Nicholas Smith. Signed Nicholas Smith. Delivered in presence of Thos. Turner, Wm. Underwood. Recorded 3 November 1721 E. Turbervile.

1:27 - DEED OF RELEASE - 3 November 1721 - Nicholas Smith of Sittenbourn Parish, gentleman, to Richard Tutt of same, planter. 100 pounds sterling for 227A described in lease. Signed Nicholas Smith. Delivered in presence of Thos. Turner,Wm. Underwood. Recorded 3 November 1721 E. Turberville.

1:29 - BOND - 3 November 1721 - Nicholas Smith bound to Richard Tutt for 200 pounds sterling. Condition such that if terms of deeds of lease and release are met, obligation is void. Signed Nicholas Smith. Delivered in presence of Thos. Turner, Wm. Underwood. Recorded 3 November 1721 E. Turbervile.

1:30 - POWER OF ATTORNEY - 2 November 1721 - Katherine Fewel, relict of Stephen Fewell, dec'd, appoints John Farguson to release her right of dower to 100A sold by son Henry Fewel to John Skinner by deed of release dated 1 and 2 April 1720. Signed Katherine Fewell. Delivered in presence of Thomas Steward, Charles Steward. Recorded 3 November 1721 E. Turbervile.

1:31 - DEED OF LEASE - 2 November 1721 - Alexander Beach of Hanover Parish, planter to Charles Morgan of same, planter. 5 shillings sterling to lease 150A bounded by lands of Edward Price, Morgan Darnall, Alexander Scot, Mark Harden. Signed Alexander Beech, Charles Morgan. Delivered in presence of Hen. Mackie, Jeremia Bronaugh, Dennis Raredon. Recorded 3 November 1721 E. Turbervile.

1:32 - DEED OF RELEASE - 3 November 1721 - Alexander Beech of Hanover Parish to Charles Morgan of same, planter. 500 pounds of tobacco for 150A described in lease. Signed Alex. Beach, Charles Morgan. Delivered in presence of Hen. Mackie, Jeremia Bronaugh, Dennis Raredon. Recorded 3 November 1721 E. Turbervile.

1:34 - DEED OF LEASE - 17 October 1721 - Augustin Smith of Spotsylvania County, gentleman, to George Proctor and William Proctor of King George County, planters. 40 pounds and 10 shillings sterling to lease 300A for a term of 89 years. Formerly granted unto Francis Plato by patent dated 1654. Plato Powell of the parish of St. Ann's in Essex county was lawfully seized of that tract which lies in the fork of Lambs Creek by virtue of a lease dated 11 November 1710 unto Augustin Smith for a term of 99 years. Signed Aug. Smith. Delivered in presence of Robert Richards, George Bronough, Jos. Crouch. Recorded 1 December 1721 E. Turbervile.

1:36 - DEED OF LEASE - 6 November 1721 - George Bronaugh of St. Mary's Parish in Essex County to William Sarjant of the city of Bristol, merchant. 5 shillings sterling to lease 100A lying on north side of Rappahanock River. Bounded by Henry Wilton, Colonel Mathews, part of land fallen to William Bronaugh, dec'd, by the death of his father David Bronaugh. The said William Bronaugh in his life time granted and made over unto the said George Bronaugh by deed bearing date 4 December 1699. Signed Geo. Bronaugh. Delivered in presence of Patrick McKey, Rowland Williams, E. Turbervile. Recorded 1 December 1721 E. Turbervile.

1:37 - DEED OF RELEASE - 7 November 1721 - George Bronaugh of St. Mary's Parish in Essex County to William Sarjant of the city of Bristol, merchant. 40 pounds sterling for 100A described in lease. Bounded by Henry Wilton, heirs of Colonel Mathews, part of land fallen to William Bronaugh, dec'd, by the death of his father David Bronaugh. Agnes Bronaugh, wife of George Bronaugh, appoints Joseph Crouch her attorney to acknowledge right of dower and thirds, acknowledged by Patrick McKey, Rowland Williams. Signed Geo. Bronaugh. Delivered in presence of Patrick McKey, Rowland Williams, E. Turbervile. Recorded 1 December 1721 E. Turbervile.

1:39 - DEED OF LEASE - 30 November 1721 - Charles Cale and Alice Cale his wife of Hanover Parish to Mrs. Ann Fawlk Fitzhugh. 5 shillings sterling to lease 1A on the south side of a run called Cleyborns Run. 1A owned by Charles and Alice Cale by inheritance in pure and absolute fee simple. Signed Charles Cale, Alice Cale. Delivered in the presence of Mungo Roy, La. Pepper, Henry Connyers. Recorded 1 December 1721 E. Turbervile.

1:40 - DEED OF RELEASE - 1 December 1721 - Charles Cale and Alice his wife to Mrs. Ann Fowlks Fitzshugh. 500 pounds of tobacco for 1A described in lease. Having their corn for them and their children ground free during their lives at a mill built by Thomas Fitzhugh upon the land herein conveyed. Signed Charles Cale, Alice Cale. Delivered in presence of Mungo Roy, Ls. Pepper, Henry Connyers. Recorded 1 December 1721 E. Turbervile.

1:42 - DEED OF LEASE - 30 November 1721 - James Key of Hanover Parish, planter to John Dinwiddie of same, gentleman. 5 shillings sterling to lease 97A lying upon the branches of Haugh Creek and commonly known by the name of Keys Ponds. Being part of a 1680A grant to Colonel Gerard Fowlkes and Mr.

Richard Hubourd dated 23 March 1664; sold by Hubourd (he being the survivor) to James Key, grandfather to the aforesaid James Key who came by it by inheritance. Bounded by the lands of Capt. Samuel Mathews, dec'd, and Charles Steward. Signed James Kay, Mary Kay. Delivered in presence of Patrick McKey, Rowland Williams, E. Turbervile. Recorded 1 December 1721 E. Turbervile.

1:44 - DEED OF RELEASE - 1 December 1721 - James Key of Hanover Parish, planter to John Dinwiddie of same, gentleman. 30 pounds sterling for 97A described in lease. Mary, wife of James Kay, relinquishes her right of dower and thirds. Signed James Kay, Mary Kay. Delivered in the presence of John Farguson, Charles Cale. Recorded 1 December 1721 E. Turbervile.

1:46 - DEED OF LEASE - 30 October 1721 - John England and Susanna his wife to William Marshall Junior. 2 shillings sterling to lease 100A formerly belonging to Thomas Grimsly. Bounded by Alexanders, Thomas Grimsly. Signed John England. Delivered in presence of Richard Tankersly, Saml. Wharton. Recorded 1 December 1721 E. Turbervile.

1:47 - DEED OF RELEASE - 30 October 1721 - John England and Susanna his wife to William Marshall, Jr.. 4000 pounds of good tobacco for 100A described in lease. Susanna, wife of John England, relinquishes her right of dower and thirds. Signed John England. Delivered in the presence of Richard Tankersly, Saml. Wharton. Recorded 1 December 1721 E. Turbervile.

1:49 - DEED OF SALE - 30 January 1721 - William Meconicoe to John Smith. 1200 pounds of tobacco for 50A being part of 550A tract bought by William Smith from Alexander Swan and Judeth his wife 30 May 1691. Said Smith willed it to William Meconicoe. Signed William Meconicoe. Delivered in the presence of Jno. Grayson, Jno. Manifield. Recorded 7 January 1721 E. Turbervile.

1:51 - RECEIPT - 9 October 1719 - To acknowledge receipt from Colonel William Robinson and Mr. John Gilbert, executors of the last will and testament of Mr. John Burket who willed to Elizabeth, Anne, and Margaret our wives, our equal part of the said estate. Signed George White, Cor. Edmonds, John Pratt. Testes: Tho. Sharp, Eleanor Hughs, John Murphey. Recorded 5 January 1721 E. Turbervile.

1:51 - POWER OF ATTORNEY - 27 May 1721 - John Taylor and John Lomas, merchants in Virginia; and Philip Elway of Sidney in the county of Glour. to buy any parcels of land, iron ore, and wood as to them shall seem needed for the use and benefit of iron works of listed partners. Signed John King, Jeremy

Innys, Jno. Lewis, Saml. Jacob, Lyonel Lyde,Walt. King, Jno. Templeman, Saml. Dyke. Delivered in presence of James Baker, George Williams, Stephen Williams. Recorded 2 February 1721 E. Turbervile.

1:52 - DEED OF GIFT - 11 November 1721 - Bind and oblige my heirs to pay to Richd. Rhymer, son of Ann Rymer of King George county, two young cows of four years old at his arriving at twenty-one years of age. Allso 3 pewter dishes, three pewter basons new ones, a pot and pothooks, and a frying pan. Signed John Patison. Testes: Mungo Roy, John Waugh. Recorded 2 March 1721 E. Turbervile.

1:53 - POWER OF ATTORNEY - 16 February 1721 - I, Robert Carter, Esq. of the county of Lancaster agent and attorney for the right honorable Thomas Lord Fairfax and William Cage, Esq., proprietors of the Northern Neck, appoint Thomas Hooper of the county of Stafford, gentleman to be my attorney substitute and surveyor: to survey and give bounds to all ungranted and surplus lands that he shall from time to time receive warrants from me for the laying out and admeasuring and also to take entrys for any quantity of land in the said county not exceeding 400A in one tract and to fill up blank warrants. Signed Robert Carter. Delivered in presence of G. Eskridge, William Daniel, Robert Briscoe. Recorded 2 March 1721 E. Turbervile.

1:54 - DEED OF LEASE - 1 March 1721 - Thomas Stone of Charles County in the Province of Maryland, gentleman to William Thornton of King George County, gentleman. 5 shillings current money to lease 200A about a mile below the falls of the Rappahanack River. Part of 2000A grant to Colonel John Cattlett by patent bearing date 2 June 1666, 500A of which became the property of Edward Maddock, late of Stafford County, who willed 200A to John Robbins, son of Robert Robins of Maryland, by will dated 3 June 1694 and duly proved in Stafford County court 11 December 1694, on condition that if John Robbins died without sons of his body, the land descended to John Stone, son of John Stone elder of Maryland, who also died without sons of his body. Land descended to his brother Thomas Stone, only brother of John Stone. Catherine, wife of Thomas Stone, relinquishes her right of dower. Signed Thomas Stone. Delivered in presence of E. Turberville, M. Battaley. Recorded 2 March 1721 E. Turbervile.

1:55 - DEED OF RELEASE - 2 March 1721 - Thomas Stone of Charles County, province of Maryland, gentleman to William Thornton, gentleman. 30 pounds current money for 200A described in lease. Catherine, wife of Thomas Stone, relinquishes her right of dower. Signed Thomas Stone. Delivered in presence of E. Turbervile, M. Battaley. Recorded 2 March 1721 E. Turbervile.

1:58 - BOND - Thomas Stone of Charles county, province of Maryland, bound to William Thornton of King George county for 100 pounds sterling. Condition such that if agreements made in deeds of lease and release are met, obligation to be void. Signed Thomas Stone. Delivered in presence of E. Turbervile, M. Battaley. Recorded 2 March 1721 E. Turbervile.

1:58 - DEED OF LEASE - 28 November 1721 - William Kendall of Washington Parish in Westmoreland County, planter to Samuel Kendall of Hanover Parish, planter. 5 shillings of good and lawful money of England to lease 50A on the lower side of Powltridges Creek. Bounded by Edwin Conway, John Green. Signed Wm. Kendill. Delivered in presence of Isaac Arnold, Edward Feagens. Recorded 2 March 1721 E. Turbervile.

1:59 - DEED OF RELEASE - 29 November 1721 - William Kendall of Washington Parish in Westmoreland County to Samuel Kendell of Hanover Parish, his brother. 3000 pounds of good tobacco for 50A described in lease. Part of a grant to Thomas Kendall for 100A. Signed Wm. Kendell. Delivered in presence of Isaac Arnold, Edward Feagens. Recorded 2 March 1721 E. Turbervile.

1:61 - DEPOSITION - 6 July 1722 - Thomas Turner deposed that on May court last Captain Dinwiddie said that the gentlemen of the court would neither build a courthouse or prison whilst he was sheriff and if any of them should send a prisoner to him he would send him back to him again and he might wipe his ars with the mittimus and he did not care if the devil geld his dominions and some of the justices. William Strother, Jr. deposed that he heard Captain Dinwiddie say at Walter Anderson's house in company that the court was a parcell of goal birds and scoundrels and all damned rogues excepting two which were good civil gentlemen.

1:61 - POWER OF ATTORNEY - 30 April 1722 - Thomas Guibert and Rebecca his wife of St. Mary's County in Maryland depute Thomas Grigsby their lawful attorney to recover debts due them. Signed Thomas Guibert, Rebecca Gui.. Delivered in presence of John Travis, Sam. Burton. Recorded 6 July 1722 E. Turbervile.

1:62 - COMMISSION - 14 March 1721 - Peter Beverley of the county of Gloucester, Esquire, Surveyor General of the colony, commissioned John Savage, gentleman, to be surveyor of the county of King George. Recorded 6 July 1722 E. Turbervile.

1:63 - OATH - 2 February 1716 - Mr. John Jones presented accounts from Micajah Perry and son Richard Perry, London merchants, both deceased, showing amount due to him. Recorded 6 July 1722 E. Turbervile.

1:64 - DEED OF LEASE - 4 April 1722 - William Tippett of Hanover Parish, planter to Edmund Dunnoho of same, planter. 5 shillings of good and lawful money of Great Britain to lease 80A lying on the lowermost side of the main branch of Powltridges Creek. Bounded on the west side by said branch, on the north side by Henry Wood, dec'd, on the south side by John Anderson, dec'd, and on the east side by John Willis. Signed William Tippet. Delivered in presence of Isaac Arnold, John Green, John Harvey. Recorded 6 July 1722 E. Turbervile.

1:65 - DEED OF RELEASE - 5 April 1722 - William Tippet of Hanover Parish, planter to Edmond Dunnoho of same, planter. 3000 pounds of good and well conditioned leaf tobacco for 80A described in lease. Mary Tippet, wife of William Tippet, appoints loving friend John Green to acknowledge her reliquishment of dower rights and thirds. Signed Mary Tippet. Acknowledged by Isaac Arnold, John Harvey. Signed William Tippet. Delivered in presence of Isaac Arnold, John Green, John Harvey. Recorded 6 July 1722 E. Turbervile.

1:67 - DEED OF LEASE - 4 July 1722 - Alexander Clement of Hanover Parish to George Allen of same, carpenter. 5 shillings of lawful money of England to lease 100A being part of a tract of 200A granted to said Alexander Clement by patent dated 16 June 1716. Bounded by Thomas Evans. Signed Alexander Clement. Delivered in presence of Henry Connyers, Darby Calloham. Recorded 6 July 1722 E. Turbervile.

1:68 - DEED OF RELEASE - 5 July 1722 - Alexander Clement of Hanover Parish, planter to George Allen of same, carpenter. 1500 pounds of good tobacco for 100A described in lease. Signed Alexr. Clement. Delivered in presence of Henry Connyers, Darby Callaham. Recorded 6 July 1722 E. Turbervile.

1:71 - DEED OF LEASE - 20 January 1721 - George Proctor and William Proctor both of Hanover Parish, planters to William Sarjant of the city of Bristol, merchant. 53 pounds sterling to lease 100A lying on Lambs Creek, formerly belonging to William Wood and 2A formerly belonging to William Wilton. Bounded by land of William Proctor purchased of Augustin Smith. Signed George Procter, Wm. Procter. Delivered in presence of Jos. Couch, E. Turbervile. Recorded 6 July 1722 E. Turbervile.

1:72 - BOND - 20 January 1721 - George Procter of Hanover Parish bound unto William Sarjant of the city of Bristol, merchant for 100 pounds sterling. Condition such that if terms of deed of lease are fullfilled, bond is void. Signed

George Procter. Delivered in presence of Jos. Couch, E. Turbervile. Recorded 6 July 1722 E. Turbervile.

1:73 - POWER OF ATTORNEY - 23 February 1721 - John Pope of Great Britain, mercer, appoints Thomas Martin of the city of Bristol, merchant, and William Winston of the colony of Virginia, merchant, his true and lawful attorneys to receive of Robert Burgis, late of Great Britain, coller maker, the sum of 26 pounds and interest. Signed John Pope. Delivered in the presence of John Thomas, Nathaniel Pope. Recorded 3 August 1722 E. Turbervile.

1:73 - DEED OF LEASE - 15 June 1722 - John Plaile of Sittenburn Parish and Catherin his wife to Joseph Minton of same. 5 shillings to lease 80A being all the land between Joseph Minton and a swamp which divides the said land from the land of William Monroe. Part of 1000A granted to Thomas Whitlock by patent dated 20 February 1662, 550A of which was sold by said Whitlock to Thomas Swinbourne, except one acre sold to the said William Monroe to build a mill now in the possession of Thomas Evans. Signed John Plail, Catherine Plail. Delivered in presence of Jno. Gilbert, Luke Tippett. Recorded 3 August 1722 E. Turbervile.

1:74 - DEED OF RELEASE - 16 June 1722 - John Plaile of Sittenburn Parish and Catherin his wife to Joseph Minton of same. 5000 pounds of good tobacco and 20 shillings for 80A described in lease. Signed John Plaile, Catherin Plaile. Delivered in presence of John Gilbert, Luke Tippet. Recorded 3 August 1722 E. Turbervile.

1:76 - DEED OF LEASE - 2 August 1722 - John Green of Hanover Parish, planter to Anthony Thornton of St. Paul's Parish in Stafford County, gentleman. 5 shillings of lawful money of England to lease 65A bounded by Francis Thornton's land whereon lives one William Giffy and John Kendall. Signed John Green, Abigail Green. Delivered in presence of Fran. Thornton, Will Strother. Recorded 7 September 1722 E. Turbervile.

1:77 - DEED OF RELEASE - 3 August 1722 - John Green of Hanover Parish, planter to Anthony Thornton of St. Paul's Parish in Stafford County, gentleman. 4000 pounds of good tobacco for 65A described in lease. Abigail, wife of John Green, relinquishes her right of dower and thirds. Signed John Green, Abigail Green. Delivered in presence of Francis Thornton, Wm. Strother. Recorded 7 September 1722 E. Turbervile.

1:79- DEED OF LEASE - 27 July 1722 - David Ball of Lancaster County, gentleman to James Ball of same. 5 shillings sterling to lease 200A given to said David Ball by the last will of his father William Ball. Signed David Ball.

Delivered in presence of Geo. Murdoch, Henry Still. Recorded 5 October 1722 E. Turbervile.

1:80 - DEED OF RELEASE - 28 July 1722 - David Ball of Lancaster County, gentleman to James Ball of same, gentleman. 65 pounds sterling for 200A described in lease. Signed David Ball. Delivered in presence of Geo. Murdach, Henry Still. Recorded 5 October 1722 E. Turbervile.

1:81 - DEED OF LEASE - 4 October 1722 - John Underwood of Hanover Parish, planter to John King, Esquire, and Company, merchants in Bristol and owner of the Bristol Iron Works in the parish aforesaid. 5 shillings to lease 140A at the mouth of a branch called Sandy Valley. Being part of a tract of 1400A granted to Robert Bird by patent dated 29 July 1650. NOT signed or witnessed. Recorded 5 October 1722 E. Turbervile.

1:82 - DEED OF RELEASE - 5 October 1722 - John Underwood of Hanover Parish, planter to John King, Esquire, and Company, merchants in Bristol and owner of the Bristol Iron Works in the parish aforesaid. 56 pounds sterling for 140A described in lease. NOT signed or witnessed. Recorded 5 October 1722 E. Turbervile.

1:85 - DEED OF LEASE - 1 October 1722 - Mot Doniphan of Overwharton Parish in Stafford County and Robert Doniphan of Hanover Parish of the one part to John Dinwiddie of Hanover Parish, gentleman of the other. 5 shillings to lease 27A between the lands of the said Robert Doniphan and George Proctor. Signed Mot Doniphan, Robert Doniphan. Delivered in presence of Jno. Gilbert, Willm. Tharp. Recorded 5 October 1722 E. Turbervile.

1:86 - DEED OF RELEASE - 2 October 1722 - Mot Doniphan of Overwharton Parish in Stafford County and Robert Doniphan of Hanover Parish to John Dinwiddie of Hanover Parish. 60 pounds sterling for 27A between the lands of Robert Doniphan and George Proctor. Said land was formerly purchased by Alexander Doniphan, dec'd, father of the said Mot and Robert Doniphan from one William Griffin by deed dated 4 April 1692, being part of a patent granted unto John and George Mott for 15,654A dated 17 October 1670. Signed Mot Doniphan, Robert Doniphan. Delivered in presence of Jno. Gilbert, Willm. Tharp. Recorded 5 October 1722 E. Turbervile.

1:88 - BOND - 2 October 1722 - Mot Doniphan and Robert Doniphan bound unto John Dinwiddie for 500 pounds sterling. Condition such that if covenants of certain deeds of lease and release are fulfilled, obligation to be void. Signed Mot Doniphan, Robert Doniphan. Delivered in presence of Jno. Gilbert, Willm. Tharp. Recorded 5 October 1722 E. Turbervile.

1:88 - DEED OF LEASE - 1 October 1722 - Robert Doniphan of Hanover Parish to John Dinwiddie of same, gentleman. 5 shillings sterling to lease 173A bounded by George Proctor, John Dinwiddie. Signed Robart Doniphan. Delivered in presence of Jno. Gilbert, Willm. Tharp. Recorded 5 October 1722 E. Turbervile.

1:89 - DEED OF RELEASE - 2 October 1722 - Robert Doniphan of Hanover Parish to John Dinwiddie of same, gentleman. 100 pounds sterling for 172A Bounded by George Proctor, John Dinwiddie. Being part of a patent granted unto John and George Mott for 15,654A dated 17 October 1670 which has since become the freehold and inheritance of Robert Doniphan. Signed Robert Doniphan. Delivered in presence of Jno. Gilbert, Willm. Tharp. Recorded 5 October 1722 E. Turbervile.

1:91 - BOND - 2 October 1722 - Robert Doniphan bound to John Dinwiddie for 500 pounds sterling. Condition such that if covenants in certain deeds of lease and release bearing equal date are kept according to the true intent and meaning, the obligation shall be void. Signed Robart Doniphan. Delivered in presence of Jno. Gilbert, Willm. Tharp. Recorded 5 October 1722 E. Turbervile.

1:92 - DEED OF EXCHANGE - 30 October 1722 - Nicholas Smith of Sittenburn Parish to Daniel White of same, planter, and Ann his wife. Nicholas Smith, in consideration of 188A granted by the said Daniel and Ann his wife, give, grant, and confirm unto the said Ann White, in free and liberal exchange, one tract of land containing 196A. 150A where of the said Nicholas Smith purchasesd of Richard Jordan and Cicely his wife by deed dated 4 March 1694; 30A Nicholas Smith purchased of Thomas Richardson and Thomas Brock and Cecil his wife by deed dated 29 October 1709 as surveyed by Edward Barrow, surveyor of Richmond County; the other 16A purchased by Nicholas Smith from Thomas Brock and Cecil his wife by deed dated 29 October 1709. The said 188A being upon Charles' bever dam between Capt. Spicer's and William Carter's, formerly belonging to Francis Taylor and Elizabeth his wife. Then sold to David Sterne by deed dated 25 August 1687 and since come to Daniel White and his wife Ann. Signed Daniel White, Ann White. Delivered in presence of Jno. Gilbert, George White, J. Mercer. Recorded 2 November 1722 E. Turbervile.

1:94- POWER OF ATTORNEY - 30 October 1722 - Ann, wife of Daniel White, appoints John Gilbert her true and lawful attorney to relinquish all right, title, and interest whatever to a certain parcel of land deeded to Nicholas Smith bearing equal date. Signed Ann White. Delivered in presence of George White,

J. Mercer. Recorded 2 November 1722 E. Turbervile.

1:94 - DEED OF GIFT - 5 April 1722 - I, William Strother of Hanover Parish, planter, for diverse goods and other considerations, but expecially for the natural love I bear to my eldest son William Strothers, do give, grant all land that my father by his will left me, excepting the 60A that Mr. Samuel Skinner now holds. Signed William Strothers. Testes: Francis Strothers, Thomas Grimsly. Recorded 2 Novemher 1722 E. Turbervile.

1:95 - DEED - Not dated - John Brown and Mary his wife of Northumberland County to John Crump of same. 70 pounds sterling already received for 178A being part of a tract of 427A granted to John Brown and William Allen by patent dated 1 January 1710. Signed John Brown. Delivered in presence of William Mathbe, Henry E____ Recorded 2 November 1722 E. Turbervile.

1:96 - POWER OF ATTORNEY - 28 October 1722 - Mary Brown, wife of John Brown, gives Peter Lehen power of attorney to relinquish her right of dower. Signed Mary Brown. Delivered in presence of Willm. Lunsford, Edwd. Lunsford. Recorded 2 November 1722 E. Turbervile.

1:96 - DEED OF GIFT - 6 December 1722 - Honour Richardson of Sittenbourne Parish to daughters Elizabeth Richardson and Mary Richardson. A tract to be divided equally upon mother's death. 600A being the land of John Barrow, dec'd, and by him given by his last will and testament dated 3 February 1684 unto his three sons Moses, Alexander, and Jonathan Barrow, and for want of heirs of their bodies to his two daughters Honour and Cicelly, and since the death of Cicelly is become the inheritance of Honour. Signed Honour Richardson. Delivered in the presence of Rowland Thornton, Robert Spence. Recorded 7 December 1722 E. Turbervile.

1:98 - DEED OF EXCHANGE - 30 October 1722 - Nicholas Smith of Sittenbourne Parish, gentleman to Daniel White of same. Nicholas Smith, in consideration of 188A granted to him by Daniel White and Ann his wife, grants 196A unto them. 150A whereof the said Nicholas Smith purchased from Richard Jourdon and Ciceley his wife by deed dated 4 March 1694; another parcel of 30A Nicholas Smith purchased from Thomas Richardson and Thomas Brock and Cecil his wife by deed dated 29 October 1709 and surveyed by Edward Barrow; and 16A Nicholas Smith purchased of Thomas Brock and Cecil his wife by deed dated 29 October 1709. The 188A was sold by Francis Taylor and Elizabeth his wife to David Storin by deed dated 25 August 1687 and has since come to Daniel White and Ann his wife. Signed Nicholas Smith. Delivered in presence of Jno. Gilbert, George White, John Mercer. Recorded 2 November 1722 E. Turbervile.

1:100 - POWER OF ATTORNEY - 30 October 1722 - Ann , wife of Daniel White, gives power of attorney to John Gilbert to take and accept the acknowledgement of a certain deed of exchange between Nicholas Smith of the one part and my husband and myself of the other part. Signed Ann White. Delivered in presence of George White, Jno. Mercer. Recorded 2 November 1722 E. Turbervile.

1:101 - DEED OF LEASE - 5 November 1722 - John Underwood of Sittenbourne Parish, planter to John King Esquire and Company, merchants in Bristoll and owners of the Bristoll Iron Works. 5 shillings sterling to lease 140A beginning at the mouth of a branch called Sandey Valley, bounded by Foxhalls Mill Run. Part of a tract of 1400A granted to Robert Bird by patent dated 29 July 1650. Signed John Underwood. Delivered in presence of Richard Tutt, John Hooe, Jno. Mercer. Recorded 7 December 1722 E. Turbervile.

1:103 - DEED OF RELEASE - 6 November 1722 - John Underwood of Sittenbourne Parish, planter to John King Esquire and Company, merchants in Bristoll and owners of the Bristoll Iron Works. 56 pounds sterling for 140A described in lease. Signed John Underwood. Delivered in presence of Richard Tutt, John Hooe, Jno. Mercer. Recorded 5 December 1722 E. Turbervile.

1:106 - POWER OF ATTORNEY - 6 December 1722 - Elizabeth Underwood, the wife of John Underwood of Sittenbourne Parish, appoints Major Nicholas Smith her true and lawful attorney to relinquish her right and title of dower and thirds to land sold by her husband John Underwood to John King Esquire and Company. Signed Elizabeth Underwood. Delivered in presence of John Underwood, Margaret Thornborough. Recorded 7 December 1722 E. Turbervile.

1:107 - DEED OF LEASE - 31 August 1722 - Robert Doniphan of Hanover Parish, planter to Edward Price of same, planter. 5 shillings sterling to lease 50A adjoining to the plantation of said Edward Price, lying between lines of Edward Price and Lawrance Taliaferroe. Part of a patent granted to John and George Mott for 15,654A 17 October 1672. Signed Robart Doniphan. Delivered in presence of John Cobern,Charles Jones. Recorded 5 January 1722.

1:108 - DEED OF RELEASE - 1 September 1722 - Robert Doniphan of Hanover Parish, planter to Edwrd Price of same, planter. 70 pounds sterling for 140A described in lease. Signed Robart Doniphan. Delivered in presence of John Coburn, Charles Jones. Recorded 5 January 1722 E. Turbervile.

1:110 - DEED OF LEASE - 3 January 1722 - George Eskridge of Westmoreland County, gentleman to William Thornton of King George County, gentleman. 5 shillings to lease 256A being part of a tract containing 2060A granted to said Eskridge by deed dated 27 December 1716. Bounded by land taken up by William Russel and by him sold to William Thornton. Boundary beginning at a marked Spanish Oak standing in a small island lying in the Marsh Run opposite to the lower end of the Elk marsh. Signed G. Eskridge. Delivered in the presence of Wil. Robinson, Jos. Strother, E. Turbervile. Recorded 4 January 1722 E. Turbervile.

1:111 - DEED OF RELEASE - 4 January 1722 - George Eskridge of Westmoreland County, gentleman to William Thornton of King George County, gentleman. 25 pounds 6 shillings sterling for 256A described in lease. Signed G. Eskridge. Delivered in presence of Wil. Robinson, Jos. Strother, E. Turbervile. Recorded 4 January 1722 E. Turbervile.

1:113 - DEED OF LEASE - 12 September 1719 - Ann Glendinin, widow, and John Glendining her son of Hanover Parish to Joseph Armstrong and Elizabeth Armstrong his wife of same. 250 pounds of tobacco every year during their natural lives. Adjoining Richard Pearl's plantation, beisng the plantation whereon John Armstrong, Sr. formerly did live. Boundary beginning at a little branch at the lower side of Richard Pearl's plantation, from thence up to the main road, from thence down the said road to the road of the deep branch, down along the said branch to Muddy Creek. Signed Ann Glendinning, Jno. Glendining, Joseph Armstrong, Elizabeth Armstrong. Delivered in presence of Richard White, Margt. White. Recorded 1 February 1722 E. Turbervile.

1:114 - DEED OF SALE - 14 January 1722 - Waugh Darnell, John Kenyen, Abraham Kenyen of Hanover Parish to James Ball of Mary's White Chapple Parish in Lancaster County, gentleman. 36 pounds sterling for 100A part of 1600A formerly granted to William Ball and Thomas Chitwood, being late in the occupation of Thomas Stone. Signed Waugh Darnall, John Kenyon, Abraham Kenyon. Delivered in presence of Jos. Ball, Travors Downman, Fran. Conway, Jonath. Gibson, Jr. Recorded 1 February 1722 E. Turbervile.

1:116 - DEED OF LEASE - 21 January 1722 - James Kay of Hanover Parish, planter to John Popham of Westmoreland County, planter. 5 shillings sterling to lease 126A bounded by John Price, Benjamin Stribling, Charles Steward. Signed James Kay. Delivered in presence of John Farguson, Ja. Robertson. Recorded 1 February 1722 E. Turbervile.

1:117 - DEED OF RELEASE - 20 January 1722 - James Kay of Hanover Parish, planter to John Popham of Westmoreland County, planter. 10,000 pounds of good tobacco for 126A bounded by John Price, Benjamin Stribling, Charles Steward. Part of a patent granted to James Kay by Colonel Thomas Lee, agent and then attorney for the proprietors of the Northern Neck, for 2180A - June 1715. 500A being surplus land and 1680A being formerly granted to Col. Gerard Fawlks and Mr. Richard Haiberd by patent dated 23 March 1664 and by the said Heibard (he being the survivor) sold to James Kay, grandfather to the present James Kay. Signed James Kay. Delivered in presence of John Farguson, Ja. Robertson. Recorded 1 February 1722 E. Turbervile.

1:119 - BOND - 20 January 1722 - James Kay of Hanover Parish bound to John Popham of Westmoreland County in the sum of 20,000 pounds of good, sound tobacco and cask. Condition such that if conditions of certain deeds of lease and release bearing equal date are observed, obligation to be void. Signed James Kay. Delivered in presence of John Farguson, Ja. Robertson. Recorded 1 February 1722 E. Turbervile.

1:120 - DEED OF LEASE - 7 January 1722 - William Lampton of Hanover Parish, planter to John Dinwiddie of same, gentleman. 5 shillings sterling to lease 136A formerly belonging to John Fossaker, dec'd. Bounded by lands of Col. George Mason, dec'd, John Glendinning, and western most branch of Lambs Creek. Part of a patent for 15,654A granted 17 October 1672 to John and George Mott which has since become the freehold and inheritance of William Lampton in fee simple. Hester, wife of William Lampton, relinquishes her right of dower. Signed William Lampton. Delivered in presence of Edwd. Price,George Procktor, James Grant, Charles Seale. Recorded 1 February 1722.

1:121 - DEED OF RELEASE - 8 January 1722 - William Lampton of Hanover Parish, planter to John Dinwiddie of same, gentleman. 50 pounds sterling for 136A described in lease. Hester, wife of William Lampton, relinquishes her right of dower. Signed William Lampton. Delivered in presence of Edward Price, James Grant,, George Procktor, Charles Seale. Recorded 1 February 1722 E. Turbervile.

1:122 - BOND - 8 January 1722 - William Lampton bound to John Dinwiddie for 100 pounds sterling. Condition such that if all covenants in deeds of lease and release bearing even date with these are kept, obligation is void. Signed William Lampton. Delivered in presence of Edward Price, James Grant, George Procktor, Charles Seale. Recorded 1 February 1722 E. Turbervile.

1:123 - POWER OF ATTORNEY - 9 January 1722 - William Lampton of Hanover Parish authorizes John Coburn of same to acknowledge in his name certain deeds of lease and release and bond for performace of covenants. Signed William Lampton. Delivered in presence of Edward Price, James Grant, George Procktor, Charles Seale. Recorded 1 February 1722 E. Turbervile.

1:124 - DEED OF LEASE - 30 January 1722 - John Plaile of Sittenburn Parish, planter and Catherin his wife to Meriday Price of same, gentleman. 5 shillings current money to lease 50A bounded by Thatchers, the main road, Munroe, Samuel Nicholls. Signed Jno. Plaile, Catherin Plaile. Delivered in presence of Thomas Monroe, Andrew Baker. 1 February 1722 E. Turbervile.

1:125 - DEED OF RELEASE - 31 January 1722 - John Plaile of Sittenburn Parish, planter and Catherin his wife to Meriday Price of same, gentleman. 5000 pounds of tobacco for 50A bounded by Thatchers, the main road, Munroes, Samuel Nicholls. Part of a patent of 1000A granted 12 February 1660 to Thomas Whitlock and since descended to the aforesaid Catherin. Signed Jno. Plaile, Catherin Plaile. Delivered in presence of Thomas Monroe, Andrew Baker. Recorded 1 February 1722 E. Turbervile.

1:127 DEED OF LEASE - 1 April 1723 - Edward Taylor of Hanover Parish, planter to Archibald Allen of Washington Parish in Westmoreland County, planter. 5 shillings sterling to lease 150A bounded by a branch commonly called Cool Spring branch, land of Robert Alexander, dec'd, Joshue Davis, dec'd, William Hutson Land formerly belonging to John Brown, being part of a patent granted unto William Brown and William Bastrop for 744A 7 August 1669 which by several conveyances has become freehold and inheritance of Edward Taylor. Signed E. Taylor. Delivered in presence of Ann Coomb, Jno. Taylor, E. Turbervile. Recorded 5 April 1723 E. Turbervile

1:129 - DEED OF RELEASE - 2 April 1723 - Edward Taylor of Hanover Parish, planter to Archibald Allen of Washington Parish in Westmoreland County, planter. 6000 pounds of good tobacco for 150A formerly belonging to John Brown who sold to Thomas White. Part of patent described in lease. Signed E. Taylor. Delivered in presence of Ann Coomb, Jno. Taylor. John Taylor, by virtue of a power of attorney, acknowledges Sara Taylor's thirds or Right of Dower. Recorded 5 April 1723 E. Turbervile.

1:131 - BOND - 2 April 1723 - Edward Taylor of Hanover Parish, planter bound to Archibald Allen of Westmoreland county, planter for 20,000 pounds of tobacco and cask. Condition such that if Edward Taylor does fulfill all covenants of deeds of lease and release bearing even date with these present, obligation is void. Signed E. Taylor. Delivered in presence of Ann Comb, Jno. Taylor, E. Turbervile. Recorded 5 April 1723 E. Turbervile.

1:132 - POWER OF ATTORNEY - 4 April 1723 - Sara Taylor, wife of Edward Taylor of Hanover Parish, planter, deputes well-beloved son John Taylor her true and lawfull attorney to relinquish her right of dower and thirds unto Archibald Allen. Signed Sara Taylor. Delivered in presence of Ann Comb, E.

Turbervile. Recorded 5 April 1723 E. Turbervile.

1:133 - DEED OF SALE - 5 December 1718 - Edward Leman of London, linen draper, son and heir of Edward Leman, late citizen and tallow chandler of London, dec'd, to John Lomax of Essex County in Virginia, gentleman. 21 pounds lawful money of Great Britain for 400A being part of a patent granted to Thomas Chetwood and John Prosser, planters, for 5275A 28 September 1667. Divided between them 26 July 1668. 400A of Chetwood's to Cuthbert Potter of Middlesex County, gentleman, by deed dated 14 November 1668. Then by indenture dated 10 April 1688 to Edward Leman, Sr., Cuthbert Potter was to pay 115 pounds 9 shillings within seven years or lose the land. He did not pay, so land was forfeited and now being sold to John Lomax. Signed Edward Leman. Delivered in presence of Ann Turner, Sarah Turner, G. Braxton, John Saltor, William Mossley, Jere. Murdock. Edward Leman appoints Thomas Turner and William Thornton to act in his place to acknowledge the deed to John Lomax in Richmond County court. Recorded 4 May 1720 by M. Beckwith. Recorded in King George County court 5 April 1723 E. Turbervile.

1:138 - DEED OF LEASE - 2 April 1723 - James Key of Hanover Parish, planter to Benjamin Stribling of St. Paul Parish in Stafford county, planter. 5 shillings sterling to lease 80A being part of a tract granted to said James Key containing 2180A by patent dated 13 June 1715. Bounded by Henry Berry, John Popham Benjamin Stribling, James Key near Hale's Road. Mary, wife of James Kay, relinquishes her right of dower. Signed James Kay, Mary Kay, John Price, Thomas Goostry. Recorded 5 April 1723 E. Turbervile.

1:139 - DEED OF RELEASE - 3 April 1723 - James Key of Hanover Parish, planter to Benjamin Stripling of St. Paul Parish in Stafford county. 3600 pounds of tobacco for 80A described in lease. Remainder of deed missing.

1:141 and 142 missing.

1:143 - DEED OF RELEASE - 27 November 1722 - Thomas Green of Hanover Parish, planter to Neal Mickormick of same, planter. 2000 pounds of good tobacco for the land now in Neal Mickormick's possession by lease, given and left to Thomas Green by his father George Green. Together with 65A part of a 885A patent granted to George Green 15 December 1708. Mary, wife of Thomas Green, relinquishes her right of dower. Signed Thomas Green, Mary Green. Delivered in presence of Isaac Arnold, Thomas Arnold, Margaret Arnold. Recorded 3 May 1723 E. Turbervile.

1:145 - DEED OF LEASE - 2 May 1723 - Robert Doniphon, planter to William Thornton, gentleman. 5 shillings current money to lease 227A. Part of the tract the said Doniphan now lives on, and includes the plantation whereon James Grant now lives as a tenant. Bounded by John Dinwiddie, Lambs Creek, Edward Price, Elinore Shippy. Part of 15,680A patent granted to John and George Mott 17 October 1672 out of which patent sundry parcels were sold by John and George Mott in their life time. The residue by George's will dated 31 March 1674 and by John's will dated 8 October 1675, both of which were proved in Rappahannock County, left to George's four daughters Elizabeth, Margaret, Ann, and Elinor. The land now leased is part of what was alotted for Margaret, the second daughter of George Mott and the mother of Robert Doniphon, her oldest son. Signed Robart Doniphan. Delivered in presence of Benja. Berryman, Henry Connyers. Recorded 3 May 1723 E. Turbervile.

1:147 - DEED OF RELEASE - 3 May 1723 - Robert Doniphon, planter to William Thornton, planter. 32 pounds sterling and 12,700 pounds of tobacco for 227A described in lease. Signed Robart Doniphan. Delivered in presence of Benja. Berryman, Henry Connyers. Recorded 3 May 1723 E. Turbervile.

1:150 - BOND - 3 May 1723 - Robert Donophan bound to William Thornton for 200 pounds sterling. Condition such that if conditions in deeds are met, obligation is void. Signed Robart Doniphan. Delivered in presence of Benja. Berryman, Henry Connyers. Recorded 3 May 1723 E. Turbervile.

1:151 - DEED OF LEASE - 4 July 1723 - Benjamin Taylor of St. Mary's Parish in Essex County, planter to Edward Turbervile of Hanover Parish, planter. 5 shillings sterling to lease 150A. Part of 400A given by John and George Mott, deceased, unto John Vickars, also deceased, and by him to his son Nathaniel Vickars and by him sold unto Thomas Taylor, deceased, father of Benjamin Taylor. Bounded by Peter Gallon, dec'd, and since belonging to Alexander Doniphan, gentleman, also dec'd. Elinor, wife of Benjamin Taylor, relinquishes her right of dower and thirds. Signed Benjamin Taylor. Delivered in presence of Aaron Thornley, Mosley Battaley. Recorded 2 August 1723 E. Turbervile.

1:153 - DEED OF RELEASE - 5 July 1723 - Benjamin Taylor of St. Mary's Parish in Essex County, planter to Edward Turbervile of Hanover Parish, planter. 5000 pounds of good tobacco and cask for 150A described in lease. Elinor, wife of Benjamin Taylor, relinquishes her right of dower and thirds. Signed Benjamin Taylor. Delivered in presence of Aaron Thornley, Mosley Battaley. Recorded 2 August 1723 E. Turbervile.

1:155 - DEED OF LEASE - 30 July 1723 - Benjamin Henslee and Elizabeth his wife to Thomas Reiley and Elizabeth his wife of Stafford County. 5 shillings to lease 100A. Part of tract given by will to William Berry and his sister Martha Berry by their father Henry Berry and since bought of William Berry by

Benjamin Henslee. Bounded by land formerly belonging to Robert Peck and Henry Berry. Elizabeth, wife of Benjamin Henslee, relinquishes her right of dower. Signed Benja. Henslee, Eliz. Henslee. Delivered in the presence of Tho. Gregsby, James Kay. Recorded 2 August 1723 E. Turbervile.

1:156 - DEED OF RELEASE - 31 July 1723 - Benjamin Henslee and Elizabeth his wife to Thomas Bailey and Elizabeth his wife of Stafford County. 5000 pounds of tobacco for 100A described in lease. Elizabeth, wife of Benjamin Henslee, relinquishes her right of dower. Signed Benja. Henslee, Eliza. Henslee. Delivered in presence of Tho. Gregsby, James Kay. Recorded 2 August 1723 E. Turbervile.

1:158 - BOND - 1 October 1723 - John Brown, Senior, of Hanover Parish, planter bound to Archibald Allen of Westmoreland county for 2000 pounds of tobacco and cask. Condition such that if John Brown, Senior, conveys 20A parcel of land to Alexander Allen, obligation to be void. Land is bounded by George Peach on one side and Gingoteague Swamp on the other on the head of land belonging to Mr. Benjamin Strother. Signed John Brown. Delivered in presence of Benja. Parker, Eleanor Dunfee. Recorded 1 November 1723 Thos. Turner.

1:159 - DEED OF LEASE - 4 September 1723 - Patrick Grady of Stafford County, planter to Samuel Skinkor of Hanover Parish, merchant. 5 shilllings current money to lease 250A granted to the said Grady by patent dated 1 June 1715. Lying on the south side of the Great Marsh and bounded by William Allen, Phillip Ludwoll, Esq. Signed Patrick Grady. Delivered in presence of John Farguson, Waltor Anderson, Richard Long. Recorded 6 September 1723 Thos. Turner.

1:161 - DEED OF RELEASE - 5 September 1723 - Patrick Grady of Stafford County, planter to Samuel Skinkor of Hanover Parish, merchant. 4000 pounds of tobacco for 250A described in lease. Signed Patrick Grady. Delivered in presence of John Farguson, Waltor Anderson, Richard Long. Recorded 6 September 1723 Thos. Turner.

1:163 - DEED OF LEASE - 2 October 1723 - Waugh Darnell of Hanover Parish, planter to James Kenney of Spotsylvania County, planter. 5 shillings sterling to lease 300A near to the head branch of Muddy Creek. Bounded by Newton's, Ball's, Kenyon's, John Jones, Rowland Thornton. Signed Waugh Darnell. Delivered in presence of Jno. Grayson, Amb. Grayson, John Grayson, Jr. Recorded 4 October 1723 Thos. Turner.

1:165 - DEED OF RELEASE - 3 October 1723 - Waugh Darnell of Hanover

Parish, planter to James Kenney of Spotsylvania County, planter. 6000 pounds of tobacco for 300A described in lease. Signed Waugh Darnell. Delivered in presence of John Grayson, Ambr. Grayson, John Grayson, Jr. Recorded 4 October 1723 Thos. Turner.

1:168 - DEED OF LEASE - 7 December 1723 - Henry Long, Senior of Hanover Parish to William Size of same. 5 shillings lawful money to lease 50A bounded by Samuel Wharton, John Ester, John Reynolds. Signed Henry Long. Delivered in presence of Wm. Marshall, Charles Seale. Recorded 6 December 1723 Thos. Turner.

1:169 - DEED OF RELEASE - 7 December 1723 - Henry Long, Senior of Hanover Parish to William Size of same. 12 pounds sterling and 1600 pounds of tobacco for 50A described in lease. Signed Henry Long. Delivered in presence of Charles Seale, Wm. Marshall. Recorded 6 December 1723 Thos. Turner.

1:172 - BOND - 7 December 1723 - Henry Long bound to William Size for 32 pounds sterling. Condition such that if terms of deeds of lease and release are met, obligation to be void. Signed Henry Long. Delivered in presence of Charles Seale, William Marshall. Recorded 6 December 1723 Thos. Turner.

1:173 - INDENTURE - 5 December 1723 - William Thornton, gentleman and William Cleark, a servant. The said William Clark being a servant to Patrick Grady of Stafford County in a very sick and weak condition and obliged to serve the said Grady until the 26th day of this instance come two years did agree with the said Thornton that if he would purchase him of his master, he would serve him the said Thornton until the first day of next July come two years as a good and faithful servant. Signed William Thornton, Wm. Cleark. Delivered in presence of William Strother, Junr., George Parsons. Recorded 6 December 1723 Thos. Turner.

1:173 - POWER OF ATTORNEY - 7 August 1723 - John King, Esq., Lyonell Lyde, Esq., John Lewis, merchant, Jeremiah Innys, merchant, and Thomas Longman, merchant,,all of the city of Bristoll, partners of the iron works lately set up, appoint Walter King of the city of Bristoll, merchant (another one of the said partners) to be their true and lawful attorney of and for said company to direct and order the future management of said company. Signed John King, Lyonell Lyde, John Lewis, Jeremy Innys, Thos. Longman. Delivered in presence of James Vandermark, James Jones, Chrs. Tarkett. Recorded 6 December 1723 Thos. Turner.

1:175 - DEED OF LEASE - 2 December 1723 - Richard Buttler of Hanover Parish, planter to Rush Hudson of same, planter. 5 shillings to lease 30A whereon Wm. Hoaking now lives. Part of a patent granted unto John Washington for 1700A. Lying on the lower side of Bald Eagle Run. Bounded by George Green, William Tippett, Rowland Thornton, and a branch called Deep Branch. Signed Richard Butler. Delivered in the presence of Isaac Arnold, Thomas Arnold. Recorded 6 December 1723 Thos. Turner.

1:177 - DEED OF RELEASE - 3 December 1723 - Richarad Butler of Hanover Parish, planter to Rush Hutson of same, planter. 5000 pounds of tobacco for 30A whereon William Hoakins now lives. Part of 1700A patent to John Washington. Signed Richard Butler. Delivered in presence of Isaac Arnold, Thos. Arnold. Recorded 6 December 1723 Thos. Turner.

1:180 - DEED OF LEASE - 24 January 1723 - James Kay, planter to Samuel Skinker, gentleman. 5 shillings current money to lease 198A. Part of tract of land James Kay now lives on and includes the plantation with David Jones now holds as tenant, and also joins upon a parcel of land lately sold by the said James Kay to Hanover Parish for a Gleib. Bounded by Benjamin Stripling. Part of a patent dated 23 March 1664 formerly granted to Col. Gerard Fawkes and Richard Haiberd and sold by Haiberd (he being the survivor) to James Kay, grandfather of the present James Kay to whom the said land descended by inheritance, his father having made no disposition of same in his lifetime and he being the only heir thereof. Signed James Kay. Delivered in presence of John Farguson, Thomas Goostree, Evan Hopkins. Recorded 8 February 1723 Thos. Turner.

1:182 - DEED OF RELEASE - 24 January 1723 - James Kay, planter to Samuel Skinker, gentleman. 6500 pounds of tobacco for 198A described in lease. Mary, wife of James Kay, relinquishes her right of dower and thirds. Signed James Kay. Delivered in presence of John Farguson, Thomas Gostree, Evan Hopkins. Recorded 8 February 1723 Thos. Turner.

1:185 - DEED OF LEASE - 3 February 1723 - James Kay of Hanover Parish, planter to Benjamin Stripling of St. Paul's Parish in Stafford County. 5 shillings sterling to lease 20A. Part of a patent dated 13 June 1715 granted unto the said James Kay. Bounded by John Popham, Benjamin Stripling. Signed James Kay. Delivered in presence of John Banton, John Raw. Recorded 8 February 1723 Thos. Turner.

1:186 - DEED OF RELEASE - 4 February 1723 - James Kay of Hanover Parish, planter to Benjamin Stripling of Stafford County. 1000 pounds of tobacco for 20A described in lease. Mary wife of said James Kay, relinquishes her right of dower and thirds. Signed James Kay. Delivered in presence of John Banton, John Race. Recorded 8 February 1723 Thos. Turner.

1:190 - DEED OF LEASE - 3 February 1723 - James Kay of Hanover Parish, planter to Benjamin Stribling of St. Paul's Parish in Stafford County. 5 shillings sterling to lease 54A. Part of tract of land granted unto the said James Kay by patent dated 13 June 1715. Bounded by the 80A formerly purchased by the said Ben Stribling of James Kay, James Kay. Signed James Kay. Delivered in presence of John Banton, John Raw. Recorded 8 February 1723 Thos. Turner.

1:192 - DEED OF RELEASE - 4 February 1723 - James Kay of Hanover Parish to Benjamin Stribling of St. Paul's Parish in Stafford County. 2700 pounds of tobacco in cask for 54A described in lease. Mary, wife of James Kay, relinquishes her right of dower. Signed James Kay. Delivered in presence of John Banton, John Raw. Recorded 8 February 1723 Thos. Turner.

1:195 - DEED OF LEASE - 2 January 1723 - William Strother, Junior of Hanover Parish to James Robertson of same. 5 shillings sterling to lease 40A bounded by John Lomax. Line runs up the Old House Swamp to the main county road. Signed Wm. Strother. Delivered in presence of Benja. Strother, James Bowcock. Recorded 8 February 1723 Thos. Turner.

1:197 - DEED OF RELEASE - 3 January 1723 - William Strother, Junior of Hanover Parish to James Robertson of same. 40 pounds sterling for 40A described in lease. Signed Will. Strother. Delivered in presence of Benjamin Strother, James Bowcock. Recorded 8 February 1723 Thos. Turner.

1:200 - POWER OF ATTORNEY - 8 February 1723 - Margaret, wife of Wm. Strother, Junior of Hanover Parish appoints her loving brother Benja. Strother her true and lawful attorney to acknowledge in her name her right of dower and thirds in land sold to James Robertson. Signed Margaret Strother. Delivered in presence of Neall McCormick, Isaac Johnson. Recorded 8 February 1723 Thos. Turner.

1:201 - DEED OF LEASE - 5 March 1723 - Walter Frances and George Procter of Hanover Parish to William Thornton of same. 5 shillings to lease 200A bounded by Jeremiah Bronaugh, Jr., Jeremiah Bronaugh, Sr., Edward Price, William Thornton, John Dinwidie. Purchased by the said Walter Frances of Alvin Mounjoy by deed dated 3 April 1700 and given by the said Walter after his decease to the said George Procter by a deed of gift dated 2 August 1714. Signed Walter Francis, George Procter. Delivered in presence of Mosley Battley, Thos. Turner. Recorded 6 March 1723 Thos. Turner.

1:203 - DEED OF RELEASE - 6 March 1723 - Walter Francis and George Procter of Hanover Parish to William Thornton of same. 150 pounds sterling for 200A purchasesd by the said Walter Francis of Alvin Mountjoy by deed dated 3

April 1700 and given by the said Walter Francis after his decease to George Proctor by deed of gift dated 2 August 1714. Signed Walter Francis, George Procter. Delivered in presence of Mosley Battaly, Thos. Turner. Recorded 6 March 1723 Thos. Turner.

1:206 - DEED OF LEASE - 5 March 1723 - Edward Price of Hanover parish, planter to William Thornton of same, gentleman. 5 shillings current money to lease 120A. Being what his father Edward Price bought of William Griffin and all that parcel of land bought of Robert Doniphan containing 50A. Signed Edward Price. Delivered in presence of Benja. Strother, Thos. Turner. Recorded 6 March 1723 Thos. Turner.

1:207 - DEED OF RELEASE - 6 March 1723 - Edward Price of Hanover Parish, planter to William Thornton of same, gentleman. 100 pounds sterling for 120A described in lease. Signed Edward Price. Delivered in presence of Benja. Strother, Thos. Turner. Recorded 6 March 1723 Thos. Turner.

1:210 - DEED OF LEASE - 21 January 1723 - Edward Price of Hanover Parish, planter to John Dinwiddie of same, gentleman. 5 shillings sterling to lease 427A bounded by land surveyed for Morgan Darnall. Land and premises being granted by Thomas Lee, Esqr., agent and attorney for the proprieters of the Northern Neck, unto the said George Price by patent dated 2 August 1715. Signed Edward Price. Delivered in presence of Thos. Turner, Saml. Skinker. Recorded 6 March 1723 Thos. Turner.

1:212 - DEED OF RELEASE - 22 January 1723 - Edward Price of Hanover Parish, planter to John Dinwiddie of same, gentleman. 8000 pounds of good tobacco and cask for 427A described in lease. Signed Edward Price. Delivered in presence of Thos. Turner, Saml. Skinker. Recorded 6 March 1723 Thos. Turner.

1:214 - BOND - 6 March 1723 - Edward Price bound to John Dinwiddie for 20,000 pounds of good tobacco and cask. Condition such that if covenants in deeds of lease and release are met, obligation is void. Signed Edward Price. Delivered in presence of Thos. Turner, Saml. Skinker. Recorded 6 March 1723 Thos. Turner.

1:215 - DEED OF LEASE - 24 March 1723 - William Grant of Sittenburn Parish and George Eskridge of Westmoreland County to George White of King George County. 5 shillings of lawfull money to lease tract of land in Sittenburn Parish where the said Wm. Grant now lives and one tract of land in Hanover Parish, formerly purchasesd of Cornelius Edmonds, where on his son John Grant now lives and six negroes: Sambo, Pall, George, Harry, Jack and Pegg to have and to hold during the natural life of said Wm. Grant. After his decease, land in Sittenburn Parish and two negroes to go to son William Grant, Jr. Land in Hanover Parish and other four negroes to be divided between sons John Grant and Daniel Grant. If any son dies without lawful heirs, property reverts to his brothers and their heirs. Signed William Grant. Delivered in presence of Ralph Elston, Andrew Greenhorne. Recorded 4 March 1723 Thos. Turner.

1:217 - DEED OF LEASE - 1 April 1724 - George Green of Hanover Parish, planter to Rush Hutson of same, planter. 5 shillings to lease 65A lying on the lower side of the western main branch of Poultridge's Creek, which is known as Bald Eagle Run. Bounded by land of the said Rush Hutson, Richard Butler, Rowland Thornton, Elizabeth Green, mother of the said George Green. Part of a 885A patent granted unto George Green, father to the said George Green. Sarah, wife of George Green, relinquishes her right of dower and thirds. Signed George Green. Delivered in presence of Isaac Arnold, John Kendell. Recorded 3 April 1724 Thos. Turner.

1:219 - DEED OF RELEASE - 2 April 1724 - George Green of Hanover Parish, planter to Rush Hutson of same, planter. 6000 pounds of good tobacco for 65A described in lease. Sarah, wife of George Green, relinquishes her right of dower and thirds. Signed George Green, Sarah Green. Delivered in presence of Isaac Arnold, John Kendell. Recorded 3 April 1724 Thos. Turner.

1:221 - POWER OF ATTORNEY - 3 April 1724 - Mary Doniphan, wife of Robert Doniphan of Hanover Parish, appoints William Patishall to be her true and lawfull attorney to relinquish her right of dower in 227A heretofore sold to William Thornton. Signed Mary Doniphan. Delivered in presence of John Ambros, William Taylor. Recorded 3 April 1724 Thos. Turner.

1:221 - DEED OF SALE - 29 April 1724 - Ann Glendening of Hanover Parish, widow, to David Seal and Jeal his wife and daughter of the said Ann Glendening. 3000 pounds of tobacco and 5 shillings lawful money for 100A. Bounded by Richard Fossiker, John Dinwiddie, the main branch of Lambs Creek, and the main road. Part of a patent granted to John Mott and George Mott 17 October 1670 and bequeathed by George Mott, father of the said Ann Glendening, to his four daughters Elizabeth, Margaret, Ann, and Ellen in joint tenantcy by his will dated 31 March 1674 and proved 27 May 1674. Land being afterwards divided between the sisters. Bounded by land leased to Richard Pearle and the main road. Signed Ann Glendening. Delivered in presence of Simon White, Richard Pearle, William Welsh. Recorded 1 May 1724 Thos. Turner.

1:226 - DEED OF SALE - 27 April 1724 - Ann Glendening of Hanover Parish, widow, to Joseph Armstrong and Elizabeth his wife and daughter of the said Ann Glendening. 3000 pounds of tobacco and 5 shillings sterling for 100A. Bounded by land leased to Richard Pearle and the main road. Part of a patent granted to John Mott and George Mott 17 October 1670 and bequeathed by George Mott, father of the said Ann Glendening, to his four daughters Elizabeth, Margaret, Ann, and Ellen by his will dated 31 March 1674 and proved 27 May 1674. Land being afterwards divided between the sisters. Signed Ann Glendening. Delivered in presence of Simon White, Richd. Pearle, William Welsh. Recorded 1 May 1724 Thos. Turner.

1:230 - DEED OF SALE - 29 April 1724 - Ann Glendening of Hanover Parish, widow, to William Grant and Margaret his wife and daughter of the said Ann Glendening. 3000 pounds of tobacco and 5 shillings for 100A. Part of a patent granted to John Mott and George Mott 17 October 1670 and bequeathed by George Mott, father of the said Ann Glendening to his four daughters Elizabeth,, Margaret, Ann, and Ellen by his will dated 31 March 1674 and proved 27 May 1674. Land being afterwards divided between the sisters. Bounded by the main road and Richard Fossiker. Signed Ann Glendening. Delivered in presence of Simon White, Richard Pearle, William Welsh. Recorded 1 May 1724 Thos. Turner.

1:234 - DEED OF SALE - 29 April 1724 - Ann Glendening of Hanover Parish, widow, to John Armstrong and Ellen his wife and daughter of the said Ann Glendening. 3000 pounds of tobacco and 5 shillings for 100A. Part of a patent granted to John Mott and George Mott 17 October 1670 and bequeathed by George Mott, father of the said Ann Glendening, to his four daughters Elizabeth, Margaret, Ann, and Ellen by his will dated 31 March 1674 and proved 27 May 1674. Land being afterwards divided between the sisters. Bounded by Joseph Armstrong and Muddy Creek to the mouth of a branch called Back Branch. Signed Ann Glendening. Delivered in presence of Simon White, Richard Pearle, William Welsh. Recorded 1 May 1724 Thos. Turner.

1:239 - DEED OF LEASE - 5 June 1724 - James Kay of Hanover Parish, planter, to Samuel Skinker of same. 5 shillings sterling to lease 255A being part of the dividend whereon the said Kay now lives. Bounded by Mathews, Dinwiddie, John Price, John Popham, Benjamin Stribling. Mary, wife of James Kay, relinquishes her right of dower and thirds. Signed James Kay. Delivered in presence of Richard Longman, George Downing, Moses Caddy. Recorded 5 June 1724 Thos. Turner.

1:240 - DEED OF RELEASE - 5 June 1724 - James Kay of Hanover Parish, planter, to Samuel Skinker of same. 15,000 pounds of tobacco for 255A described in lease. Mary, wife of James Kay, relinquishes her right of dower and thirds. Signed James Kay. Delivered in presence of Richd. Longman, George Downing, Moses Caddy. Recorded 5 June 1724 Thos. Turner.

1:243 - POWER OF ATTORNEY - 29 May 1724 - Thomas Guibert of Maryland deputes William Robinson of King George County his true and lawful attorney to ask, demand, and sue for such sums that are due . Signed Thos. Guibert. Delivered in presence of Thos. McWilliams, Thos. Grigsby, Anne Walter, Rose Grigsby. Recorded 3 July 1724 Thos. Turner.

1:243 - BOND - 3 July 1724 - Jonathan Gibson, William Thornton, and William Strothers bound to their sovereign lord the King for 1000 pounds sterling. Condition such that if Jonathan Gibson, gentleman, do faithfully and truly perform the said office of sheriff of King George county, the obligation is void. Signed Jonathan Gibson, Wm. Thornton, Wm. Strother.

1:244 - DEED OF LEASE - 2 July 1724 - John Elzy of Stafford County, planter to John Jones the Younger of King George County, planter. 5 shillings sterling to lease 100A being part of 500A bought by Thomas Elzy, father of the said John Elzy, from John Waugh of Stafford County by deed dated 8 October 1690. Said 500A was part of 2000A bought by the said John Waugh, clerk of Thomas Comer, who bought the same of Richard Whitehead, gentleman. Thomas Elzy by will dated 19 May 1698 and proved 10 November 1698 bequeathed the land unto his three sons. 200A to Thomas Elzy and 300A to be divided between Wm. Elzy and John Elzy. Bounded by former Simon Thomas line, Wm. Elzy, Thomas Elzy. Bridget, wife of said John Elzy, relinquishes her right of dower and thirds. Signed John Ellzey. Delivered in presence of Jonath. Gibson, Charles Seale, Henry Conyers. Recorded 7 August 1724 Thos. Turner.

1:245 - DEED OF RELEASE - 3 July 1724 - John Elzy of Stafford County, planter, to John Jones the Younger of King George County, planter. 8000 pounds of tobacco for 100A described in lease. This being the remaining part of the said John Elzy's 150A, the said John having sold about 40A unto Francis Waddington. Bridget, wife of John Elzy, relinquishes her right of dower and thirds. Signed John Ellzey. Delivered in presence of Jonath. Gibson, Charles Seale, Henry Conyers. Recorded 7 August 1724 Thos. Turner.

1:248 - POWER OF ATTORNEY - 9 April 1724 - John Becher of the city of Bristol, Esqr., appoints Samuel Skinker his true and lawful attorney to ask, demand, and receive the sum of 18 pounds, five shillings, and 5 pence from George Mason. Signed John Becher. Delivered in presence of Richd. Lewis, Wm. Cowhird. Recorded 7 August 1724 Thos. Turner.

1:249 - DEED OF LEASE - 3 March 1723 - Charles Cale and Alice his wife of

Hanover Parish to William Thornton of same. 5 shillings to lease 35A. Part of 2000A granted to Colonel John Catlet 2 June 1666, 500A of which at length became the property of Edward Maddock of Stafford county who by will dated 23 June 1694 and proved 11 December 1694 bequeathed 200A to Alice, wife of said Charles Cale. Bounded by east side of the mouth of Claburne Run, land bought by Wm. Thornton from Thomas Stone, Fitzhughs' mill pond. Signed Charles Cale, Alice Cale. Delivered in presence of Thomas Benson, John Hall, Wm. Hall. Recorded 7 August 1724 Thos. Turner.

1:251 - DEED OF RELEASE - 4 March 1723 - Charles Cale and Alice his wife of Hanover Parish to William Thornton of same. 14 pounds current money for 35A described in lease. Signed Charles Cale, Alice Cale. Delivered in presence of Thomas Benson, John Hall, Wm. Hall. Recorded 7 August 1724 Thos. Turner.

1:253 - INDENTURE - 24 August 1724 - John Harman of Hanover Parish, planter, to James Hackley of same, house carpenter. John Harman puts himself apprentice to James Hackley to learn the art and mystery of a house carpenter to serve him from the day's date for the term of four years. At the expiration of said term, James Hackley to give John Harman a set of house carpenter's tools fit for any common work and a fashionable suit of holyday new clothes. Signed John Harman, James Hackley. Delivered in presence of Wm. Thornton, Richd. Curtis. Recorded 4 September 1724 Thomas Turner.

1:253 - DEED OF LEASE - 11 August 1724 - James Kay of Hanover Parish to Samuel Skinker of same. 5 shillings to lease 647A bounded by parcel of land sold by said Kay to above parish for a Glebe house, Benjamin Stripling, John Popham, John Price. Mary, wife of James Kay, relinquishes her right of dower and thirds. Signed James Kay. Delivered in presence of Richd. Longman, John Farguson, James Hall. Recorded 2 October 1724 T. Turner.

1:255 - DEED OF RELEASE - 12 August 1724 - James Kay of Hanover Parish to Samuel Skinker of same. 21,000 pounds of tobacco and 58 pounds 4 shillings sterling for 647A. Containing 198A formerly sold by the said James Kay to the said Samuel Skinker by deed dated 24 January 1723; 255A sold by Kay to Skinker by deed dated 5 June 1724; and 194A now being sold by the said James Kay to the said Samuel Skinker. Part of a patent granted to Col. Gerard Fowks and Mr. Richard Haibert 23 March 1664. Mr. Haibert being the survivor sold it to James Kay, grandfather of the said James Kay to whom the said land descended by inheritance, his father having made no disposition of the same in his lifetime and he being the only heir. Mary, wife of James Kay, relinquishes her right of dower and thirds. Signed James Kay. Delivered in presence of Richard Longman, John Farguson, James Hall. Recorded 2 October 1724 T.

Turner.

1:259 - POWER OF ATTORNEY - 15 August 1724 - John Dinwiddie, merchant, appoints Mr. Thomas Monteith, merchant, to be his true and lawful attorney to ask, demand, and receive from all and every person all sums of money, debts, goods, wares, merchandise, effects, and anything whatsoever found due, owing, payable, belonging and coming unto the said constituant. Signed John Dinwiddie. Delivered in presence of Mungo Roy, Jeremiah Bronaugh. Recorded 3 October 1724 T. Turner.

1:260 - BOND - 4 September 1724 - William Allen of Stafford County, planter, bound unto John Brown of Northumberland county, tailor, for 500 pounds sterling. Condition such that if the two patents taken up by Brown and Allen dated 25 September 1710 and 1 January 1710 are not contested in any manner, obligation is void. Signed William Allen. Delivered in presence of Edward Taylor, Mosely Battaly. Recorded 4 December 1724 T. Turner.

1:261 - BOND - 4 December 1724 - John Brown bound to William Allen for 500 pounds sterling. Condition such that if John Brown and his heirs permit William Allen and his heirs to peaceably possess and enjoy lands taken up between Brown and Allen in patents dated 25 Sseptember 1710 and 1 January 1710 by title of survivorship, obligation is void. Signed John Brown. Delivered in presence of Edward Taylor, Moseley Battaly. Recorded 4 December 1724 T. Turner.

1:262 - DEED OF LEASE - 1 January 1724 - Henry Long, Senior of Hanover Parish to Robert Johnson of same. 5 shillings to lease 100A lying on north side of the Gravelly Run and formerly belonging to Cornelius and John Reynolds. Signed Henry Long. Delivered in presence of T. Turner, Wm. Hambleton. Recorded 1 January 1724 T. Turner.

1:263 - DEED OF RELEASE - 1 January 1724 - Henry Long, Senr. of Hanover Parish to Robert Johnson of same, planter. 3000 pounds of tobacco for 100A described in lease. Signed Henry Long. Delivered in presence of T. Turner, William Hambleton. Recorded 1 January 1724 T. Turner.

1:265 - POWER OF ATTORNEY - 5 September 1724 - Merchants and partners of the Iron Works with others of the city of Bristoll appoint Paul Micon the Younger and John Micon, both of Essex county, either of them or both of them, to be our true and lawfull attorneys of and for all the said company and partners. Signed John King, Jno. Lewis, Jeremiah Innys, Lyonel Lyde. Delivered in presence of Thomas Hall, Wm. Pitts. Recorded 1 January 1724 T. Turner.

1:266 - DEED OF LEASE - 4 September 1723 - Rowland Thornton of Hanover Parish to Humphrey Sawyer of same. 200 pounds tobacco yearly to lease 150A lying on the north side of a branch of Muddy Run. Formerly devised to Patrick Gibbons. To be let by Humphrey Sawyer and Frances his wife and their heirs until the full end and expiration of the natural lives of three persons, (viz): Humphrey Sawyer, Richard Martin, and Thomas Martin both sons-in-law to the said Humphrey Sawyer. Signed Rowland Thornton, Humphrey Sawyer. Delivered in presence of Richd. Pearle, Wm. Pearle. Recorded 5 February 1724 T. Turner.

1:268 - DEED OF GIFT - 2 March 1724 - John Owen, planter, in consideration of the love, good will, and affection which he bears towards his loving brothers William Owens and Richard Owens, gives and grants them a tract of land containing 200A bounded by Howson's line and land sold to Nathaniel Elkins. Signed John Owen. Delivered in presence of Wm. Redman, Seth Bryan, Richd. Bryan. Recorded 2 April 1725 T. Turner.

1:269 - DEED OF LEASE - _ April 1725 - William Rowley of Hanover Parish to Thomas Grigsby of St. Paul's Parish in Stafford County. 5 shillings to lease 50A being the plantation thereon Richard Griffis now lives. Part of 500A which belonged to Catherine the daughter and heiress of Hugh Williams, late the wife of John Rowley, dec'd. Escheated by William Wood by deed dated 23 February 1705 and who by will dated 6 June 1706 bequeathed it to the aforesaid William Rowley. Bounded by Richard Rosser, Mr. Gregg's line, Hall's line. Mary, wife of William Rowley, relinquishes her right of dower and thirds. Signed Will. Rowley. Delivered in presence of Benjam. Berryman, Mosley Battaly. Recorded 2 April 1725 T. Turner.

1:271 - DEED OF RELEASE - 2 April 1725 - William Rowley of Hanover Parish to Thomas Grigsby of St. Paul's Parish in Stafford County. 2000 pounds of tobacco for 50A described in lease. Mary, wife of William Rowley, relinquishes her right of dower and thirds. Signed Will. Rowley. Delivered in presence of Benjamin Berryman, Mosley Battaly. Recorded 2 April 1725 T. Turner.

1:273 - BOND - 2 April 1725 - William Rowley of Hanover Parish bound to Thomas Grigsby of St Paul's Parish in Stafford County in the full and just sum of 100 pounds sterling. Condition such that if terms of certain deeds of lease and release are kept, obligation to be void. Signed Wm. Rowley. Delivered in presence of Benja. Berryman, Mosley Battaley. Recorded 2 April 1725 T. Turner.

1:274 - RECEIPT - 1 April 1725 - Received of Mr. Thomas Grigsby 5 shillings being the consideration within mentioned. Received of Mr. Thomas Grigsby 2000 pounds of tobacco being the consideration within mentioned. Signed Will. Rowley. Recorded 7 May 1725 T. Turner.

1:274 - DEED OF LEASE - 1 April 1725 - James Kay of Hanover Parish, planter, to John Tayloe of North Farnham Parish in Richmond County, gentleman. 5 shillings to lease 170A bounded by George Jones, Mr. Diskins, Glebe land, Mr. Skrine, Mr. Skinker. Mary, wife of James Kay, relinquishes her right of dower and thirds. Signed James Kay. Delivered in presence of Jno. Price, Francis Payne, John Fewell. Recorded 1 May 1725 T. Turner.

1:276 - DEED OF RELEASE - 2 April 1725 - James Kay of Hanover Parish, planter, to John Tayloe of North Farnham Parish in Richmond County, gentleman. 30 pounds 12 shillings sterling for 170A described in lease. Mary, wife of James Kay, relinquishes her right of dower and thirds. Signed James Kay. Delivered in presence of Jno. Price, Fran. Payne, Jno. Fewell. Recorded 7 May 1725 T. Turner.

1:279 - DEED OF LEASE - 28 April 1725 - James Kay of Hanover Parish, planter, to John Diskin of same. 5 shillings to lease 104A being part of a 2334A patent granted to James Kay 12 December 1722. Bounded by Glebe land, Col. Corbins, George Jones. Mary, wife of James Kay, relinquishes her right of dower and thirds. Signed James Kay. Delivered in presence of Jno. Price, Francis Payne, Jno. Fewell. Recorded 7 May 1725 T. Turner.

1:281 - DEED OF RELEASE - 28 April 1725 - James Kay of Hanover Parish, planter, to John Diskin of same. 50 pounds sterling for 104A described in lease. Mary, wife of James Kay, relinquishes her right of dower and thirds. Signed James Kay. Delivered in presence of Jno. Price, Francis Payne, John Fewell. Recorded 7 May 1725 T. Turner.

1:284 and 285 are blank.

1:286 - BOND - 28 April 1725 - James Kay, planter of King George County, bound to John Diskin of Richmond County for 400 pounds sterling. Condition such that if covenants of deeds are met, obligation to be void. Signed James Kay. Delivered in presence of John Price, Francis Payne, John Fewell. Recorded 7 May 1725 T. Turner.

1:287 - DEED OF SALE - 3 February 1724 - Ann Glendening of Hanover Parish, widow to John Glendening, the only son of the said Ann Glendening, of same and Pheaby his wife. 3000 pounds of tobacco and 5 shillings for 250A. Part of a tract of land granted unto Jno. Mott and George Mott by patent dated

17 October 1760. Which tract was bequeathed by the said George Mott, father to the said Ann Glendening, unto his four daughters Elizabeth, Margaret, Ann, and Ellen by his last will and testament dated 31 March 1674 and proved in Rappahanack court 27 May 1674. The said John Glendening is not to disturb or molest the said Ann Glendening in her house and plantation where she now liveth. She may peaceably occupy, possess, and enjoy the house and plantation during her natural life. If said John Glendening leaves no heirs to inherit said land, it is to be divided among his four sisters and their next and nearest heirs. Signed Ann Glendening. Delivered in presence of Richd. Pearle, Simon White, Willm. Welsh. Recorded 7 May 1725 T. Turner.

1:291 - DEED OF GIFT - 1 July 1725 - Henry Long, Senr. of Hanover Parish, planter, gives unto his daughter Martha Wharton, the wife of John Wharton, one negro boy called Toby five years of age last March 1724/5. Signed Henry Long. Delivered in presence of Sam. Wharton,, Ann Wharton. Recorded 6 August 1725 T. Turner.

1:292 - DEED OF LEASE - 6 January 1724 - Rowland Thornton of Hanover Parish to John Allen and Mary his wife and Mary Allen, daughter of John Allen. To lease 100A lying upon the western most branches of Muddy Creek, near to Potomack Rowling Road. Lease to run for the full end and duration of the natural life of the longest liver. First 5 years rent free. 500 pounds of tobacco from the sixth year on upon every feast of St. Thomas, December 21. Signed John Allen, Rowld. Thornton. Delivered in presence of John Jones, Elizabeth Jones. Recorded 6 August 1725 T. Turner.

1:294 - POWER OF ATTORNEY - 29 May 1725 - Alexander McFarland of the city of Glasgow, merchant, makes Capt. William Strother of King George County his true and lawful attorney. Signed A. McFarlane. Delivered in presence of Wm. Thornton, Catesby Cocke. Recorded 6 August 1725 T. Turner.

1:295 - DEED OF SALE - 2 July 1725 - William Allen of Stafford County, planter, to William Hackney. 100A in consideration of several services done for assisting about, finding out, and helping survey a tract of land. Part of a 1490A tract granted to William Allen in 1718. Begins at the mouth of Beaver Dam Branch. Bounded by Philip Ludwell, John Roberts. Signed William Allen. Delivered in presence of Henry Long, Sr., Jno. Page, Mosely Battaley. Recorded 6 August 1725 T. Turner.

1:296 - DEED OF LEASE - 3 June 1725 - William Allen of Stafford County, cordwainer, to William Strother, Junr. of King George County, gentleman. 5 shillings sterling to lease 740A bounded by Daniel Marr. Begins on east side of the Marsh Run. Part of a 1490A grant to William Allen dated 17 February

1718/19. Signed William Allen. Delivered in the presence of Mosley Battaley, Antho. Hayne, George Parsons. Recorded 6 August 1725 T. Turner.

1:298 - DEED OF RELEASE - 4 June 1725 - William Allen of Stafford County, cordwainer, to William Strother, Junr. of King George County, gentleman. 120 pounds sterling for 740A described in lease. Thomas Turner, Gent., by the power of attorney from Margaret, wife of William Allen, relinquishes her right of dower and thirds. Signed Wm. Allen. Delivered in presence of Moseley Battaley, Anth. Hayne, George Parsons. Recorded 6 August 1725 T. Turner.

1:300 POWER OF ATTORNEY - 14 April 1725 - Margaret, wife of William Allen of Stafford County, authorizes Thomas Turner to be her good and lawful attorney to acknowledge and relinquish her right of dower of, in, and to one certain tract of land sold to William Strother, Gent. Signed Margaret Allen. Delivered in presence of Henry Connyers, Mosely Battaley, Catesby Cocke. Recorded 6 August 1725 T. Turner.

1:301 - DEED OF SALE - 2 September 1725 - Rice Curtis, Junr. and Martha his wife of Christ Church Parish in Middlesex County to Nicholas Smith of Sittenburne Parish, gentleman. 57 pounds 10 shillings current money of Virginia for 116A. Part of a 464A patent which hath been lately held by Henry Thacker, dec'd. Bounded by a branch called Spring Branch, Nicholas Smith. Martha, wife of Rice Curtis, Jr., relinquishes her right of dower and thirds. Signed Rice Curtis Jr., Martha Curtis. Delivered in presence of G. Eskridge, John Spicer, Charles Deane. Recorded 3 September 1725 T. Turner.

1:303 - DEED OF LEASE - 2 September 1725 - Joshua Davis of Overwharton Parish in Stafford County and Samuel Davis of Washington Parish in Westmoreland County to William Duff of Hanover Parish, taylor. 5 shillings sterling to lease 476A surveyed by William Horton. Parcel of land formerly sold by Malathy Peale of Stafford County unto Joshua Davis, Gent., father to the said Joshua and Samuel by deed dated 27 January 1696. Part of a patent granted by Sir William Barkeley unto Robert Alexander, John Alexander and Christopher Lunn for 1428A. Bounded by Edward Taylor, Malathy Peale. Catherine Butler, now wife of James Butler, mother of the said Joshua and Samuel Davis, relinquishes her right of dower and thirds. Signed Joshua Davis, Saml. Davis. Delivered in presence of Walter Anderson, Will. Jordan. Recorded 3 September 1725 T. Turner.

1:305 - DEED OF RELEASE - 3 September 1725 - Joshua Davis of Overwharton Parish in Stafford County and Samuel Davis of Washington Parish in Westmoreland County to William Duff of Hanover Parish, taylor. 80 pounds sterling for 476A described in lease. Catherine Butler, mother of Joshua and

Samuel Davis, relinquishes her right of dower and thirds. Signed Joshua Davis, Saml. Davis. Delivered in presence of Walter Anderson, Will. Jordon. Recorded 3 September 1725 T. Turner.

1:308 - BOND - 1 September 1725 - Joshua Davis of Overwharton Parish in Stafford County and Samuel Davis of Washington Parish in Westmoreland County, planters, bound unto William Duff of Hanover Parish, taylor, in the full and just sum of 160 pounds sterling. Condition such that if agreements in conveyances are met, obligation to be void. Signed Joshua Davis, Saml. Davis. Delivered in presence of Walter Anderson, Will. Jordan. Recorded 3 September 1725 T. Turner.

1:309 - DEED OF LEASE - 27 August 1725 - Alxdr. Beach of Stafford County to Timothy Reading of King George County. 5 shillings to lease 456A beginning upon the road branch of the run issueing out of the side of Marsh Run. Bounded by Alexander Beach, Charles Morgan, Morgan Darnall, Edward Price, Alxdr. Scott, Mark Harding, and William Russell. Signed Allaxd. Beach. Delivered in presence of James Warren, Thomas Wellch. Recorded 3 September 1725 T. Turner.

1:310 - DEED OF RELEASE - 28 August 1725 - Alexander Beach of Stafford County to Timothy Reading of King George County, planter. 6000 pounds of tobacco for 456A described in lease. Signed Alexdr. Beach. Delivered in presence of James Warren, Thomas Wellch. Recorded 3 September 1725 T. Turner.

1:312 - BOND - 1 October 1725 - William Thornton bound unto William Strother for 500 pounds sterling. Condition such that whereas in the year 1718 William Thornton did in partnership with William Cocke Esq., Ch----Corbin Thacker and Francis Thornton Junr. survey and take up 6000A in Essex, now Spotsylvania County, and by reason that the said William Thornton was surveyor, he was advised to put in the name of a friend which might after convey the land to him and be a means for the grant more ready to pass. Upon which the said Thorton did put in the said William Strother. Now the said William Thornton having disposed of the land to George Prockter of Spotsylvania county has prevailed with the said William Strother to sign deed of lease and release to convey the said land to the said Procter. And the said William Strother has taken this bond as a cautionary security that he nor his heirs shall hereafter be anyway damnified for so doing. If no trouble, cost or damage whatsoever shall happen or come unto the said William Strother or his heirs by means of his executing the said deeds of lease and release, the above obligation to be void. Signed Wm. Thornton. Delivered in presence of Henry Connyers, Mosley Battaley. Recorded 2 October 1725 T. Turner.

1:313 - BOND - No date - John Prince of Hanover Parish, rector, and James Markham of same, gentleman, are bound unto Walter Anderson of King George County and Edward Price of Spotsylvania County for 210 pounds current money of Virginia. Condition such that Walter Anderson and Edward Price stand security for Margaret Runer, executrix of the last will and testament of Mark Runer, dec'd, and if the bounden do for and on behalf of the said Markham Runer save harmless and indemnify the said Walter Anderson and Edward Price, then obligation is to be void. Signed John Prince, James Markham. Recorded 2 October 1725 T. Turner.

1:314 - DEPOSITION - 26 October 1725 - Ann Hopkins, wife of John Hopkins, about thirty years, being first sworn, saith that she is the daughter of Mary Hinson and heir to William Wood, late of Stafford county deceased, and that about twenty years ago she was saved by the Indians that committed the murders at John Rowley's plantation and in a small time after the said murder her Uncle William Wood carried this deponent to the house of Evan Jones and that she staid there till her mother came from Pennsylvania and carried her down to James River and further this deponent saith not. Pursuant to an order of King George county court dated the second day of October 1725, this deposition was taken before us the twenty-sixth day of October 1725. Signed Saml. Skinker, T. Turner. Then came Hester Lampton, widow, and presented the above deposition and her motion, the same was ordered to be recorded and is accordingly. Recorded 8 November 1725 T. Turner.

1:314 - DEPOSITION - 26 October 1725 - Mary Rowley, aged about fifty-three years, being first sworn, saith that Ann Hinson, daughter of Mary Hinson and now wife of John Hopkins, is the same girl that was saved by the Indians when they committed the murders at John Rowley's plantation and this deponent further saith that she was present when her uncle William Wood made his will and therein left the said Ann Hinson 100A of land binding on the land of John Gregsby and that some time after the deponent and her husband sent the said Ann word of the said land being left her by her uncle upon which she being at James River, she returned again and further this deponent saith not. Pursuant to an order of King George county court dated the second day of October 1725, this deposition was taken before us the twenty-sixth day of October 1725. Signed Saml. Skinker, T. Turner. Then came Hester Lampton, widow, and presented the above deposition and her motion, the same was ordered to be recorded and is accordingly. Recorded 8 November 1725 T. Turner.

1:315 - DEPOSITION - 26 October 1725 - Ann Harris, aged about sixty-three years, being first sworn, saith that Ann Hinson, who is now Ann Hopkins and wife to John Hopkins and about thirty years of age, is as the deponent verily believes the same person that one William Wood, late of Stafford County deceased, left 100A of land, the said land being then in Stafford, now in King George County, and binding on the land of John Gregsby, the said William Wood being uncle to the said Ann Hinson and further this deponent saith not. Pursuant to an order of King George County court dated the second day of October 1725, this deposition was taken before us the twenty-sixth day of October 1725. Signed Saml. Skinker, T. Turner. Then came Hester Lampton, widow, and presented the above deposition and her motion, the same was ordered to be recorded and is accordingly. Recorded 8 November 1725 T. Turner.

1:316 - DEPOSITION - 26 October 1725 - William Rowley, aged about sixty years, being first sworn, saith that Ann Hinson, who is now about thirty years of age and intermarried with John Hopkins, is the daughter of Mary Hinson and the same person that William Wood of Stafford County, who was her uncle, bequeathed 100A of land to by his last will and testament, the said land binding on the land of John Gregsby and further this deponent saith not. Pursuant to an order of King George County Court dated the second day of October 1725, this deposition was taken before us the twenty-sixth day of October 1725. Signed Samuel Skinker, T. Turner. Then came Hester Lampton, widow, and presented the above deposition and her motion, the same was ordered to be recorded and is accordingly. Recorded 8 November 1725 T. Turner.

1:316 - DEPOSITION - 26 October 1725 - Mary Cheshire, aged about forty-one years, being first sworn, saith that about twenty-one years ago Ann Hinson, the daughter of Mary Hinson, between nine or ten years age, was brought by her uncle William Wood to Evan Jones house and that she there staid two or three months and by a certain mark on her body she, this deponent, knows her to be the same girl that at this present time is the now wife of John Hopkins and further this deponent saith not. Pursuant to an order of King George County Court dated the second day of October 1725, this deposition was taken before us the twenty-sixth day of October 1725. Signed Samuel Skinker, T. Turner. Then came Hester Lampton, widow, and presented the above deposition and her motion, the same was ordered to be recorded and is accordingly. Recorded 8 November 1725 T. Turner.

1:317 - BOND - 3 December 1725 - Thomas Bartlett, William Miller, Thomas Dickinson, Henry Long Junr., and Robert Johnson, all of the county of King George, are firmly bound unto Sam Wharton of same in the sum of 500 pounds sterling. Condition such that whereas the above named Samuel Wharton at the instants and request of Elizabeth Jones, then widow of Lewis Jones and now wife of the above bound Thomas Bartlett, did become bound in the sum of 500 pounds sterling that the aforesaid Elizabeth should faithfully administer the goods, chatells and credits of the said Lewis, dec'd; if the said Thomas Bartlett and his heirs do and shall at all times hereafter save and keep harmless and indemnified the said Samuel Wharton and his heirs from all manner of arrest, actions, charges and damages whatsoever that may arise by reason of the said revised bond or anything relating to or concerning the same, then the obligation to be void. Signed Thos. Bartlett, Thos. Dickinson, Henry Long, Robt. Johnson. Recorded 3 December 1725 T. Turner.

1:318 - DEED OF LEASE - 14 December 1725 - William Hamett of Hanover Parish, planter, to John Dougins of Westmoreland County, planter. 5 shillings to lease 100A on the head of the main branch of Gingotague. Part of a 116A patent to William Hamett dated 10 July 1724. Bounded by Nicholas Downton, Thomas Newton, John Dodd, George Peach. Elizabeth, wife of William Hamett, relinquishes her right of dower. Signed William Hamett, Elizabeth Hamett. Delivered in presence of Isaac Arnold, Isaac Arnold, Jr., John Goff. Recorded 7 January 1725.

1:320 - DEED OF RELEASE - 15 December 1725 - William Hamett of Hanover Parish, planter, to John Dougins of Westmoreland County. 4000 pounds of good tobacco for 100A described in lease. Elizabeth, wife of William Hamett, relinquishes her right of dower. Signed William Hamett, Elizabeth Hamett. Delivered in presence of Isaac Arnold, Isaac Arnold, Jr., John Goff. Recorded 7 January 1725 T. Turner.

1:322 - BOND - 15 December 1725 - William Hamett of Hanover Parish bound to John Dougins for 8000 pounds of good tobacco. Condition such that if all agreements made in deeds of lease and release are met, obligation to be void. Signed William Hamett. Delivered in presence of Isaac Arnold, Isaac Arnold, Jr., John Goff. Recorded 7 January 1725 T. Turner.

1:323 - DEED OF SALE - 29 December 1725 - Joseph Berry of Stafford County, planter to Andrew Harrison of Westmoreland County and Richard Griffis of King George County, planters. 4000 pounds of tobacco in cask for a certain mill standing on the Doeg Run, likewise a small parcel of land adjacent and opposite to the said mill. Signed Joseph Berry. Delivered in presence of Thomas Stribling, William Harrison. Recorded 7 January 1725 T. Turner.

1:324 - DEED OF LEASE - 27 December 1725 - Benjamin Henslee and Elizabeth his wife of King George County to John Holdsworth of same. 5 shillings to lease 50A being all the remaining part of a tract of land which the said Benjamin Henslee holds by virture of a deed of lease and release dated 5 April 1720 from William Berry, son of Henry Berry, dec'd. Bounded by Thomas Reiley, Thomas Williams, John Berry and Robert Strother. Elizabeth;, wife of Benjamin Henslee, relinquishes her right of dower. Signed Benja. Henslee,

Eliza. Henslee. Delivered in presence of Joseph Berry, James Kay. Recorded 7 January 1725 T. Turner.

1:325 - DEED OF RELEASE - 28 December 1725 - Benjamin Henslee and Elizabeth his wife of King George County to John Holdsworth of same. 4000 pounds of tobacco for 50A described in lease. Elizabeth, wife of Benjamin Henslee, relinquishes her right of dower. Signed Benja. Henslee, Eliza. Henslee. Delivered in presence of Joseph Berry, James Kay. Recorded 7 January 1725 T. Turner.

1:326 - DEED OF LEASE - 3 February 1725 - James Markham of Hanover Parish, planter, to Thomas Turner of same. 5 shillings to lease 200A beginning on the main branch of Gingoteague. Being part of a tract containing 450A granted to John Griffin by patent dated 11 March 1694/5. Signed James Markham. Delivered in presence of Wm. Thornton, Rowld. Thornton. Recorded 4 February 1725 T. Turner.

1:327 - DEED OF RELEASE - 4 February1725 - James Markham of Hanover Parish, planter, to Thomas Turner of same. 3000 pounds of good, sound, merchantable tobacco for 200A described in lease. Signed James Markham. Delivered in presence of Wm. Thornton, Rowld. Thornton. Recorded 4 February 1725 T. Turner.

1:329 - BOND - 4 February 1725 - James Markham of Hanover Parish bound to Thomas Turner of same for 200 pounds sterling. Condition such that if agreements made in deeds of lease and release are met, obligation to be void. Signed James Markham. Delivered in presence of Wm. Thornton, Rowld. Thornton. Recorded 4 February 1725 T. Turner.

1:330 - DEED OF GIFT - 21 January 1725 - Mary Raw of King George County for the love and affection she bears towards her well beloved son Abraham Raw give a young mare and her future increase, a chest and small deal box, a gun, an iron pot holding about four gallons and pot hook, a pied heifer named Star and all her future female increase. Signed Mary Raw. Delivered in presence of Joseph Berry, Patrick Hamrick. Recorded 4 February 1725 T. Turner.

1:330 - PATENT ASSIGNMENT - 4 February 1695/6 - Margaret Lady Culpeper, Thomas Lord Fairfax, Katherin his wife and Alexander Culpeper Esq., proprietors of the Northern Neck of Virginia, grant to John Griffin 450A bounded by Ralph Whiting, James Mathews, Esqr., Grg. Wormley. Signed Will. Fitshugh. All the right, title, and interest of all and singular provisions contained within the patent are assigned to Ralph Whiteing for 18,000 pounds of tobacco. Signed John Griffing, Elizabeth Griffing. Delivered in presence of John Caryll,

Ann Lawrence. Than came Samuel Wharton and presented into court the within patent together with this assignment from John Griffin and Elizabeth his wife to Ralph Whiteing and on his motion they are both admitted to record. Recorded 1 April 1726 T. Turner.

1:332 - DEED OF LEASE - 31 March 1726 - Rice Hooe, Junr. and Catherin his wife of St. Paul's Parish in Stafford County to Thomas Turner of Hanover Parish. 5 shillings current money of Virginia to lease 43A. Being part of a tract of land sold to Richard Taliaferro by John Reynolds containing 200A which land descended to Richard Taliaferro, son to the aforesaid Richard Taliaferro and brother to the aforesaid Catherin and now on the decease of Richard Taliaferro the son, the said 43A descend to the said Catherin; the same being one third part of what is left of Richard Taliaferro's land in a survey made in the year 1714 between Col. Wm. Fitzhugh,, Mr. John Lomax and others called the Nansamond Patent. Signed Rice Hooe, Katherine Hooe. Delivered in presence of Fran. Thornton, Benja. Strother. Recorded 1 April 1726 T. Turner.

1:333 - DEED OF RELEASE - 1 April 1726 - Rice Hooe, Jr. and Catherin his wife of St. Paul's Parish in Stafford County to Thomas Turner of Hanover Parish. 10 pounds current money for 43A described in lease. Signed Rice Hooe, Katherine Hooe. Delivered in presence of Fran. Thornton, Benja. Strother. Recorded 1 April 1726 T. Turner.

1:334 - BOND - 1 April 1726- Rice Hooe, Junr. of Stafford County bound to Thomas Turner of King George County for 200 pounds sterling. Condition such that if agreements made in deeds of lease and release are met, obligation to be void. Signed Rice Hooe. Delivered in presence of Fran. Thornton, Benja. Strother. Recorded 1 April 1726 T. Turner.

1:335 - DEED OF LEASE - 25 March 1726 - Robert Hughs of Sittenbourn Parish, taylor, to Nicholas Smith of same, gentleman. 5 shillings sterling to lease 122A bounded by Nicholas Smith, Wm. and Mary Quissenberry, Wm. Grant, Alexander Hinsen, and Humphry Quisssenberry. The land having been purchased of Robert Hinson, David Dickey, and John Jenings by deeds of sale in Richmond county court. Signed Robert Hughs. Delivered in presence of Catesby Cocke, Edw. Barradall, T. Turner. Recorded 1 April 1726 T. Turner.

1:336 - DEED OF RELEASE - 26 March 1726 - Robert Hughs of Sittenburn Parish, taylor, to Nicholas Smith of same, gentleman. 5500 pounds of tobacco for 122A described in lease. Signed Robert Hughs. Delivered in presence of Catesby Cocke, Edw. Barradall, T. Turner. Recorded 1 April 1726 T. Turner.

1:337 - DEED OF LEASE - 31 March 1726 - John Jones and George Jones of

Hanover Parish to Hugh French of Westmoreland County. 5 shillings to lease 200A being part of 500A bought by Sampson Dorell of John Fossaker and Elizabeth his wife. Bounded by Fitzhugh, John and George Jones, John Simson, Hugh Mason, Daniel French. Signed John Jones, George Jones. Delivered in presence of Hen. McKie, Aaron Thornley. Recorded 1 April 1726 T. Turner.

1:338 - DEED OF RELEASE - 1 April 1726 - John Jones and George Jones of Hanover Parish to Hugh French of Westmoreland County. 200A . Whereas a certain Sampson Dorell did by deed dated 16 April 1692 purchase of John Fossaker and Elizabeth his wife 500A of land and whereas the said Sampson Dorrell did on 22 May 1699 convey unto Mary French, sister to the above mentioned Hugh, 200A, part of the above 500A, adjoining the land which Hugh French, father of the said Mary French, had bought of John Fossaker ; and whereas judgment is granted by the court unto Hugh French for his 200A to be laid off according to the said Dorell's deed to Mary French, which if it were, would include and take in the plantation whereon the said John Jones now liveth, John and George Jones to release these 200A unto Hugh French; also, the above named John and George Jones did purchase the 300A remaining of the 500A. Bounded by Fitzhugh, John and George Jones, John Simson, Hugh Mason, Daniel French. Signed John Jones, George Jones. Delivered in presence of Hen,. McKie, Aaron Thornley. Recorded 1 April 1726 T. Turner.

1:340 - DEED OF LEASE - 31 March 1726 - Daniel Marr of Hanover Parish, planter, to John Hudnall of same, planter. 5 shillings to lease 235A being part of a tract of 713A granted to William Allen and John Brown by deed dated 25 September 1710, being one third in length of the said land. Signed Daniel Marr. Not Witnesssed. Recorded 1 April 1726 T. Turner.

1:341 - DEED OF RELEASE - 1 April 1726 - Daniel Marr of Hanover Parish, planter, to John Hudnall of same, planter. 35 pounds sterling for 235A described in lease. Signed Daniel Marr. Not Witnesssed. Recorded 1 April 1726 T. Turner.

1:342 - DEED OF SALE - 1 March 1725 - Francis Triplet of Washington Parish in Westmoreland County, mariner, to Robert French of Sittenbourne Parish, planter. 2000 pounds of good tobacco for 210A. Tract of land which said Triplet's grandfather Francis Triplet once bought of John Wright and by his last will and testament bequeathed it to the said Francis Triplet. Bounded by Wm. Smart, dec'd. Signed Francis Triplett. Delivered in presence of William Browne, Francis Triplitt. Recorded 1 April 1726 T. Turner.

1:344 - DEPOSITION - Constance Pain of King George County, aged sixty-three or there abouts, saith that she knew James Kay, Senior, and William

Kay his brother and that they were always reputed to be Lancashire men and that James Kay was the elder and that the said James Kay married with one Sarah Joeson and had five children: James, Robert, Ann, William, and Richard, and that James was the elder. This deponent further saith that the said James Kay the son intermarried with one Mary Pannell and had five by her: a son named James, who is the eldest and only son now living of the said James Kay the son, inherited all the lands which his said father died possesssed of in this colony and this deponent further saith that she was in the room when the said James Kay the grandson was born and further this deponent saith not. Signed Constance Pain. This deposition was presented into court by James Kay and the said Constance Pain made oath in open court to the truth of what is therein mentioned which at the instance of James Markham is admitted to record. Recorded 1 April 1726 T. Turner.

1:344 - DEPOSITION - Grace Steward of King George County, aged fifty-four years or there abouts, saith she knew James Kay Jr. who intermarried with Mary Pannell and had issue by her five children of which James is the eldest and only son now living. This deponent was in the room when the said James the son was born and saith he inherited all the lands which his said father died possessed of within the colony. Signed Grace Steward. Deposition presented in court by James Kay and the said Grace Steward made oath in open court to the truth of what is therein mentioned which at the instance of James Markham is admitted to record. Recorded 1 April 1726 T. Turner.

1:345 - DEPOSITION - Henry Long of King George County, aged seventy-six years or there abouts, saith he knew James Kay and William Kay, two brothers who often told this deponent that they were Lancashire men, and that the said James Kay was the elder and this deponent saith that the said James Kay intermarried with one ----- Joeson and had issue by her four children that this deponent knew: James, who was the eldest, Robert, Ann, Richard, and the said James Kay the son intermarried with one Mary Pannell and had issue by her a son named James and other children which said James was the eldest son of the said James Kay the son and now inherits all his said father's lands within this colony. Signed Henry Long. Deposition presented into court by James Kay and the said Henry Long made oath in open court to the truth of what is therein mentioned which at the instance of James Markham is admitted to record. Recorded 1 April 1726 T. Turner.

1:345 - DEPOSITION - William Smith of King George County, aged eighty-five years or there abouts, saith he knew James Kay, grandfather of James Kay now of the county of King George aforesaid, and William Kay his brother and saith they were Lancashire men and that James was the eldest and that the said James Kay's wife was named Sarah and that he had issue by her four children which this deponent knew: James, who was the eldest, Robert, Ann, and William, and further this deponent saith not. Signed William Smith. Deposition presented into court by James Kay and the said William Smith made oath in open court to the truth of what is therein mentioned which at the instance of James Markham is admitted to record. Recorded 1 April 1726 Thomas Turner.

1:346 - INDENTURE - 1 April 1726 - The Worshipful Court of King George County and Jeremiah Bronaugh, Sr. of said county, planter. Said court hath bound William Raredon, being a poor orphan, apprentice unto Jeremiah Bronaugh to learn the trade and mystery of planter to the age of twenty-one, he being seventeen years old the fifteenth of October next. Signed Jera. Bronaugh. Recorded 1 April 1726 T. Turner.

1:346 - INDENTURE - 1 April 1726 - The Worshipful Court of King George County and John Stewart of the said county, planter. Said court hath bound Joseph Raredon, being a poor orphan, apprentice unto John Stewart until he shall arrive to the age of twenty-one years, he being fifteen years old the nineteenth day of October next. Signed John Steward. Recorded 1 April 1726 Thomas Turner.

1:347 - INDENTURE - No Date - The Worshipful Court of King George County and Robert Doniphan of said county, planter. Said court hath bound Elizabeth Raredon, being a poor orphan, apprentice unto Robert Doniphan to learn the trade and mystery of a spinstor. She shall abide with Doniphan until she shall arrive at the age of eighteen years, she being twelve years old the eleventh day of September last. Signed Robert Doniphan. Recorded 1 April 1726 T. Turner.

1:347 - POWER OF ATTORNEY - 26 March 1726 - William Sarjant of Bristol, merchant, appoints Thomas Wareing, Edmund Bagge, and Jeremiah Bronaugh the Elder his true and lawful attorneys to ask, demand, and receive of and from any person all and every debt owing and belonging to him. Signed Willm. Sarjant. Delivered in presence of John Farguson, John Corbin, Mungo Roy. Recorded 1 April 1726 T. Turner.

1:348 - DEED OF LEASE - 19 April 1726 - Archibald Allen of Washington Parish in Westmoreland County, planter, to William Duff of Hanover Parish, planter. 5 shillings sterling to lease 150A whereon Edward Taylor now lives, nigh a branch commonly called Cool Spring branch. Bounded by Robert Alexander, deceased; Joshua David, deceased; William Hutson; and land formerly belonging to John Brown nigh the mouth of a branch called Clay Spring branch. Being part of a patent granted unto William Brown and William

Baltrop for 744A dated 7 August 1669 which by several conveyances is since become the freehold and inheritance of Archibald Allen in fee simple; it being the residue and remainder of all land belonging to and appertaining to the said Edward Taylor. Signed Archibald Allan. Delivered in presence of Saml. Davis, Robert Green. Recorded 6 May 1726 T. Turner.

1:349 - DEED OF RELEASE - 20 April 1726 - Archibald Allen of Washington Parish in Westmoreland County, planter, to William Duff of Hanover Parish, planter. 6000 pounds tobacco for 150A described in lease. Bounded by land formerly belonging to John Brown and by him sold to Thomas White, deceased. Signed Archibald Allan. Delivered in presence of Saml. Davis, Robert Green. Recorded 6 May 1726 T. Turner.

1:351 - BOND - 20 April 1726 - Archibald Allen of Washington Parish in Westmoreland County, planter, bound unto William Duff of Hanover Parish, planter, for 20,000 pounds of good tobacco. Condition such that if agreements in certain deeds of lease and release bearing even date are kept, obligation to be void. Signed Archibald Allan. Delivered in presence of Saml. Davis, Robert Green. Recorded 6 May 1726 T. Turner.

1:352 - BOND - 2 May 1726 - Archibald Allen of Washington Parish in Westmoreland County, planter, bound unto William Duff of King George County for 2000 pounds of tobacco and cask. Condition such that if Archibald Allen upon the request and cost of William Duff will attest that 20A, bounded by George Peach on one side and Gingcotege Swamp on the other , on the head of the land belonging to Benjamin Strother be the same more or less clearly acquired and discharged from all and all manner of former bargains and sales, gifts, grants, charges, troubles, incumbrances whatsoever, obligation to be void. Signed Archibald Allan. Delivered in presence of Saml. Davis, Robert Green. Recorded 6 May 1726 T. Turner.

1:353 - DEED OF LEASE - 28 June 1726 - Henry Calfee of King George County to John Morehead of same. 5 shillings to lease 200A being part of a tract of land surveyed for the said Henry Calfee by John Coppedge in April 1723. Signed Henry Calfee. Delivered in presence of Peter Ker, John Calfee. Recorded 1 July 1726 T. Turner.

1:353 - DEED OF RELEASE - 29 June 1726 - Henry Calfee of King George County to John Morehead of same. 1330 pounds tobacco for 200A described in lease. Signed Henry Calfee. Delivered in presence of Peter Ker, John Calfee. Elinor, wife of Henry Calfee, relinquishes her right of dower. Recorded 1 July 1726 T. Turner.

1:354 - POWER OF ATTORNEY - 25 June 1726 - Eleanor Calfee, wife to Henry Calfee of King George County, nominated Capt. William Strother her true and lawful attorney to relinquish her right of dower. Signed Eleanor Calfee. Delivered in presence of Michael Mildrum, William Hackney. Recorded 1 July 1726 T. Turner.

1:355 - DEED OF LEASE - 6 April 1726 - John Spicer of Sittenbourne Parish, Gent., to Nicholas Smith of same, Gent. 5 shillings current money of Virginia to lease 300A a little above Charles' Beaver Dam Swamp. Bounded by William Carter's orchard fence and a branch that falls into Ireland Swamp. Formerly the land of Captain Arthur Spicer, deceased, father of the said John Spicer. Signed John Spicer. Delivered in presence of Charles Deane, Herman Arige, Crestofar Pretchet, George Paine, Edw. Barradall. Recorded 1 July 1726 T. Turner.

1:356 - DEED OF RELEASE - 7 April 1726 - John Spicer of Sittenbourne Parish, Gent., to Nicholas Smith of same, Gent. 12,000 pounds tobacco for 300A described in lease. Signed John Spicer. Delivered in presence of Charles Deane, Herman Arige, Crestofar Pretchet, George Paine, Edw. Barradall. Mary, wife of John Spicer, relinquishes her right of dower. Delivered in presence of Charles Deane, Robert Wilsone, Wm. Baptie. Recorded 1 July 1726 T. Turner.

1:358 - BOND - 7 April 1726 - John Spicer of Hanover Parish, Gent., bound unto Nicholas Smith of same for 200 pounds current money of Virginia. Condition such that if agreements in a certain indenture of release bearing even date are kept, obligation to be void. Signed John Spicer. Delivered in presence of Charles Deane, Herman Arige, Crestofar Pretchet, George Paine, Edw. Barradall. Recorded 1 July 1726 T. Turner.

1:359 - POWER OF ATTORNEY - 7 April 1726 - John Spicer, Gent., of King George County authorizes Mr. Thomas Turner of same to be his lawful attorney to acknowledge unto Colonel Nicholas Smith deeds of lease and release for 300A bearing equal date. Signed John Spicer.. Delivered in presence of Charles Deane, George Paine, Wm. Baptie. Recorded 1 July 1726 T. Turner.

1:359 - POWER OF ATTORNEY - 7 April 1726 - Mary Spicer, wife of John Spicer, authorizes Mr. Thomas Turner to acknowledge her relinquishment of dower to 300A conveyed to Nicholas Smith. Signed Mary Spicer. Delivered in presence of Charles Deane, Robert Wilsone, Wm. Baptie, George Paine. Recorded 1 July 1726 T. Turner.

1:360 - DEED OF LEASE - 29 June 1726 - Samuel Hoyles of Hanover Parish, planter, to Samuel Skinker of same, Gent. 5 shillings lawful money of England to lease 119A. Part of a patent of 600A taken up by Charles Grymes 4

September 1654 who by his last will and testament bequeathed half of the patent to his daughter in law Ann Debuam which said Ann did intermarry with a certain Edward Hoyles by whom she had issue the above named Samuel Hoyles. Bounded by Cattail Swamp. Signed Samuel Hoyle. Delivered in presence of William Alsup, Alexr. Snelling, Jno. Warner. Recorded 1 July 1726 T. Turner.

1:362 - DEED OF LEASE - 16 June 1726 - Mark Hardin of Hanover Parish, planter, to Richard Buckner of Essex County and William Strother and Thomas Turner, both of King George County. 5 shillings to lease 92A whereon the said Mark Hardin now dwelleth. Signed Mark Hardin. Delivered in presence of Archibald McPherson, William Brent, Eliz. Stidston, Jean Bowers. Recorded 1 July 1726 T. Turner.

1:363 - DEED OF RELEASE - 17 June 1726 - Mark Hardin of Hanover Parish, planter, to Richard Buckner of St. Mary's Parish in Essex County and William Strother and Thomas Turner, both of Hanover Parish. Two Negro slaves and two white servants, each to have five years to serve him, for 92A whereon the said Mark Hardin now dwelleth. Signed Mark Hardin. Delivered in presence of Archibald McPherson, William Brent, Eliz. Stidston, Jean Bowers. Mary, wife of Mark Hardin, relinquishes her right of dower and thirds through her attorney Charles Seale by oaths of Timothy Reading and William Harkney. Recorded 1 July 1726 T. Turner.

1:365 - BOND - 17 June 1726 - Mark Hardin of Hanover Parish, planter, bound unto Richard Buckner, William Strother, and Thomas Turner in the sum of 300 pounds sterling. Condition such that if agreements made in one pair of indentures bearing equal date are observed , obligation to be void. Signed Mark Hardin. Delivered in presence of Archibald McPherson, William Brent, Eliz. Stidston, Jean Bowers. Recorded 1 July 1726 T. Turner.

1:366 - POWER OF ATTORNEY - 17 June 1726 - Mary Hardin, wife of Mark Hardin, authorizes Charles Seale to relinquish her right of dower of, in and to a tract of land sold and conveyed unto Richard Buckner, William Strother, and Thomas Turner. Signed Mary Hardin. Witnesses: Timothy Reading, William Harkney. Recorded 1 July 1726 T. Turner.

1:366 - DEED - 17 June 1726 - Richard Buckner of Essex County and William Strother and Thomas Turner, both of King George County, have purchased of Mark Hardin 92A by a deed of release and have hereby mutually covenanted and agreed by and between them that they nor heirs of them shall or will take any advantage of survivorship at, upon or after the death of any or either of them. The heirs or assigns of either of them shall and may inherit, possess, and enjoy the right of property. Signed Richard Buckner, W. Strother, T. Turner.

Delivered in presence of Archibald McPherson, William Brent, Eliz. Stidston. Recorded 1 July 1726 T. Turner.

1:367 - ESTATE ADMINISTRATION - No Date - Sarah Brown, administratrix of the estate of John Brown, deceased, presented amounts against said estate: Anthony Seale, Anthony Seale, Junr., Saml. Skinker. Recorded 2 September 1726 T. Turner.

1:367 - DEPOSITION - Edward Taylor of King George County, aged eighty years or there about, sayeth that he knew James Kay and William Kay who were reputed to be Lancashire men and that James was the elder and intermarried with one Sarah Joeson by whom he had issue five children (to wit: James, Robert, Ann, Richard) of which James was the eldest and the said James Kay the son intermarried with one Mary Pannell and had issue of several children of which James was his eldest son who is now from the county of King George aforesaid and inherits all his said father's land within this colony and further this deponent saith not. Signed Edward Taylor. This deposition was presented into court by James Markham and the said Edward Taylor made oath before the court that what is therein contained is the truth, the whole truth, and nothing but the truth. Recorded 2 September 1726 T. Turner.

1:368 - DEED OF LEASE - 4 May 1726 - John Green of Stafford County, planter, to William Pitman of Hanover Parish, planter. 5 shillings of good and lawful money of England to lease 50A together with plantation whereon John Fox, blacksmith, now liveth. Bounded by a small branch which leads into Poultridges Creek, Sammuel Rendall, Edwin Conway, a line formerly Mary Gunstocker's, Thomas Goff. Part of a patent for 105A granted by William Fitzhugh and George Brown, agents for the proprietors of the northern neck of Virginia, unto Thomas Rendall. Signed John Green. Delivered in presence of Isaac Arnold, Neall McCormick, John McCormick. Recorded 2 September 1726 T. Turner.

1:369 - DEED OF RELEASE - 5 May 1726 - John Green of Stafford County, planter, to William Pitman of Hanover Parish, planter. 15 pounds current money of Virginia for 50A described in lease. (John Green's wife Abigail named in body of deed.) Signed John Green. Delivered in presence of Neall McCormick, John McCormick, Isaac Arnold. Recorded 2 September 1726 T. Turner.

1:371 - BOND - 5 May 1726 - John Green of Stafford County bound unto William Pitman of Hanover Parish in the sum of 30 pounds current money of Virginia. Condition such that if agreements in said deeds of lease and release are performed, obligation to be void. Signed John Green. Delivered in presence of Isaac Arnold, Neal McCormick, John McCormick. Recorded 2 September 1726

T. Turner.

1:371 - DEED OF LEASE - 1 September 1726 - Thomas Reiley and Elizabeth his wife of Stafford County to John Holdsworth of King George County. 5 shillings to lease 100A bounded by lands formerly belonging to Robert Peck and Henry Berry, and by land of Thomas Reiley. Purchased by Reiley from Benjamin Henslee by deed dated 1 July 1723. Signed Thomas Reiley, Elizabeth Reiley. Delivered in presence of Joseph Berry, Thomas Williams. Elizabeth, wife of Thomas Reiley, relinquishes her right of dower. Recorded 2 September 1726 T. Turner.

1:373 - DEED OF RELEASE - 2 September 1726 - Thomas Reiley and Elizbeth his wife of Stafford County to John Holdsworth of King George County. 2500 pounds of good, sound merchantable tobacco for 100A described in lease. Signed Thomas Reiley, Elizabeth Reiley. Delivered in presence of Joseph Berry, Thomas Williams. Elizabeth, wife of Thomas Reiley, relinquishes her right of dower and thirds. Recorded 2 September 1726 T. Turner.

1:374 - DEED OF LEASE - 30 June 1726 - Timothy Reading of Hanover Parish, planter, to Thomas Turner of same, chyrurgeen. 5 shillings current money of Virginia to lease 300A adjoining to the land whereon Mark Hardin now dwelleth. Part of a deed of 606A granted Alexander Beach 15 December 1719. Signed Timothy Reading. Delivered in presence of Harry Beverly, W. Strother, T. Lewis, Richard Buckner. Recorded 2 September 1726 T. Turner.

1:375 - DEED OF RELEASE - 1 July 1726 - Timothy Reading of Hanover Parish, planter, to Thomas Turner of same, chyrurgeen. 12 pounds current money and 1250 pounds tobacco for 300A described in lease. Signed Timothy Reading. Delivered in presence of Harry Beverly, W. Strother, T. Lewis, Richard Buckner. Recorded 2 September 1726 T. Turner.

1:377 - DEED OF LEASE - 6 September 1726 - Thomas Turner of Hanover Parish to Richard Buckner and William Strother. 5 shillings current money to lease 200A being part of 300A bought by the said Turner of Timothy Reading. Signed Thomas Turner. Delivered in presence of Edw. Barradall, Saml. Skinker. Recorded 7 October 1726 T. Turner.

1:377 - DEED OF RELEASE - 7 September 1726 - Thomas Turner of Hanover Parish to Richard Buckner and William Strother. 8 pounds current money and 833 pounds tobacco for 200A described in lease. Signed Thomas Turner. Delivered in presence of Edw. Barradall, Saml. Skinker. Recorded 7 October 1726 T. Turner.

1:379 - DEED OF LEASE - 3 October 1726 - John Wheeler of Stafford County to Evan Price of Westmoreland County. 5 shillings sterling to lease 266A . Signed John Wheeler. Delivered in presence of Hugh French, John Savage, Henry Field. Diana, wife of John Wheeler, relinquishes her right of dower. Recorded 7 October 1726 T. Turner.

1:380 - DEED OF RELEASE - 4 October 1726 - John Wheeler of Stafford County to Evan Price of Westmoreland County. 3500 pounds tobacco for 266A bounded by the southeast side of the head of a small branch issuing out of the lower side of the Summer Duck run,being a branch issuing out of Rappahannock between the Great Marsh and the Deep Run. Signed John Wheeler. Delivered in presence of Hugh French, John Savage, Henry Field. Diana, wife of John Wheeler, relinquishes her right of dower and thirds. Recorded 7 October 1726 T. Turner.

1:381 - BOND - No Date - John Wheeler bound unto Evan Price in the sum of 20,000 pounds of good tobacco. Condition such that if covenants in indentures of lease and release bearing equal date are kept, obligation to be void. Signed John Wheeler. Delivered in presence of John Savage, Hugh French, Henry Field. Recorded 7 October 1726 T. Turner.

1:382 - DEED OF SALE - 7 September 1726 - Anthony Seale the Younger of Hanover Parish to Thomas Turner of same. Whereas William Seale, late of Hanover Parish, was lawfully seized of a tract of 200A lying on Gingoteague Swamp adjoining to the plantation whereon Saml. Wharton now dwelleth and which the said William Seale purchased of one Samuel Wharton by deeds of lease and release dated 25 November 1713 and 26 November 1713 and acknowledged in Richmond County Court 2 December 1713; and whereas this said Wm. Seale hath for about the span of eight years past departed this colony and having left no lawful issue of his body to claim the said land, the right of reversion and inheritance thereof is in the said Anthony Seale the Younger as his at law. A certain James Markham has entered into bond in the sum of 200 pounds sterling to the said Thomas Turner that the said James Markham will warrant and forever defend the above mentioned 200A of land from the aforesaid William Seale, his heirs or assigns, unto the said Thomas Turner and his heirs and assigns. Signed Anthony Seale. Delivered in presence of Moseley Battaley, Edw. Barradall. Recorded 7 October 1726 T. Turner.

1:384 - DEED OF SALE - 20 April 1726 - James Kay of Hanover Parish, planter, to John Taylor or Richmond County, Gent. 10 pounds of good and lawful money of Great Britain for 42A bounded by Charles Stuart, Capt. Dinwiddie, and Capt. Mathews. Signed James Kay. Delivered in presence of Sus. Fewell, Richd. Jarvis, John Champe, Junr. Memorandum that on 8 July

1726 the within named James Kay delivered possession unto John Taylor.
Signed James Kay. Delivered in presence of Jno. Burn, John Champe. Recorded
7 October 1726 T. Turner.

1:385 - BOND - 7 October 1726 - James Kay of Hanover Parish, planter, bound
unto James Markham of same, planter, in the sum of 600 pounds sterling. James
Kay agrees to make over to James Markham all the estate and interest of his in
certain lands and hereditaments in the county of Lancaster within the Kingdom
of Great Britain and the rents and legacies due him by virtue of the last will of
Susan Medowcross, deceased, in consideration of 3200 pounds tobacco paid by
the said James Markham and also in consideration of the great trouble and
expense the said James Markham will be at in going to England to recover the
said land, rents and legacies. The said James Markham by one letter of attorney
bearing even date is herewith authorized and impowered to recover and receive
the said arrears of rent and legacies and to sell or lease the said lands and
hereditaments. Condition such that if James Kay permits James Markham to
receive and take the legacies, rents, and arrears of rent without giving any
amount thereof to the said James Kay and to possess the said lands and
hereditaments without any hindrances, obligation to be void. Signed James Kay.
Delivered in presence of John Farguson, Jere. Murdock. Recorded 7 October
1726 T. Turner.

1:386 - DEED OF LEASE - 2 November 1726 - Blumfield Long of Hanover
Parish and Elizabeth his wife to Henry Long, Junr. of same. 5 shillings current
money of Virginia to lease 40A being part of a patent of land formerly granted
to Renolds. Bounded on the north and east by Henry Long, on the south by the
main road and lands of Blumfield Long, and on the west by Simon Miller.
Signed Blumfield Long, Elizabeth Long. Delivered in presence of Saml.
Wharton, Robt. Johnson. Recorded 5 November 1726 T. Turner.

1:387 - DEED OF RELEASE - 4 November 1726 - Blumfield Long and
Elizabeth his wife of Hanover Parish to Henry Long, Junr. of same. 40A
described in lease in consideration of value to them paid. Signed Blumfield
Long, Elizabeth Long. Delivered in presence of Saml. Wharton, Robt. Johnson.
Recorded 5 November 1726 T. Turner.

1:389 - DEED - 4 November 1726 - George Allen of Hanover Parish to John
Marr of same. 2250 pounds tobacco for 100A being part of a tract of 200A
granted unto Alexander Clement by patent dated 16 July 1716. Bounded by
Thomas Evans, Alexander Clement. Signed Geo. Allen, John Marr. Delivered in
presence of John Savage, Alexr. Clement, Daniel Marr. Recorded 4 November
1726 T. Turner.

1:390 - BOND - 13 August 1726 - George Allen of Hanover Parish bound unto John Marr for 4500 pounds of good, merchantable tobacco. Condition such that if George Allen shall make his personal appearance at the court of this county and acknowledge and relinquish to John Marr his sole right and title to the plantation whereon the said George Allen now dwells with one hundred acres of land, obligation to be void. Signed George Allen. Delivered in presence of Peter Ker, Tobias Kelly. Recorded 4 November 1726 T. Turner.

1:391 - DEED OF LEASE - 2 November 1726 - Robert Johnson of Hanover Parish to Henry Long, Senr. of same. 5 shillings to lease 100A lying on the north side of the Gravley Run, being the same, more or less, the said land formerly belonging to Henry Long, Senr. and by him sold to the aforesaid Robert Johnson, being all the land now held by Johnson on that side of Gravley Run. Signed Robert Johnson. Delivered in presence of Saml. Wharton, Blomfield Long. Recorded 4 November 1726 T. Turner.

1:392 - DEED OF RELEASE - 3 November 1726 - Robt. Johnson of Hanover Parish, planter, to Henry Long, Senr. of same. 1300 pounds good merchantable tobacco for 100A described in lease. Signed Robert Johnson. Delivered in presence of Samuel Wharton, Blomfield Long. Recorded 4 November 1726 T. Turner.

1:393 - DEED OF LEASE - 3 November 1726 - Henry Long, Senr. of Hanover Parish to Blumfield Long of same. 5 shillings current money of Virginia to lease 50A. Part of tract taken up by the said Henry Long and lying between the line of William Reynolds and the line of Samuel Wharton and the main road of the county. Signed Henry Long. Delivered in presence of Samuel Wharton, Robert Johnson. Recorded 4 November 1726 T. Turner.

1:394 - DEED OF RELEASE - 4 November 1726 - Henry Long, Senr. of Hanover Parish to Blumfield Long of same. 4000 pounds tobacco for 50A described in lease. Signed Henry Long. Delivered in presence of Samuel Wharton, Robert Johnson. Recorded 4 November 1726 T. Turner.

1:395 - SURVEYS made by John Savage in King George County from the year 1722 to June 1726 - 7 May 1722 for Waugh Darnall 300A on ye branches of Muddy Creek joyning to Ball's land, Keynian's land, Jones's land and the land of Rowland Thornton - 3 August 1722 for the Worshipfull Court 2A lying about the Court House - 19 September 1722 for Mr. John Dinwiddie 173A joining ye land whereon Dinwiddie now lives, Geo. Prockter, and Robert Doniphan - 12 December 1722 for James Kay 2334A on ye N. side Rappa. River below a place commonly called the Hop Yard - 13 December 1722 for George Jones 100A being part of Kay's tract lying between Kay's Swamp and Doog Swamp - 13

December 1722 for John Price 124A being part of ye said Kay's tract - 14 December 1722 for John Popham 126A being part of ye sd. Kay's joining to the said Price's land - 14 December 1722 for Benja. Stripling 80A being part of the sd. Kay's tract - 5 April 1723 for the Worshipfull Court 10A for prison bounds - 22 April 1723 for Mr. Willliam Thornton 227A joyning to ye land of John Dinwiddie and Robert Doniphan - 8 July 1723 for James Kay 104A being the land whereon John Diskins now lives wch. Joyns to the land of ye aforesd. Jones - 10 August 1723 for James Kay 42A being part of said Kay's Great Tract and lying on the west end thereof - 31 August 1723 for Wm. Sarjant 253A being on Lambs Creek and the branches thereof - 7 September 1723 for Wm. Hammet 116A on branch of Chingoteague - 1 January 1723 for John Dinwiddie 137A joyning to the land of Colson and ye land of Glendening on Muddy Creek branches - 2 January 1723 for Wm. Marshall 100A being part of the land whereon Old Grimsley lives - 3 January 1723 for Mr. Saml. Skinker 197A being on ye Greab Swamp and joyning to the back line of ye sd. Grebe - 4 March 1723 for Mr. Willliam Skrine 2000A on the N. side of Rappa. River above a place called the Hopp Yard - 6 March 1723 for Richard Cary __A below ye mouth of Lambs Creek on ye N. side of Rappa. River being part of ye aforesd. Tract of 2000A surveyed for ye sd. Wm. Skrine - 1 April 1724 for Henry Berry 702A joyning to ye land of James Kay and on the branches of ye Doge Swamp - 20 April 1724 for Mark Hardin 230A joining to Berrymans land, Beache's land, ye land of Joshua Buttler and ye sd. Hardin's land, on a run called ye Dutchmans run - 6 June 1724 for Henry Long 113A lying on ye N. side Rappa. River and between the land of Thomas Turner and another tract of ye sd. Longs - 30 June 1724 for Mr. Samuel Skinker 542A nigh Rappa. Marsh and joyning to the land of Philip Ludwell, Esqr. - 24 September 1724 for the Honbl. Mann Page, Esqr. 2360A on ye N. side of Rappa. River above the mouth of Poytresses Creek - 2 November 1724 for Wm. Peck 591A being on ye head branch of the Doog run or swamp - 3 November 1724 for Benja. Hensly 100A being part of the land whereon ye sd. Hensly lives - 22 January 1724 for Patrick White 800A on the branches of little Summer Duck run and adjoyning to the land of Col. Philip Ludwell - 8 March 1724 for Mr. Cha. Carter 1425A on the Rockey run of Rappa. River and adjoyning to a tract of the said Carters called the Red Oak Land - 11 June 1725 for John Edy 279A on the branches of the Marsh run of Rappa. and adjoyning to the land of John Crump - 20 August 1725 for Dinnis Morgan 424A lying on the Uper Great run of Rappa. about 40 miles above the falls - 21 October 1725 for James McCullaugh 467A on the head branch of Summer Duck run and joyning Mr. Cha. Carters land - 21 October 1725 for John Hudnall 253A joyning to the aforesd. McCullaugh lying on the branches of Browns run - 1 January 1725 for Edwd. Twentymen 800A lying on ye N. side of Rappa. river and adjoyning to the land of Col. Ludwell - 4 January 1725 for Thomas Duncan 226A lying on Rappa. river about 35 miles above the falls - 5 January 1725 for William Thompson 88A a parcell of land on the lower Great run of Rappa. and adjoyning to ye land of Collo. Rice Hoo - 2 February 1725 for Robert Duncan 500A of land being the land whereon the sd. Duncan lives and lying on Summer Duck run - 5 April 1726 for Capt. Augustn. Washington 4560A on the branches of Deep run - 10 April 1726 for Capt. George Turbervile 459A on the branches of the Hors Pen run joyning to the land of Mr. Hancock Lee and ye land of John Waugh - 26 April 1726 for Edward Neugent 322A lying on the Great run of Rappa. and adjoyning to the land of Thoms. Welch - Recorded 7 October 1726 T. Turner.

1:397 - DEED OF LEASE - 18 November 1726 - William Gleeks of Hanover Parish to Joseph Allen of Overwharton Parish in Stafford County. 5 shillings of good lawfull money of England to lease 124A taken up and patented by the said William Gleeks 11 June 1725. Bounded by William Brooks, a branch of Deep run, Gleeks spring branch run, and the Great Marsh Path. Signed William Gleede. Delivered in presence of Benja. Strother, William Harkney, Thomas Duncan. Hanah, the wife of ye sd. William, relinquished her right of dower and thirds. Recorded 2 December 1726 T. Turner.

1:399 - DEED OF RELEASE - 19 November 1726 - William Gleeks of Hanover Parish to Joseph Allen of Overwharton Parish in Stafford County. 1650 pounds good tobacco for 124A described in lease. Signed William Gleeks. Delivered in presence of William Harkney, Benja. Strother, Thoms. Duncan. Hanah, the wife of ye sd. William, relinquished her right of dower and thirds. Recorded 2 December 1726 T. Turner.

1:401 - POWER OF ATTORNEY - 19 November 1726 - Hanah Gleeks, the now wife of Wm. Gleeks of Hanover Parish, authorizes Benja. Strother to be her true and lawfull atturnie for the next court held in this county to relinquish her right of dower to land in indentures of lease and release bearing date with these presents. Signed Hanah Gleeks. Delivered in presence of Alexander Clements, Mark Ghitwood. Recorded 2 December 1726 T. Turner.

1:401 - DEED OF LEASE - 13 November 1726 - Aaron Thornley of Hanover Parish to Thomas Turner of same. 5 shillings sterling to lease 200A lying on ye north side of Rappahannock river, being part of a tract of land Capt. Simon Miller left by will to his son William Miller and sold by him to one Andrew Harrison and sold by said Harrison to Aaron Thornley. Bounded by land of Thomas Turner formerly belonging to Robt. Paine. Signed Aaron Thornley. Delivered in presence of Mosley Battaley, Edw. Barradall. Mary, wife of the sd. Aaron, relinquished her right of dower. Recorded 2 December 1726 T. Turner.

1:402 - DEED OF RELEASE - 1 December 1726 - Aaron Thornley of Hanover Parish to Thomas Turner of same. 80 pounds sterling for 200A described in lease. Signed Aaron Thornley. Delivered in presence of Mosley Battaley, Edw. Barradall. Mary, wife of the said Aaron, relinquished her right of dower and thirds. Recorded 2 December 1726 T. Turner.

1:403 - BOND - 3 December 1726 - Aaron Thornley of Hanover Parish bound unto Thomas Turner of same in the full and just sum of 200 pounds sterling. Condition such that if all agreements made in certain deeds of lease and release bearing date the thirtieth day of November and the first day of December 1726 are kept, obligation to be void. Signed Aaron Thornley. Delivered in presence of Mosley Battaley, Edw. Barradall. Recorded 2 December 1726 T. Turner.

1:404 - DEED OF LEASE - 21 November 1726 - Henry Long, Senr. of Hanover Parish to Aaron Thornley of same. 5 shillings to lease 100A lying on the north side of Gravelly run, being more or less the land formerly belonging to Cornelious and John Reynolds and now binding on the land of William Sise, Henry Long, Junr., and Giles Ester. Signed Henry Long. Delivered in presence of T. Turner, John Short, Isaac Johnson. Christian, the wife of Henry Long, Senr., relinquished her right of dower and thirds. Recorded 2 December 1726 T. Turner.

1:405 - DEED OF RELEASE - 22 November 1726 - Henry Long, Seniour of Hanover Parish, planter, to Aaron Thornley of same, planter. 4000 pounds tobacco for 100A described in lease. Signed Henry Long. Delivered in presence of T. Turner, John Short, Isaac Johnson. Christian, wife of Henry Long, Sr., relinquished her right of dower and thirds. Recorded 2 December 1726 T. Turner.

1:407 - DEED OF LEASE - 7 December 1726 - Thomas Vivion and Mary his wife of Sittonbourn Parish, Gent., to William Robinson of same, Gent. 10 shillings lawfull money of England to lease 320A being the plantation tract and parcell of land late in the possession of Thomas Paise, deceased. Signed Thomas Vivion, Mary Vivion. Delivered in presence of John Hill, William Deverins, James Hill. Mary, wife of the said Thomas, relinquished her right of dower and thirds. Recorded 6 January 1726 T. Turner.

1:408 - DEED OF RELEASE - 8 December 1726 - Thomas Vivion and Mary his wife of Sittenbourn Parish, Gent., to William Robinson of same, Gent. 200 pounds lawfull money of England for 320A. Part of a tract of land left by Alexander Fleming to Alactia his daughter and for want of heirs of her decended and came to Elizabeth Thornton her sister who by deed dated 1 July 1699 sold and conveyed the said land to Thomas Paise who by his last will did bequeath the land unto Mary his wife, party to these presents. Signed Thomas Vivion, Mary Vivion. Delivered in presence of John Hill, William Deverins, James Hill.

Mary, wife of the said Thomas, relinquished her right of dower and thirds. Recorded 6 January 1726 T. Turner.

1:410 - DEED OF LEASE - 17 December 1726 - Patrick Hamrick and Margaret his wife and Robert Inglesh and Sarah his wife to Saml. Skinker. 5 shillings to lease 100A lying in Stafford County (indenture dated 20 October 1709) conveyed by Sem Coxe to Robert Ingles. Signed Patrick Hamrick, Margaret Hamrick, Robert Ingles, Sarah Ingles. Delivered in presence of Paul Micow, Junr., Jno. Long, John Archard. Recorded 6 January 1726 T. Turner.

1:411 - DEED OF RELEASE - 17 December 1726 - Patrick Hamrick of King George County and Margaret his wife and Robert Ingles and Sarah his wife of Stafford County to Saml. Skinker of King George County, merchant. 3500 pounds tobacco for 100A lying in Stafford County. Conveyed by Sem Coxe to Robt. Ingles by indenture dated 20 October 1709 and lying between the land of Simmons and ye Gleebe land. Bounded by Simmons, Kays pattent, Glebe land, and Mr. Bambury's line. Signed Patrick Hamrick, Margaret Hamrick, Robert Ingles, Sarah Ingles. Delivered in presence of Paul Micow, Jr., Jno. Long, Jno. Archard. Margaret Hamrick and Sarah Ingles relinquished their right of dower and thirds. Recorded 6 January 1726 T. Turner.

1:413 - BOND - 17 December 1726 - Patrick Hamrick of the county of King George and Robert Ingles of the county of Stafford bound unto Saml. Skinker of King George County in ye sum of 500 pounds. Condition such that if agreements in indenture of release bearing date with these are kept, obligation to be void. Signed Patrick Hamrick, Robert Ingles. Delivered in presence of Paul Micow, Junr., Jno. Long, Jno Archard. Recorded 6 January 1726 T. Turner.

1:414 - DEED OF LEASE - 3 February 1727 - Lazarus Damarel of Hanover Parish, planter, to Jno. Stewart of same, planter. 5 shillings sterling to lease 660A butting upon the south side of William Brooks and upon the north side of Col. Carters. Signed Lazarus Damarel. Delivered in presence of Jos. Crouch, Jno. Glendining, Richd. Bryan. Recorded 4 February 1726 T. Turner.

1:415 - DEED OF RELEASE - 2 February 1727 - Lazarus Damarel of Hanover Parish, planter, to John Stewart of same, planter. 3000 pounds good tobacco and five barrels of Indian corn for 660A described in lease. Signed Lazarus Damarel. Delivered in presence of Jos. Crouch, Jno. Glendening, Richard Bryant. Recorded 4 February 1726 T. Turner.

1:416 - DEED OF LEASE - 2 March 1726 - John Rose and Frances his wife of Hanover Parish to Thomas Turner of same. 5 shillings sterling to lease 50A the same more or less bought by William Sise of Henry Long. Lying on the North

Side of ye Gravely run. Bounded by said Turner, Henry Long, Aaron Thornton. Signed John Rose, Frances Rose. Delivered in presence of Edw. Barradall, Francis Thornton. Recorded 3 March 1726 T. Turner.

1:417 - DEED OF RELEASE - 3 March 1726 - John Rose of Hanover Parish and Frances his wife to Thomas Turner of same. 1000 pounds tobacco for 50A described in lease. Signed John Rose, Frances Rose. Delivered in presence of Edw. Barradall, Francis Thornton. Recorded 3 March 1726 T. Turner.

1:419 - DEED OF LEASE - 4 November 1726 - Jeremiah Bronaugh, Junior of Hanover Parish, planter, to Bryan Chadwell and Anne his wife of same, carpenter. 500 pounds tobacco yearly and every year to lease 150A being the plantation whereon David Bronaugh formally lived. Signed Jeremiah Bronaugh, Bryant Chadwell. Delivered in presence of Ann Bronaugh, Frances Steel. Recorded 3 March 1726 T. Turner.

1420 - DEED - 7 April 1727 - Thomas Turner of King George County to Richard Buckner of Essex County and William Strother of King George County. 200A purchased 1 July 1726 by Thomas Turner of Timothy Reading and Nept. adjoyning to the land whereon Mark Hardin now dwelleth. It is hereby mutually agreed between Richard Buckner and William Strother that they nor either of them shall or will take any advantage of survivorship at upon or after the death of either of them but that the heirs of either shall and may inherit, possess, and enjoy the right of property. Signed Richard Buckner, William Strother. Delivered in presence of G. Eskridge, Fran. Thornton, Joseph Minton. Recorded 7 April 1727 T. Turner.

1:421 - DEED OF LEASE - 28 January 1726 - Joseph Nutt of Northumberland County to Samuel Blackwell of Saint Stephens Parish in same. 5 shillings lawfull money of Great Britain to lease 280A granted unto Joseph Nutt by the proprietors of the Northern Neck of Virginia by deed dated 23 September 1724. Signed Joseph Nutt. Delivered in presence of Thomas Webb, John Hudnall, Saml. Blackwell, Junr. Recorded 5 May 1727 T. Turner.

1:422 - DEED OF RELEASE - 28 January 1726 - Joseph Nutt of Northumberland County to Samuel Blackwell of St. Stephens Parish in same. 1400 pounds tobacco and 20 shillings for 280A bounded by Blagrove Hopper, John Baley, Jeffry's run being a branch of Deep Run, Brooks and Conway. Signed Joseph Nutt. Delivered in presence of Thomas Webb, John Hudnall, Samuel Blackwell, Junr. Mary Nutt, the wife of Joseph Nutt, relinquished her right of dower and thirds. Recorded 5 May 1727 T. Turner.

1:424 - POWER OF ATTORNEY - 28 January 1726 - Mary, wife of Joseph

Nutt of the county of Northumberland, appoints Thomas Turner her true and lawfull attorney to acknowledge her right of dower in a certain tract of land which is sold by her husband unto Samuel Blackwell. Signed Mary Nutt. Delivered in presence of John Hudnall, Samuel Blackwell, Junr. Recorded 5 May 1727 T. Turner.

1:424 - DEED OF LEASE - 2 September 1726 - John Hudnall of Hanover Parish, Gent., to William Strother of same, Gent. 5 shillings lawfull money of Virginia to lease 235A being part of a 713A tract granted to William Allen and John Brown by deed dated 25 September 1710, being one third part in length of the said land. Signed John Hudnall. Delivered in presence of Lazarus Dameron, Timothy Reading, John Morehead, Darby Callihan. Recorded 5 May 1727 T. Turner.

1:425 - DEED OF RELEASE - 2 September 1726 - John Hudnall of Hanover Parish, planter to William Strother of same, Gent. 20 pounds current money of Virginia and 3000 pounds tobacco for 235A described in lease. Signed John Hudnall. Delivered in presence of Lazarus Dameron, Timothy Reading, John Morehead, Darby Callihan. Sarah, wife of John Hudnall, relinquishesd her right of dower and thirds. Recorded 5 May 1727 T. Turner.

1:427 - POWER OF ATTORNEY - 1 May 1727 - Sarah, wife of John Hudnall, Junr. of Northumberland County, appoints Thomas Turner, Gent. Clerk of the County Court, her true and lawfull attorney to acknowledge her right of dower of, in and to a certain tract of land sold by her husband to William Strother and to approve and execute the said deed on her behalf. Signed Sarah Hudnall. Delivered in presence of Saml. Blackwell, Saml. Blackwell, Junr. Recorded 5 May 1727 T. Turner.

1:428 - DEED OF LEASE - 4 May 1727 - Francis Sterne of St. Marys Parish in Essex County, planter, to Thomas King of Washinton Parish in Westmoreland County, planter. 5 shillings lawfull money of Great Britain to lease 175A lying in Sittenbourne Parish. Part of a greater tract of land that was given and devised by Francis Sterne the Elder, father to the aforesaid Francis, to him the said Francis and his brother David Sterne to be equally divided between them. Signed Fran. Sterne. Delivered in presence of Jere. Bronaugh, Edwd. Barradall. Recorded 5 May 1727 T. Turner.

1:429 - DEED OF RELEASE - 5 May 1727 - Francis Sterne of St. Marys Parish in Essex County, planter, to Thomas King of Washington Parish in Westmoreland County, planter. 80 pounds lawfull money of Great Britain for 175A described in lease. Signed Fran. Sterne. Delivered in presence of Jere. Bronaugh, Edwd. Barradall. Recorded 5 May 1727 T. Turner.

1:430 - BOND - 5 May 1727 - Francis Sterne of St. Marys Parish in Essex County bound unto Thomas King of Washington Parish in Westmoreland County in the sum of 100 pounds sterling. Condition such that if agreements made in certain indenture of release bearing even date with these are kept, obligation to be void. Signed Fran. Sterne. Delivered in presence of Jeremiah Bronaugh, Edwd. Barradall. Recorded 5 May 1727 T. Turner.

1:431 - DEED OF RELEASE - 1 March 1726 - William Robinson of Sittenbourn Parish, Gent., to Thomas Vivion of same, Gent. 10 shillings lawfull money of England to lease 320A formerly belonging to Thomas Paise, deceased. Signed William Robinson. Delivered in presence of James Hill, Simon Hughes, Jones Katen. Recorded 5 May 1727 T. Turner.

1:432 - DEED OF RELEASE - 2 March 1726 - William Robinson of Sittenbourne Parish, Gent., to Thomas Vivion of same, Gent. 200 pounds lawfull money of England for 320A. Part of a tract of land left by Alexander Fleming to Alactia his daughter and for want of heirs of her decended and came to Elizabeth Thornton her sister who by deed dated 1 July 1699 sold and conveyed the land to Thomas Paise who by his last will did bequeath the same unto Mary his wife who by deed of release dated 8 December last did convey the same unto William Robinson. Signed William Robinson. Delivered in presence of James Hill, Simon Hughes, Jones Katen. Recorded 5 May 1727 T. Turner.

1:434 - DEED OF GIFT - 5 July 1727 - I, William Robinson of Sittenbourn Parish, gentleman, for divers good causes and considerations but more especially for the natural love and affection that I have for my beloved son Maximilian Robinson give, grant, assign and make over to said son 600A of land lying in Sittenbourn Parish, being one half of the tract of land I now dwell. Together with the following gifts: Negroes Jack, Pompey, long George, Will, Jamsy, Mark, Harry, Sepoo, Bristol, Nanny, Ponder, Winney, Kate, Betty, Lotty, forty head of cattle, twenty sheep, fifty hoggs, twelve silver spoons, one gallon tankard, two porrengers, two sallts, one salvor, two cannes a tea, post and lamp, one milk pott, two castors, six tea spoons, a pair of tea tonges, one silver straner, one blew conopy bed and furniture, a cabinett, a dressing table and glass, six black cain chairs, one yellow canopy bed and furniture, chest of draws, one black dressing table and large looking glass, one iron back, a pair of scouches, six chairs gilt and flowerd with gold, one large Japand looking glass, one flowerd ovall table, a pair of scounces, one iron back, six gilt leather chairs flowerd and a couch of the same, one Japand hanging cupboard, one large looking glass, two oval tables, twelve cain chairs and all the other furniture in the hall as pictures, one bed and furniture, six black cain chairs flowerd with goald, a dressing table with three more beds and furniture. Signed Wil.

Robinson. Delivered in presence of T. Turner, Jere. Murdock. Recorded 6 July 1727 T. Turner.

1:435 - DEED OF LEASE - 6 July 1727 - Elizabeth Vivion, widow of Christ Church Parish in Middlesex County, to Nicholas Smith of Sittenbourn Parish, Gent. 5 shillings lawfull money of Virginia to lease 116A between the land which Nicholas Smith purchased of Rice Curtis and Martha his wife and the land of Thomas Vivion and according to a division made by Edward Barrow surveyor of Richmond County as by his survey dated 2 August 1720. Signed Elizabeth Vivion. Delivered in presence of Wil. Robinson, T. Turner. Recorded 6 July 1727 T. Turner.

1:436 - DEED OF RELEASE - 7 July 1727 - Elizabeth Vivion, widow of Christ Church Parish in Middlesex County, to Nicholas Smith of Sittenbourn Parish, Gentleman. 100 pounds lawfull money of Virginia for 116A described in lease. Part of a patent taken up and granted to John Paine who gave the same to Elizabeth his grandaughter who by her last will and testament bequeathed the same to her four daughters to be equally divided which said division was made and alotted to Elizabeth, party to these presents. Signed Elizabeth Vivion. Delivered in presence of Wil. Robinson, T. Turner. Recorded 6 July 1727 T. Turner.

1:438 - DEED OF LEASE - 15 March 1726 - Richard Butler of Hanover Parish to Rowland Thornton of same. 5 shillings sterling to lease 100A. Part of a patent granted to Majr. John Washington for 1700A dated 1 January 1664 and purchased by the said Richard Butler of John Hampford. Bounded by the land of the said Rowland Thornton, William Tippet, and Henry Wood. Signed Richard Butler. Delivered in presence of Francis Velden, John Kindol, John Hawkens, William Taylor. Mary, wife of Richard Butler, relinquishsed her right of dower and thirds. Recorded 6 July 1727 T. Turner.

1:439 - DEED OF RELEASE - 16 March 1726 - Richard Butler of Hanover Parish to Rowland Thornton of same. 5500 pounds tobacco for 100A described in lease. Signed Richard Butler. Delivered in presence of Francis Velden, John Kindol, John Hawkens, William Taylor. Mary, wife of said Richard, relinquishes her right of dower and thirds. Recorded 6 July 1727 T. Turner.

1:440 - BOND - 3 April 1726 - Richard Butler of Hanover Parish bound unto Rowland Thornton of same in the full sum of 12000 pounds tobacco. Condition such that if Richard Butler keeps all and every covenant in certain deeds of lease and release bearing date the fifteenth and sixteenth day of March 1726, obligation to be void. Signed Richard Butler. Delivered in presence of Francis Velden, John Kindol, John Hawkens, William Taylor. Recorded 6 July 1727 T.

Turner.

1:440 - DEED - No Date - Henry Berry of Spotsylvania County to Christopher Rodgers and Margaret his wife of King George County. As Christopher Rodgers paid an equal part in proporsion to the proprietor of the northern neck and their agents for the takeing up and pattenting of a tract of land in King George County granted to the said Henry Berry 3 August 1724 and is in actual possession of the premises, Henry Berry allows the said possession to be legal and utterly acquits and relinquishes all his right and property of, in and unto the said land. Signed Henry Berry. Delivered in presence of Joseph Berry, Robert Strother, Benja. Hensley. Recorded 4 August 1727 T. Turner.

1:441 - BOND - 18 May 1727 - Robert Finch of Sittenbourn Parish bound unto Francis Selden and Thomas Charles, both of Hanover Parish, in the sum of 8000 pounds of good tobacco. Condition such that if said Robert Finch will and truly observe agreements in deeds of lease and release bearing even date, obligation to be void. Signed Robert Finch. Delivered in presence of Isaac Arnold, Thomas Thatcher, John Fox. Recorded 4 August 1727 T. Turner.

1:442 - DEED OF LEASE - 17 May 1727 - Robert Finch of Sittenbourn Parish, planter, to Francis Selden and Thomas Charles, both of Hanover Parish, salors. 5 shillings good and lawfull money of England to lease 210A commonly called and known by the name of Tripletts old fields. Bounded by Mr. William Smart, deceased. Signed Robert Finch. Delivered in presence of Isaac Arnold, Thos. Thatcher, John Fox. Recorded 4 August 1727 T. Turner.

1:443 - DEED OF RELEASE - 18 May 1727 - Robert Finch of Sittenbourn Parish, planter, to Francis Velden and Thos. Charles, both of Hanover Parish, sailors. 8000 pounds good tobacco for 210A described in lease. Signed Robert Finch, Mary Finch. Delivered in presence of Isaac Arnold, Thos. Thatcher, John Fox. Mary, wife of Robert Finch, relinquishes her right of dower and thirds. Recorded 4 August 1727 T. Turner.

1:445 - DEED OF LEASE - 3 August 1727 - William Strother to Saml. Skinker. 5 shillings lawfull money of England to lease 410A formerly in possession of Wm. Strother, Senr., deceased, where the said Samuel Skinker now lives. Signed William Strother. Delivered in presence of Harry Beverly, Mosley Battaley, Enoch Innis. Recorded 1 September 1727 T. Turner.

1:445 - DEED OF RELEASE - 4 August 1727 - William Strother of Hanover Parish, Gent., to Samuel Skinker of same. 250 pounds sterling for 410A. 300A part here of conveyed to said Strother by his mother Margret Strother in deed of gift dated 1 August 1727 and the residue decended to him from his deceased father William Strother. Memorandum: half an acre of land for burying places is excepted on each of the within mentioned plantations and reserved out of the sale to be laid off in squares to include the graves that are now there as near the middle of the said squares as may be. Signed William Strother. Delivered in presence of Harry Beverly, Mosley Battaley, Enoch Innis. Recorded 1 September 1727 T. Turner.

1:447 - DEED OF LEASE - 11 August 1727 - Enoch Innis of Hanover Parish, Gent., to Thomas Harwood of same, Gent. 5 shillings sterling to lease 200A bounded by main county road and land of deceased brother James Innis as by their deceased father's will does appear. Signed Enoch Innis. Delivered in presence of William Strother, Mosley Battaley, Anthony Thornton. Recorded 1 September 1727 T. Turner.

1:447 - DEED OF RELEASE - 12 August 1727 - Enoch Innis of Hanover Parish, Gent., to Thomas Harwood of same, planter. 100 pounds sterling for 200A described in lease. Signed Enoch Innis. Delivered in presence of William Strother, Mosley Battaley, Anthony Thornton. Recorded 1 September 1727 T. Turner.

1:449 - DEED OF LEASE - 10 August 1727 - Thomas Harwood of King George County, planter, and Margaret his wife to William Strother of same, Gent. 5 shillings sterling to lease 150A on the head of the Rappahannock River below the falls. Between the land of Mr. Brent and John Robins. By deed dated 14 September 1710 granted unto Maurice Clerk, late of the county of Richmond, and by sundry conveyances vested in ye said Thomas Harwood and Margaret his wife. Signed Thomas Harwood, Margaret Harwood. Delivered in presence of Anthony Thornton, Mosley Battaley, Enoch Innis. Recorded 1 September 1727 T. Turner.

1:450 - DEED OF RELEASE - 11 August 1727 - Thomas Harwood of King George County, planter, and Margaret his wife to William Strother of same, Gent. 80 pounds sterling for 150A described in lease. Signed Thomas Harwood, Margaret Harwood. Delivered in presence of Anthony Thornton, Moseley Battaley, Enoch Innis. Recorded 1 September 1727 T. Turner.

1:451 - DEED - 31 August 1727 - Joseph Strother and Jno. Farguson, both Vestrymen in Hanover Parish, to Samuel Skinker of same, merchant. 2200 pounds tobacco for 92A commonly known by the name of the glebe land. Bounded on the west side by land of John Owen, on the north side by land of Mr. Bambury, on the east by Patrick Hamrick, and on the south by Kay's pattent. Sem Coxe in his last will and testament dated 18 October 1710 did bequeath said land to the two churches of the northside of St. Mary's Parish in

Richmond county (now Hanover Parish in King George County) in case Joseph Downing should happen to die without issue after the decease of his mother Ann. The same will made Benjamin Deveret and George Downing his executors. Signed Joseph Strother, John Farguson. Delivered in presence of Nicholas Porter, Benjamin Hensley, Junr., John Burn. Recorded 1 September 1727 T. Turner.

1:452 - DEED OF GIFT - 30 August 1727 - Isaac Arnold of Hanover Parish, planter, to Thomas Arnold, son of the said Isaac, of same, planter. In consideration of the natural love, good will, and affection that the said Isaac Arnold hath and now beareth to and towards his loving son, the said Thomas Arnold, and Mary his now wife, he hath given, granted, bargained, made over, and lawfully conveyed unto the said Thomas Arnold and his heirs forever all that plantation and parcel of land whereon the said Thomas Arnold now liveth together with 60A bounded by Robert Elliston, a small branch which leads into the Western main branch of Gingoteague, Henry Long, James Arnold. After the death of the survivor and longest liver of Thomas and Mary, property to go to Humphrey Arnold, son of the said Thomas and Mary. Signed Isaac Arnold. Delivered in presence of Ralph Saise, William Harvey. Recorded 1 September 1727 T. Turner.

1:453 - DEED OF GIFT - 1 August 1727 - Margret Strother of Hanover parish, widow, for the natural love and affection that she bears to her son William Strother does give, grant, and confirm unto her son 300A of land being formerly given by deed of gift by her grandfather Anthony Savage to her father Francis Thornton, Gent. and her mother Alice for their natural lives. Excepting always and reserving to myself and to my heirs, one half acre of land for a burying place to be laid of squares and ye angles to be East, West, North, and South, encluding ye graves that now are and they to be in ye centre. Signed Margret Strother. Delivered in presence of Harry Beverley, Mosley Battaley, Enoch Innis. Recorded 1 September 1727 T. Turner.

1:454 - DEED OF GIFT - 2 September 1727 - Margt. Strother of the county of King George, widow, for the natural love and affection she bears to her son Francis Strother has sent to him for a certain time, that is to say during his natural life, one young negro wench named Phyllis and all her future increase. At the expiration of the life of her son Francis, the said negro and all her increase goes to her grandson William Strother, son of the said Francis Strother, and his heirs provided he shall live to the age of twenty-one or shall have lawfull issue. But if he departs this life before he arrives to the age or have lawfull issue, then the said negro and her issue are to be equally divided amongst the surviving children of Francis Strother. Signed Margret Strother. Delivered in presence of Edw. Barradall, John Gilbert, Jere. Bronaugh.

Recorded 2 September 1727 T. Turner.

1:454 - BOND - 16 July 1727 - Joseph Strother, William Robinson and William Strother, Gent., are firmly bound unto their sovereign lord the King, his heirs and successors, in the full and just sum of 1000 pounds sterling. Condition such that whereas Joseph Strother is admitted Sheriff for the county of King George for the ensuing year now if the said Joseph Strother do truly and faithfully perform the said office of sheriff, obligation to be void. Signed Jos. Strother, Wil. Robinson, W. Strother. Delivered in presence of T. Turner, F. Thornton, Junr. Recorded 6 July 1727 T. Turner.

1:455 - DEED OF LEASE - 4 July 1727 - Anthony Thornton of St. Paul's Parish in Stafford County to Rowland Thornton of Hanover Parish, Gent. 5 shillings lawfull money of England to lease 65A in the head of a valley that falls into Crows Swamp. Bounded by John Kindall. Signed Anthony Thornton. Delivered in presence of Chas. Seale, Antho. Strother, Wm. Thornton. Recorded 7 October 1727 T. Turner.

1:456 - DEED OF RELEASE - 5 July 1727 - Anthony Thornton of St. Paul's Parish in Stafford County to Rowland Thornton of Hanover Parish, Gent. 20 pounds sterling for 65A described in lease. Signed Anthony Thornton. Delivered in presence of Chas. Seale, Anthony Strother, Wm. Thornton. Recorded 7 October 1727 T. Turner.

1:457 - BOND - 1 September 1727 - Anthony Thornton of St. Paul's Parish in Stafford County bound unto Rowland Thornton of Hanover Parish in the sum of 20 pounds sterling. Condition such that if Anthony Thornton observes all agreements made in certain deeds of lease and release bearing date the fourth and fifth days of July 1727 and if Winifred Thornton, wife of the said Anthony Thornton, relinquishes her right of dower and thirds, obligation to be void. Signed Anthony Thornton. Delivered in presence of Charles Seale, Anthony Strother, Wm. Thornton. Recorded 7 October 1727 T. Turner.

1:458 - DEED OF LEASE - 5 October 1727 - David Sterne of Essex County, planter, to Jno. Triplett of Sittenbourn Parish. 5 shillings to lease 175A bounded by lands of Wm. Triplett, Senr. and Fran. James on the south, Thomas Slowper on the west, and Thomas King and his line to Underwoods beaver dams. It being a full Moyety of all the lands left by Francis Sterne of the said Parish and county, deceased, between his two sons Frans. and David by his last will and testament dated 19 January 1712. Signed David Stern. Delivered in presence of Xtopha. Edrington, Aaron Thornley. Recorded 7 October 1727 T. Turner.

1:459 - DEED OF RELEASE - 6 October 1727 - David Stern of Essex County, planter, to John Triplett of Sittenbourn Parish. 35 pounds sterling for 175A described in lease. Signed David Stern. Delivered in presence of Xtopher. Edrington, Aaron Thornley. Recorded 7 October 1727 T. Turner.

1:460 - DEED OF SALE - 5 October 1727 - John Owen of Hanover Parish, planter, to Nathaniell Ellkins of same, carpenter. 35A bounded by lines of Major John Fitzhugh, Mr. Thomas Grigsby, Edward Humsteed. Signed John Owen, Ellinor Owen. Delivered in presence of Richard Ellkins, Junr., Jos. Crouch. Elinor, the wife of John Owen, relinquishes her right of dower and thirds. Recorded 7 October 1727 T. Turner.

1:461 - DEED OF LEASE - 30 November 1727 - Thomas Vivion of Sittenbourn Parish, Gent., to Nicholas Smith of same, Gent. 10 shillings lawfull money of England to lease 116A lying on Pepetak Creek. Being one fourth part of a tract of land formerly granted by patent to John Payne, deceased, and from him decended to Elizabeth his grandaughter who by her last will bequeathed it to be equally divided between her four daughters Elizabeth, Frances, Martha and Littice which said Frances was the wife to Thomas Vivion. Signed Thos. Vivion. Delivered in presence of Wil. Robinson, John Scott, Max. Robinson. Recorded 1 December 1727 T. Turner.

1:462 - DEED OF RELEASE - 1 December 1727 - Thomas Vivion of Sittenbourn Parish, Gent., to Nicholas Smith of same, Gent. 200 pounds lawfull money of England for 116A described in lease. Signed Thos. Vivion. Delivered in presence of Wil. Robinson, John Scott, Max. Robinson. Recorded 1 December 1727 T. Turner.

1:466 - BOND - 1 December 1727 - Thomas Vivion of Sittenbourn Parish, Gent., bound unto Nicholas Smith of same, Gent., in the sum of 400 pounds of lawfull money of England. Condition such that if Thomas Vivion observes the agreements mentioned in one pair of indentures bearing equal date with these, obligation to be void. Signed Thos. Vivion. Delivered in presence of Wil. Robinson, John Scott, Max. Robinson. Recorded 1 December 1727 T. Turner.

1:467 - DEED OF LEASE - 30 November 1727 - Nicho. Hawkins of St. George Parish in Spotsylvania County to Thomas Davis of Sittenbourn Parish. 5 shillings sterling to lease xxxxxA (50A) formerly in the possession of James Trent and by the last will and testament of the said James Trent given and devised to his daughter Anne Trent and bought by the said Nicho. Hawkins of one John James who intermaried with the said Ann. Signed Nicho. Hawkins. Delivered in the presence of Thos. Chew, George White, John Grant. Recorded 1 December 1727 T. Turner.

1:469 - DEED OF RELEASE - 1 December 1727 - Nicho. Hawkins of St. George Parish in Spotsylvania County to Thomas Davis of Sittenbourn Parish. 2700 pounds tobacco for xxxA (30A) described in lease. Signed Nicho. Hawkins. Delivered in presence of Thos. Chew, George White, John Grant. Recorded 1 December 1727 T. Turner.

1:472 - DEED OF GIFT - 1 March 1727 - John Steward of Hanover Parish, planter, to Joseph Steward of same. John Steward in consideration of the naturall love, good will, and brotherly affection which he hath and doth bear towards the above Joseph Steward his brother, as also for and in consideration of 20 pounds sterling, hath given, granted, bargained, sold, transferred, made over, and by these presents doth freely, clearly, and absolutely give, grant, bargain, sell, transfer, and make over unto the said Joseph Steward 260A. Part of a tract of 460A purchased by the said Jno. Steward of a certain Lazarus Dameron being on the branches of Deep Run. Bounded by the land of the said John Steward and the land of the said Lazarus Dameron. Signed John Steward. Delivered in presence of John Warner, Jerh. Bronaugh. Recorded 1 March 1727 T. Turner.

1:473 - POWER OF ATTORNEY - No Date - Elizabeth Dameron, wife of Lazarus Dameron, appoints Jeremiah Bronaugh her attorney in King George County Court to acknowledge her right and title of dower and thirds at the common law in and to a parcell of land being 660A sold by her husband to John Steward. Signed Elizabeth Dameron. Delivered in presence of John Warner, Joseph Steward. Recorded 1 March 1727 T. Turner.

1:473 - DEED OF LEASE - 10 October 1727 - Samuel Kendell of Washington Parish in Westmoreland County, planter, to William Pittman of Hanover Parish, planter. 5 shillings good and lawful money of England to lease 20A joyning upon the north side of the Rappahannock River. Bounded by Ralph Wormly, Esqr., deceased, Thomas Dickason, John Willis, Junr. Being part of a patent of land granted unto John Willis, Senr., deceased. Signed Samuel Kendall. Delivered in presence of Isaac Arnold, Isaac Arnold, Junr. Recorded 1 March 1727 T. Turner.

1:475 - DEED OF RELEASE - 11 October 1727 - Samuel Kendell of Washington Parish in Westmoreland County, planter, to William Pittman of Hanover Parish, planter. 3000 pounds good tobacco for 20A described in lease. Signed Samuel Kendal. Delivered in presence of Isaac Arnold, Isaac Arnold, Junr. Recorded 1 March 1727 T. Turner.

1:476 - BOND - 11 October 1727 - Samuel Kendell of Washington Parish in Westmoreland County bound unto William Pittman of Hanover Parish in the sum of 3000 pounds good tobacco. Condition such that if Samuel Kendell keeps all and every agreement contained in deeds of lease and release, obligtion to be void. Signed Samuel Kendal. Delivered in presence of Isaac Arnold, Isaac Arnold, Junr. Recorded 1 March 1727 T. Turner.

1:477 - DEED OF LEASE - 1 December 1727 - James Warren of Hanover Parish to William Flowers of same. 5 shilllings to lease 168A bounded by hors pen run a little below William Russels spring. Signed James Warren. Delivered in presence of Mosley Battaly, William Hackney. Recorded 1 March 1727 T. Turner.

1:478 - DEED OF RELEASE - 2 December 1727 - James Warren of Hanover Parish to William Flowers of same. 3000 pounds tobacco for 168A described in lease. Signed James Warren. Delivered in presence of Mosley Battaly, William Hackney. Recorded 1 March 1727 T. Turner.

1:479 - DEED OF LEASE - 4 April 1728 - John Triplett of Sittenbourne Parish to John King, Esqr. and Company of the city of Bristol, merchants and owners of certain iron works set up by them in the county of King George. 5 shillings current money of Virginia to lease 175A. Bounded on the east with the land of William Triplett, Senr. and Francis James, on the south with the land of Thomas Slowper, on the west with the lands of Thomas King and with his line to Underwoods beaver dams. Being one full moiety of all the land left by Francis Stern, deceased, between his two sons, Francis and David, and sold by the said David unto the said John Triplett. Signed John Triplett. Delivered in presence of Walter Anderson, John Warner. Recorded 4 April 1728 T. Turner.

1:480 - DEED OF RELEASE - 5 April 1728 - John Triplett of Sittenbourn Parish, planter, to John King, Esqr. and Company of the city of Bristol, merchants and owners of certain ironworks in the county of King George. 45 pounds lawfull money of England for 175A described in lease. Signed John Triplett. Delivered in presence of Walter Anderson, John Warner. Recorded 4 April 1728 T. Turner.

1:481 - DEED OF LEASE - 22 February 1727 - George Evans of Stafford County, planter, to George Rust of same, Gent. 5 shillings lawfull money of Great Britain to lease 338A lying in Hanover Parish formerly granted to Thomas Evans by deed dated 28 July 1715. Bounded by a branch of Horse pen run. Signed George Evans. Delivered in presence of Enoch Innis, Thos. Reilly, Lawr. Pepper, Peter Hodgman. Recorded 3 May 1728 T. Turner.

1:482 - DEED OF RELEASE - 3 February 1727 - George Evans of Stafford County, planter, to George Rust of same, Gent. 40 pounds sterling for 338A described in lease. The said Thomas Evans being the lawfull father of the above George Evans. Signed George Evans. Delivered in presence of Enoch Innis, Thos. Reilly, Law. Pepper, Peter Hodgman. Recorded 3 May 1728 T. Turner.

1:484 - DEED OF LEASE - 2 May 1728 - Willliam Strother of Hanover Parish to John Williams of Sittenbourne Parish. 5 shillings to lease 50A being one moiety of a tract of land for 100A bought by the said Wm. Strother of Thos. Turner. Signed William Strother. Delivered in presence of Mungo Roy, David Stern. Recorded 3 May 1728 T. Turner.

1:485 - DEED OF RELEASE - 3 May 1728 - William Strother of Hanover Parish to John Williams of Sittenbourne Parish. 10 pounds current money of Virginia for 50A described in lease. Signed William Strother. Delivered in presence of Mungo Roy, David Stern. Margaret, wife of William Strother, relinquished her right of dower. Recorded 3 May 1728 T. Turner.

1:487 - POWER OF ATTORNEY - 3 May 1728 - Margaret Strother, wife of William Strother, authorizes Mr. Thomas Turner to acknowledge her relinquishment of dower of this date to fifty acres of land unto John Williams. Signed Margaret Strother. Delivered in presence of Wm. Taylor, Ann Leitch. Recorded 3 May 1728 T. Turner.

1:487 - DEED OF LEASE - 2 May 1728 - Thomas Turner of Hanover Parish to John Williams of Sittenbourne Parish. 5 shilllings current money of Virginia to lease 100A lying in Hanover Parish. Being one third part of 300A bought by the said Thomas Turner of Timothy Reading, the other two-thirds also sold by Turner to Richd. Buckner and Wm. Strother. Signed T. Turner. Delivered in presence of Mongo Roy, David Stern. Recorded 3 May 1728 T. Turner.

1:488 - DEED OF RELEASE - May 1728 - Thomas Turner of Hanover Parish to John Williams of Sittenbourne Parish. 20 pounds current money of Virginia for 100A described in lease. Signed T. Turner. Delivered in presence of Mungo Roy, David Stern. Sarah, wife of Thomas Turner, relinquished her right of dower. Recorded 3 May 1728 T. Turner.

1:490 - POWER OF ATTORNEY - 3 May 1728 - Sarah Turner, wife of Thomas Turner, authorizes Charles Seale to acknowledge her relinquishment of dower of this date to 100A of land unto John Williams. Signed Sarah Turner. Delivered in presence of John Lomax, T. Turner. Recorded 3 May 1728 T. Turner.

1:490 - DEED OF LEASE - 2 May 1728 - William Strother and Thomas Turner, both of Hanover Parish, to John Williams of Sittenbourn Parish. 5 shillings current money of Virginia to lease two thirds of 92A. It being the land whereon Mark Hardin now lives. The 92A being sold by Mark Hardin unto Richard Buckner, William Strother, and Thomas Turner and equally to be divided between them. Signed William Strother, T. Turner. Delivered in presence of Mungo Roy, David Sterne. Recorded 3 May 1728 T. Turner.

1:491 - DEED OF RELEASE - 3 May 1728 - William Strother and Thomas Turner, both of Hanover Parish, to John Williams of Sittenbourne Parish. 25 pounds sterling to each of them for two thirds of 92A described in lease. Signed William Strother, T. Turner. Delivered in presence of Mungo Roy, David Stern. Margaret Strother, wife of Wm. Strother, and Sarah Turner, wife of Thos. Turner, relinquish their right of dower. Recorded 3 May 1728 T. Turner.

1:493 - POWER OF ATTORNEY - 3 May 1728 - Margaret Strother, wife of Wm. Strother, and Sarah Turner, wife of Thomas Turner, both of King George County, authorize Charles Seale to acknowledge their relinquishment of dower of this date to sixty-one acres and a third of land unto John Williams. Signed Margaret Strother, Sarah Turner. Delivered in presence of Wm. Taylor, Anne Leitch, John Lomax, T. Turner. Recorded 3 May 1728 T. Turner.

1:493 - DEED OF LEASE - 1 May 1728 - Christopher Pritchet of Sittenbourne Parish, planter, to Martin Gollashum of Washington Parish in Westmoreland County, planter. 5 shillings sterling to lease 150A being by the road commonly called Maddox Road. Part of a tract of land formerly pattented by John Lord who sold the above mentioned 150A to Martin Fisher who sold it to the said Christopher Pritchet. Signed Christopher Pritchet. Delivered in presence of Charles Deane, James Gahagan. Recorded 3 May 1728 T. Turner.

1:494 - DEED OF RELEASE - 2 May 1728 - Christopher Pritchet of Sittenbourne Parish, planter, to Martin Gollathan of Washington Parish in Westmoreland County, planter. 5200 pounds tobacco for 150A described in lease. Signed Christopher Pritchet. Delivered in presence of Charles Deane, James Glahagan. Recorded 3 May 1728 T. Turner.

1:496 - DEED OF LEASE - 2 May 1728 - Anne Lampton of King George County to Robt. Richards of Westmoreland County. 5 shillings sterling to lease 100A. Tract of land which was formerly Robt. King's, being part of a greater dividend lying between the counties of King George and Westmoreland. Bounded by a road commonly called Falls Road, Benja. Newton, Sem Cox, Anthony Hoggard. Signed Anne Lampton. Delivered in presence of Jeremiah Bronaugh, Mungo Roy, James Jones. Recorded 3 May 1728 T. Turner.

1:497 - DEED OF RELEASE - 3 May 1728 - Anne Lampton of King George

County to Robert Richards of Westmoreland County. 42 shillings and one choice negro for 100A described in lease. Signed Anne Lampton. Delivered in presence of Jeremiah Bronaugh, Mungo Roy, Jas. Jones. Easter Jones relinquishsed her right of dower and thirds at the common law in and to the lands and premises by the said release. Recorded 3 May 1728 T. Turner.

1:499 - BOND - 3 May 1728 - Anne Lampton of King George County bound unto Robert Richards in the sum of 80 pounds sterling. Condition such that if Anne Lampton keeps all and every covenant in one indenture of lease and release bearing equal date with this and Easter Jones in open court relinquishes and disclaims all her right of dower and thirds unto the said land, obligation to be void. Signed Anne Lampton. Delivered in presence of Mungo Roy, James Jones. Recorded 3 May 1728 T. Turner.

1:500 - DEED OF LEASE - 6 April 1728 - William Thornton of King George County to William Hackney of same and his heirs, but not assigns. Yearly rent hereafter mentioned to lease 300A on the upper side of the Great Marsh including part of the same, by the side of a great savana, with the back line towards mount pleasant. From the twenty-fifth day of September next for and during the natural lives of the said William Hackney, Gemima Hackney, the wife of the said Wm., and John Hackney, the son of the said Wm., and no longer so that when all these three persons named are dead and departed this life, this lease is at an end. The said Wm. Hackney doth hereby oblige himself his heirs Exr. and admrs. to pay and deliver unto the said Wm. Thornton, his heirs, at the said Thornton's dwelling plantation at some time between the first of November and twenty-fifth of December yearly twenty swine shoats well grown in good plight and thriving condition, clear of scabs or mange to be geld or spaied and well of the same and three months old at least and likewise pay the yearly quittrents for the said three hundred acres. Always obliging himself and his heirs that whenever the lease shall become void, the said plantation shall be in good repairs, tenantable. Signed William Thornton, William Hackney. Delivered in presence of Max. Robinson, Charles Lewis. Recorded 3 May 1728 T. Turner.

1:501 - DEED OF LEASE - 18 April 1728 - William Thornton of King George County to Henry Calfee of same and his heirs, but not assigns. Yearly rent hereafter mentioned to lease 250A. 200A lying on the upper side of the Great Marsh including part of the same. It being the remainder part of the said Thornton's tract of land over and above what is heretofore leased to Wm. Hackney. 50A on a knowle or ridge of land in one other tract of land. The said Thornton doth oblige himself to build as soon as conveniatly as he can next winter one dwelling house twenty feet long and sixteen feet wide and to cause to be cleared and fenced at least ten thousand corn hills under a good substantial fence. To have and to hold for and during the natural lives of Henry Calfee, his wife Elenor Calfee, and his son John Calfee and no longer. Paying yearly at some time between the first of November and the twenty-fifth of December and to be delivered to the said Thornton's dwelling for the first five years five swine shoats of three months old at least well grown in a thriving condition, clear of scabs and mange, to be gilt or spaid and well of the same, and for the next five years to pay ten of the like shoats, and for every year after fifteen of the like shoats and likewise pay the yearly quittrents for the said 250A. Always obliging himself and his heirs that when this lease shall become void that the land and plantation shall be left tenantable and in good repair. Signed William Thornton, Henry Calfee. Delivered in presence of Max. Robinson, Robt. Stuart. Recorded 3 May 1728 T. Turner.

1:502 - DEPOSITION - 3 May 1728 - Bryant Hanly of St. Paul's Parish in the county of Stafford, planter, aged about thirty-seven years, came before this court and being sworn says that Henry Kelly came into the colony of Virginia with him in a ship called the Brittania and that the Captain's name was Peirce and the merchant's name was Grenslett and the deponent says he can't remember their Christian names, the deponent further declares that they took shipping near a place called Ballyhark in Waterford river in Ireland and that the above said Kelly came on board the ship by the name of Henry Kelly, the deponent believes it to be about thirty years since they came from Ireland to this colony and upon his oath affirms that this same Henry Kelly is the same person who was his shipmate and for whom he gives his evidence before this court. Signed Bryant Hanly. Recorded 3 May 1728 T. Turner.

1:502 - DEPOSITION - 3 May 1728 - James Gahagan, aged forty-seven years or there abouts, of Washington Parish in the county of Westmoreland, planter, being sworn before the court saith that Henry Kelly came into the colony of Virginia with him this deponent in a ship called the Brittania Capt. Pearce commd. and merchant's name Grinslett their Christian names the deponent can't charge his memory with; this deponent further declares as reported that the said Kelly was kidnapt and believes it to be about thirty years since they came from Ireland to this colony and the deponent further saith that this Henry Kelly who appears in person now in this Court is the same person who was called Henry Kelly on board said ship and for whom this evidence is given and to which he has given his oath before this Court. Signed James Gahagan. Recorded 3 May 1728 T. Turner.

1:503 - POWER OF ATTORNEY - 5 April 1728 - Katherine Triplet, wife of John Triplet of the county of King George, authorizes Mr. Thomas Turner to acknowledge her relinquishment of dower and thirds at the common law to a certain tract or dividend of land containing 175A sold unto John King, Esqr. and Company, owners of the Bristol Iron Works. Signed Catherine Triplet.

Delivered in presence of Francis Triplet, Nathan Turner, Archd. Coombs. Recorded 7 June 1728 T. Turner on the motion of John Williams, agent for the said company.

1:503 - POWER OF ATTORNEY - 26 October 1727 - Edward Tronghear of the parish of Criplegate in the county of Middlesex, innholder, for Henry Tronghear his son, Elizabeth Atkinson of the parish of St. Andrews Holebourne in the said county, spinster, William Harrison of Whithaven in the county of Cumberland, mason, and Ruth his wife, Rachel Bacon of the same, widow, and William Marshal of the same, mariner, and Mary his wife who are the four daughters of Elianer Atkinson of Whithaven aforesaid sister of Joseph Tronghear, late of Essex County in Virginia deceased appoint Richard Kelsick of Whitehaven aforesaid, mariner, their true and lawfull attorney for them and in their names and for their use to ask, demand and receive of Jane Tronghear, widow of the said Joseph Tronghear and of his executors Francis Thornton, Francis Conway, Thomas Catlett, John Catlett and Jonathan Gibson, Junr. all such sums of money as now are or hereafter shall become due from them or any of them. Signed Edward Tronghere, Elizabeth Atkinson, William Harrison, Ruth Harrison, Rachel Brown, William Marshall, Mary Marshall. Delivered in presence of John Bacon, Richd. Skelton, Thos. Watson, Robert Lund. Recorded 7 June 1728 T. Turner.

1:505 - POWER OF ATTORNEY - 7 June 1728 - By virtue of the within Letter of Attorney from William Harrison, Ruth Harrison, Rachel Bacon, William Marshall and Mary Marshall now duly proved in Court, Richard Kelsick grants Col. William Robinson all the powers which are therein contained and appoints the said Col. Willliam Robinson attorney for them. Signed Richd. Kelsick. Delivered in presence of Mungo Roy, Max. Robinson. Recorded 7 June 1728 T. Turner.

1:506 - DEED OF LEASE - 29 May 1728 - Benjamin Berryman of Washington Parish in Westmoreland County, Gentleman, to Benjamin Berryman, Junior of Hanover Parish, gentleman. 5 shillings sterling to lease 200A. Part of a parcel of 400A that was formerly escheated by the said Benjamin Berryman from Jacob Daniel, John Farmer, and Samuel Dudley by three several pattents all dated 15 December 1710. Bounded by Rappahannock River, Thomas Grigsby, and 350A now occupied by Benjamin Berryman, Junr. Signed Benjamin Berryman. Delivered in presence of Thomas Sharpe, Evan Price. Recorded 7 June 1728 T. Turner.

1:507 - DEED OF RELEASE - 30 May 1728 - Benjamin Berryman of Washington Parish in Westmoreland County, gentleman, to Benjamin Berryman, Junr. of Hanover Parish, Gentleman. 20 shillings sterling for 200A described in lease. Signed Benja. Berryman. Delivered in presence of Thomas Sharpe, Evan Price. Recorded 7 June 1728 T. Turner.

1:509 - DEED - 7 June 1728 - George Davis and Patience his wife, which said Patience Davis is the daughter and sole heiress of Thomas Brock and Cicely his wife late of the parish of Sittenbourn deceased, to William Morton of Sittenbourn Parish. 150 pounds current money of Virginia for 150A. Part of a patent of land granted to John Barrow 13 October 1657 which was surveyed by Edward Barrow 25 March 1709 and divided between the aforesaid Thomas Brock and William Richason. Adjoins land of John Burckett, deceased. Signed George Davis, Patience Davis. Delivered in presence of Wm. Jordon, James Willson, John Jennings, Alein Motthershed. Received of Wm. Morten the sum of 150 pounds current money of Virginia. Signed George Davis, Patience Davis. Delivered in presence of John Champe, Thomas Davis. Recorded 7 June 1728 T. Turner.

1:511 - DEED OF LEASE - 6 June 1728 - Edwin Conway of Christ Church Parish in Lancaster County, Gent., to Jeremiah Murdock of Hanover Parish, merchant. 5 shillings lawfull money of England to lease 136A. Bounded by Blagg's land, a branch that falls into the Bristol Ironworks Creek, Moyakin land, Coombs lline, near a rowling road which leadeth from Potomack, Anderson's land. Signed Edwin Conway. Delivered in presence of Max. Robinson, William Woodford, Francis Conway. Recorded 7 June 1728 T. Turner.

1:512 - DEED OF RELEASE - 7 June 1728 - Edwin Conway of Christ Church Parish in Lancaster County, Gent., to Jeremiah Murdock of Hanover Parish, merchant. 28 pounds lawfull money of England for 136A described in lease. Signed Edwin Conway. Delivered in presence of Max. Robinson, Wm. Woodford, Fran. Conway. Recorded 7 June 1728 T. Turner.

1:514 - DEED OF LEASE - 4 June 1728 - Edwin Conway of Christ Church Parish in Lancaster County, Gent., to Jeremiah Murdock of Hanover Parish, merchant. 10 shillings lawfull money of England to lease 80A. Bounded by William Pittman, a creek known by the name of Indian Heds but formerly called Poytresses Creek. It being the land whereon Jeremiah Murdock now dwells. Signed Edwin Conway. Delivered in presence of Charles Wright, John Burch, John Williams. Recorded 7 June 1728 T. Turner.

1:515 - DEED OF RELEASE - 5 June 1728 - Edwin Conway of Christ Church Parish in Lancaster County, Gent., to Jeremiah Murdock of Hanover Parish, merchant. 60 pounds lawfull money of England for 80A described in lease. Signed Edwin Conway. Delivered in presence of Charles Wright, John Burch, John Williams. Recorded 7 June 1728 T. Turner.

1:517 - BOND - 5 June 1728 - Edwin Conway bound unto Jeremiah Murdock in the sum of 120 pounds sterling. Condition such that if agreements in a pair of indentures bearing equal date with these are kept, obligation to be void. Signed Edwin Conway. Delivered in presence of Charles Wright, John Burch, John Williams. Recorded 7 June 1728 T. Turner.

1:518 - POWER OF ATTORNEY - No Date - Anne Conway constitutes and ordains Thomas Turner, Gent., of the county of King George to be her lawfull attorney to relinquish her right of dower in all lands sold by her husband Edwin Conway to Jeremiah Murdock situated in the county of King George being part of a pattent granted to Nicholas Meriwether 13 April 1655 for 2000A and renewed by John Walker, Esqr. the 21 September 1663. Signed Anne Conway. Delivered in presence of Jos. Farguson, Charles Burges. Recorded 7 June 1728 T. Turner.

1:518 - DEED OF LEASE - 7 June 1728 - John Jones the Younger of King George County, planter, to Wm. Flowers of same. 5 shillings sterling to lease 100A. Bounded by former line of Simon Thomas, land that was William Elzy's, land of Thomas Elzy, deceased, bought of John Waugh of Stafford County by deed bearing date of 8 October 1690 and bequeathed by Thomas Elzy in his last will and testament 19 May 1698 to his son Thomas Elzy. Signed John Jones. Delivered in presence of Richard Bryan, Andr. Leitch, Fran. Triplett. Recorded 7 June 1728 T. Turner.

1:519 - DEED OF RELEASE - 7 June 1728 - John Jones the Younger of King George County, planter, to William Flowers of same, planter. 30 pounds sterling for 100A described in lease. Signed John Jones. Delivered in presence of Richd. Bryan, Andr. Leitch, Frans. Triplett. Anne, the wife of John Jones, relinquished her right of dower and thirds. Recorded 7 June 1728 T. Turner.

1:521 - DEED OF LEASE - 10 June 1728 - William McBee of Hanover Parish, planter, to Thomas Barnes of Washington Parish in Westmoreland county, merchant. 5 shillings current money of Virginia to lease 342A lying on both sides of Marr's run being a branch falling into the Great Marsh run. Formerly granted unto the said Wm. McBee by deed dated 2 March 1722. Bounded by line of the land surveyed for Mr. John Coppedge. Signed William McBee. Delivered in presence of Abraham Barnes, John Graham, William Greenaway, Elizabeth Tracey. Recorded 2 August 1728 T. Turner.

1:523 - DEED OF RELEASE - 11 June 1728 - William McBee of Hanover Parish, planter, to Thomas Barnes of Washington Parish in Westmoreland county, planter. 200 pounds sterling and 4000 pounds tobacco for 342A described in lease. Signed William McBee. Delivered in presence of Abraham

Barnes, John Graham, William Greenaway, Elizabeth Tracey. Susannah, the wife of McBee, relinquished her right of dower and thirds. Recorded 2 August 1728 T. Turner.

1:525 - DEED OF LEASE - 5 September 1728 - Ralph Falkner of Sittenbourne Parish to John Williams of same. 5 shilllings current money of Virginia to lease 80A bounded by James Warren, Joseph King, Mr. Coppedge. Signed Ralph Falkner. Delivered in presence of Will. Skrine, T. Turner. Recorded 6 September 1728 T. Turner.

1:526 - DEED OF RELEASE - 6 September 1728 - Ralph Falkner of Sittenbourne Parish to John Williams of same. 8 pounds current money of Virginia for 80A described in lease. Signed Ralph Falkner. Delivered in presence of Willm. Skrine, Thos. Turner. Eliz. Falkner, wife of Ralph Falkner, relinquished her right of dower. Recorded 6 September 1728 T. Turner.

1:527 - POWER OF ATTORNEY - 6 September 1728 - Elizabeth Falkner, wife of Ralph Falkner, authorizes Mr. Thomas Turner to asknowledge her relinquishment of dower of this date to 80A sold unto John Williams. Signed Elizabeth Falkner. Delivered in presence of Roger Proser, Ralph Falkner. Recorded 6 September 1728 T. Turner.

1:528 - DEED OF LEASE - 5 September 1728 - Benjamin Johnson of St. Ann's Parish in Essex County, planter, to John King, Esqr. and Company of Bristol, merchants and owners of the Ironworks in King George County. 5 shillings sterling to lease 100A beginning at a marked Spanish oak saplin upon the north side of Rappahannock River in a branch called the Sandy Valley close to the said river and near unto Foxhall's Mill upon the westward side thereof. Bounded by lands of Nathaniel Pope and Edward George. Signed Benj. Johnson. Delivered in presence of John Harvie, Thos. Turner. Recorded 6 September 1728 T. Turner.

1:529 - DEED OF RELEASE - 6 September 1728 - Benjamin Johnson of St. Ann's Parish in Essex County, planter, to John King, Esqr. and Company, merchants and owners of the Ironworks in King George County. 20 pounds current money for 100A described in lease. Bounded by land sold unto Robert Mindawe by William Underwood. Signed Benjamin Johnson. Delivered in presence of John Harvie, T. Turner. Margaret Johnson, wife of Benjamin Johnson, relinquished her right of dower. Recorded 6 September 1728 T. Turner.

1:531 - POWER OF ATTORNEY - 4 September 1728 - Margaret Johnson, wife of Benjamin Johnson of Essex County, authorizes Thomas Turner to acknowledge her relinquishment of dower to 100A of land being conveyed by her husband unto John King, Esqr. and Company. Signed Margaret Johnson. Delivered in presence of John Harvie, Caleb Hundley. Recorded 6 September 1728 T. Turner.

1:531 - DEED OF LEASE - 4 September 1728 - Richard Buckner of St. Marie's Parish in Caroline county, Gent. to John Williams of Sittenbourne Parish. 5 shillings sterling to lease 100A which was formerly sold by Timothy Reading unto Thomas Turner and by the said Thomas Turner sold to the said Richard Buckner. Also one-third of 92A whereon Mark Hardin now lives conveyed by Harding unto the said Richard Buckner, Willliam Strother, and Thomas Turner. Signed Richard Buckner. Delivered in presence of Thomas Buckner, Archd. McPherson, Eliz. Stidston. Recorded 6 September 1728 T. Turner.

1:532 - DEED OF RELEASE - 5 September 1728 - Richard Buckner of St. Marie's Parish in Caroline County, Gent., to John Williams of Sittenbourne Parish. 50 pounds sterling for a 100A tract and one-third of a 92A tract described in lease. Signed Richard Buckner. Delivered in presence of Thos. Buckner, Archd. McPherson, Elizabeth Stidston. Eliz. Buckner, wife of the said Buckner, relinquished her right of dower. Recorded 6 September 1728 T. Turner.

1:534 - POWER OF ATTORNEY - 6 September 1728 - Elizabeth Buckner authorizes Mr. Thomas Turner to be her attorney and in her name to relinquish her right of dower to the lands sold by her husband Richard Buckner to John Williams. Signed Elizabeth Buckner. Delivered in presence of Thos. Buckner, Archd. McPherson. Recorded 6 September 1728 T. Turner.

1:535 - DEED - 4 October 1728 - John Warner of Stafford County to John Champ of King George County. Robert Carter, Esqr., Willm. Thornton, John Fitzhugh and Charles Carter, Gent., Directors of the town of Falmouth in the county of King George did by this deed dated 1 October 1728 convey unto the said John Warner one lott or half acre of land within the town of Falmouth numbered twenty-eight according to the plat thereof made and laid of unto lotts by John Warner, surveyor of King George county for 4 pounds current money. Signed John Warner. Delivered in presence of Thomas Benson, Francis Woffendalle. Recorded 4 October 1728 T. Turner.

1:536 - BILL EXCHANGE - 5 March 1723 - Sir. Virginia March 5 1723. Exchange for 8 pounds at sixty days right after this my second of Exchange my first and third not paid. Pay'd pay unto Mr. Richd. Johnson or order the sum of eight pounds sterling money it being for value here recvd. at time make good payment and paee the same to the account of Ja. your humble sert. To Mr.

Artdr. Lee, mercht. in London. Signed James Booth. Delivered in presence of Richd. Johnson, Will. Marshall, Anth. Thornton. No date of recording.

1:536 - DEED OF LEASE - 12 September 1728 - Thomas Quissenbury of Sittenbourn Parish, planter, to John Finch of Washington Parish in Westmoreland County, planter. 5 shillings to lease two tracts of land. 100A formerly in the possession of Martin Fisher. Part of 300A of land formerly purchasesd by the said Martin Fisher's father of one William Jennings. 30A formerly purchased by the aforesaid Martin Fisher's father of one William Payne. The inheritance of which came to David Dickey who by deed dated 31 December 1719 conveyed the same to Humphry Quissenbury, deceased, who in his last will and testament did give and devise the same unto his son the said Thomas Quissenbury. Signed Thomas Quissenbury. Delivered in presence of David Wise, Robert Tomkins, Edward Barradall. Recorded 1 November 1728 T. Turner.

1:537 - DEED OF RELEASE - 13 September 1728 - Thomas Quissenbury of Sittenburn Parish, planter, to John Finch of Washington Parish in Westmoreland county, planter. 12,000 pounds tobacco for two tracts of land, 100A and 30A, described in lease. Signed Thomas Quissenbury. Delivered in presence of David Wise, Robert Tomkins, Edw. Barradall. Recorded 1 November 1728 T. Turner.

1:539 - INDENTURE - 6 November 1725 - Joyce Smith of Washington Parish in Westmoreland County apprentices her son Henry _____ to Christopher Pritchett of Hanover Parish until he shall reach the full age of twenty-one, he being eleven the twelfth day of next January. Signed Joyce Smith, Christopher Pritchett. Delivered in presence of Fran. Smith, Mary Donoly. Recorded 1 November 1728 T. Turner.

1:540 - INDENTURE - 6 November 1725 - Mary Donoly of Washington Parish in Westmoreland County for divers good causes binds her son John Pritchett an apprentice or servant unto Christopher Pritchett of Hanover Parish untill he shall arrive unto the age of twenty-one years he being now agoing in seven since the first day of last July. Signed Mary Donoly, Christopher Pritchett. Delivered in presence of Fran. Smith, Joyce Smith. Recorded 1 November 1728 T. Turner.

1:540 - BOND - 2 November 1728 - Joseph Strother, Samuel Skinker and William Strother bound to our Sovereign Lord the King his Heirs and Successors in the quantity of 84,150 pounds tobacco to the which payment will and truly to be made. Condition such that if the bounden Josesph Strother, Gent., Sheriff of the county of King George has the collection of the said county amounting to 42,075 pounds of tobacco this day put into his hands to collect now if the said Joseph Strother do faithfully collect and duly pay the same to the respective creditors according to law then obligation to be void. Signed Jos. Strother, Sam. Skinker, Will. Strother. Delivered in presence of Thomas Turner. Recorded 2 November 1728 T. Turner.

1:541 - BOND - 13 September 1728 - Thomas Quissenbury of Sittenburn Parish, planter, bound unto John Finch of Washington Parish in Westmoreland county for 100 pounds sterling. Condition such that if agreements in a certain indenture of release bearing even date are kept, obligation to be void. Signed Thomas Quissenbury. Delivered in presence of David Wise, Robt. Tomkins, Edward Barradall. Recorded 1 November 1728 T. Turner.

1:542 - DEED OF LEASE - 2 December 1728 - Richarad Gill of St. Mary's Parish in the county of King George, planter to Marmaduke Beckwith of Northfarnham Parish in the county of Richmond, Gent. 5 shillings lawfull money of England to lease 55A above the falls of Rappahannock River. Land granted to the said Gill by deed dated 15 October 1726. Bounded by the lower side of Deep Run, James Jones, land of said Marmaduke Beckwith, Robert Carter, Esqr. Signed Richard Gill. Delivered in presence of L. Lewis, Edw. Barradall. Recorded 3 January 1728 T. Turner.

1:543 - DEED OF RELEASE - 3 December 1728 - Richard Gill of St. Mary's Parish in the county of King George, planter to Marmaduke Beckwith of Northfarnham Parish in Richmond county, Gent. 1500 pounds tobacco for 55A described in lease. Signed Richard Gill. Delivered in presence of L. Lewis, Edw. Barradall. Recorded 3 January 1728 T. Turner.

1:545 - BOND - 3 December 1728 - Richard Gill of St. Mary's Parish in King George County bound unto Marmaduke Beckwith of Northfarnham Parish in Richmond county in the sum of 3000 pounds good tobacco. Condition such that if all conditions mentioned in certain indentures of lease and release for 55A of land bearing equal date with these are fulfilled, obligation to be void. Signed Richard Gill. Delivered in presence of L. Lewis, Edw. Barradall. Recorded 3 January 1728 T. Turner.

1:546 - INDENTURE - 2 January 1728 - William Roof of Hanover Parish, planter, bound unto Richard Griffith of same, planter, from the day of the date hereof for and during the term of three years in consideration of 1340 pounds good tobacco and good and sufficient meat, drink, washing and lodging, and cloaths according to the custom of servants in such cases. Signed William Roof. Delivered in presence of Benja. Rush, Jos. Crouch. Recorded 3 January 1728 T. Turner.

1:546 - DEED - 3 January 1728 - Robert Doniphan of Hanover Parish, planter, to William Thornton of same, Gent. 56 pounds sterling for 150A bounded by John Dinwiddie, the river, Rowland Williams, land Doniphan formerly sold to William Thornton. Signed Robert Doniphan. Delivered in presence of Francis Conway, Rowland Thornton, John Ambrose. Recorded 3 January 1728 T. Turner.

1:548 - DEED - 5 March 1728 - John Quissenbury and William Quissenbury, both of Sittenburn Parish, planters, to Nicholas Smith of same, Gent. 100 pounds sterling for 130A bounded by a line formerly a dividing lline between John and William Jennings, a branch of Payers Beaver Dam, land of Nicholas Smith party to these presents formerly belonging to George Irwin, deceased, and Perpetua Creek. Being part of a 300A tract granted to John Jennings by William Berkly by patent dated 11 March 1662 and since conveyed by John Jennings, grandson to the aforesaid John Jennings, unto Humphry Quissenbury by deed dated 3 November 1718 and since given by the last will of Humphry Quissenbury unto the said John and William Quissenbury. Signed John Quissenbury, William Quissenbury. Delivered in presence of Charles Deane, George Fishpool, Thomas Moore. Elizabeth Quissenbury, wife of John Quissenbury, relinquished her right of dower. Recorded 7 March 1728 T. Turner.

1:550 - POWER OF ATTORNEY - 5 March 1728 - Elizabeth Quissenbury, wife of John Quissenbury of Sittenbourn Parish, authorizes Thomas Turner to acknowledge her relinquishment of dower to 130A conveyed this day to Nicholas Smith by her husband. Signed Elizabeth Quissenbury. Delivered in presence of Charles Deane, Geo. Fishpool, Thomas Moore. Recorded 7 March 1728 T. Turner.

1:551 - DEED - 5 March 1728 - Nicholas Smith of Sittingbourn Parish, Gentleman, to John Quissenbury of same. 100 pounds sterling for 300A a little above Charles' Beaver Dam Swamp and formerly belonging to John Spicer, being sold by him to Nicholas Smith 7 April 1726. Bounded by William Carter's orchard fence. Signed Nicholas Smith. Delivered in presence of Charles Deane, George Fishpool, Thomas Moore. Elizabeth Smith, wife of Nicholas Smith, relinquished her right of dower. Recorded 7 March 1728 T. Turner.

1:553 - DEED - 1 October 1728 - Robert Carter, William Thornton, John Fitzhugh, Charles Carter, Directors and Trustees of the town of Falmouth in the county of King George to Mann Page, Esqr. of Gloucester County. 9 pounds 10 shillings current money of Virginia for two lots or one acre of land lying within the said Falmouth Town numbered 6 and 26 according to the platt thereof and as laid of unto lotts by John Warner, surveyor of King George County. The said Mann Page shall build on each lot one framed house of brick, stone, or wood of the dimensions twenty foot square and nine foot pitch at least within two years after the date of this present deed, otherways this grant to be void and the lotts herein granted and not built upon to be reinvested in the Trustees of the said town. Signed Robert Carter, Willm. Thornton, John Fitzhugh, Charles Carter. Delivered in presence of Catesby Cocke, Benj. Rush, Robert Jones, John Warner. Recorded 7 March 1728 T. Turner.

1:554 - POWER OF ATTORNEY - 5 March 1728 - Nicholas Smith appoints Edward Barradall his true and lawfull attorney to acknowledge in the County Court a certain deed between him and John Quissenbury bearing even date with these presents for the conveying of 300A and to acknowledge a certain deed also bearing even date with these presents made between John and William Quissenbury and him the said Nicholas Smith. Signed Nicholas Smith. Delivered in presence of Geo. Fishpool, Charles Deane. Recorded 7 March 1728 T. Turner.

1:555 - DEED - 1 October 1728 - Robert Carter, William Thornton, John Fitzhugh, Directors and Trustees of the town of Falmouth in the county of King George to Charles Carter of Lancaster County. 7 pounds current money of Virginia for one lott and half being three quarters of an acre of land being with the said Falmouth Town numbered five and fifteen according to the platt thereof made and laid of into lotts by John Warner, surveyor, he paying the yearly quit rents for the said lotts. Signed Robert Carter, William Thornton, John Fitzhugh. Delivered in presence of Catesby Cocke, Benja. Rush, Robert Jones, John Warner. Recorded 7 March 1728 T. Turner.

1:557 - DEED - 1 October 1728 - Robert Carter, William Thornton, John Fitzhugh, Charles Carter, Directors and Trustees of the town of Falmouth in the county of King George to John Warner of King George county. 8 pounds current money of Virginia for 2 lotts or half acres of land lying within the said town of Falmouth numbered 22 and 28 according to the platt thereof made and laid of into lotts by John Warner, surveyor. Signed Robert Carter, Wm. Thornton, John Fitzhugh, Charles Carter. Delivered in presence of Catesby Cocke, Robert Jones, Benja. Rush, John Harvey. Recorded 7 March 1728 T. Turner.

1:558 - DEED - 1 October 1728 - Robert Carter, William Thornton, John Fitzhugh, Charles Carter, Directors and Trustees of the town of Falmouth in the county of King George to Robert Carter, Junr. Esqr. of Lancaster County. 7 pounds current money of Virginia for two lotts or half acres being within the said town of Falmouth numbered 16 and 24 according to the platt thereof made and laid of into lotts by John Warner, surveyor. Signed Robert Carter, Willm. Thornton, John Fitzhugh, Charles Carter. Delivered in presence of Catesby

Cocke, Robt. Jones, Jno. Warner, Jno. Harvey, Benja. Rush. Recorded 7 March 1728 T. Turner.

1:559 - DEED - 1 October 1728 - Willliam Thornton, John Fitzhugh, Charles Carter, Directors and Trustees of the town of Falmouth in the county of King George to Robert Carter, Esqr. of Lancaster County. 9 pounds current money of Virginia for 2 lotts or half acres being within the said Falmouth Town numbered 2 and 26 according to the platt thereof made and laid of into lotts by John Warner, surveyor. Signed William Thornton, John Fitzhugh, Charles Carter. Delivered in presence of Catesby Cocke, Robert Jones, Benja. Rush, John Warner. Recorded 7 March 1728 T. Turner.

1:561 - DEED - 1 October 1728 - Robert Carter, William Thornton, John Fitzhugh, Charles Carter, Directors and Trustees of the town of Falmouth in the county of King George to William Beverly of Essex County. 5 pounds current money of Virginia for one lott or half acre of land being within the said Falmouth Town numbered three according to the platt thereof made and laid of into lotts by John Warner, surveyor. Signed Robert Carter, Willm. Thornton, John Fitzhugh, Charles Carter. Delivered in presence of John Warner, Robert Jones, Benja. Rush. Recorded 7 March 1728 T. Turner.

1:562 - DEED - 1 October 1728 - Robert Carter, William Thornton, John Fitzhugh, Charles Carter, Directors and Trustees of the town of Falmouth in the county of King George to Nicholas Smith of King George County. 5 pounds 10 shillings current money of Virginia for one lott or half acre of land being with the said Falmouth Town numbered eight according to the platt thereof made and laid of into lotts by John Warner, surveyor. Signed Robert Carter, William Thornton, John Fitzhugh, Charles Carter. Delivered in presence of Catesby Cocke, Robert Jones, Benja. Rush, John Warner. Recorded 7 March 1728 T. Turner.

1:564 - DEED - 1 October 1728 - Robert Carter, Nicholas Smith, William Thornton, John Fitzhugh, Charles Carter and Henry Fitzhugh the Younger, Directors and Trustees of the town of Falmouth in the county of King George to William Thornton of King George County. 8 pounds current money of Virginia for two lotts or one acre of land being within the said Falmouth Town numbered nine and seventeen according to the platt thereof made and laid of into lotts by John Warner, surveyor. Signed Robert Carter, John Fitzhugh, Charles Carter. Delivered in presence of Catesby Cocke, John Warner, Benja. Rush, Robt. Jones. Recorded 7 March 1728 T. Turner.

1:566 - DEED - 1 October 1728 - Robert Carter, Wm. Thornton, John Fitzhugh, Charles Carter, Directors and Trustees of the town of Falmouth in the county of

King George to John Williams of King George County. 8 pounds current money of Virginia for two lotts or one acre of land being within the said Falmouth Town numbered thirteen and nineteen according to the platt thereof made and laid of into lotts by John Warner, surveyor. Signed Robert Carter, Wm. Thornton, John Fitzhugh, Charles Carter. Delivered in presence of Catesby Cocke, John Warner, Robt. Jones, Benja. Rush, John Harvey. Recorded 7 March 1728 T. Turner.

1:567 - DEED - 1 October 1728 - Robert Carter, William Thornton, John Fitzhugh, Charles Carter, Directors and Trustees of the town of Falmouth in the county of King George to John Carter, Esqr. 8 pounds current money of Virginia for two lotts or half acres of land being within the said Falmouth Town numbered twenty and twenty-one according to the platt thereof made and laid of into lotts by John Warner, surveyor. Signed Robert Carter, Wm.Thornton, John Fitzhugh, Charles Carter. Delivered in presence of Catesby Cocke, Robt. Jones, John Warner, Benja. Rush. Recorded 7 March 1728 T. Turner.

1:569 - DEED - 1 October 1728 - Robert Carter, William Thornton, John Fitzhugh, Charles Carter, Directors and Trustees of the town of Falmouth in the county of King George to Robert Jones of King George County. 9 pounds 10 shillings current money of Virginia for two lotts or one acre of land being within the said Falmouth Town numbered seven and fourteen according to the platt thereof made and laid of into lotts by John Warner, surveyor. Signed Robert Carter, Wm. Thornton, John Fitzhugh, Charles Carter. Delivered in presence of Catesby Cocke, John Warner, Benja. Rush, John Harvey. Recorded 7 March 1728 T. Turner.

1:571 - POWER OF ATTORNEY - 5 March 1728 - Elizabeth Smith, wife of Nicholas Smith of Sittingbourn Parish, authorizes Thomas Turner to acknowledge her relinquishment of dower of this date to 300A of land conveyed unto John Quissenbury by her husband. Signed Elizabeth Smith. Delivered in presence of Charles Deane, Geo. Fishpoole. Recorded 7 March 1728 T. Turner.

1:571 - POWER OF ATTORNEY - 3 January 1728 - Margaret Strother, wife of William Strother, authorizes Mr. Thomas Turner her good and lawfull attorney to acknowledge unto Samuel Skinker her right of dower in 350A sold unto him by her husband. Signed Marg. Strother. Delivered in presence of M. Battaley, Thos. Smith. Recorded 7 March 1728 T. Turner.

1:572 - DEED OF LEASE - 3 December 1728 - Enoch Innis of King George County to Robert Carter, Esqr. of Lancaster County. 5 shillings current money of Virginia to lease 150A between the main road that leads from the falls up to the Marsh, the tract of land which belongs to the said Carter called the falls

Plantation and a line of Waughs great tract. Part of a greater tract given and devised to the said Innis by his father. Signed Enoch Innis. Delivered in presence of Charles Brent, Richd. Chapman, John Harvey. Recorded 7 March 1728 T. Turner.

1:574 - DEED OF RELEASE - 4 December 1728 - Enoch Innis of King George County to Robert Carter, Esqr. of Lancaster County. 30 pounds current money of Virginia for 150A described in lease. Signed Enoch Innis. Delivered in presence of Charles Brent, Richd. Chapman, John Harvey. Recorded 7 March 1728 T. Turner.

1:577 - DEED OF LEASE - 27 November 1728 - William Russell of the county of Stafford to John Bradford of Hanover Parish. 5 shillings lawfull money of England to lease 125A at a place called the Marsh Land and being part of a tract of 316A granted to the said William Russell by a patent dated 2 July 1712. Lying on a branch of the Marsh Run called the Horse Pen branch on the westward of the said branch a little below the lick where stands a Great Horse Pen belonging to the said Russell. Bounded by land of John Marr, Junr. and John Hopper. The said 316A divided by Mr. William Thornton, surveyor, between the said William Russell and Alexander Beach of the county of Stafford. Signed William Russell. Delivered in presence of Robert Fanny, Andrew Forbes. Recorded 7 March 1728 T. Turner.

1:578 - DEED OF RELEASE - 28 November 1728 - William Russell of Stafford County to John Bradford of Hanover Parish. 5000 pounds tobacco for 125A described in lease. Being now in the tenure and occupation of David Denny, blacksmith. Signed William Russell. Delivered in presence of Robert Fanny, Andrew Forbes. Recorded 7 March 1728 T. Turner.

1:582 - DEED OF LEASE - 27 February 1728 - William Skrine of Hanover Parish, Gent., to Nicholas Smith of Sittingbourn Parish, Gent. 10 shillings lawfull money of England to lease 833A. Bounded by east side of a branch falling into the southwest branch of Deep Run known by the name of Hoppers branch and at a small distance from the upper fork of the said branch, a small branch falling into Browns Run otherwise known by the name of the Easterly branch of the Marsh Run issuing out of Rappahannock River about thirty miles above the falls, a branch of Marrs Run being another branch of the said Marsh Run formerly known by the name of Horse Pen branch. Being granted unto the said William Skrine by deed from the proprietors office dated 4 January 1719. Signed Willliam Skrine. Delivered in presence of Samuel Skinker, John Farguson, Jere. Bronaugh, Thos. Turner. Margaret Skrine, wife of William Skrine, relinquished her right of dower. Recorded 7 March 1728 T. Turner.

1:584 - DEED OF RELEASE - 28 February 1728 - William Skrine of Hanover Parish, Gent., to Nicholas Smith of Sittenbourn Parish, Gent. 12,800 pounds tobacco for 833A described in lease. Signed William Skrine. Delivered in presence of Sam. Skinker, John Farguson, Jere. Bronaugh, Thos. Turner. Margaret, wife of William Skrine, relinquished her right of dower. Recorded 7 March 1728 T. Turner.

1:587 - POWER OF ATTORNEY - 28 February 1728 - Margaret Skrine, wife of William Skrine of King George County, authorizes Mr. Thomas Turner to acknowledge her relinquishment of dower to 833A conveyed unto Nicholas Smith this day by her husband. Signed Margaret Skrine. Delivered in presence of Saml. Skinker, John Farguson, Jere. Bronaugh. Recorded 7 March 1728 T. Turner.

1:588 - DEED - 3 December 1728 - Joseph Allen of Stafford County to John Morehead of King George County. 2000 pounds tobacco and divers good causes and considerations for 124A. Bounded by Gleeks line, Gleeks spring branch, Stafford road, Thomas Brooks line, and a branch of Deep Run. Signed Joseph Allen, Mary Allen. Delivered in presence of John Hudnall, Jos. Hudnall. Recorded 7 March 1728 T. Turner.

1:590 - DEED OF LEASE - 3 April 1729 - Christopher Rodgers and Margaret his wife (in whom the right lyes) of Hanover Parish to Joseph Strother of same. 5 shillings sterling to lease 50A formerly taken up by Willm. Berry and Sem Coxe and by the said Sem Coxe sold to the said Margaret Rodgers and her heirs forever. Bounded by Robert Harrison, Doog Swamp, Simson's patent. Signed Christopher Rodgers, Margaret Rodgers. Delivered in presence of John Coburn, Baldwin Matthews. Recorded 5 April 1729 T. Turner.

1:592 - DEED OF RELEASE - 4 April 1729 - Christopher Rodgers and Margaret his wife (in whom the right lies) of Hanover Parish to Joseph Strother of same. 1000 pounds tobacco for 50A described in lease. Signed Christopher Rodgers, Margaret Rodgers. Delivered in presence of John Coburn, Baldwin Matthews. Recorded 5 April 1729 T. Turner.

1:595 - DEED OF LEASE - 3 April 1729 - William Strother of Hanover Parish to John Williams of Sittenbourne Parish. 5 shillings current money of Virginia to lease 50A and all title and interest in a certain copper mine on the land. Being one moiety or half part of 100A lately bought by the said William Strother of Thomas Turner who was sold the land by Timothy Reading. Signed William Strother. Delivered in presence of Edw. Barradall, Richd. Barns, Thos. Turner, Jere. Murdock, Edw. Rowell. Recorded 2 May 1729 T. Turner.

1:596 - DEED OF RELEASE - 4 April 1729 - William Strother of Hanover Parish, Gent., to John Williams of Sittenbourne Parish. 25 pounds for 50A described in lease. Signed William Strother. Delivered in presence of Edw. Barradall, Richd. Barnes, Jere. Murdock, Edw. Rowell. Margaret Strother, wife of William Strother, relinquished her right of dower. Recorded 2 May 1729 T. Turner.

1:598 - POWER OF ATTORNEY - 2 May 1729 - Margaret Strother, wife of William Strother, impowers Mr. Thomas Turner for her and in her name to relinquish her right of dower and thirds to a certain tract of land together with a certain copper mine sold to Capt. John Williams by her husband. Signed Margaret Strother. Delivered in presence of James Markham, Linefield Sharpe. Recorded 2 May 1729 T. Turner.

1:599 - DEED OF LEASE - 30 April 1729 - Thomas Davis of Sittenbourne Parish to William Remey of same. 4600 pounds tobacco to lease 125A being the one half of 250A which James Trent left to his daughter Anne. Bounded by lands of William Carter, John Quissenbury formerly belonging to Capt. John Spicer, and Joseph Carpender. Signed Thomas Davis, Elizabeth Davis. Delivered in presence of Gyles Carter, Will. Clator. Recorded 2 May 1729 T. Turner.

1:601 - DEED OF RELEASE - 1 May 1729 - Thomas Davis of Sittenbourn Parish, planter, to William Remey of same, carpenter. 4600 pounds tobacco for land described in lease. Formerly belonging to James Trent who by his last will and testament left to his daughter Ann Trent and by Nicholas Hawkins sold unto the within named Thomas Davis. Signed Thomas Davis. Delivered in presence of Gyles Carter, Will. Cleater. Recorded 2 May 1729 T. Turner.

1:602 - POWER OF ATTORNEY - 1 May 1729 - Elizabeth Davis, wife of Thomas Davis, appoints William Grant her lawfull attorney to acknowledge her relinquishment of dower and thirds to land sold to William Remey in a certain deed of release bearing date 1 May 1729. Signed Elizabeth Davis. Delivered in presence of Gyles Carter, Willm. Clater. Recorded 2 May 1729 T. Turner.

1:603 - POWER OF ATTORNEY - 4 December 1728 - Mary Allen of Stafford County deputes William Hackney her true and lawfull attorney to acknowledge in her name to John Morehead full and peaceable possession all that tract of land which by indenture bearing date 3 December 1728 was sold to him by her husband. Signed Mary Allen. Delivered in presence of John Hudnall, Joseph Hudnall. Recorded 2 May 1729 T. Turner.

1:603 - POWER OF ATTORNEY - 4 December 1728 - Henry and Eleanor

Calfee depute William Hackney of King George County their true and lawfull attorney to acknowledge in John Hudnall full and peaceable possession to that tract of land which by indenture bearing date 20 November 1728 was sold to him. Signed Eleanor Calfee. Delivered in presence of Joseph Hudnall, John Hudnall. Recorded 2 May 1729 T. Turner.

1:604 - DEED OF GIFT - 6 June 1729 - John Lomax of St. Maries Parish in Caroline County, Gent., for divers good causes and considerations but more especially for the natural love and affection that he has for his beloved son Lunsford Lomax makes over unto his son and the woman he shall happen to marry his plantation called Shillings over against Taliaferro's Mount in King George County to enjoy until he shall enjoy his mother's land at Postebage. Also he gives all his right, title and interest to the three following plantations: Old Nanzemond, Tobias Quarter, and the Court House Quarter. Also sixteen working Negroes: Sambo, Cook, Dogo, Toby, Hector, Jeffery, Hanibal, Juba, Essie, Judy, Phillis, Frank, Nan, Vennus, Sonny, and Jubia and seven younger Negroes: Robin, Rose, Harry, Sarah, Judy, Aggy and Betty together with all his stocks of horses, cattle, hoggs and sheep. Signed John Lomax. Delivered in presence of Jere. Murdock, Edw. Barradall, Thomas Turner. Recorded 6 June 1729 T. Turner.

1:605 - POWER OF ATTORNEY - 6 January 1728/29 - David, Robert, Isabell and Betty Oswald, lawfull children to the deceased Thomas Oswald, shipman in Kirkaldy, and brothers and sisters to the deceased eldest brother Henry Oswald of Virginia, with consent of Walter Kay, husband of Isabell, appoint Thomas Ramsey, shipman in Kirkaldy husband to the said Betty Oswald, their factor and special errand bearer to receive all whatsoever belonged to Henry Oswald their brother at the time of his decease. Signed David Oswald, Isabell Oswald, Walter Kay, Betty Oswald. Witnesses: George Cunningham, Alexander Oswald, Alexander Angus. The provost and bailies of the Burgh of Kirkaldy in the county of Fife North Britain certify and declare David, Robert, Isobell, and Betty Oswald lawfull children to the deceased Thomas Oswald and brothers and sisters and nearest of kin to Henry Oswald of Virginia. Consequently by the law of this country have right to all which belonged to the deceased Henry Oswald. Signed William Jeffreys, Provost, James Duncans and Alexr. Sterdman, Bailies. Recorded 6 June 1729 T. Turner.

1:607 - BOND - 6 June 1729 - Thomas Vivion, William Thornton, Thomas Turner firmly bound to their Sovereign Lord the King in the sum of 1000 pounds sterling. Condition such that whereas the above bound Thomas Vivion, admitted Sheriff of the county of King George, does truly and faithfully perform the said office for the year, obligation to be void. Signed Thomas Vivion, William Thornton, Thomas Turner. Recorded 6 June 1729 T. Turner.

1:607 - DEED OF GIFT - 3 June 1729 - Edward Taylor of Hanover Parish doth for the natural love good will and affection that he hath and now beareth towards his son John Taylor and for his advancement and settlement by the way of marriage and for the settling and establishing the premises herein after mentioned and expressed in the blood and posterity of his said son John Taylor, doth fully, freely, clearly give unto the said John Taylor a tract of land containing eighty choice acres bounded by lines of Ralph Wormley, Esqr. deceased, and William Freak and by the westernmost side of a branch running into Powtriges Creek. Signed Edward Taylor. Delivered in presence of Isaac Arnold, William Tutt. Recorded 4 July 1729 T. Turner.

1:609 - DEED OF LEASE - 1 August 1729 - John Dodd, Junr. of Sittenbourn Parish, planter, to Simon Hughs of Hanover Parish, taylor. 350 pounds tobacco together with the quitrents every year during the natural lives of Simon Hughs, Mary his wife, and William Hughs, son of the said Simon and Mary, whoever the survivor and longest liver may be, to lease 50A being the moiety of a tract formerly bought by John Dodd, father of the said John party to these presents, of John Brown deceased. Lying near the head of the main branch of Chingateague, along the line of Thomas White, and by the land of Joseph Dodd, brother to the said John Dodd party to these presents. The said Simon Hughs to plant and maintain 100 apple trees and to build a sixteen foot square dwelling house and that then the said John Dodd shall allow the said Simon Hughs one whole year's rent. Signed John Dodd, Junr. Delivered in presence of Will. Turbervile, Will. Gearing, James Dishman. Recorded 1 August 1729 T. Turner.

1:611 - DEED OF GIFT - 1 August 1729 - John Dodd, Senr. of Washington Parish in the county of Westmoreland to John Dodd, Junr. of Sittenbourn Parish. For divers good causes and considerations hath given 50A being part of a tract of land formerly granted to William Brown and William Baltrope by patent dated 1669. By the last will and testament of the said William Brown given to John Brown and Maxfield Brown and by the said John Brown sold to John Dodd, Senr. Signed John Dodd, Senr. Delivered in presence of Will. Turbervile, Will. Gearing, James Dishman. Recorded 1 August 1729 T. Turner.

1:612 - ESTATE ADMINISTRATION - 31 July 1729 - Accounts of the estate of John Dinwiddie presented by Jere. Bronaugh and Rose his wife, administrators. Amounts paid to John Carter, Esqr., Mungo Roy, Mr. Turner, three claims for taking up Peter a runaway Negro, Robt. Pullen, John Mercer, Widow King, Thomas Cattlet, Rev. Alexander Scott, Mr. Harry Beverly, Mr. Barradall, Mr. Battaley, John Payton, John Coburn. Amounts received from Joseph Berry, David Waugh, Widow Nugent. Recorded 1 August 1729 T. Turner.

1:613 - DEED OF LEASE - 3 September 1729 - Tobias Ingram of St. Ann's Parish in Essex County, planter, to Samuel Skinker of Hanover Parish, merchant. 5 shillings to lease the tract of land left by Henry Berry to be divided between his son William Berry and Martha Berry his daughter and the mother of the above said Tobias Ingram. Signed Tobias Ingram. Delivered in presence of Saml. Newbald, Hannah Newbald, Thomas Grigsby, Edw. Barradall. Recorded 5 September 1729 T. Turner.

1:614 - DEED OF RELEASE - 4 September 1729 - Tobias Ingram of St. Ann's Parish in Essex county, planter to Samuel Skinker of Hanover Parish, merchant. 15 pounds current money of Virginia for land described in lease. Signed Tobias Ingram. Delivered in presence of Saml. Newbald, Hannah Newbald, Thomas Grigsby, Edw. Barradall. Recorded 5 September 1729 T. Turner.

1:617 - DEED OF LEASE - 2 October 1729 - Thomas Grigsby of Stafford County, gentleman, and Rose his wife, one of the daughters and coheiress of Gerrard Newton, late of Richmond County deceased, to Samuel Skinker of the county of King George, Gent. 5 shillings lawfull money to lease 550A now divided between the said Thomas Grigsby and Rose his wife and Matthew Guibert of the Province of Maryland and Elizabeth his wife, the other daughter and coheiress of the said Gerrard Newton, deceased. Signed Thomas Grigsby, Rose Grigsby. Delivered in presence of Jere. Bronaugh, Junr., Edw. Barradall. Recorded 3 October 1729 T. Turner.

1:618 - DEED OF RELEASE - 3 October 1729 - Thomas Grigsby of Stafford County, Gent. and Rose his wife, one of the daughters of Gerrard Newton, late of Richmond county deceased, to Samuel Skinker of King George county, Gent. 30 pounds current money of Virginia for 250A being one half part of 500A divided between the said Thomas Grigsby and Rose his wife and Matthew Guibert of the province of Maryland and Elizabeth his wife, the other daughter of Gerrard Newton. Bounded by Rappahannock River. Signed Thomas Grigsby, Rose Grigsby. Delivered in presence of Jeremiah Bronaugh, Junr., Edward Barradall. Recorded 3 October 1729 T. Turner.

1:620 - DEED OF LEASE - 24 September 1729 - Thomas Turner of Hanover Parish, Gent., to Samuel Wharton of same, planter. 5 shillings to lease 200A being part of a 450A tract situated on Gingoteague Creek granted to John Griffin by patent dated 11 March 1694/95. Signed Thomas Turner. Delivered in presence of Saml. Wharton, Isaac Johnson, Edw. Rowell. Recorded 3 October 1729 T. Turner.

1:621 - DEED OF RELEASE - 25 September 1729 - Thomas Turner of Hanover Parish, Gent., to Samuel Wharton of same. 15 pounds sterling for

200A described in lease. Signed Thomas Turner. Delivered in presence of Samuel Wharton, Isaac Johnson, Edward Rowell. Sarah Turner, wife of Thomas Turner, relinquished her right of dower. Recorded 3 October 1729 T. Turner.

1:623 - POWER OF ATTORNEY - 25 September 1729 - Sarah Turner, wife of Thomas Turner of King George County, authorizes Benja. Rush to acknowledge her relinquishment of dower to two hundred acres of land conveyed this day to Samuel Wharton by her husband. Signed Sarah Turner. Delivered in presence of William Stevenson, William Strother. Recorded 3 October 1729 T. Turner.

1:624 - DEED OF LEASE - 24 September 1729 - Samuel Wharton of Hanover Parish, planter, to Thomas Turner of same. 5 shillings to lease 150A beginning on the northside of a branch of Gingoteague creek called the Gravelly Run, in the line of Henry Long near the ferry crossing, to the plantation whereon John Wharton now dwells, and thence to the ferry road. It being the land whereon Edward Turbervile now dwells and part of a patent for 250A granted Ralph Whiteing 11 March 1694/95. Signed Saml. Wharton. Delivered in presence of Samuel Wharton, Isaac Johnson, Edwd. Rowell. Recorded 3 October 1729 T. Turner.

1:625 - DEED OF RELEASE - 25 September 1729 - Samuel Wharton of Hanover Parish, planter, to Thomas Turner of same, Gent. 100 pounds sterling for 150A described in lease. Signed Samuel Wharton. Delivered in presence of Samuel Wharton, Isaac Johnson, Edward Rowell. Ann Wharton, wife of Samuel Wharton, relinquished her right of dower. Recorded 3 October 1729 T. Turner.

1:627 - POWER OF ATTORNEY - 25 September 1729 - Ann Wharton, wife of Samuel Wharton, authorizes Mr. Benja. Rush to be her true and lawfull attorney for her and in her name to relinquish her right of dower and thirds to 150A of land conveyed by her husband unto Thomas Turner. Signed Ann Wharton. Delivered in presence of Samuel Wharton, Edwd. Rowell. Recorded 3 October 1729 T. Turner.

1:628 - INDENTURE - 7 November 1729 - John Conner of Hanover Parish, planter, hath of his own free will bound himself apprentice to William Stringfellow, blacksmith, to learn the art, trade or mistery of a locksmith to serve him from the date of these presents during the term of seven years next ensuing. The said William Stringfellow at the expiration of the time to give him a pare of smith bellows, one pair of vice, two hammers, one sledge and the other a hand hammer, one anvil, half a dozen files, and a pair of tongs. Signed William Stringfellow. Delivered in presence of Iten McKie, Willm. Corban. Recorded 7 November 1729 T. Turner.

1:629 - INDENTURE - 7 November 1729 - John Conner of Hanover Parish, planter, hath of his own free will bound himself unto William Stringfellow, blacksmith, to learn the art, trade or mistery of a locksmith after the manner of an apprentice to serve him from the date of these presents for and during the term of seven years next ensuing all which term the said apprentice shall not absent himself day or night from his said masters service without his leave and shall not fail to do any lawfull imployment the said master shall set him about, but in all things shall behave himself as a faithfull apprentice ought to do. Signed John Conner. Delivered in presence of Iten McKie, Willm. Corban. Recorded 7 November T. Turner.

1:630 - DEED OF LEASE - 16 April 1729 - John Travis of Stafford County to Joseph Crouch of King George County. To lease 50A on the north side of Rappahannock River. Part of a dividend of 1300A bought by Capt. William Hubbart by Francis Naile and after given by the said Nailes to John Owens and sold by Owens to Stephen Fewell and after the decease of Stephen Fewell sold by Henry Fewell, son of Stephen Fewell, to Margt. Hubbart and now the said John Travis is married to the said Margaret Hubbart. Bounded by south side of a branch of Poplar Swamp, Mr. Hugh Willliams, James Lamb. To lease during the term of the natural lives of him the said Joseph Crouch and Ann his wife having the same two years rent free and paying the next 500 pounds tobacco during the term. The said John Travis is to find 1500 tenpenny nails and 1500 eightpenny nails. Signed John Travis. Delivered in presence of Richd. Bryan, Richd. Griffith. Recorded 7 November 1729 T. Turner.

1:631 - INDENTURE - 16 April 1729 - John Travis of Stafford County to Joseph Crouch of King George County. 50A described in lease. If the rent be unpaid sixty days after the last day of January of lawfull demand then it shall and may be lawfull for the said John Travis to reenter into the said tenement as if there had been a lease never made. Signed Joseph Crouch. Delivered in presence of Richd. Bryan, Richd. Griffith. Recorded 7 November 1729 T. Turner.

1:633 - DEED OF LEASE - 4 December 1729 - Richard Griffis of King George County to William Rowley of same, planter. 5000 pounds tobacco in cask for all right, title, and interest to half of a certain mill standing on the Douge river and a small parcel of land of a 100A joyning to the line of Robert Harrison, James Kay, Col. Corbin. Signed Richard Griffis. Delivered in presence of William Baily, William Sudard. Recorded 5 December 1729 T. Turner.

1:633 - BOND - December 1729 - Richard Griffis of Hanover Parish, planter, bound unto William Rowley of same, planter, in the sum of 40 pounds good lawfull money of Virginia. Condition such that if Richard Griffis shall forever warrant and defend the half a mill standing on the Douge run and parcel of land containing 100A bounded by Col. Corbin, James Kay, and Andrew Harrison from the claim of any manner of person whatever, obligation to be void. Signed Richard Griffis. Delivered in presence of William Baily, Willm. Sudard. Recorded 5 December 1729 T. Turner.

1:634 - DEED - 4 December 1729 - William Rowley of King George county, planter to Richard Griffis of same, planter. 5000 pounds tobacco for 75A that John Sowel lately lived upon. Bounded by poplar swamp, a spring branch that belonged to William Smith, cleared ground where John Mard lived, Absolom Spicer's line. Signed William Rowley. Delivered in presence of William Baily, William Sudard. Recorded 5 December 1729 T. Turner.

1:635 - DEED OF LEASE - 5 December 1729 - William Thornton of King George County to Thomas Acres Ayers of same. For the yearly rent hereafter mentioned to lease 150A including two small houses lately built. To have and to hold during the natural lives of the said Thomas Acres Ayres, his wife Elizabeth and his daughter Henneretta. Between the first day of November and the twenty-fifth day of December and to be delivered to Thorntons dwelling for the first five years five swine shoats clear of scabs and mange; for the next five years succeeding to pay ten of such like shoats and every year after fifteen of the like shoats. Signed William Thornton, Thomas Akers Ayers. Delivered in presence of John Gilbert, Willm. Hackney, Thos. Turner. Recorded 5 December 1729 T. Turner.

1:637 - DEED OF LEASE - 4 December 1729 - Alice Cale of Hanover Parish, widow to William Strother of same, gentleman. 5 shillings to lease 200A on Claibournes Run now in the possession of Alice Cale. Bounded by land late in the possession of Thomas Fitzhugh, gent. deceased, the land now in the possession of Burwells Pophams and the land of Majr. William Thornton which he bought of Mr. Thomas Stone. Said land was bequeathed to the said Alice by the will of Edward Maddox, gent. deceased, excepting always out of the said 200A a certain part thereof sold to the said William Thornton for 35A by the said Alice Cale and Charles Cale deceased her late husband. Signed Alice Cale. Delivered in presence of Edw. Barradall, John Mercer. Recorded 5 December 1729 T. Turner.

1:638 - DEED OF RELEASE - 5 December 1729 - Alice Cale of Hanover Parish, widow to William Strother of same, gentleman. 50 pounds sterling for 200A described in lease. Signed Alice Cale. Delivered in presence of Edw. Barradall, John Mercer. Recorded 5 December 1729 T. Turner.

1:641 - DEED OF LEASE - 19 November 1729 - John Williams of the city of

Bristol, mariner, to Lyonel Lyde, Esqr., John Lewis, William Williams, Gent., of the city of Bristol, and John Taylor of Richmond County in Virginia, gentleman. 5 shillings to lease several parcels of land. One tract of 92A conveyed by Mark Hardin unto Richard Buckner, William Strother and Thomas Turner by deeds of lease and release dated 16 and 17 June 1726. One tract of 300A adjoyning the sd 92A tract, and conveyed by Timothy Reading unto Thomas Turner by deeds of lease and release dated 30 June and 1 July 1726. Part of 606A deeded to Alexander Beach 15 December 1719 and conveyed by Beach to Reading to Turner to Williams. One tract of 80A granted to Ralph Falkner by the proprietors 23 January 1726 and by the said Falkner to John Williams. Signed John Williams. Delivered in presence of John Slater, Willm. Garland, William Champney, John Smith. Recorded 5 December 1729 T. Turner.

1:643 - DEED OF RELEASE - 20 November 1729 - John Williams of the city of Bristol, mariner, to Lyonel Lyde, Esqr., John Lewis, William Williams, of the city of Bristol, and John Taylor of Richmond County in the colony of Virginia, gentleman. 120 pounds lawfull money of Great Britain for three tracts described in lease. Signed John Willliams. Delivered in presence of John Slater, Willm. Garland, Willm. Champney, John Smith. Recorded 5 December 1729 T. Turner.

1A:1 - DEED OF LEASE - Date illegible - Robert Elliston and Elinor his wife of Hanover Parish to Thomas Turner of same. 5 shillings current money to lease 200A bequeathed to the said Elinor Elliston by the last will and testament of Simon Miller deceased, father to the said Elinor, dated 1 December 1719. The said will recorded in Richmond County. Signed Robert Elliston, Elinor Elliston. Delivered in presence of Jonathan Gibson, William Thornton. Recorded 6 February 1729 T. Turner.

1A:1 - DEED OF RELEASE - 5 February 1729 - Robert Elliston and Elinor his wife of Hanover Parish to Thomas Turner of same. 80 pounds sterling for 200A described in lease. Signed Robert Elliston, Elinor Elliston. Delivered in presence of Jonathan Gibson, William Thornton. Recorded 6 February 1729 T. Turner.

1A:3 - DEED OF LEASE - 4 February 1729 - John Grayson of Spotsylvania County, Gent., to Thomas Turner of King George County. 5 shillings current money to lease 619A being the upper or half part of a 1238A tract granted unto Andrew Jackson of Lancaster County by deed from the proprietors' office dated 29 July 1704. Lying between Deep Run and Richland Run about twelve miles above the falls of the Rappahannock. Signed John Grayson. Delivered in presence of Jonathan Gibson, William Thornton. Recorded 6 February 1729 T. Turner.

1A:4 - DEED OF RELEASE - 5 February 1729 - John Grayson of Spotsylvania County, Gent., to Thomas Turner of King George County. 64 pounds 10 shillings current money for 619A described in lease. Signed John Grayson. Delivered in presence of Jonathan Gibson, William Thornton. Susannah, wife of John Grayson, relinquished her right of dower and thirds. Recorded 6 February 1729 T. Turner.

1A:6 - POWER OF ATTORNEY - 1 February 1729 - Susannah Grayson, wife of John Grayson of the county of Spotsylvania, constitutes Benja. Rush of King George County to be her lawfull attorney to relinquish her right of dower and thirds at the common law for a certain dividend or tract of land containing 619A in the county of King George being conveyed unto Thomas Turner by her husband. Signed Susannah Grayson. Delivered in presence of James Strother, Jonas Williams. Recorded 6 February 1729 T. Turner.

1A:6 - DEED OF LEASE - 4 February 1729 - Thomas Turner of Hanover Parish, gent., to Elinor Elliston of same. 5 shillings current money to lease 200A. Part of a tract of land containing 1238A formerly granted unto Andrew Jackson of Lancaster County by the proprietors' office dated 29 July 1704. Beginning at the mouth of the Deep Run about twelve miles above the falls of the Rappahannock River. Signed Thomas Turner. Delivered in presence of Jonathan Gibson, William Thornton. Recorded 6 February 1729 T. Turner.

1A:7 - DEED OF RELEASE - 5 February 1729 - Thomas Turner of Hanover Parish, Gent., to Elinor Elliston of same. 20 pounds current money for 200A described in lease. Signed Thomas Turner. Delivered in presence of Jonathan Gibson, William Thornton. Recorded 6 February 1729 T. Turner.

1A:9 - DEED OF LEASE - 21 August 1729 - John Travis and Margaret his wife, late Margaret Heabard, of the parish of Overwharton and county of Stafford to Catesby Cocke, Gent., of same. 5 shillings lawfull money of England to lease 50A beginning on the southside of a branch of poplar swamp. Bounded by Hugh Williams, John Owens, and James Lamb. Conveyed to the said Margaret by certain deeds dated 6 October 1721 by Henry Fewell. Signed John Travis, Margaret Travis. Delivered in presence of Edwd. Barradall, John Grant, T. Lewis, John Gregg. Recorded 6 February 1729 T. Turner.

1A:10 - DEED OF RELEASE - 22 August 1729 - John Travis and Margaret his wife, late Margaret Steward, of Overwharton Parish in the county of Stafford to Catesby Cocke of same. 3000 pounds tobacco for 50A described in lease. Signed John Travis, Margaret Travis. Delivered in presence of Edwd. Barradall, John Grant, T. Lewis, John Gregg. Recorded 6 February 1729 T. Turner.

1A:13 - DEED OF LEASE - 4 March 1729 - Martin Gollathan of Washington Parish in Westmoreland County, planter, to John Birkley of Cople Parish in Westmoreland County, planter. 5 shillings current money of Virginia to lease 150A beginning at the head of a small branch that comes out of cattail branch. Signed Martin Gollathan. Delivered in presence of Danl. McCarty, John Briscoe. Recorded 6 March 1729 T. Turner.

1A:14 - DEED OF RELEASE - 5 March 1729 - Martin Gollathan of Washington Parish in Westmoreland County, planter, to John Birkley of Cople Parish in Westmoreland County, planter. 7000 pounds tobacco for 150A near to Maddox Road. Part of a tract formerly patented and taken up by John Lord who sold it to one Martin Fisher who sold the same to Christopher Pritchett who by deeds dated 1 and 2 May 1728 sold it to the said Martin Gollathan. Signed Martin Gollathan. Delivered in presence of Danl. McCarty, John Briscoe. Recorded 6 March 1729 T. Turner.

1A:17 - BOND - 5 March 1729 - Martin Gollathan of Washington Parish in Westmoreland County, planter, bound unto John Birkley of Cople Parish in Westmoreland County, planter, in the sum of 14,000 pounds tobacco. Condition such that if Martin Gollathan truly keeps all agreements in certain indentures of lease and release bearing even date with these presents, obligation to be void. Signed Martin Gollathan. Delivered in presence of Danl. McCarty, John Briscoe. Recorded 6 March 1729 T. Turner.

1A:18 - DEED OF SALE - 5 March 1729 - John Quissenbury of Sittenbourn Parish to John Dodd of Washington Parish in Westmoreland County. 4000 pounds tobacco for 60A. Bounded by lands of William Remey which formerly belonged to James Trent, a branch of wool pit creek, and William Carter. Signed John Quissenbury. Delivered in presence of Thomas Clayter, William Clayter. Elizabeth, wife of John Quissenbury, relinquished her right of dower and thirds. Recorded 6 March 1729 T. Turner.

1A:19 - POWER OF ATTORNEY - 5 March 1729 - Elizabeth Quissenbury, wife of John Quissenbury, appoints William Remey her true and lawfull attorney to acknowledge a certain indenture made between John Quissenbury and John Dodd bearing date of 5 March 1729 and to acknowledge the relinquishment of her right of dower and thirds in and to the land and premises. Signed Elizabeth Quissenbury. Delivered in presence of Thomas Clayter, William Clayter. Recorded 6 March 1729 T. Turner.

1A:20 - INVENTORY - November 1729 - Inventory list of the estate of Adam Christie presented by Robert Jones, Thomas Smith, and Thos. Harwood. Recorded 6 February 1729 T. Turner.

1A:20 - DEED OF LEASE - 2 April 1730 - Robert Doniphan of Hanover Parish and Mott Doniphan of Overwharton Parish in the county of Stafford, planters, to Stephen Hansford of Hanover Parish, mariner. 5 shillings to lease 165A including the plantation whereon William _____ now lives. Part of a 315A tract formerly purchased by Capt. Alexander Doniphan, late of Richmond County deceased, of Joshua Davis 1 June 1704. Signed Robert Doniphan, Mott Doniphan. Delivered in presence of Joseph Crouch, William Stringfellow, M. Battaley. Recorded 3 April 1730 T. Turner.

1A:21 - DEED OF RELEASE - 3 April 1730 - Robert Doniphan of Hanover Parish and Mott Doniphan of Overwharton Parish in the county of Stafford, planters, to Stephen Hansford of Hanover Parish, mariner. 300 pounds tobacco and 12 pounds sterling for 165A including the plantation whereon William Summerton now lives and part of a tract described in lease. Signed Robert Doniphan, Mott Doniphan. Delivered in presence of M. Battaley, Joseph Crouch, William Stringfellow. Recorded 3 April 1730 T. Turner.

1A:24 - BOND - 3 April 1730 - Robert Doniphan of Hanover Parish and Mott Doniphan of Stafford County bound unto Stephen Hansford of Hanover Parish in the sum of 500 pounds sterling. Condition such that if Robert Doniphan and Mott Doniphan do truly observe, fullfill, and keep the several clauses, articles and covenants in one deed of release of land bearing equal date with this present obligation, obligation to be void. Signed Robert Doniphan, Mott Doniphan. Delivered in presence of M. Battaley, Joseph Crouch, William Stringfellow. Recorded 3 April 1730 T. Turner.

1A:24 - DEED - 28 November 1718 - The Right Honble. Catherine Lady Fairfax Sole Proprietor of the Northern Neck of Virginia and Thomas Lee, Esqr., of Westmoreland County. For and in consideration of compensation to me paid and the annual rent hereafter do by these presents grant, make over, and confirm unto Thomas Lee 4200A of land in Richmond County beginning at a corner marked on the Northwesterly side of the great run and at the distance of a quarter of a mile from the said run being the Northwesterly corner of a tract of land taken up by Col. Rice Hooe near half a mile below the main fork of the said run. (Cider Run, Turkey Run, Licking Run, southwest branch of Occoquon River named). Signed Jenings. Recorded in folio 1209 by Danl. Jenings, Clk. Proprietors office. Recorded 3 April 1730 T. Turner.

1A:26 - DEED OF SALE - 29 April 1730 - Archibald Combes of Hanover Parish, planter, to Mary Tutt of same. 1400 pounds tobacco for the parcel of land whereon Mary Tutt now dwelleth. Signed Archibald Combes. Delivered in presence of John Gilbert, Adam Cuningham. Memorandum signed by William Tutt, Adam Cuningham, John Gilbert. Recorded 1 May 1730 T. Turner.

1A:28 - DEED OF GIFT - 10 April 1730 - Elizabeth Lomax, widow, to Lunsford Lomax of King George County. 5 shillings and in consideration of the natural love and affection which she hath and doth bare to her son and for divers other good causes and considerations hath given granted bargained sold and transferred those three quarters and plantations upon Nansemond Tract of land now in the actural possession of her son the said Lunsford Lomax. Signed Elizabeth _____. Delivered in presence of John Champe, Chas. Seale, Richd. Jarvis, James Vaughan. Recorded 1 May 1730 T. Turner.

1A:29 - DEED OF LEASE - Date Illegible - Thomas Thatcher of the county of King George to William Wheeler of the county of Westmoreland. 5 shillings sterling to lease 110A. Part in King George County, part in Westmoreland County, and part in Stafford County. Part of 220A left to Thatchers wife by her deceased father William Pannell. Bounded by Henry Berry, Robert Peck, George King, John Pearce, the Beaver Dam of Indian Ridge, and Thomas Porter. Said land was first deeded to Thomas Harvey 2_ July 1697 and by several conveyances became William Pannells who divided it between his two daughters Katherine and Mary. Signed Katherine Thatcher, Thomas Thatcher. Delivered in presence of Chas. Seale, Benja. Strother, Francis Lacon. Recorded 1 May 1730 T. Turner.

1A:30 - DEED OF RELEASE - Date Illegible - Thomas Thatcher of King George County, planter, to William Wheeler of the county of Westmoreland, planter. Amount not given for 110A described in lease. Signed Katherine Thatcher, Thomas Thatcher. Delivered in presence of Chas. Seale, Benja. Strother, Francis Lacon. Recorded 1 May 1730 T. Turner.

1A:32 - BOND - Date Illegible - Thomas Thatcher of the county of King George bound unto William Wheeler of the county of Westmoreland for 8000 pounds of good tobacco. Condition such that if agreements made in deeds of lease and release bearing equal date are kept, obligation to be void. Signed Thomas Thatcher. Delivered in presence of Francis Lacon, Chas. Seale, Benja. Strother. Recorded 1 May 1730 T. Turner.

1A:34 - DEED OF LEASE - 30 April 1730 - William Robinson of Sittenbourn Parish, Gent., to Maximilian Robinson of same. 5 shillings sterling to lease 600A being the plantation and land the said Max. Robinson now lives on. Signed Will. Robinson. Delivered in presence of Mungo Roy, Mosely Battaley, Willm. Thornton. Recorded 1 May 1730 T. Turner.

1A:35 - DEED OF RELEASE - 1 May 1730 - William Robinson of Sittenbourn Parish, gent., to Maximilian Robinson of same. 500 pounds sterling for 600A described in lease. Signed Wil. Robinson. Delivered in presence of Mungo Roy,

Mosely Battaley, Willm. Thornton. Recorded 1 May 1730 T. Turner.

1A:36 - DEED OF LEASE - 1 April 1730 - John Edy of Westmoreland County to Thomas Osbourne and Tobias Pussell both of the county of King George. ___ sterling money of England to lease 954A granted unto the said John Edy by patent dated 17 April 1727. Signed John Edy. Delivered in presence of Richard Jarvis, Thos. Phillips. Recorded 1 May 1730 T. Turner.

1A:38 - DEED OF RELEASE - 2 April 1730 - John Edy of Westmoreland County to Thomas Osbourne and Tobias Pussell. 3200 pounds tobacco for 954A described in lease. Signed John Edy. Delivered in presence of Richard Jarvis, Thomas Phillips. Recorded 1 May 1730 T. Turner.

1A:41 - DEED OF LEASE - Date Illegible - Thomas Riphley of King George County, carpenter, to William McBee of same, planter. 5 shillings lawfull money to lease 259A taken up by Grace Riphley, alias Butler, now wife of the said Thomas Riphley, in the time of her widowhood by deed dated 14 July 1727. Signed Thomas Riphley, Grace Riphley alias Butler. Delivered in presence of John Wright, Charles Morgan. William Strother acknowledged this lease by virtue of a power of attorney. Recorded 1 May 1730 T. Turner.

1A:42 - DEED OF RELEASE - 28 April 1730 - Thomas Riphley of the county of King George, carpenter, to William McBee of same, planter. 2000 pounds good sound merchantable tobacco and cask at the Rowling house within this county for 259A described in lease. Bounded by William Russell, Joshua Butler, and Joseph King. Signed Thomas Riphley, Grace Riphley alias Butler. Delivered in presence of John Wright, Charles Morgan. William Strother acknowledged this release by virtue of a power of attorney. Recorded 1 May 1730 T. Turner.

1A:43 - POWER OF ATTORNEY - 28 April 1730 - Thomas Riphley and Grace Riphley alias Butler, wife of the said Thomas Riphley, appoint their trusty and well beloved friends Capt. William Strother and John Bradford their true and lawfull attorneys to sell and in their behalves to acknowledge good and lawfull deeds of lease and release together with the right of dower of two hundred and fifty-nine acres and also to act and proceed in all and every respects for the more sure making and confirming of the said land unto William McBee. Signed Thomas Riphley, Grace Riphley alias Butler. Delivered in presence of John Wright, Chas. Morgan. Recorded 1 May 1730 T. Turner.

1A:44 - DEED - 1 May 1730 - Nicholas Smith and William Thornton, gentlemen, Directors and Trustees of the Town of Falmouth in the county of King George to Hancock Lee of Northumberland County. 5 pounds current money of Virginia for one lott, or half acre, number four according to the plat thereof made and laid of into lotts by John Warner, surveyor. Signed Nicho. Smith, Wm. Thornton. Delivered in presence of T. Turner. Recorded 1 May 1730 T. Turner.

1A:45 - DEED - 5 June 1730 - Richard Griffis of the county of King George, planter, to Mary Harrison of the county of Westmoreland, widow. 1000 pounds tobacco for one moiety or half part of one acre of land and the mill thereon formerly purchased by Andrew Harrison late of the county of Westmoreland deceased and the said Richard Griffis of Joseph Berry by deed dated 9 December 1725. Signed Richard Griffis. Delivered in presence of Edw. Barradall, T. Turner. Recorded 5 June 1730 T. Turner.

1A:47 - BOND - 5 June 1730 - Richard Griffis of the county of King George bound unto Mary Harrison of the county of Westmoreland, widow, in the sum of twenty pounds sterling. Condition such that if Richard Griffis keeps all covenants in a certain deed bearing even date with these presents, obligation to be void. Signed Richard Griffis. Delivered in presence of Edwd. Barradall, T. Turner. Recorded 5 June 1730 T. Turner.

1A:48 - DEED OF LEASE - 4 June 1730 - Rice Hooe and Catherine his wife of St. Paul's Parish in the county of Stafford to Thomas Turner of Hanover Parish. 5 shillings current money of Virginia to lease 43A lying on the north side of the Rappahannock River. Part of a 200A tract sold to Mr. Richard Taliaferro by John Reynolds which descended to Richard Taliaferro son to the aforesaid Richard Taliaferro and brother to the aforesaid Catherine and on the decease of Richard Taliaferro the son the said forty-three acres descends to the said Catherine the same being one-third of what is left of the deceased Richard Taliaferro's land in a survey made the year 1714 between Col. William Fitzhugh and Mr. John Lomax and others called the Nansemond Patent. Signed Rice Hooe, Katherine Hooe. Delivered in presence of Thomas Catlett, Edward Clement. Recorded 5 June 1730 T. Turner.

1A:50 - DEED OF RELEASE - 5 June 1730 - Rice Hooe and Katherine his wife of St. Paul's Parish in the county of Stafford to Thomas Turner of Hanover Parish. 10 pounds current money of Virginia for 43A described in lease. Signed Rice Hooe, Katherine Hooe. Delivered in presence of Thomas Catlet, Edward Clement. Recorded 5 June 1730 T. Turner.

1A:52 - DEED OF LEASE - 25 April 1730 - William Lampton, planter, of Hanover Parish to James Jones, bricklayer, of same. 5 shillings to lease 220A being part of 320A formerly purchased by Sem Cox of Robert Peck. Then 100A was sold by Sem Cox to one Edward Roch and the other 220A was formerly sold unto Thomas White. Bounded by Edward Rock, Sem Cox, Samuel Duchinnia, John Thomas, Hales, William Cash. Signed William Lampton. Delivered in presence of Jeremiah Bronaugh, Senr., Richard Bryan, John Steward. Recorded 5 June 1730 T. Turner.

1A:53 - DEED OF RELEASE - 25 April 1730 - William Lampton, planter, of Hanover Parish to James Jones, bricklayer, of same. 80 pounds sterling for 220A described in lease. Signed William Lampton. Delivered in presence of Jere. Bronaugh, Senr., Jere. Bronaugh, Junr., John Steward. Memorandum - Recd. of James Jones two slaves under four foot high for the two hundred and twenty acres of land which I am content. Signed William Lampton. Recorded 5 June 1730 T. Turner.

1A:57 - DEED OF LEASE - 1 July 1730 - Samuel Kendall of Hanover Parish, planter, to Jeremiah Murdock of same, gentleman. 5 shillings good and lawfull money of England to lease 12A. Part of a 105A patent made unto Thomas Kendall, deceased, father to the said Samuel Kendall. Bounded by Murdocks line on a creek called Indian Nedds and land of Samuel Kendall. Signed Samuel Kendall. Delivered in presence of Isaac Arnold, Thomas James, Francis Attwood. Recorded 3 July 1730 T. Turner.

1A:59 - DEED OF RELEASE - 2 July 1730 - Samuel Kendall of Hanover Parish, planter, to Jeremiah Murdock of same. 750 pounds good tobacco for 12A described in lease. Signed Samuel Kendall. Delivered in presence of Isaac Arnold, Thomas James, Francis Attwood. Recorded 3 July 1730 T. Turner.

1A:61 - BOND - 2 July 1730 - Samuel Kendall of Hanover Parish bound unto Jeremiah Murdock of same in the sum of fifty pounds current money of Virginia. Condition such that if the said Samuel Kendall faithfully keeps all agreements therein contained according to the true intent and meaning of the deeds, obligation to be void. Signed Samuel Kendall. Delivered in presence of Isaac Arnold, Thomas James, Francis Attwood. Recorded 3 July 1730 T. Turner.

1A:62 - ADMINISTRATION ACCOUNT - No Date - Account of William Pattishall deceased. Monies paid to Thomas Jefrey, Doctor Livingstone, John Ambrose, William Flowers, Lunsford Sharp, John Obanion, Mr. Ambrose Grayson, Charles Brunt, Mr. Walter Anderson, Mr. John Savage, and Charles Deuat. The account was presented into Court by Adam Christie. Recorded 1 May 1730 T. Turner.

1A:62 - DEED OF SALE - 5 December 1728 - Samuel Green of Hanover Parish, planter, to Francis Settle of same, planter. 1500 pounds good tobacco for

50A which is all that tract which his father George Green willed and bequeathed unto him. Signed Samuel Green. Delivered in presence of Statford Lightbourn, John Kindall. Recorded 7 August 1730 T. Turner.

1A:64 - DEED OF LEASE - 3 August 1730 - John Pope of Washington Parish in Westmoreland County to Joshua Farguson of Hanover Parish. 5 shillings good lawfull money of England to lease 80A whereon Joshua Farguson now liveth. All the remaining part of 300A formerly sold by Capt. William Underwood, deceased, unto Nathaniel Pope alias Bridges, father to the said John Pope party to these presents, by deed dated 3 August 1696. Bounded by line of Capt. Jeremiah Murdock, Abraham Blagg, and the former line of William Underwood's deed to Nathaniel Pope. The remaining part of 100A bought of the said William Underwood by William Wheeler and by William Wheeler sold to the said Nathaniel Pope by deed dated 4 December 1689. Signed J. Pope. Delivered in presence of Josiah Farguson, Moss Knighton. Recorded 7 August 1730 T. Turner.

1A:65 - DEED OF RELEASE - 4 August 1730 - John Pope of Washington Parish in Westmoreland County to Joshua Farguson of Hanover Parish. 30 pounds current money of Virginia for tracts described in lease. Signed J. Pope. Delivered in presence of Josiah Farguson, Moses Knighton. Recorded 7 August 1730 T. Turner.

1A:68 - BOND - 4 August 1730 - John Pope of Washington Parish in Westmoreland County bound unto Joshua Farguson in the sum of 60 pounds current money of Virginia. Condition such that if John Pope faithfully keeps all agreements in one deed of lease and one deed of release for the same land bearing date the 3 and 4 August 1730, obligation to be void. Signed J. Pope. Delivered in presence of Josiah Farguson, Mosses Knighton. Recorded 7 August 1730 T. Turner.

1A:69 - POWER OF ATTORNEY - 4 August 1730 - Elizabeth Pope, wife of John Pope of Westmoreland County, authorizes Thomas Turner, Gent., to acknowledge her relinquishment of dower unto Joshua Farguson of 100A of land more or less conveyed by her husband by deeds bearing equal date with these presents. Signed Elizabeth Pope. Delivered in presence of John Burch, George Parsons. Recorded 7 August 1730 T. Turner.

1A:70 - DEED OF SALE - 18 August 1730 - Samuel Green of Hanover Parish, planter, to Francis Settle of same, planter. 1500 pounds good tobacco for 50A bequeathed unto Samuel Green by his father George Green being joyned upon his mother's land. Signed Samuel Green. Delivered in presence of Statford Lightbourn, William Harrison, John Hudson, Francis Wolfendale. Recorded 4

September 1730 T. Turner.

1A:71 - DEED OF LEASE - 2 September 1730 - John Diskin of Hanover Parish, planter, to Samuel Skinker of same, gent. 5 shillings lawfull current money of Virginia to lease 104A. Part of a 2234A tract granted unto James Kay by deed dated 12 December 1722 then granted unto John Diskin by James Kay. Bounded by Glebe land, Colonel Corbyn, and George Jones. Signed John Diskin. Delivered in presence of John Farguson, John Farguson, Junr., Joshua Farguson. Recorded 4 September 1730 T. Turner.

1A:72 - DEED OF RELEASE - 3 September 1730 - John Diskin of Hanover Parish, planter, to Samuel Skinker of same, Gent. 24 pounds and 15 shillings lawfull current money of Virginia for 104A described in lease. Signed John Diskin. Delivered in presence of John Farguson, John Farguson, Junr., Joshua Farguson. Recorded 4 September 1730 T. Turner.

1A:74 - DEED OF LEASE - 4 September 1730 - George Rust of Overwharton Parish in the county of Stafford, gent., and Sarah his wife to Enoch Innis of same, Gent.. 5 shillings sterling to lease 275A lying upon a run known by the name of great gravelly run falling into the Rappahannock River about two miles above the falls. Bounded by the said run, the Rappahannock River, land late in the tenure of Mr. Jackson, and the land of Colo. Carter. Part of a greater tract of 975A formerly granted to Mr. James Innis by patent dated 1 June 1704. Signed George Rust, Sarah Rust. Delivered in presence of James Markham, Charles Seale, John Champe. Recorded 4 September 1730 T. Turner.

1A:75 - DEED OF RELEASE - 4 September 1730 - George Rust of Overwharton Parish in the county of Stafford, gent., and Sarah his wife to Enoch Innis of same, gent.. 80 pounds sterling for 275A described in lease. Bequeathed by James Innis to his daughter Sarah by his last will and testament dated 25 December 1709. Signed George Rust, Sarah Rust. Delivered in presence of James Markham, Charles Seale, John Champe. Recorded 4 September 1730 T. Turner.

1A:77 - DEED OF LEASE - 5 August 1730 - Lincefield Sharp of Hanover Parish, planter, to Muttoone Lewis of same, planter. 5 shillings sterling to lease 100A whereon the said Muttoone Lewis now liveth. Part of a 1250A tract granted to Thomas Knight of Northumberland County by patent dated 5 June 1704. Given by Thomas Knight by his will to Lincefield Sharp and John Sharp to be equally divided between them. Signed Lincefield Sharp. Delivered in presence of Thomas Moore, Edward Turbervile, Wil. Turbervile. Recorded 2 October 1730 T. Turner.

1A:78 - DEED OF RELEASE - 6 August 1730 - Lincefield Sharp of Hanover Parish, planter, to Muttone Lewis of same, planter. 5000 pounds good tobacco for 100A described in lease. Signed Lincefield Sharp. Delivered in presence of Thomas Moore, Edward Turbervile, Will. Turbervile. Recorded 2 October 1730 T. Turner.

1A:81 - BOND - 6 August 1730 - Lincefield Sharp of Hanover Parish, planter, bound unto Muttoone Lewis of same, planter, in the sum of 100 pounds sterling. Condition such that if Lincefield Sharp truly observes all covenants in certain deeds of lease and release bearing date even with these presents, obligation to be void. Signed Lincefield Sharp. Delivered in presence of Thomas Moore, E. Turbervile, Will. Turbervile. Recorded 2 October 1730 T. Turner.

1A:82 - POWER OF ATTORNEY - 18 September 1730 - Jeremiah Murdock of Hanover Parish, gent., appoints Thomas Turner to be his true and lawfull attorney to ask, demand, sue and receive of all and every person all such debts and sums of money and tobacco rents and arrears of rents due and payable unto him and also for him and in his name to commence and proscecute any other action or suit either in law or equity as said attorney shall deem necessary for his interest to be done. Signed Jere. Murdock. Delivered in presence of Edw. Barradall, Francis Attwood. Recorded 2 October 1730 T. Turner.

1A:83 - POWER OF ATTORNEY - 5 September 1730 - Elizabeth Diskin, wife of John Diskin of Hanover Parish, appoints Thomas Turner her true and lawfull attorney to relinquish her right of dower to a certain piece or parcel of land containing 104A conveyed by her husband unto Saml. Skinker by deeds of lease and release bearing date the second and third days of this instant September. Signed Elizabeth Diskin. Delivered in presence of John Farguson, Timothy Goode. Recorded 2 October 1730 T. Turner.

1A:83 - DEED OF LEASE - 1 October 1730 - Bloomfield Long of Hanover Parish, blacksmith, and Elizabeth his wife to Thomas Turner of same, gent.. 5 shillings sterling to lease 136A in three parcels. A 34A tract part of 84A tract formerly belonging to William Reynolds, father to the said Elizabeth, the other 50A being conveyed to Henry Long, Junr. in exchange for 50A conveyed to the said Bloomfield Long by Henry Long, Senr. by deeds dated 3 and 4 November 1726. A 52A tract formerly belonging to John Reynolds and by him conveyed unto the said Bloomfield Long by deeds dated 1 and 2 April 1713. A 50A tract conveyed to the said Bloomfield Long by Henry Long, Senr. by deeds dated 3 and 4 November 1726. Adjoining unto the lands of Thomas Turner, Simon Miller, and the main county road. Signed Bloomfield Long, Elizabeth Long. Delivered in presence of John Mercer, John Miller. Recorded 2 October 1730 T. Turner.

1A:85 - DEED OF RELEASE - 2 October 1730 - Bloomfield Long of Hanover Parish, blacksmith, and Elizabeth his wife to Thomas Turner of same, gent.. 80 pounds sterling for three tracts of land containing 136A described in lease. Signed Bloomfield Long, Elizabeth Long. Delivered in presence of John Mercer, John Miller. Recorded 2 October 1730 T. Turner.

1A:87 - BOND - 2 October 1730 - Bloomfield Long of Hanover Parish bound unto Thomas Turner in the sum of 160 pounds current money. Condition such that if Bloomfield Long keeps all agreements in certain indentures of lease and release the lease dated the day before and the release bearing even date with these presents, obligation to be void. Signed Bloomfield Long. Delivered in presence of Jno. Mercer, John Miller. Recorded 2 October 1730 T. Turner.

1A:89 - ACCOUNT OF ESTATE - 2 October 1730 - Account submitted by John Miller on behalf of Simon Miller, son of Will. Miller deceased. The balance due to Simon Miller is 1493 pounds of tobacco, 34 barrels of Indian corn, 15 bushels of wheat, and two shares of tobacco and corn and one share of wheat for this present year 1730 deducting one _____ same 9 barrels of corn for him and his negro wench and child's accomodation. Signed John Miller. Recorded 2 October 1730 T. Turner.

1A:89 - DEED OF LEASE - 4 November 1730 - Samuel Wharton of Hanover Parish, planter, to Robert Johnson of same, planter. 5 shillings to lease 80A on the main branch of the Gingoteague. Part of a 450A tract granted to John Griffin by patent dated 11 March 1694/5. Bounded by Thomas Turner, Samuel Wharton, and James Mathews. Signed Samuel Wharton. Delivered in presence of Richard Tutt, William Marshall. Ann Wharton, wife of Samuel Wharton, relinquished her right of dower. Recorded 6 November 1730 T. Turner.

1A:91 - DEED OF RELEASE - 5 November 1730 - Samuel Wharton of Hanover Parish to Robert Johnson of same. 15 pounds sterling for 80A described in lease. Signed Samuel Wharton. Delivered in presence of Richard Tutt, William Marshall. Ann Wharton, wife of Samuel Wharton, relinquished her right of dower. Recorded 6 November 1730 T. Turner.

1A:92 - DEED OF LEASE - 1 October 1730 - Thomas Welch of Hanover Parish, planter, to Samuel Bronaugh and Jeremiah Bronaugh his brother of same. 5 shillings sterling to lease 600A being part of a tract whereon he now lives. Bounded by Nathanels Hedgman, George Eskridge, and Charles Morgan. Signed Thomas Welch. Delivered in presence of Jeremiah Bronaugh, Junr., John Wright, Henry McKie. Recorded 6 November 1730 T. Turner.

1A:94 - DEED OF RELEASE - 2 October 1730 - Thomas Welch of Hanover

Parish, planter, to Samuel Bronaugh and Jeremiah Bronaugh his brother of same, planters. 10,000 pounds tobacco for 600A described in lease. Part of a tract of 1267A taken up by him in the countys of Stafford and King George. Signed Thomas Welch. Delivered in presence of Jeremiah Bronaugh, Junr., John Wright, Hen. McKie. Doras Welch, wife of Thomas, relinquished her right of dower. Recorded 6 November 1730 T. Turner.

1A:96 - POWER OF ATTORNEY - 19 September 1730 - Dorias Welch of Hanover Parish appoints her trusty and well beloved friends Capt. William Strother and Capt. John Wright her true and lawfull attorneys to acknowledge, transfer, and make over all her right, title, and interest of Dowery in a piece of land containing six hundred acres unto Mr. Jeremiah Bronaugh, Senr. Signed Dorias Welch. Delivered in presence of Christopher Marr, Alexander Clement, James McDaniel. This power of attorney from Doras Welch to William Strother, gent., and John Wright was proved by the oath of Christopher Marr, Alexr. Clement, and James McDonnell and admitted to record. Recorded 6 November 1730 T. Turner.

1A:96 - DEED OF LEASE - 4 November 1730 - James Kay of Hanover Parish, planter, to Samuel Skinker of same, merchant. 5 shillings sterling to lease 27A bounded on the lines of John Price, John Dinwiddie, and the said Samuel Skinker. Part of a certain tract of land granted by patent to Colo. Jerrard Fowke and Mr. Richard Heabard dated 23 March 1664. Surveyed and sold by the said Heabard to James Kay deceased Grandfather to the present James Kay to whom the said land descends by inheritance. Signed James Kay. Delivered in presence of Joel Berry, William Edgar, John Burn. Recorded 6 November 1730 T. Turner.

1A:97 - DEED OF RELEASE - 5 November 1730 - James Kay of Hanover Parish, planter, to Samuel Skinker of same, merchant. 1500 pounds good, sound merchantable tobacco for 27A described in lease. Signed James Kay. Delivered in presence of Joel Berry, William Edgar, John Burn. Mary Kay, wife of James Kay, relinquished her right of dower. Recorded 6 November 1730 T. Turner.

1A:99 - POWER OF ATTORNEY - 20 August 1730 - Angus Mackay of Invorness of the Kingdom of Great Britain now of the county of King George appoints William Strother his true and lawfull attorney to ask, demand, and sue for, recover and receive all such debt and debt sums and sums of mony and tobacco due, dutys and demands whatsoever which now are or at any time hereafter shall become due and payable to him. Signed Angus Mackay. Delivered in presence of Thomas Moore, Nicho. Smith, Edw. Barradall. Recorded 6 November 1730 T. Turner.

1A:100 - DEED OF LEASE - 29 September 1730 - William McBee of the county of King George, planter, to Emmanuel Cumbee of same. 5 shillings lawfull money to lease 200A upon the horse penn branch. Bounded by William Russell, Joshua Butler, Joseph King, and Mark Hardin. Part of 259A taken up by Grace Butler in the time of her widowhood the deeds thereof bearing date 14 July 1727. Signed William McBee. Delivered in presence of James McDonnel, Daniel Blackman. Recorded 6 November 1730 T. Turner.

1A:101 - DEED OF RELEASE - 30 September 1730 - William McBee of the county of King George, planter, to Emmanuel Cumbee of same. 12 pounds current money for 200A described in lease. Signed William McBee. Delivered in presence of James McDonnal, Daniel Blackburn. By virtue of a power of attorney, Susannah McBee, wife of William, relinquishes her right of dower. Recorded 6 November 1730 T. Turner.

1A:102 - POWER OF ATTORNEY - 3 October 1730 - Susannah McBee of the county of King George appoints her trustee and well beloved friend James McDonnal her true and lawfull attorney to acknowledge, transfer, and make over all her right, title, and interest of Dower in and to a certain tract of land made over by her husband William McBee unto Emmanuel Cumbee. Signed Susannah McBee. Delivered in presence of John Hamman, William McBee. Recorded 6 November 1730 T. Turner.

1A:103 - DEED OF SALE - 28 September 1730 - William Morton of Sittenbourn Parish in Richmond County to John Piper of Washington Parish in the county of Westmoreland. 90 pounds current money of Virginia for 150A sold by George Davis and Patience Davis his wife unto the said William Morton 7 June 1728. Part of a patent granted John Barrow 13 October 1657 which was surveyed on 25 March 1709 and divided between Thomas Brock, father to the aforesaid Patience Davis, and one William Richardson. It is that part which did belong to Brock and is next adjoining to the land late of John Burkett deceased. Signed William Morton, Ann Morton. Delivered in presence of Thomas Frank, Thomas Thompson, Samuel Reeds. Recorded 6 November 1730 T. Turner.

1A:105 - POWER OF ATTORNEY - 28 September 1730 - Ann Morton the now wife of William Morton does of her own free will and power accord relinquish all her right of dower and thirds to one hundred and fifty acres of land sold by her husband William Morton unto John Piper and puts in her place in the open Court of King George County her loving friend Samuel Reeds her attorney to make this relinquishment. Signed Ann Morton. Delivered in presence of Thomas Frank, Thomas Thompson. Recorded 6 November 1730 T. Turner.

1A:105 - DEED OF SALE - 6 November 1730 - Thomas Smith and Anne Foulke Smith his wife to Henry Willis of Spotsylvania County, gent.. 28 pounds for all the right, title, interest and property that they the said Thomas Smith and Ann Foulk Smith have unto the land whereon they now live and on which Thomas Fitzhugh deceased late husband of the said Ann Foulk Smith formerly lived being one third part as her Dower of the said land together with all her dower of the mills formerly belonging to the said Fitzhugh and adjoining to the said land. Signed Thomas Smith, Ann Fowks Smith. Delivered in presence of Chas. Seale, John Gregsby. Recorded 6 November 1730 T. Turner.

1A:106 - DEED OF SALE - 6 November 1730 - Elizabeth Kitchen, widow, of Sittenbourn Parish to Margaret Tutt of same. 20 shillings sterling for 50A whereon the said Margaret now liveth. Bounded by Claytors Swamp, Samuel Prims, and Ireland. Signed Elizabeth Kitchen. Delivered in presence of Benja. Rush, John Drake. Recorded 6 November 1730 T. Turner.

1A:107 - DEED OF LEASE - 27 October 1730 - Thomas Conway of St. Stephen's Parish in the county of Northumberland to Bryant Bredin and Elizabeth his wife of Hanover Parish. Yearly rent of 96 pounds of tobacco or eight shillings sterling in cash to lease 50A now in the possession of Bryant Bredin and Elizabeth his wife. Lying on the north side of Deep Run and joyning on the land of William Blackwell and the land of Samuel Earles. The said Bryant Bredin and Elizabeth his wife shall peaceably and quietly have hold use occupy possess and enjoy the said 50A and premises during their two natural lives. Signed Thomas Conway, Bryant Bredin. Delivered in presence of George Conway, Andrew Hunt. Memorandum - That quiet peaceable possession and seizure of the within granted fifty acres of land and premises was this day given in the presence of Blag Grovehopper, Thomas Harper. Recorded 6 November 1730 T. Turner.

1A:108 - DEED OF LEASE - 5 November 1730 - William Lampton of Hanover Parish, planter, and John Gregsby of Overwharton Parish in the county of Stafford, blacksmith, and Ann his wife to James Jones of Hanover Parish, bricklayer. 5 shillings current money of Virginia to lease 100A lying partly in King George County and partly in Stafford County. William Lampton deceased formerly purchased of one John Hopkins and Ann his wife and by his last will and testament bequeathed to his son Samuel Lampton and if he died before he arrived to the age of eighteen years then to be equally divided between his other three children - the above named William Lampton, Anne now the wife of the above named John Gregsby, and Joshua Lampton who became seized of one third part of the said parcel of land. Bounded by lands of William Grigsby, son of John Grigsby late of Stafford County deceased, Major John Fitzhugh, and Richard Rosser. Signed William Lampton, John Grigsby, Ann Grigsby.

Delivered in presence of Richard Bryan, Thomas Vivion, Richard Tutt. Recorded 6 November 1730 T. Turner.

1A:109 - DEED OF RELEASE - 6 November 1730 - William Lampton of Hanover Parish, planter, and John Grigsby, Junr. of the county of Stafford and parish of Overwharton, blacksmith, and Ann his wife to James Jones of Hanover Parish. 30 pounds current money of Virginia for 100A described in lease. Signed William Lampton, John Grigsby, Ann Grigsby. Delivered in presence of Richard Bryan, Thomas Vivion, Richard Tutt. Recorded 6 November 1730 T. Turner.

1A:111 - POWER OF ATTORNEY - No Date - Rosemond Steward, wife to John Steward, appoints Benjamin Rush her attorney to acknowledge all her right of dower and thirds at the common law in and to a parcel of land being 260A given by her husband to Joseph Steward. Signed Rosemond Steward. Delivered in presence of John Dunkin, Thomas Steward. Recorded 6 November 1730 T. Turner.

1A:112 - DEED OF LEASE - 3 December 1730 - Baldwin Mathews of Hanover Parish, gent., to John Champ of same, merchant. 5 shillings lawfull current money of Virginia to lease 400A. Part of 2000A granted unto Lt. Col. Samuel Mathews, great grandfather of the said Baldwin Mathews, by patent 7 September 1654. Beginning at a place commonly called the hopsyard upon the Rappahannock River, thence up the said river to the mouth of a creek commonly called Skrines Mill Creek, thence along said creek to the back line of the said tract of 2000A, thence along the said back line to the land of Col. John Tayloe, thence along the said Tayloes line to the first beginning. Signed Baldwin Mathews. Delivered in presence of Robert Richards, Cornelus McCarty, Hugh Kennedy. Recorded 4 December 1730 T. Turner.

1A:113 - DEED OF RELEASE - 4 December 1730 - Baldwin Mathews of Hanover Parish, gent., to John Champe of same, merchant. 290 pounds lawfull current money of Virginia for 400A described in lease. Signed Baldwin Mathews. Delivered in presence of Robert Richards, Cornelus McCarty, Hugh Kennedy. Recorded 4 December 1730 T. Turner.

1A:115 - BOND - 2 December 1730 - Baldwin Mathews of Hanover Parish, gent., bound unto John Champ of same, merchant, for 600 pounds lawfull current money of Virginia. Condition is such that if Baldwin Mathews keeps all agreements in one indenture of release bearing even date with these presents between the said Baldwin Mathews and the said John Champ, obligation to be void. Signed Baldwin Mathews. Delivered in presence of Robert Richards, Cornelius McCarty, Hugh Kennedy. Recorded 4 December 1730 T. Turner.

1A:115 - DEED OF LEASE - 3 December 1730 - Timothy Reading of Hanover Parish, planter, to John Tayloe, Lyonel Lyde, John and Andrew Lewis, and William and John Williams, gentlemen. 5 shillings sterling to lease 104A adjoining to the 300A sold by the said Reading to Capt. John Williams and is the remainder of the 456A bought by the said Reading of Alexander Beach. Signed Timothy Reading. Delivered in presence of Lunsford Lomax, Ralph Falknor, John Toward. Recorded 4 December 1730 T. Turner.

1A:117 - DEED OF RELEASE - 4 December 1730 - Timothy Reading of Hanover Parish, planter, to John Tayloe, Lyonel Lyde, John and Andrew Lewis, and William and John Williams, gentlemen. 26 pounds current money for 104A described in lease. Signed Timothy Reading. Sarah Reading, wife of Timothy Reading, relinquished her right of dower and thirds. Delivered in presence of Ralph Falkner, Lunsford Lomax, John Toward. Recorded 4 December 1730 T. Turner.

1A:119 - POWER OF ATTORNEY - 4 November 1730 - Sarah Reading authorizes Thomas Turner to be her true and lawfull attorney for her and in her name to acknowledge her dower and thirds of 104A of land in King George County to John Tayloe and Company adventurers in the Coppermine at the marsh as may appear by the deeds conveyed to them by her husband Timothy Reading. Signed Sarah Reading. Delivered in presence of James McDonnell, Timothy Reading, Margt. Combes. Recorded 4 December 1730 T. Turner.

1A:120 - DEED OF GIFT - 3 December 1730 - Henry Long of Hanover Parish gives unto his daughter Mary Tankersley, the wife of George Tankersley, a Negro boy named Ben the age of five years old the last day of last June to her and her heirs forever. Signed Henry Long. Delivered in presence of John Wharton, Christian Long. Recorded 4 December 1730 T. Turner.

1A:120 - DEPOSITION - 5 February 1730 - Ann Mackfereson of Stafford County aged about sixty-three years sayeth that Francis Golbie came to her and asked whether or no she was the daughter of Francis Warringtons wife which the aforesaid Ann said she was then replyed Francis Golbee you are my own cousin for your mother and my mother is two sisters. Deponant further says that her mother which was then Warringtons wife but sometime before had been the wife of John Martin deceased informed her several times that Francis Golbee was her own sisters child and the deponant further declareth the aforesaid Francis Golbee which was afterwards the wife of Thomas White deceased always acknowledged Warringtons wife to be her aunt and further the deponant sayeth not. Signed Ann Mackfereson. On the motion of James Jones the above deposition was admitted to record. Recorded 5 February 1730 T. Turner.

1A:120 - DEPOSITION - 5 February 1730 - Mary Reynolds of King George County aged about ninty-one years sayeth that Francis Golbee, afterward wife of Thomas White deceased, informed her about thirty odd years ago that she had heard that Francis Warrintons wife, who some time before was the widow of John Martin deceased, was her kinswoman and desired the said Mary Reynolds to go with her the said Francis Golbee to know the certainty whether or no Warringtons wife was related to her which the said Mary did. When they came to Warringtons house, Warringtons wife after some discorse with the aforesaid Francis Golbee concerning the place of their nativity, Frances Golbee asked Warringtons wife if she knew such a woman which the aforesaid Warringtons wife replyed I did know her very well some years ago for she is my own sister. Then replyed Frances Golbee you are my Aunt. Then says Warringtons wife you are my own sisters child and the aforesaid Mary Reynolds further declares that Warringtons wife as far as ever she heard afterwards ever went for Frances Golbee's Aunt and further the deponant sayeth not. Signed Mary Reynolds. On the motion of James Jones, the above deposition was admitted to record. Recorded 5 February 1730 T. Turner.

1A:121 - DEED OF LEASE - 1 April 1731 - Jerimiah Bronaugh, Junr. and Rose his wife, Thomas Montieth and Jeremiah Bronaugh, Senr. Executors of the last Will and Testament of John Dinwiddie, Gent. deceased, to William Stevenson of Washington Parish in the county of Westmoreland, physition. 5 shillings current money of Virginia to lease 200A. 173A being sold unto the said John Dinwiddie by Robert Donaphan and the other 27A by Mott and Robert Donaphan by deeds of lease and release both bearing date of 1 and 2 October 1722. Signed Jeremiah Bronaugh, Junr., Rose Bronaugh, Thomas Montieth, Jeremiah Bronaugh, Senr. Delivered in presence of Ralph Falkner, Lunsford Lomax, William Tyler. Recorded 2 April 1731 T. Turner.

1A:122 - DEED OF RELEASE - 2 April 1731 - Jeremiah Bronaugh, Junr. and Rose his wife, Thomas Montieth, and Jeremiah Bronaugh, Senr., Executors of the Last Will and Testament of John Dinwiddie, Gent. deceased, to William Stevenson of Washington Parish and county of Westmoreland, phisition. 240 pounds current money of Virginia for 200A described in lease. Signed Jere. Bronaugh, Junr., Rose Bronaugh, Thos. Montieth, Jere. Bronaugh, Senr.. Rose Bronaugh relinquished her right of dower and thirds at the common law in and to the said land. Delivered in presence of Ralph Falkner, Lunsford Lomax, William Tyler. Recorded 2 April 1731 T. Turner.

1A:125 - BOND - 2 April 1731 - Jeremiah Bronaugh, Junr., Thomas Montieth, and Jeremiah Bronaugh, Senr. bound unto William Stevenson of Washington Parish in Westmoreland County, Physition, in the sum of 240 pounds lawfull money of Virginia. Condition such that if the above bound fulfill all and singular covenants contained in one indenture of release bearing equal daate with these presents purposing to be a conveyance to the said William Stevenson of 200A of land, obligation to be void. Signed Jerem. Bronaugh, Junr., Thomas Montieth, Jerem. Bronaugh, Senr.. Delivered in presence of Ralph Falkner, Lunsford Lomax, William Tyler. Recorded 2 April 1731 T. Turner.

1A:126 - DEED OF LEASE - 1 April 1731 - John Seamans of Farnham Parish in Richmond County, planter, to Edward Burges of Hanover Parish, planter. 5 shillings to lease 100A lying on the main ridge between the Rivers of Rappahannock and Pertomack. Part in King George and part in Stafford County. Bounded by Benjamin Stribling, Henry Berry, Majr. John Fitzhugh, the Rowling Road, land formerly belonging to Mr. William Bunbury, and land formerly granted to Mr. Sem Cox. Part of a tract granted to Mr. Sem Cox by patent 1 March 1694/95, sold by the said Sem Cox to Joseph Seamans of Lancaster County by deed 26 October 1709, and devised to the said John Seamans by the last will and testament of the said Joseph Seamans, father to the said John Seamans, dated 20 November 1729. Signed John Seamans. Elizabeth, wife of the said John, relinquished her right of dower and thirds. Delivered in presence of Thos. Catlett, Wm. Strother, Jos. Berry. Recorded 7 May 1731 T. Turner.

1A:127 - DEED OF RELEASE - 2 April 1731 - John Seamans of Farnham Parish in the county of Richmond, planter, to Edward Burges of Hanover Parish, planter. 6000 pounds good merchantable tobacco for 100A described in lease. Signed John Seamans. Elizabeth, wife of the said John, relinquished her right of dower and thirds. Delivered in presence of Thos. Catlett, Wm. Strother, Jos. Berry. Recorded 7 May 1731 T. Turner.

1A:129 - BOND - 2 April 1731 - John Seamans of Farnham Parish in the county of Richmond stands firmly indebted to Edward Burges of Hanover Parish in the just sum of 12,000 pounds of good, sound merchantable tobacco. Condition such that if John Seamans fulfills all covenants mentioned in indenture of release bearing date with these presents entered into between the said John Seamans and the said Edward Burges, obligation to be void. Signed John Seamans. Delivered in presence of Thos. Catlett, Wm. Strother, Jos. Berry. Recorded 7 May 1731 T. Turner.

1A:129 - DEED OF LEASE - 4 March 1730 - William Sarjant of the city of Bristol in the Kingdom of Great Britain, merchant, to William Stringfellow of King George County, blacksmith. 5 shillings sterling to lease 100A lying on the north side of Rappahannock River. Bounded by Henry Wilton and the heirs of Colonel Mathews. Signed Willm. Sarjant. Thomas Waring, by virtue of a power of attorney, relinquished the right of dower of Jane Sarjant, wife of William

Sarjant. Delivered in presence of T. Waring, Richard Bryan, M. Battaley. Recorded 7 May 1731 T. Turner.

1A:131 - DEED OF RELEASE - 5 March 1730 - William Sarjant of the city of Bristol in the Kingdom of Great Britain, merchant, to William Stringfellow of Hanover Parish, blacksmith. 10,000 pounds tobacco for 100A described in lease. Signed William Sarjant. Jane Sarjant, wife of William Sarjant, relinquished her right of dower and thirds. Delivered in presence of Thos. Waring, Richd. Bryan, M. Battaley. Recorded 7 May 1731 T. Turner.

1A:133 - POWER OF ATTORNEY - 14 July 1729 - Jane Sarjant, wife of William Sarjant, of the city of Bristol, deputes Thomas Waring of Essex County in the Colony of Virginia Gent. her true and lawfull attorney to relinquish her Right of Dower to all lands and tenements which her husband is now in possession of in King George County or any other county in the Colony of Virginia. Signed Jane Sarjant. Admitted to record in Essex County 6 December 1729 by W. Beverley. Delivered in presence of Willm. Lloyd, Joseph Smith. Recorded 7 May 1731 T. Turner.

1A:133 - DEED OF LEASE - 30 April 1731 - Robert Doniphan of King George County, planter, to William Thornton of same, gent.. 5 shillings to lease 180A whereon Peter Lowd now lives. Bounded by land the said Doniphan formerly sold to Mr. John Dinwiddie and lately purchased by Doctr. William Stevenson, cleared ground of the plantation whereon the said Doniphan now liveth, Mrs. Elenor Shippey now in the possession of Mary Williams, and land the said Doniphan formerly sold to the said William Thornton. Part of a patent dated 17 October 1670 formerly granted to John and George Mott for 15,654A out of which patent sundry parcells were sold by John and George Mott in their lifetime. The residue was by the last will and testament of the said George dated 31 March 1674 and by the last will of the said John Mott dated 8 October 1675 given and bequeathed to the four daughters of the said George Mott - Elizabeth, Margaret, Ann, and Elinor. Upon an equal and just division by William Mosley, surveyor, this land now leased is part of what was alotted for Margaret mother of the present mentioned Robert Doniphan to whom the land descends by inheritance. Signed Robert Doniphan. Edward Barradall by virtue of a power of attorney, relinquished the right of dower and thirds for Mary Doniphan, wife of Robert. Delivered in presence of Max. Robinson, Rowld. Thornton, John Jones. Recorded 7 May 1731 T. Turner.

1A:135 - DEED OF RELEASE - 1 May 1731 - Robert Doniphan of King George County, planter, to William Thornton of same, Gent.. One Negro man named Edenborough and 100 pounds current money of Virginia for 180A described in lease. Signed Robert Doniphan. Edward Barradell, by virtue of a power of attorney, relinquished the right of dower and thirds of Mary Doniphan, wife of Robert. Delivered in presence of Max Robinson, Rowld. Thornton, John Jones. Recorded 7 May 1731 T. Turner.

1A:137 - POWER OF ATTORNEY - 7 May 1731 - Mary Doniphan, wife of Robert Doniphan of Hanover Parish, appoints Mr. Edward Barradall her true and lawfull attorney for her and in her name to acknowledge and relinquish all her Right of Dower or otherwise of, in, or to a certain parcell of land containing 180A lately sold by her husband Robert Doniphan to William Thornton. Signed Mary Doniphan. Delivered in presence of Rowd. Thornton, Edward Pearl. Recorded 7 May 1731 T. Turner.

1A:138 - DEED OF LEASE - 6 May 1731 - John Grayson of the county of Spotsylvania, Gent., to Joseph Strother of the county of King George. 5 shillings current money to lease 619A. The lower or half part of a tract for 1,238A granted unto Andrew Jackson of Lancaster County 29 July 1704 between the Deep Run and the Richland Run about twelve miles above the falls of the Rappahannock River. To be laid off with a proportionable breadth upon the River. Signed John Grayson. Delivered in presence of Thos. Stribling, Robert Stuart. Recorded 7 May 1731 T. Turner.

1A:139 - DEED OF RELEASE - 7 May 1731 - John Grayson of the county of Spotsylvania, Gent., to Joseph Strother of King George County. 70 pounds current money for 619A described in lease. Signed John Grayson. Benjamin Rush by virtue of a power of attorney from Susanna, wife of John Grayson, relinquished her Right of Dower and Thirds. Delivered in presence of Thomas Stribling, Robert Stuart. Recorded 7 May 1731 T. Turner.

1A:140 - BOND - 7 May 1731 - John Grayson of the county of Spotsylvania bound unto Joseph Strother of the county of King George in the sum of 140 pounds current money of Virginia. Condition such that if John Grayson shall keep all and singular agreements contained in one indenture of release bearing equal date with these presents between the said John Grayson and Joseph Strother purporting to be a conveyance of 619A of land, obligation to be void. Signed John Grayson. Delivered in presence of Thos. Stribling, Robt. Stuart. Recorded 7 May 1731 T. Turner.

1A:141 - POWER OF ATTORNEY - 6 May 1731 - Susanna Grayson the now wife of John Grayson of Spotsylvania County appoints Mr. Benjamin Rush to be her true and lawfull attorney to relinquish her Right of Dower and Thirds unto a certain tract of land about six hundred acres binding upon the Richland Run and Rappahannock River sold by her husband unto Capt. Joseph Strother. Signed Susanna Grayson. Delivered in presence of James Strother, John

Stanley, John Ambros. Recorded 7 May 1731 T. Turner.

1A:141 - DEED OF LEASE - 21 April 1731 - The Honoble. Robert Carter of
the county of Lancaster, Esq., to Nicholas Smith of the county of King George,
Gent.. 5 shillings to lease 500A commonly called by the name of the Round
Hills. Part of a tract of 1000A granted unto Sylvester Thatcher by patent dated
18 March 1660. Formerly purchased by the said Robert Carter of Robert Carey
of London, merchant, and Elizabeth his wife 31 December 1725. Signed Robert
Carter. Delivered in presence of T. Turner, William Stevenson, Edw. Barradall.
Recorded 7 May 1731 T. Turner.

1A:142 - DEED OF RELEASE - 22 April 1731 - The honble. Robert Carter of
the county of Lancaster, Esqr., to Nicholas Smith of the county of King George,
Gent.. 150 pounds sterling for 500A described in lease. Signed Robert Carter.
Delivered in presence of T. Turner, William Stevenson, Edw. Barradall.
Recorded 7 May 1731 T. Turner.

1A:145 - DEED OF LEASE - No date given - William Duff of Hanover Parish
to William Hambleton of same. 500 pounds tobacco and cask every year to
lease 100A bought by the said William Duff of Robert Smith. Lease is during
the term and space of the natural lives of the said William Hambleton and
Hannah Hambleton, wife of the said William, or the longest liver of them.
Signed William Duff. Delivered in presence of Rush Hudson, Robt. Strother.
Memorandum - William Hambleton is not to put any tenant upon the above
mentioned land. Recorded 7 May 1731 T. Turner.

1A:146 - ESTATE ACCOUNT - No date given - George White and Francis
James securities for the Executrix of Humphry Quisenberry deceased. Amounts
paid to Doctor Turner, Mr. Barradall, Willm. Jett, Capt. Strother, and Thos.
Clayter. In obediance to an order of Court bearing date 8 May 1731 the
subscribers have stated and settled all the matters in differences between James
Quisenberry plt. and George White and Frances James defts. and find due from
the defendants to the said planif twenty-two pounds nineteen shillings and one
penny half penny current money. Signed Wil. Robinson, Nichs. Smith.
Recorded 4 June 1731 T. Turner.

1A:146 - ESTATE ACCOUNT - No Date Given - At a Court held for King
George County the fifth day of December 1724 - In the suit in Chancery
depending between the orphans of Jett agst. Elizabeth Jett by consent of both
parties Nichos. Smith, Gent., is desired to audit, state and settle all accounts
belonging to the estate of Francis Jett deceased and make report thereof to the
next Court. Persuant to the within order Nicholas Smith did within a few days
after the date thereof mentioned and found yet remaining eleven pounds eleven

shillings and six pence of the estate of Francis Jett in the hands of his son Wm. Jett. This report was presented into court by Will. Jett and on his motion admitted to record. Recorded 6 November 1730 T. Turner.

1A:147 - BOND - 2 July 1731 - John Champe, Thos. Vivion, and William Strother gent. are firmly bound to their Sovereign Lord the King in the sum of 1000 pounds sterling. Condition such that if the said John Champe do truly and faithfully perform the office of sheriff for the county of King George the ensuing year, obligation to be void. Signed John Champe, Thos. Vivion, Willm. Strother. Recorded 2 July 1731 T. Turner.

1A:147 - DEED OF SALE - 6 August 1731 - Samuel Wharton, Senior of Hanover Parish, planter, to Thomas Turner of same. 20 shillings current money of Virginia for 2A bounded by line of Robt. Johnson, main branch of Gingoteague Creek, and plantation whereon Andrew Beard now dwells. Part of a 200A tract formerly sold by the said Thomas Turner to the said Samuel Wharton. Signed Saml. Wharton. Ann, wife of Samuel Wharton, relinquished her right of dower and thirds. Delivered in presence of Wm. Taliaferro, Francis Conway, Wm. Tutt. Recorded 6 August 1731 T. Turner.

1A:149 - DEED OF LEASE - 3 August 1731 - Thomas Turner and Sarah his wife of Hanover Parish to Edward Barradall of same. 5 shillings current money of Virginia to lease 43A on the north side of Rappa. River. Part of a 200A tract of land sold to Mr. Richd. Taliaferro by John Reynolds. Land descended to Richard Taliaferro, son to the aforesd. Richard Taliaferro and brother to the aforesd. Sarah, the same being one-third part of what is left of the said Richard Taliaferro's land in a survey made in the year 1714 between Colonel William Fitzhugh and Mr. John Lomax and others called the Nansamond Patent. Signed T. Turner, Sarah Turner. Delivered in presence of Jno. Taliaferro, Archd. Mcpherson, Catesby Cocke. Recorded 6 August 1731 T. Turner.

1A:150 - DEED OF RELEASE - 4 August 1731 - Thomas Turner and Sarah his wife of Hanover Parish to Edward Barradall of same. 10 pounds current money of Virginia for 43A described in lease. Signed T. Turner, Sarah Turner. Delivered in presence of John Taliaferro, Archd. Mcpherson, Catesby Cocke. Recorded 6 August 1731 T. Turner.

1A:151 - OBLIGATION - 23 May 1728 - Saml. Barron obliges himself unto Samuel Skinker that if a two hundred pound bill of exchange which he received of the said Skinker draft on Mr. Thos. Longman, mercht. in Bristol, should be protested that he will indemnifie ye said Skinker from any charge or charges proceeding from the same. He further obliges himself that in case the next proceeds of his tobacco now in ye hand of the said Skinker and by him to be shipt. on his own account to Mr. Thos. Longman in Bristol should not amount to the sum of two hundred pounds sterling, he than and in such case oblige himself to be accountable to the said Skinker and what money should be wanting to compleat the sum. Signed Saml. Barron. Delivered in presence of Saml. Hearn, Robt. Cawl. Recorded 6 August 1731 T. Turner.

1A:152 - DEED OF SALE - 5 August 1731 - John Gilbert and Sarah his wife of Sittenburn Parish to Mary Tutt of Hanover Parish. 100 pounds sterling for 200A on the northside of Rappa. River. Bounded by the line of John Underwood. Signed John Gilbert, Sarah Gilbert. Delivered in presence of Thos. Vivion, Peter Daniell. Memorandum delivered in presence of Richd. Tutt, Willm. Tutt. Recorded 6 August 1731 T. Turner.

1A:153 - DEED OF LEASE - 5 August 1731 - Edward Barradall of Hanover Parish to Thomas Turner of same. 5 shillings current money of Virginia to lease 43A lying on northside of Rappa. River. Part of a 200A tract of land sold to Mr. Richard Taliaferro by John Reynolds which descended to Mr. Richard Taliaferro, son of the aforesaid Richard Taliaferro. And now on the decease of Richard Taliaferro the son, the 43A decends to Sarah, wife of the said Thomas Turner. It being one-third part of what is left of the said Richard Taliaferro's land in a survey made in the year 1714 between Colonel William Fitzhugh and Mr. John Lomax and others called the Nansamond Patent. Signed Edward Barradall. Delivered in presence of Mercer, M. Batteley, Catesby Cocke. Recorded 6 August 1731 T. Turner.

1A:154 - DEED OF RELEASE - 6 August 1731 - Edward Barradall of Hanover Parish to Thomas Turner of same. 15 pounds current money of Virginia for 43A described in lease. Signed Edward Barradall. Delivered in presence of Mercer, M. Batteley, Catesby Cocke. Recorded 6 August 1731 T. Turner.

1A:155 - DEED OF LEASE - 3 September 1731 - William Sarjant of the city of Bristol, merchant, to John Champe of Hanover Parish, merchant. 30 pounds current money to lease two tracts of land. 100A according to the bounds agreed upon between William Wilton and William Wood lying at Lambs Creek. Formerly belonging to William Wood. 2A formerly belonging to William Wilton. Bounded on the north with the land which formerly belonged to the said William Wood, on the south part with the Rowling Road, on the east part with a creek called Pye Creek, and on the west part with some of the land formerly belonging to the said William Wilton and now in the possession of the said William Sarjant. Said land was purchased of Augustine Smith by George and William Proctor and sold by them to the said William Sarjant. Signed William Sarjant. Thomas Waring, by virtue of a power of attorney of Jane Sarjant, relinquished her right of dower to the said lands. Delivered in presence of

Walter Anderson, Saml. Hearn, T. Warring. Recorded 3 September 1731 T. Turner.

1A:156 - BOND - 3 September 1731 - John Champe, Junr. of Hanover Parish bound unto William Sarjant of the city of Bristol in the sum of 16,000 pounds of tobacco. Condition such that if John Champe does indemnify and save harmless the above named Willm. Sarjant from any suit, trouble or damage he shall receive from John McCarty of Hanover Parish, planter, by reason of certain articles of agreement made between him the said Willm. Sarjant and the above named John Mccarty, then this obligation to be void. Signed John Champe. Delivered in presence of Walter Anderson, T. Waring, Saml. Hearn. Recorded 3 September 1731 T. Turner.

1A:157 - DEED OF LEASE - 12 June 1730 - William Procter of the county of King George, planter, to John Champ of same, merchant. 60 pounds good and lawful money of Virginia and 5000 nails to lease 182A during the term of seventy-nine years. Land whereon the said William Procter now lives. Augustine Smith by virtue of a lease dated 17 October 1721 let it to farm unto William Procter to hold the same during the term of eighty and nine years. Tract was formerly granted unto Francis Place of the county of Essex by patent in the year 1654. Signed William Proctor. Delivered in presence of Jeremiah Bryan, John Coburn, John McCarty. Recorded 3 September 1731 T. Turner.

1A:158 - DEED OF LEASE - 3 May 1731 - Baldwin Matthews of Hanover Parish, gent., to John Champe of same, merchant. 5 shillings lawfull current money of Virginia to lease 500A. Part of 2000A granted unto Lt. Col. Samuel Matthews, great grandfather to the said Baldwin Matthews, by patent dated 7 September 1654. Bounded by a certain place commonly called the hopyard, extending up the Rappa. River, and thence NE by N to the back line of the tract that is parallel to the River. Signed Balwin Matthews. Delivered in presence of Robt. Richards, Cornelius Mccarty, Hugh Kennedy. Recorded 3 September 1731 T. Turner.

1A:159 - DEED OF RELEASE - 4 May 1731 - Baldwin Matthews of Hanover parish, gent., to John Champe of same, merchant. 290 pounds lawful current money of Virginia for 500A described in lease. Signed Baldwin Matthews. Delivered in presence of Robert Richards, Cornelius McCarty, Hugh Kenady. Recorded 3 September 1731 T. Turner.

1A:161 - BOND - 4 May 1731 - Baldwin Matthews of Hanover parish, gent., bound unto John Champe of same, merchant, in the sum of 600 pounds lawful current money of Virginia. Condition such that if Baldwin Matthews will truly keep all and singular agreements contained in a certain deed of release bearing even date with these presents purporting to be a conveyance from the said Baldwin Matthews to the said John Champe of 500A of land, obligation to be void. Signed Baldwin Matthews. Delivered in presence of Robt. Richards, Cornelius McCarty, Hugh Kenady. Recorded 3 September 1731 T. Turner.

1A:161 - INDENTURE OF DEFERANCE - 4 May 1731 - John Champe of Hanover Parish, merchant, and Baldwin Mathews of same, gent.. The said Baldwin Matthews hath granted and conveyed unto the said John Champe the fee simple and inhertance of 500A of land as by the said deeds of lease and release which were made and intended to be made only as for a collateral security from the said Baldwin Matthews to the said John Champe for the warranting the right and title of him the said Baldwin Mathews to the said John Champe for a certain parcel of land containing 400A and for no other use, intent or purpose whatever. The said John Champe promises the said Baldwin Matthews and his heirs that they may possess and enjoy the said 500A of land without trouble or hindrance of him the said John Champe until he the said John Champe his heirs or assigns shall be molested or disturbed out of or in the possession of the said 400A of land. In case the said John Champe or his heirs or assigns shall not be molested or disturbed out of or in the possession of the said 400A of land within the space of ninety-nine years either by Baldwin Mathews or his heirs or any other person or persons whatever, then the aforesaid recited indentures of lease and release shall be utterly void. Signed John Champe. Delivered in presence of Robt. Richards, Cornelius McCarty, Hugh Kenady. Recorded 3 September 1731 T. Turner.

1A:162 - BOND - 4 May 1731 - John Champe of Hanover Parish, merchant, bound unto Baldwin Matthews of same, gent., in the sum of 600 pounds lawfull current money of Virginia. Condition such that if John Champe will truly observe all and singular conditions contained in a certain indenture bearing even date with these presents in all things according to the true intent and meaning of the said indenture, obligation to be void. Signed John Champe. Delivered in presence of Robt. Richards, Cornelius McCarty, Hugh Kenady. Recorded 3 September 1731 T. Turner.

1A:163 - DEED OF SALE - 17 April 1731 - Francis Velden of the Parish of St. Mary's White Chapple in the county of Lancaster, mariner, to William Brown of same. 35 pounds lawfull money of Virginia for 210A being one moiety of a certain tract the said Velden and Thos. Charles purchased of Robt. French commonly called by the name of Tripletts Old Fields. Bounded by land lately in the tenure and occupation of William Smart, deceased. Signed Francis Velden. Delivered in presence of James McDonnell, Thos. Charles, Robt. Boatman, Jno. Boatman. Recorded 3 September 1731 T. Turner.

1A:164 - BOND - 16 February 1730 - Francis Velden of the Parish of St. Mary's White Chapple in the county of Lancaster bound unto William Brown of same in the sum of seventy pounds current money. Condition such that if Francis Velden shall within three months next coming convey unto the said William Brown all his estate right title and interest in fee unto the said William Brown forever of, in, and to a moiety of said land, obligation to be void. Signed Francis Velden. Delivered in presence of Cha. Burges, Thos. Harwood, Chas. Ewell. Recorded 3 September 1731 T. Turner.

1A:165 - DEED OF LEASE - 30 September 1731 - Jeremiah Bronaugh the Elder of the county of King George, planter, and Jeremiah Bronaugh the Younger of the county of Prince William, planter, and Rose his wife, late widdow and relect of John Dinwiddie, to John Tayloe of the county of Richmond, Gent.. 5 shillings lawful current money of Virginia to lease 97A upon the branches of haugh creek issuing out of Rappahannock River commonly known by the name of Kay's pond. Formerly purchased by John Dinwiddie of one James Kay 30 November and 1 December 1721. John Dinwiddie in his will dated 21 August 1714 appointed his loving wife Rose together with Thomas Montieth and Jeremiah Bronaugh the elder Executors and declared that all his lands should be sold to the highest bidder except that tract he bought part of Robert Doniphan and part of Mott Doniphan. Signed Jereh. Bronaugh, Jerh. Bronaugh, Junr., Rose Bronaugh. Rose, wife of Jeremiah Bronaugh the younger, relinquished her right of dower and thirds. Delivered in presence of John Champe, Edw. Barradall. Recorded 1 October 1731 T. Turner.

1A:166 - DEED OF RELEASE - 1 October 1731 - Jeremiah Bronaugh the Elder of the county of King George, planter, and Jeremiah Bronaugh the younger of the county of Prince William, planter, and his wife Rose, late widdow and relect of John Dinwiddie, to John Tayloe of the county of Richmond, gent.. 80 pounds lawfull current money of Virginia for 97A described in lease. Signed Jerh. Bronaugh, Jerh. Bronaugh, Junr., Rose Bronaugh. Delivered in presence of John Champe, Edw. Barradall. Recorded 1 October 1731 T. Turner.

1A:169 - BOND - 1 October 1731 - Jeremiah Bronaugh the Elder and Jeremiah Bronaugh the younger bound unto John Tayloe in the sum of 160 pounds current money. Condition such that if Jeremiah Bronaugh the Elder and Jeremiah Bronaugh the younger will truly keep all agreements in one indenture of release bearing even date with these presents made between Jeremiah Bronaugh the Elder and Jeremiah Bronaugh the younger and Rose his wife which the said Jeremiah Bronaugh the Elder and Rose Bronaugh are two of the executors of the last will and testament of John Dinwiddie, of the one part and John Tayloe of the other part, obligation to be void. Signed Jerh. Bronaugh, Jerh. Bronaugh, Junr.. Delivered in presence of John Champe, Edw. Barradall.

Recorded 1 October 1731 T. Turner.

1A:170 - DEED OF LEASE - 29 September 1731 - Baldwin Mathews of the county of King George, planter, heir and devisee of Samuel Mathews, to Robert Carter of Lancaster County, Esqr.. 5 shillings good and lawful money to lease 1200A bounded by Mr. Hancock Lee's quarter. Part of a 6350A tract granted John Waugh Clerk by patent 2 March 1691. Sold by Joseph Waugh, heir of the said John Waugh, to Samuel Mathews, father of the said Baldwin Matthews, by deed dated 5 November 1718. Devised unto his sons John Mathews and Baldwin Mathews in equal parts by the said Samuel Mathews in his will dated 16 November 1718. The said Baldwin Matthews is now the only surviving son which in the meaning of the said will and now is in the actual possession of the said lands. Signed Baldwin Mathews. Delivered in presence of John Champe, Thos. Vivion. This deed admitted to record on the motion of Edward Barradall, atto. for the said Carter. Recorded 1 October 1731 T. Turner.

1A:171 - DEED OF RELEASE - 1 October 1731 - Baldwin Mathews of the county of King George, heir and devisee of Samuel Mathews, to Robert Carter of Lancaster County, Esqr. 150 pounds good current money of Virginia for 1200A described in lease. Signed Baldwin Mathews. Delivered in presence of John Champe, Thos. Vivion. Recorded 1 October 1731 T. Turner.

1A:174 - BOND - 1 October 1731 - Baldwin Mathews of the county of King George, planter, bound unto Robert Carter, Esqr., of the county of Lancaster in the sum of 300 pounds current money of Virginia. Condition such that if Baldwin Mathews will truly observe all and every covenant expressed in one indenture of release bearing even date with these presents, obligation to be void. Signed Baldwin Mathews. Delivered in presence of John Champe, Thos. Vivion. Recorded 1 October 1731 T. Turner.

1A:175 - DEPOSITION - 30 September 1731 - Ann Glendening aged sixty years or there abouts being first sworn by virtue of the within order saith that John Taylor deceased, the son of Thos. Taylor deceased, was born in the month of February 1704. Delivered in presence of Jos. Strother, John Champe. On the motion of John Coburn, deposition was admitted to record. Recorded 1 October 1731 T. Turner.

1A:175 - DEED OF LEASE - 5 November 1731 - Katherine Hancock of Hamilton Parish in the county of Prince William to John Gilbert of Sittenburn Parish, planter, and Sarah his wife. 50 pounds sterling to lease 160A during their natural lives and the life of the survivor of them. Daniel McKenny now lives upon the land. Signed Catherine Hancock. Delivered in presence of R. Rogers, William Tutt, Jno. Quin. Recorded 5 November 1731 T. Turner.

1A:177 - BOND - 5 November 1731 - Katherine Hancock of Prince William County bound unto John Gilbert of the county of King George in the sum of 100 pounds sterling. Condition such that if the said Scarlet Hancock, heir to the land, when he shall arrive to the age of twenty-one shall refuse to acknowledge the land aforesaid to the said John Gilbert according to the intent of the same lease and the said Katherine Hancock shall pay the fifty pounds the consideration in the lease expressed to the said John Gilbert and Sarah his wife, obligation to be void. Signed Catherine Hancock. Delivered in presence of R. Rogers, William Tutt. Recorded 5 November 1731 T. Turner.

1A:177 - DEED OF LEASE - 4 November 1731 - Baldwin Mathews of the county of King George, Gent., to John Champe the Younger of same, Gent.. 5 shillings lawfull current money of Virginia to lease 2000A formerly granted to Lt. Col. Samuel Mathews, great grandfather to the said Baldwin Mathews, by patent 7 September 1654. Except a certain tract containing 400A formerly purchased by the said John Champe of the said Baldwin Mathews by indentures of lease and release dated 3 and 4 December 1730. Signed Baldwin Mathews. Delivered in presence of Thos. Stribling, John Coburn, John Fewell. Recorded 5 November 1731 T. Turner.

1A:179 - DEED OF RELEASE - 5 November 1731 - Baldwin Mathews of the county of King George, Gent., to John Champe the Younger of same, Gent. 400 pounds sterling for 2000A described in lease. The right of dower of Margaret Richards now wife of Robert Richards and late widow and relict of Samuel Mathews, father of the said Baldwin Mathews, of in and to 600A hereby granted and released. Signed Baldwin Mathews. Delivered in presence of Thos. Stribling, John Coburn, John Fewell. Recorded 5 November 1731 T. Turner.

1A:181 - BOND - 5 November 1731 - Baldwin Mathews of Hanover Parish, Gent., bound unto John Champe the Younger of same, Gent., in the sum of 800 pounds sterling. Condition such that if Baldwin Mathews do well and truly keep all and singular agreements mentioned in a certain indenture of bargain and sale bearing even date with these presents, obligation to be void. Signed Baldwin Mathews. Delivered in presence of Thos. Stribling, John Coburn, John Fewell. Recorded 5 November 1731 T. Turner.

1A:181 - DEED OF LEASE - 2 November 1731 - John Arnold of King George County to Isaac Johnson of same. Yearly rent of 530 pounds tobacco and the Quitrents to lease the plantation whereon John Arnold now lives for the space of thirty-one years ensuing the date hereof. It is part of a parcel of land given to John Arnold by his father Thomas Arnold deceased. Signed John Arnold. Delivered in presence of Richd. Tankersley, Henry Long, Charles Tankersley. Recorded 3 December 1731 T. Turner.

1A:183 - BOND - 2 November 1731 - John Arnold of King George County, planter, bound unto Isaac Johnson of same, sadler, in the sum of 50 pounds sterling. Condition such that if John Arnold do well and truly keep all and singular agreements mentioned in a certain lease bearing date with these presents, obligation to be void. Signed John Arnold. Delivered in presence of Richd. Tankersley, Henry Long, Charles Tankersley. Recorded 3 December 1731 T. Turner.

1A:184 - DEED OF RELEASE - 1 December 1731 - John Plaile, planter, and Katherine his wife of Sittenbourne Parish to William Robinson of same, Gent. 15 pounds current money for 200A whereon the said William Robinson now dwelleth. Signed Jno. Plaile, Katherine Plaile. Delivered in presence of Jno. Gilbert, Richard Plaile, Susannah Plaile. Recorded 3 December 1731 T. Turner.

1A:186 - DEED OF LEASE - 4 November 1731 - Thomas Turner of Hanover Parish, Chyrurgeon, to Simon Miller of same. 5 shillings to lease 200A. Part of 619A tract sold by John Grayson unto the said Thomas Turner.Laid off and divided by John Warner between the lands of Robert Elliston and Simon Miller. Signed Thomas Turner. Delivered in presence of Samuel Nubald, Robert Rankins, Jno. Brown. Recorded 3 March 1731 T. Turner.

1A:187 - DEED OF RELEASE - 5 November 1731 - Thomas Turner of Hanover Parish to Simon Miller of same. 20 pounds current money for 200A described in lease. Signed Thomas Turner. Delivered in presence of John Brown, Samuel Nubald, Robert Rankins, Thomas Leftwich. Recorded 3 March 1731 T. Turner.

1A:187 - DEED OF LEASE - 4 January 1731 - Simon Miller, son of William Miller deceased, of Hanover Parish, planter, to Thomas Turner of same. 5 shillings sterling to lease 200A lying on the north side of Rappahannock River. 160A of the said land being devised unto the said Simon Miller by William Miller deceased, father to the said Simon Miller, by his will dated 31 March 1726. 40A of the said land being devised by the said last will unto Benjamin Miller, son to the said William Miller and brother to the said Simon. Signed Simon Miller. Delivered in presence of Samuel Nubald, Robert Rankins, John Brown, Thomas Leftwich. Recorded 3 March 1731 T. Turner.

1A:188 - DEED OF RELEASE - 5 January 1731 - Simon Miller, son of William Miller deceased, of Hanover Parish, planter, to Thomas Turner of same, Chirurgeon. 150 pounds sterling for 200A described in lease. The said Simon being older brother and heir at law of the said Benjamin. Signed Simon Miller. Delivered in presence of Samuel Nubald, Robert Rankins, John Brown, Thomas Leftwich. Recorded 3 March 1731 T. Turner.

1A:190 - BOND - 5 January 1731 - Simon Miller, son of Wm. Miller deceased, of Hanover Parish bound unto Thomas Turner of same, Chyrurgeon, in the sum of 300 pounds sterling. Condition such that if Simon Miller well and truly keeps all and singular agreements contained in one indenture of release bearing even date with these presents, obligation to be void. Signed Simon Miller. Delivered in presence of Samuel Nubald, Robert Rankins, John Brown, Thomas Leftwich. Recorded 3 March 1731 T. Turner.

1A:191 - DEED - 5 January 1731 - Simon Miller of Hanover Parish, planter, to Thomas Turner of same, Chyrurgeon. 30 pounds sterling for 40A the said Simon Miller hath after the decease of his brother Benjamin Miller. By virtue of the last will and testament of William Miller, in case the said Benjamin should depart this life before he came to the age of twenty-one or after having no lawfull issue or making no legal deposition thereof, the said land doth belong unto the said Simon Miller. Signed Simon Miller. Delivered in presence of Samuel Nubald, Robert Rankins, John Brown, Thomas Leftwich. Recorded 3 March 1731 T. Turner.

1A:193 - BOND - 5 January 1731 - Simon Miller, son of William Miller deceased, of Hanover Parish, planter, bound unto Thomas Turner of same, Chyrurgeon, in the sum of 30 pounds sterling. Condition such that if Simon Miller keeps all and singular agreements contained in one indenture bearing even date with these presents purporting to be a conveyance of forty acres of land which the said Simon Miller in reversion as heir at law to his brother Benjamin Miller is selling to Thomas Turner, obligation to be void. Signed Simon Miller. Delivered in presence of Samuel Nubald, Robert Rankins, John Brown, Thomas Leftwich. Recorded 3 March 1731 T. Turner.

1A:193 - DEED OF LEASE - 3 February 1731 - William Woodford of the county of Caroline, Gent., to William Thornton of the county of King George, Gent. 5 shillings current money to lease his part and share of 333A which the said William Woodford and the said William Thornton bought joyntly between them of Thomas Foxhall and Elizabeth his wife by deed dated 4 April 1716. Land lies near the falls of Rappahannock River. Signed William Woodford. Delivered in presence of Lunsford Lomax, Thos. Vivion, T. Lewis. Recorded 3 March 1731 T. Turner.

1A:194 - DEED OF RELEASE - 4 February 1731 - William Woodford of the county of Caroline, Gent., to William Thornton of King George County, Gent. 20 pounds current money of Virginia for one hundred sixty-six and one half acre described in lease. Signed William Woodford. Delivered in presence of Lunsford Lomax, Thos. Vivion. Recorded 3 March 1731 T. Turner.

1A:196 - DEED OF LEASE - 21 January 1731 - Mosely Battaley of the county of King George, Gent., and Elizabeth his wife to John Champe the Younger of same, Gent. 5 shillings sterling to lease 100A which the said Mosely Battaley and Elizabeth his wife claim by virtue of the last will and testament of one John Mathews dated 6 February 1728. Part of a 2000A tract granted unto Col. Samuel Mathews by patent dated 7 September 1654. Signed Mosely Battaley, Elizabeth Battaley. Delivered in presence of Robert Richards, John Farguson, Cornelius Mackerty. Recorded 3 March 1731 T. Turner.

1A:196 - DEED OF RELEASE - 22 January 1731 - Mosely Battaley of the county of King George and Elizabeth his wife to John Champe the younger of same, Gent. 100 pounds sterling for 100A described in lease. Signed Mosely Battaley, Elizabeth Battaley. Delivered in presence of Robert Richards, John Farguson, Cornelius McKerty. Recorded 3 March 1731 T. Turner.

1A:198 - BOND - 22 January 1731 - Mosely Battaley of the county of King George, Gentleman, bound unto John Champ the younger of same, Gent., in the sum of 500 pounds sterling. Condition such that if Mosely Battaley and Elizabeth his wife keep all agreements contained in one indenture of release bearing even date with these presents, obligation to be void. Signed Mosely Battaley. Delivered in presence of Robert Richards, John Farguson, Cornelius Mackerty. Recorded 3 March 1731 T. Turner.

1A:199 - DEED OF RELEASE - 24 January 1731 - Mosely Battaley of the county of King George, Gent., and Elizabeth his wife to John Champe the Younger of same, Gent. 100 pounds sterling to release and forever quit claim all the estate right title interest claims demand whatsoever in and to all that tract or parcel of land containing 2000A granted unto Lt. Col. Samuel Mathews deceased by patent dated 7 September 1654 and lately purchased by John Champe of one Baldwin Mathews. Signed Mosely Battaley, Elizabeth Battaley. Delivered in presence of Robert Richards, John Farguson, Cornelius Mackarty. Recorded 3 March 1731 T. Turner.

1A:200 - BOND - 24 January 1731 - Mosely Battaley of the county of King George, Gent., bound unto John Champe the younger of same, Gent., in the sum of 500 pounds sterling. Condition such that if Mosely Battaley and Elizabeth his wife well and truly keep all and every the agreements contained in one indenture of release bearing even date with these presents, obligation to be void. Signed Mosely Battaley. Delivered in presence of Robert Richards, John Farguson, Cornelius Mackerty. Recorded 3 March 1731 T. Turner.

1A:201 - DEED OF LEASE - 4 May 1732 - Thomas Harwood of Hanover Parish, planter, to Charles Burges of White Chappel in the county of Lancaster,

Gent. 5 shillings current money of Virginia to lease one moiety or half of a 200A tract. Bounded by the Rappahannock River, the Mason County road, and a branch which divides the land of Enoch Innis from the land of James Innis deceased, brother to the said Enoch, as by their father's will. Includes the plantation whereon James Innis formerly dwelt. Signed Thomas Harwood. Delivered in presence of Wm. Strother, T. Lewis. Recorded 5 May 1732 T. Turner.

1A:201 - DEED OF RELEASE - 5 May 1732 - Thomas Harwood of Hanover Parish, planter, to Charles Burges of White Chappel Parish in the county of Lancaster, Gent. 30 pounds sterling and 500 pounds tobacco for one moiety described in lease. Signed Thomas Harwood. Delivered in presence of Wm. Strother, T. Lewis. Recorded 5 May 1732 T. Turner.

1A:203 - BOND - 5 May 1732 - Thomas Harwood of Hanover Parish, planter, bound unto Charles Burges of Lancaster County, Gent., for 80 pounds current money of Virginia. Condition such that if Thomas Harwood well and truly observes the covenants mentioned in a certain indenture of release bearing even date with these presents, obligation to be void. Signed Thomas Harwood. Delivered in presence of Wm. Strother, T. Lewis. Recorded 5 May 1732 T. Turner.

1A:204 - POWER OF ATTORNEY - 2 May 1732 - Margaret Harwood, wife of Thomas Harwood of King George County, authorizes and impowers Mr. Thomas Turner to acknowledge her relinquishment of dower and thirds to one moiety of a tract of land containing 200A whereon her said husband now dwells the said land being conveyed by her husband unto Charles Burges of Lancaster County. Signed Margaret Harwood. Delivered in presence of John Wybird, Thomas Dondall. Recorded 5 May 1732 T. Turner.

1A:204 - DEED OF LEASE - 29 April 1732 - John Triplett of the county of King George, planter, to John Cannada of same, planter. 5 shillings current money of Virginia to lease 73A that is part of the plantation in the occupation of Isabella Triplett, widow. Bounded by Francis Triplett, Junr., land formerly belonging to William Underwood, Capt. Augustin Washington, Samuel James, and James Hore. Signed John Triplett. Delivered in presence of Francis Triplett, Francis Triplett, Saml. James. Recorded 5 May 1732 T. Turner.

1A:205 - DEED OF RELEASE - 30 April 1732 - John Triplet of the county of King George, planter, to John Cannada of same, planter. 6000 pounds tobacco for 73A described in lease. Signed John Triplett. Delivered in presence of Francis Triplett, Francis Triplett, Samuel James. Recorded 5 May 1732 T. Turner.

1A:207 - BOND - 30 April 1732 - John Triplett of the county of King George, planter, bound unto John Cannada of same, planter, for 1200 pounds tobacco. Condition such that if John Triplett well and truly keeps all agreements contained in one indenture of release bearing even date with these presents, obligation to be void. Signed John Triplett. Delivered in presence of Francis Triplett, Francis Triplett, Samuel James. Recorded 5 May 1732 T. Turner.

1A:207 - DEED OF LEASE - 25 April 1732 - Thomas Thatcher of Sittenburn Parish, planter, and Katherine his wife to William Wheler of Washington Parish in the county of Westmoreland, planter. 5 shillings good and lawfull money of England to lease 110A being part in King George County, part in Westmoreland County, and part in Stafford County. Part of a 220A tract granted to Thomas Harvey. The moiety or half part of the grant which by conveyances became the land of William Pannel, father to the said Katherine Thatcher, whose will left it to be equally divided between his two daughters Katherine and Mary. Bounded by Henry Berry and Robert Peck, Hailes path, George King, John Pearce, and Thomas Porter. Signed Thomas Thatcher, Katherine Thatcher. Delivered in presence of Isaac Arnold, John Plunkett. Recorded 5 May 1732 T. Turner.

1A:208 - DEED OF RELEASE - 26 April 1732 - Thomas Thatcher of Sittenbourn Parish, planter, and Katherine his wife to William Wheeler of Washington Parish in the county of Westmoreland, planter. 3500 pounds tobacco for 110A described in lease. Signed Thomas Thatcher, Katherine Thatcher. Delivered in presence of Isaac Arnold, John Plunkett. Recorded 5 May 1732 T. Turner.

1A:210 - BOND - 26 April 1732 - Thomas Thatcher of Sittenbourne Parish bound unto William Wheeler of Washington Parish in the county of Westmoreland in the sum of 7000 pounds of good tobacco. Condition such that if Thomas Thatcher will faithfully keep all agreements contained in one deed of lease and one deed of release which bear dates of 25 and 26 April 1732 for one hundred and ten acres conveyed unto William Wheeler, obligation to be void. Signed Thomas Thatcher. Delivered in presence of Isaac Arnold, John Plunkett. Recorded 5 May 1732 T. Turner.

1A:211 - DEED OF LEASE - 4 May 1732 - John Hartshorn of Stafford County and Barsheba his wife to William Strother of King George County, Gent. 5 shillings sterling to lease 150A lying below the falls of the Rappahannock River and between the lands of Mrs. Brent and John Robins. Granted unto Maurice Clark 10 September 1710 and by sundry conveyances became vested in the said John Hartshorn and Barsheba his wife. Signed John Hartshorn, Barsheba Hartshorn. Delivered in presence of Wm. Thornton, Richard Barnes, Thomas Monroe. Recorded 5 May 1732 T. Turner.

1A:211 - DEED OF RELEASE - 5 May 1732 - John Hartshorn of Stafford County, miner, and Barsheba his wife to William Strother of King George County, Gent. 50 pounds sterling for 150A described in lease. Signed John Hartshorn, Barsheba Hartshorn. Delivered in presence of William Thornton, Richard Barnes, Thomas Monroe. Recorded 5 May 1732 T. Turner.

1A:213 - DEED OF SALE - 7 July 1732 - John Dishman of Washington Parish in the county of Westmoreland for divers good considerations but more especially for and in consideration of the sum of 20 pounds current money sold unto Thomas Munro six Negro slaves by name Winny and her five children Tom, Moll, Nel, Sam, and Tony; all which Negro slaves are now in the actual possession of the said Thomas Munro. Signed John Disman. Delivered in presence of Francis Stone, John Fillyer. Recorded 7 July 1732 T. Turner.

1A:213 - BOND - 7 July 1732 - Daniel Underwood and Richard Tutt bound unto William Robinson of the county of King George for and in behalf of the Court of the aforesaid county in the sum of 150 pounds sterling. Condition such that if Daniel Underwood, guardian of Elizabeth Fossaker, shall well and truly pay unto the said orphan all such estate as now is or hereafter shall come to the hands of the said Daniel as soon as the said orphan shall attain to lawfull age or thereunto required by the Justices of Peace for King George County Court, obligation to be void. Signed Daniel Underwood, Richard Tutt. 7 July 1732 T. Turner.

1A:214 - BOND - 7 July 1732 - John Jennings and William Grant bound unto John Willis in the sum of 100 pounds current money. Condition such that whereas John Jennings has this day judgmt. passed agst. him for the sum of 53 pounds 14 shillings from which judgmt. he appeals to the Ninth Day of the General Court next, now if the said John Jennings so presents the said appeal is an effect, obligation to be void. Signed John Jennings, William Grant. Delivered in presence of T. Turner. Recorded 7 July 1732 T. Turner.

1A:214 - DEED OF LEASE - 28 July 1732 - John Doyle of North Carolina to Isaac Arnold, Senior of Hanover Parish. 5 shillings current money of Virginia to lease 226A granted 23 January 1716/7 unto John Doyle, Senr., father of the said John Doyle party to these presents. Bounded by a small branch of Gengoteague Creek, land formerly granted to Prosscer and Chettwood, John Berry, Thomas Arnold's cleared ground, and Cornelius Reynolds. Signed John Doyle. Delivered in presence of Thomas Goff, John Hawkins, John Willis. Recorded 4 August 1732 T. Turner.

1A:215 - DEED OF RELEASE - 29 July 1732 - John Doyle of North Carolina to Isaac Arnold of Hanover Parish. 22 pounds 10 shillings current money of

Virginia for 226A described in lease. Signed John Doyle. Delivered in presence of Thomas Goff, John Hawkins, John Willis. Recorded 4 August 1732 T. Turner.

1A:216 - BOND - 29 July 1732 - John Doyle of North Carolina bound unto Isaac Arnold of Hanover Parish in the sum of 45 pounds current money of Virginia. Condition such that if John Doyle for ever hereafter keeps all and every the agreements contained in deeds of lease and release bearing dates 28 and 29 July 1732 for two hundred and twenty acres conveyed unto Isaac Arnold, obligation to be void. Signed John Doyle. Delivered in presence of Thomas Goff, John Hawkins, John Willis. Recorded 4 August 1732 T. Turner.

1A:217 - POWER OF ATTORNEY - 28 March 1732 - Thomas Seed of the city of Bristol, cooper, and Elizabeth his wife, one of the daughters and coheirs of Francis Barnard late of the same city merchant deceased; Francis Brown of the city of Bristol, cooper, son of Nathaniel Brown late of the said city baker deceased and on the body of Mary his wife begotten one other of the daughters and coheirs of the said Francis Barnard have appointed Jeremiah Murdock of the colony of Virginia, merchant, to be their lawfull attorney for, in, and in their names to demand and require sue for recover and receive of and from all and every person whatsoever all maner of rents of all that tract containing 200A in Washington Parish in the county of Westmoreland purchased by the said Francis Barnard from John Jones of the city of Bristol, mariner. They also grant him full power to sell and dispose of said property for the most moneys that can be got. Signed Thomas Seed, Elizabeth Seed, Fran. Brown. Delivered in presence of Daniel Williams, Thomas Smith. Recorded 4 August 1732 T. Turner.

1A:218 - DEED OF LEASE - 3 August 1732 - Richard Gill of Hanover Parish, planter, to Marmaduke Beckwith of North Farnham Parish in the county of Richmond, Gent. 5 shillings sterling to lease 100A bounded by the said Beckwith, the said Gill, James Jones, close by a little house where William M__ing now lives. Part of a deed dated 17 October 1726 for 374A granted to the said Richard Gill. Signed the mark of Richd. Gill. Delivered in presence of Edw. Barradall, T. Turner. Recorded 4 August 1732 T. Turner.

1A:219 - DEED OF RELEASE - 4 August 1732 - Richard Gill of Hanover Parish, planter, to Marmaduke Beckwith of North Farnham Parish in the county of Richmond, Gent. 4000 pounds tobacco for 100A described in lease (close by a little house where William Moreing now lives). Signed the mark of Richard Gill. Delivered in presence of Edward Barradall, T. Turner. Recorded 4 August 1732 T. Turner.

1A:221 - DEED OF LEASE - 28 August 1732 - William Duff of Hanover

Parish, planter, to William White of same. Yearly rent of 600 pounds tobacco and 4 shillings money to lease 200A. Bounded by the Ferry Road, Hudson's line, Edward Taylor's old field, the widow Nighton's spring branch, and the widow Nighton's old field. To have and to hold during the natural lives of the said William White, Katherine White his now wife, and Thomas White his son or the survivor or longest liver of them. William Duff for himself, his heirs, and assigns hereby allows the said William White free privilege to work three hands upon the plantation besides themselves. For the true performance of the said promises the partys above mentioned do bind themselves, their heirs, Extrs. and Adms. in the penial sum of 20,000 pounds of good merchantable tobacco to be paid at the breach or denial of any of the agreements. Signed William Duff, William White. Delivered in presence of Isaac Arnold, Wm. Sarjant. Recorded 1 September 1732 T. Turner.

1A:222 - DEED OF LEASE - 10 April 1732 - John Arnold of Prince William County, planter, to William Duff of Hanover Parish. 5 shillings good and lawfull money of England to lease 50A whereon Isaac Johnson now liveth. Land was given to the said John Arnold by his father Thomas Arnold. Bounded by the western Main Branch of Gengoteague, land given by the said Thomas Arnold to his son James Arnold, William Harrison's path, Capt. Joseph Strother, and Jeremiah Strother. Signed John Arnold. Delivered in presence of Isaac Arnold, Wm. Sarjant. Recorded 1 September 1732 T. Turner.

1A:223 - DEED OF RELEASE - 11 April 1732 - John Arnold of Prince William County to William Duff of Hanover Parish. 50 pounds current money of Virginia for 50A described in lease. Signed John Arnold. Margaret, wife of John Arnold, relinquished her right of dower and thirds. Delivered in presence of Isaac Arnold, Wm. Sarjant. Recorded 1 September 1732 T. Turner.

1A:224 - BOND - 11 April 1732 - John Arnold of Prince William County bound unto William Duff of Hanover Parish in the sum of 100 pounds current money of Virginia. Condition such that if John Arnold shall defend the said land and every part and parcel thereof unto William Duff according to the true intent and meaning of deeds bearing date the tenth and eleventh days of April 1732, obligation to be void. Signed John Arnold. Delivered in presence of Isaac Arnold, Wm. Sarjant. Recorded 1 September 1732 T. Turner.

1A:224 - POWER OF ATTORNEY - 11 April 1732 - Margaret Arnold, the wife of John Arnold, makes and impowers her loving friend and brother Isaac Arnold her attorney for and in her name to acknowledge her relinquishment of all her rights of dower and thirds of in and to any part or parcel of the within bargained and sold land. Signed Margaret Arnold. Delivered in presence of Wm. White, Wm. Sarjant. Recorded 1 September 1732 T. Turner.

1A:225 - DEED OF LEASE - 30 August 1732 - Joseph Ellkins of the county of King George, planter, to James Jones of same, bricklayer. 5 shillings lawfull money to lease 250A contained in two parcels of land adjoining and contiguous to each other lying in the parish of Brunswick in the county of King George. 100A in the tenure of Richard Ellkins. 150A in the tenure of Benjamin Rush. Part of a 1300A tract formerly granted 9 February 1663 to Francis Haile and William Heabert, both now deceased. Bounded by certain lands now in the possession of or belonging to Samuel Skinker, Grace Stuart, John Owens, Edward Huniston, Catesby Cocke, Richard Ellkins, Junr., and Joshua Lampton. Signed Joseph Ellkins. Delivered in presence of John Skinner, Richard Owens, Richard Griffis, Wm. Owens. Recorded 1 September 1732 T. Turner.

1A:225 - DEED OF RELEASE - 31 August 1732 - Joseph Ellkins of the county of King George, planter, to James Jones of same, bricklayer. 40 pounds current money of Virginia for 250A described in lease. Amy, now wife of Benjamin Rush, late wife and relict of James Elkins deceased, father of the said Joseph Elkins, relinquished her right of dower of in and to the 150A tract of land. Signed Joseph Ellkins. Delivered in presence of John Skinner, Richard Owens, Richard Griffis, Wm. Owens. Recorded 1 September 1731 T. Turner.

1A:227 - DEED OF LEASE - 1 August 1732 - Robert Jones, Gent., of Hamilton Parish in the county of Prince William to John Hord of Essex County, Gent. 10 shillings sterling to lease 1000A bounded by Richland Run, Deep Run, and Col. William Ball. Signed Robert Jones. Delivered in presence of Jere. Murdock, Walter Anderson. Recorded 1 September 1732 T. Turner.

1A:228 - DEED OF RELEASE - 1 September 1732 - Robert Jones of Hamilton Parish in the county of Prince William to John Hord in Essex County, Gent. 10 pounds sterling for 1000A described in lease. Signed Robert Jones. Elizabeth, wife of Robert Jones, relinquished her right of dower and thirds. Delivered in presence of Jere. Murdock, Walter Anderson. Recorded 1 September 1732 T. Turner.

1A:229 - POWER OF ATTORNEY - 1 September 1732 - Elizabeth Jones of Prince William County, now wife of Robert Jones, appoints her trusty and well beloved friend Thomas Turner her true and lawfull attorney to acknowledge unto John Hord of Essex County all her right of dower in and to a tract or parcel of land containing 1000A which her husband sold unto him. Signed Elizabeth Jones. Delivered in presence of Joseph Hidnall, Blaggrove Hopper. Recorded 1 September 1732 T. Turner.

1A:229 - BOND - 1 September 1732- William Taylor and Samuel Wharton bound unto William Robinson, Gent. of the county of King George, in behalf of the Court of the said county in the sum of ten pounds sterling. Condition such that if William Taylor, guard. of Ann Kain, shall truly pay or cause to be paid unto the sd. orphan all such estate as now is or hereafter shall come to the hands of the sd. William Taylor as soon as the orphan shall attain lawfull age or when there unto required by the Justices of Peace for King George County, obligation to be void. Signed William Taylor, Saml. Wharton. Recorded 1 September 1732 T. Turner.

1A:230 - DEED OF LEASE - 19 April 1732 - Ann Glendining of Hanover Parish to William Strother, Gent., of same. 5 shillings current money to lease 100A adjoyning to the lands of James Canney, Francis Martain, and William Flowers. Part of 15,654A granted to John and George Mott by patent bearing date 17 October 1671. Signed Ann Glendining. Delivered in presence of William Thornton, John Booth, Margt. Grant. Recorded 6 October 1732 T. Turner.

1A:230 - DEED OF RELEASE - 20 April 1732 - Ann Glendining of Hanover Parish to William Strother, Gent., of same. 20 pounds current money of Virginia for 100A described in lease. Signed Ann Glendining. Delivered in presence of William Thornton, Junior, John Booth, Margt. Grant. Recorded 6 October 1732 T. Turner.

1A:232 - DEED OF LEASE - 5 October 1732 - Christopher Pritchett of the county of King George, planter, to Martin Golothan of the county of Westmoreland, planter. 5 shillings lawfull money to lease 130A bounded by Giles Carter, William Deakins, Kitchens, Caleb Butler. Signed Christopher Pritchett. Delivered in presence of William Pannill, John Jennings. Recorded 6 October 1732 T. Turner.

1A:233 - DEED OF RELEASE - 6 October 1732 - Christopher Pritchett of the county of King George, planter, to Martin Golothan of the county of Westmoreland, planter. 30 pounds lawfull money for 130A described in lease. Signed Christopher Pritchett. Delivered in presence of Wm. Pannill, John Jennings. Recorded 6 October 1732 T. Turner.

1A:234 - BOND - 6 October 1732 - Christopher Pritchett of the county of King George, planter, bound unto Martin Golothan of the county of Westmoreland, planter, in the sum of 60 pounds lawfull money. Condition such that if Christopher Pritchett well and truly keeps all agreements in one indenture of release bearing even date with these presents, obligation to be void. Signed Christopher Pritchett. Delivered in presence of Wm. Pannill, John Jennings. Recorded 6 October 1732 T. Turner.

1A:235 - DEED - 6 _____ 1732 - Martin Golothan of Washington Parish in the county of Westmoreland to Christopher Pritchett of Sittenbourn Parish. In consideration of another tract of land granted to him by the said Christopher Pritchett to the value of 8000 pounds tobacco, the said Golothan trades 150A which is part of a 300A tract belonging to Christopher Pritchett, grandfather to the said Christopher Pritchett. Bounded by lands of Capt. Lawrence Buttler, Mr. Rolley Chinn, Garret O'Neal, and John Barklett. Said land was left by Christopher Pritchett the former owner by will unto the said Martin Golothan and granted to the said Christopher Pritchett now in possession of the said land. Signed Martin Golothan. Mary, wife of Martin Golothan, relinquished her right of dower. Delivered in presence of Wm. Pannill, Jno. Jennings. Recorded 6 October 1732 T. Turner.

1A:236 - DEED OF GIFT - __ October 1732 - Isaac Arnold of Hanover Parish to Isaac Arnold, Junior son of the aforesaid Isaac Arnold. For the natural love good will and affection which he hath and now beareth to and toward his said son Isaac Arnold, Junior, the said Isaac Arnold gives all that plantation and parcel of land whereon the said Isaac Arnold, Junior and Sarah his wife now liveth together also with 100A of land lying on the western branch of Gingoteague Creek near the church path which leads from Grace Arnold's plantation to Strothers Church and bounded by Isaac Arnold, Senior and Grace Arnold. Part of a 226A patent granted unto John Doyle deceased. After the death of the survivor and longest liver of Isaac Arnold, Junior and Sarah his wife, land to go to James Arnold son of the said Sarah Arnold and his heirs forever. Signed Isaac Arnold, Senr. Delivered in presence of Henry Head,

Thomas Dickerson. Recorded 6 October 1732 T. Turner.

1A:236 - BOND - 6 October 1732 - Thos. Phillips and Wm. Strother of Hanover Parish bound unto Our Sovereign Lord the King his Heirs and Successors in the sum of 10,000 pounds tobacco. Condition such that whereas Thomas Phillips hath obtained a license to keep an ordinary at Falmouth Town if therefore the said Thomas Phillips doth constantly find and provide good wholesome and cleanly lodging and diet for Travelers and stableage, fodder and provender or pasturage and provender as the season shall require for their horses for and during the term of one year from the said six day of October 1732 and shall not suffer and permit any unlawfull gaming in his house nor on the Sabboth day suffer any person to tipple or drink more than is necessary, obligation to be void. Signed Thomas Phillips, Wm. Strother. Recorded 6 October 1732 T. Turner.

1A:237 - BOND - 6 October 1732 - Joseph Berry and Enoch Berry of Hanover Parish bound unto Our Sovereign Lord the King his Heirs and Successors in the sum or 10,000 pounds tobacco. Condition such that whereas Joseph Berry hath obtained a license to keep an ordinary at his own house being the place which is Col. Seals ferry, if he does as the law provides for and during the term of one year from the said sixth day of October 1732, obligation to be void. (See 1A:236) Signed Joseph Berry, Enoch Berry. Recorded 6 October 1732 T. Turner.

1A:237 - BOND - 2 November 1731 - John Champe and Thomas Vivion, Gent., bound to Our Sovereign the King in the sum of 59,268 pounds tobacco. Condition such that whereas the Court of King George County hath this day paid their county levy admounting to 29,634 pounds of tobacco now if the said John Champe do faithfully collect the same and pay it to the respective creditors according to law, obligation to be void. Signed John Champe, Thos. Vivion. Recorded 3 November 1732 T. Turner.

1A:238 - DEED - 20 October 1732 - Richard Griffis of Hanover Parish, planter, to Thomas Grigsby of St. Pauls Parish in the county of Stafford, Gent. 6000 pounds tobacco for 75A. Part of Richard Rossers patent of 600A. Sold by this Richard Rosser to John Rowley by deed dated 12 January 1668 and by Wm. Rowley, son and heir of the said John Rowley, conveyed to the said Richard Griffis by deed dated 4 December 1729. Bounded by a spring branch belonging to Wm. Smith deceased, and Absalom Spicer's line. Signed Richard Griffis. Delivered in presence of John Holboock, Joseph Crouch, John Simpson. Recorded 3 November 1732 T. Turner.

1A:239 - DEED OF LEASE - 12 June 1732 - John Triplett of the county of King George, planter, to Richard Bullock of same, collier. 5 shillings current money of Virginia to lease 23A late in the occupation of Isabella Triplett, widow. Bounded by the county road, Samuel James, James Hore, the rolling path that separates the land hereby granted from land of Francis Triplett the Elder. Given and devised unto the said John Triplett (and Thomas and Francis his brothers) by their father William Triplett late of the county of Caroline, deceased, in and by his last will and testament dated 3 October 1728. Signed John Triplett. Delivered in presence of John Burch, Peter Bashaue. Recorded 3 November 1732 T. Turner.

1A:239 - DEED OF RELEASE - 13 June 1732 - John Triplett of the county of King George, planter, and Katherine his wife to Richard Bullock of same, collier. 12 pounds 4 shillings current money of Virginia for 23A described in lease. Signed John Triplett. Katherine Triplett, wife of John Triplett, relinquished her right of dower. Delivered in presence of John Burch, Peter Bashaw. Recorded 3 November 1732 T. Turner.

1A:241 - BOND - 13 June 1732 - John Triplett and Katherine his wife of the county of King George bound unto Richard Bullock of same, collier, in the sum of 24 pounds 8 shillings current money of Virginia. Condition such that if John Triplett and Katherine his wife truly keep all agreements mentioned and contained in one indenture of release bearing even date with these presents, obligation to be void. Signed John Triplett, Katherine Triplett. Delivered in presence of John Burch, Peter Bashaw. Recorded 3 November 1732 T. Turner.

1A:242 - POWER OF ATTORNEY - 6 September 1732 - Katherine Triplett, wife of John Triplett of King George County, authorizes Mr. Thomas Turner to acknowledge her relinquishment of dower to 23A conveyed by her husband unto Richard Bullock. Signed Katherine Triplett. Delivered in presence of John Fox, Thomas Reeds. Recorded 3 November 1732 T. Turner.

1A:242 - DEED OF LEASE - 4 October 1732 - Robert Doniphan of Hanover Parish to Wm. Strother, Gent., of same. 5 shillings current money to lease 200A adjoining to the lands of Francis Martin, Abraham Kenyan, and James Canny. Part of a 15,654A tract granted to John and George Mott 17 October 1670. Signed Robert Doniphan. Delivered in presence of Richard Bryan, Enoch Berry, Thos. Vivion. Recorded 3 November 1732 T. Turner.

1A:243 - DEED OF RELEASE - 5 October 1732 - Robert Doniphan of Hanover Parish to Wm. Strother, Gent., of same. 20 pounds current money of Virginia for 200A described in lease. Signed Robert Doniphan. Delivered in presence of Richard Bryan, Thos. Vivion, Enoch Berry. Recorded 3 November 1732 T. Turner.

1A:244 - DEED OF LEASE - 2 November 1732 - Charles Poe of Sittenburn Parish and county of Richmond, planter, to John Willson of Sittenburn Parish and county of King George, wood collier. 5 pounds 5 shillings to lease 100A bounded by Charles Hill, Saml. Brown, Capt. Wm. Ball, Josias Ship, Joseph Beckley. Signed Charles Spoe. Delivered in presence of John Triplett, Benja. Adie. Recorded 3 November 1732 T. Turner.

1A:245 - DEED OF RELEASE - 3 November 1732 - Charles Spoe of Sittenburn Parish and county of Richmond, planter, to John Willson of Sittenburn Parish and county of King George, wood collier. 6 pounds 6 shillings for 100A described in lease. Signed Charles Spoe. Delivered in presence of John Triplett, Benja. Adie. Recorded 3 November 1732 T. Turner.

1A:246 - DEED OF LEASE - 2 November 1732 - Lawrence Downton of the county of Westmoreland, carpenter, to Wm. Sparks of the county of King George, wheelwright. Yearly rent of 50 shillings to lease 100A bounded by

Maxfield Brown, Major Wright, John Brown. Formerly purchased by Nicholas Downton deceased. Lease is for and during the natural lives of the aforesaid Wm. Sparks and Margaret his wife and until the same be fully ended and completed. It is agreed by the aforesaid parties that the said Sparks shall be rent free this ensuing year 1733 and to pay the following year forty shillings and ever after fifty shillings. Signed Lawrence Downton. Delivered in presence of Isaac Arnold, James Strother. Recorded 3 November 1732 T. Turner.

1A:247 - BOND - 2 November 1732 - Lawrence Downton of the county of Westmoreland bound unto Wm. Sparks of the county of King George in the sum of 30 pounds current money. Condition such that if Lawrence Downton truly keeps all agreements made in one lease made by the said Lawrence Downton unto the said Wm. Sparks bearing even date with these presents, obligation to be void. Signed Lawrence Downton. Delivered in presence of Jas. Strother, Isaac Arnold. Recorded 3 November 1732 T. Turner.

1A:247 - INDENTURE - 24 November 1732 - Between John Murphey and John Edy, joyner. John Murphey doth hereby covenant, promise and agree to serve the said John Edy four years now ensuing from the date of these presents faithfully, honestly, and truly in the office of a house carpenter and joyner. In consideration whereof the said John Edy doth covenant promise grant and agree to use his best skill and endeavour to instruct and learn the said John Murphey the carpenters and joyners trade during the time aforesaid and also sufficient meat, drink, washing and lodging fit for such an apprentice and the said John Edy doth further promise and agree to give and allow to the said John Murphey at the end of the above four years one broad cloth coat and vest, one fine hat, two white linnen shirts, two neckcloths and a pr. shoes and stockins. Signed John Murphey. Delivered in presence of John Champe, Peter Daniell. Recorded 3 December 1732 T. Turner.

1A:248 - BOND - 2 February 1732 - Mary Anderson and James Jones are bound unto Our Sovereign Lord the King in the sum of 10,000 pounds tobacco. Condition such that whereas Mary Anderson has obtained a license to keep an ordinary at her dwelling plantation, if she does as the law provides for and during the term of one whole year from the date hereof, obligation to be void. (See 1A:236) Signed Mary Anderson, Jas. Jones. Recorded 6 April 1733 T. Turner.

1A:248 - DEED OF LEASE - 5 April 1733 - Samuel Wharton of Hanover Parish to Thomas Turner of same. 5 shillings sterling to lease 9A bounded on the north side with the county main road, on the east with land of Charles Wharton, on the south and on the west with the land of the said Thomas Turner. Part of a dividend of land containing 100A given to the sd. Samuel Wharton by

Samuel Wharton deceased, father to the said Samuel Wharton, by his last will and testament dated 13 November 1732. Signed Samuel Wharton. Delivered in presence of Wm. Thornton, John Champe. Recorded 6 April 1733 T. Turner.

1A:249 - DEED OF RELEASE - 6 April 1733 - Samuel Wharton of Hanover Parish to Thomas Turner of same. 550 pounds tobacco for 9A described in lease. Signed Samuel Wharton. Delivered in presence of Wm. Thornton, John Champe. Recorded 6 April 1733 T. Turner.

1A:250 - BOND - 6 April 1733 - Daniel White and Thomas Hughs of Hanover Parish bound unto Our Sovereign Lord the King his Heirs and Successors in the sum of 10,000 pounds of tobacco. Condition such that whereas Daniel White hath obtained a license to keep a ordinary at his dwelling plantation, if he does as the law provides for and during the term of one whole year from the date hereof, obligation to be void. (See 1A:236) Signed Daniel White, Thos. Hughs. Recorded 6 April 1733 T. Turner.

1A:251 - DEED OF LEASE - 5 April 1733 - William Thornton of the county of King George, Gent., to Charles Carter of Middlesex County, Esqr. 5 shillings good lawfull money to lease 333A granted to James Innis 21 December 1709 by Robt. Carter, Esq., agent to the proprietor of the Norther Neck of Virginia. James Innis left it to his daughter Elizabeth who intermarring with Thomas Foxhall did jointly sell to the said William Thornton and William Woodford of Essex County and by agreement between them William Thornton is now in actual possession. Bounded by Martha Vicaris, Charles Carter, Richard Chichester, Esq. Signed Wm. Thornton. Delivered in presence of Lunsford Lomax, T. Turner, Antho. Haynie, Edw. Barradall. Recorded 4 May 1733 T. Turner.

1A:252 - DEED OF RELEASE - 6 April 1733 - William Thornton of King George County to Charles Carter, Esq. of Middlesex County. 100 pounds current money for 333A described in lease. Signed Wm. Thornton. Delivered in presence of Lunsford Lomax, T. Turner, Antho. Haynie, Edw. Barradall. Recorded 4 May 1733 T. Turner.

1A:254 - DEED OF LEASE - 1 May 1733 - Joseph Minton of Hanover Parish, planter, to Thomas King of same, planter. 5 shillings lawfull money of Great Britain to lease 60A formerly bought of Samuel Nichols. Bounded by the main road, land that formerly belonged to Jacob Nichols, and land that formerly belonged to Francis Stern going towards Underwood's Beverdam. Signed Joseph Minton. Delivered in presence of Nicho. Smith, Thomas Moore. Recorded 4 May 1733 T. Turner.

1A:254 - DEED OF RELEASE - 2 May 1733 - Joseph Minton of Hanover Parish, planter, to Thomas King of same, planter. 10 pounds money and 1630 pounds tobacco for 60A described in lease. Signed Joseph Minton. Delivered in presence of Nicho. Smith, Thomas Moore. Recorded 4 May 1733 T. Turner.

1A:255 - BOND - 2 May 1733 - Joseph Minton of Hanover Parish, planter, bound unto Thomas King of same, planter, in the sum of 50 pounds current money. Condition such that if Joseph Minton keeps all agreements mentioned in a certain indenture of release bearing even date with these presents, obligation to be void. Signed Joseph Minton. Delivered in presence of Nicho. Smith, Thos. Moore. Recorded 4 May 1733 T. Turner.

1A:256 - DEED OF LEASE - 3 May 1733 - John Champe and John Ambrose, Church Wardens of the parish of Brunswick in the county of King George, to Rowland Thornton of Hanover Parish, Gent. 5 shillings sterling to lease 300A near William Berry's mill. Includes 30A formerly sold by Key to Thomas Williams. Signed John Champe, John Ambrose. Delivered in presence of Benja. Strother, John Gilbert, Abraham Kenyan. Recorded 4 May 1733 T. Turner.

1A:257 - DEED OF RELEASE - 4 May 1733 - John Champe and John Ambrose, Church Wardens of the parish of Brunswick in the county of King George, to Rowland Thornton of Hanover Parish, Gent. 255 pounds current money of Virginia for 300A described in lease. Signed John Champe, John Ambrose. Delivered in presence of Benja. Strother, John Gilbert, Abraham Kenyan. Recorded 4 May 1733 T. Turner.

1A:258 - BOND - 4 May 1733 - John Champe and John Ambrose, Church Wardens of the parish of Brunswick in the county of King George, bound unto Rowland Thornton of Hanover Parish for 510 pounds current money of Virginia. Condition such that if John Champe and John Ambrose and their successors keep all agreements mentioned in certain deeds of lease and release which said release bears even date with these presents, obligation to be void. Signed John Champe, John Ambrose. Delivered in presence of Benja. Strother, John Gilbert, Abraham Kenyan. Recorded 4 May 1733 T. Turner.

1A:258 - BOND - 28 April 1733 - John Kenyan of Brunswick Parish in the county of King George, planter, bound unto Abraham Kenyon of same, planter, in the sum of 1000 pounds sterling. Condition such that whereas John Kenyon deceased, father to the above bounded John Kenyon and Abraham Kenyon, by his last will and testament dated 29 August 1706 did devise unto the said Abraham and John Kenyon his sons a certain tract upon the main west branch of Muddy Creek and whereas by a late devision of the said land between the said Abraham and John Kenyon and by the free and voluntary consent of each of them the aforesaid Abraham Kenyon is to have 450A being the upper part thereof along Rappahanncock River to about a quarter of a mile above the mouth of Snow Creek, if the above bounden John Kenyon do hold the aforesaid line for his dividing line for ever, obligation to be void. Signed John Kenyon. Delivered in presence of M. Battaley, John Ambrose, John Tayler. Recorded 4 May 1733 T. Turner.

1A:259 - BOND - 28 April 1733 - Abraham Kenyon of Brunswick Parish in the county of King George, planter, bound unto John Kenyon of same, planter, in the sum of 1000 pounds sterling. Condition such that whereas Abraham and John Kenyon have this day agreed upon a dividing line of the land left to them by their father John Kenyon whereby the said John Kenyon is to have 324A being the lower part thereof, if the above bounden Abraham Kenyon do hold the aforesaid line for his dividing line for ever, obligation to be void. Signed Abraham Kenyon. Delivered in presence of M. Battaley, John Ambrose, John Tayler. Recorded 4 May 1733 T. Turner.

1A:259 - DEED OF GIFT - 3 May 1733 - Isaac Arnold of Hanover Parish to Thomas Arnold, son of the said Isaac Arnold, of same, planter. Isaac Arnold confirms unto his said son Thomas and Mary his wife all that plantation whereon the said Thomas Arnold now liveth and 60A of land during the whole term of their natural lives and after the death of the longest liver of them, the said land and premises to belong to Humphrey Arnold, oldest son of Thomas and Mary Arnold. Bounded by land formerly belonging to Mr. Jonathan Gibson, Mr. Thomas Turner, Henry Long, and line of the said Isaac Arnold. Part of a pattent for 225A granted by John Doyle unto the said Isaac Arnold. Signed Isaac Arnold. Delivered in presence of Thomas Bartlet, James Boddington. Recorded 4 May 1733 T. Turner.

1A:260 - DEED OF LEASE - 31 May 1733 - Hugh French of Overwharton Parish in the county of Stafford, Gentleman, to John Champe and John Ambris, Church Wardens of the parish of Brunswick and county of King George. 5 shillings lawfull current money of Virginia to lease 200A on the main branch of Muddy Creek. Bounded by John Simpson's tobacco ground now Owen Sullavant's. Signed Hugh French. Delivered in presence of William Walker, Peter Daniell, Jas. Jones. Recorded 1 June 1733 T. Turner.

1A:261 - DEED OF RELEASE - 1 June 1733 - Hugh French of Overwharton Parish in the county of Stafford, Gent., to John Champe and John Ambris, Church Wardens of Brunswick Parish in the county of King George. 100 pounds sterling for 200A described in lease. Signed Hugh French. Delivered in presence of William Walker, Peter Daniell, Jas. Jones. Recorded 1 June 1733 T. Turner.

1A:262 - BOND - No Date Given - Hugh French of Overwharton Parish in the county of Stafford, Gent., bound unto John Champe and John Ambriss, Church Wardens of the parish of Brunswick in the county of King George for 500 pounds lawfull current money of Virginia. Condition such that if Hugh French keeps all agreements contained in a certain indenture of release bearing even date with these presents, obligation to be void. Signed Hugh French. Delivered in presence of William Walker, Peter Daniell, Jas. Jones. Recorded 1 June 1733 T. Turner.

1A:262 - POWER OF ATTORNEY - 4 May 1733 - Mary French, wife of Hugh French of Stafford County, appoints Thomas Turner her lawfull attorney to acknowledge and relinquish all her right and title of dower of in and to a certain tract of land containing 200A conveyed by her husband to John Champe and John Ambrose, Church Wardens of the parish of Brunswick in the county of King George. Signed Mary French. Delivered in presence of Joseph Fisher, Richd. Fletcher, Mercer. Recorded 1 June 1733 T. Turner.

1A:262 - RECEIPT - 12 May 1733 - Simon Millier acknowledges to have received of Thomas Turner one young Negro man and three young Negro women of the value of eighty-one pounds sterling to his likeing the said four negroes being settled on him and the heirs of his body by Act of Assembly begun and held at the Capitol the eighteenth day of May 1732. Signed Simon Millier. Witness Benja. Adie. Recorded 1 June 1733 T. Turner.

1A:263 - DEED OF LEASE - 5 July 1733 - Thomas Williams of the county of King George, planter, and Martha his wife, one of the daughters of George Phillips, to Gawin Corbin of King and Queen County, Esq. 5 shillings current money of Virginia to lease one undivided third part of 543A of land. Bounded by Gawin Corbin's land by the mill road, Keys line, the back line of Simpsons pattent upon Thorntons land, Shropshires land, Micous line, and Walter Anderson. Part of a 2100A tract granted to John Simpson 6 June 1666. Signed Thomas Williams, Martha Williams. Delivered in presence of Tho. Catlett, Jno. Roy, Henry Berry, Joseph Williams. Recorded 6 July 1733 T. Turner.

1A:264 - DEED OF RELEASE - 6 July 1733 - Thomas Williams of the county of King George, planter, and Martha his wife, one of the daughters of George Phillips, to Gawin Corbin of the county of King and Queen, Esq. 80 pounds sterling for one undivided third part of 543A described in lease. Signed Thomas Williams, Martha Williams. Delivered in presence of Thos. Catlett, Jno. Roy, Henry Berry, Joseph Williams. Recorded 6 July 1733 T. Turner.

1A:265 - DEED OF LEASE - 5 July 1733 - William Thorn and Mary his wife, widow and relique of John Oreo late of Prince William County , and John

Glascow and Margaret his wife, daughter of the said John Oreo and Mary his wife, of same to Cornelius McKartie of Brunswick Parish. 5 shillings to lease 100A on the main branch of Omen Creek. Bounded by Samuel Dishman, Robert Peck, and Henry Berry. Part of a tract formerly granted to Robert King 18 May 1659 and sold by the said King to Robt. Peck and Henry Berry, and sold by the said Peck to John Oreo and Mary his wife during their natural lives and then to their daughter Margaret Glascow to her and her heirs forever. Signed John Glascock, Margaret Glascock. Delivered in presence of Robert Richards, William Brown, Joseph Berry. Recorded 6 July 1733 T. Turner.

1A:266 - DEED OF RELEASE - 6 July 1733 - William Thorn and Mary his wife, widow and relique of John Oreo late of Prince William County, and John Glascow and Margaret his wife, daughter to the said John Oreo and Mary his wife, of same to Cornelius McKartie of Brunswick Parish. 25 pounds current money of Virginia for 100A described in lease. Signed John Glascock, Margaret Glascock. Delivered in presence of Robt. Richards, William Browne, Joseph Berry. Recorded 6 July 1733 T. Turner.

1A:267 - BOND - 6 July 1733 - John Glasgow of Hambleton Parish in the county of Prince William bound unto Cornelius McKartie in the sum of 50 pounds current money of Virginia. Condition such that if John Glasgow fulfills the obligations mentioned in Indenture of Release bearing date with these presents for one hundred acres of land, obligation to be void. Signed John Glascock. Delivered in presence of Robt. Richards, William Brown, Joseph Berry. Recorded 6 July 1733 T. Turner.

1A:268 - DEED - 12 June 1733 - Thomas Smith of the county of Spotsylvania, planter, and Anne his wife, late widow and relict of Thomas Fitzhugh late of the county of King George, Gent., to Henry Fitzhugh of the county of Stafford, Esq. In consideration of 56 pounds 6 shillings the said Thomas Smith and Anne his wife quit claim all manner of dower and title of dower property of in to or out of all or any part of the said lands whereof the said Thomas Fitzhugh was at any time seized during the coverture between him and the said Anne. Signed Thomas Smith, Ann Smith. Delivered in presence of J. Mercer, Benja. Rush, Edw. Barradall. Recorded 6 July 1733 T. Turner.

1A:268 - RECEIPT - 6 July 1733 - Simon Miller acknowledges to have received of Thomas Turner four Negros, viz. one young Negro man and three young Nego women of the value of eighty-one pounds sterling the said four Negros being settled on him and the heirs of his body by Act of Assembly made in May 1732. Signed Simon Miller. Recorded 6 July 1733 T. Turner.

1A:269 - ESTATE ACCOUNT - 7 July 1732 - Estate of John Anderson deceased to William Brown his Executor. 1721 - To Willm. Pullen, Alex. Parker. 1722 - To Charles Brages, Walter Anderson, Dorothy Anderson. 1723 - John Price. 1732 - Mr. Barradall. Recorded 6 July 1733 T. Turner.

1A:269 - BOND - 6 July 1733 - Thomas Turner and John Champe bound unto the Justices of the county of King George in the sum of 50 pounds sterling. Conditions such that if Thomas Turner, guardian of Cyprian Anderson, shall well and truly pay or cause to be paid unto the said orphan all such estate and estates as now is or hereafter shall come to the hands of the said Thomas Turner as soon as the said orphan shall attain lawfull age or when required by the Justices of Peace for King George County, obligation to be void. Signed Thomas Turner, John Champe. Recorded 3 August 1733 T. Turner.

1A:269 - DEED OF GIFT - 6 July 1733 - William Marshall of Hanover Parish for the care that his beloved son William Marshall, Junr. is to take of him and his wife Ann during their natural lives and also for his paying all of his father's just debts, gives his said son William Marshall 180A of land whereon the father now lives together with all the rest of his estate both real and personal. Signed Wm. Marshall, Ann Marshall. Delivered in presence of Saml. Wharton, James Boddington, Wm. Wharton, Martha Slaughter. Recorded 3 August 1733 T. Turner.

1A:270 - BOND - 18 June 1733 - Peter Skinner of the county of Westmoreland, planter, bound unto Gawin Corbin of King and Queen County, Esq., for 160 pounds sterling. Condition such that if Peter Skinner and Margaret his wife shall by good and sufficient deeds convey and assure in fee simple one undivided third part of and in a certain tract containing 543A and all the estate, title and interest of them in and to the aforesaid land and if also the said Margaret shall appear before the Court and acknowledge her free and voluntary consent to the conveying such estate, obligation to be void. Signed Peter Skinner. Delivered in presence of Mungo Roy, Thomas Monteith, Jno. Livingston. Recorded 7 September 1733 T. Turner.

1A:270 - DEED OF LEASE - 6 September 1733 - Peter Skinner of the county of Westmoreland, planter, and Margaret his wife to Gawin Corbin of King and Queen County, Esqr. 5 shillings sterling to lease one undivided third part of and in a certain 543A tract. Bounded by the said Corbin's land by the mill, Keys line, back line of Simpsons pattent upon Thornton's land, Shropshires land, Micous line, and Walter Anderson. Part of a 2100A tract of land granted to John Simpson 6 June 1666. Signed Peter Skinner, Margaret Skinner. Delivered in presence of Mungo Roy, Thomas Monteith, John Livingston, Joseph Williams. Recorded 7 September 1733 T. Turner.

1A:271 - DEED OF RELEASE - 7 September 1733 - Peter Skinner of the county of Westmoreland, planter, and Margaret his wife, one of the daughters of George Phillips, to Gawin Corbin of King and Queen County, Esqr. 80 pounds sterling for one undivided third part of a 543A tract of land described in lease. Signed Peter Skinner, Margaret Skinner. Delivered in presence of John Champe, Thos. Roy, Joseph Williams. Recorded 7 September 1733 T. Turner.

1A:273 - BOND - 7 September 1733 - Benjamin Strother and Samuel Skinker bound to Our Sovereign Lord the King his Heirs and Successors in the sum of 1000 pounds sterling. Condition such that if Benjamin Strother, appointed Sheriff for the County of King George, doth true and faithfully perform his office and duty of Sheriff in all respects according to law, obligation to be void. Signed Benja. Strother, Saml. Skinker. Recorder 7 September 1733 T. Turner.

1A:273 - BOND - 2 November 1733 - Benjamin Strother and Samuel Skinker, Gent., bound to Our Sovereign Lord the King his Heirs and Successors in the quantity of 41,856 pounds of tobacco. Condition such that whereas the above bounden hath the collecion of the said county put into his hands amounting to 20,712 pounds of tobacco, if the said Benjamin Strother do faithfully collect and duely pay the same to the respected creditors as also all such Secretaries, Clerks, and Sheriffs fees that shall be put in to the hands of the said Benjamin to collect that he shall collect and pay the said fees to the respective officers, obligation to be void. Signed Benja. Strother, Saml. Skinker. Recorded 2 November 1733 T. Turner.

1A:274 - DEED OF GIFT - 30 October 1733 - William Carter, Senr. of the county of King George to William Carter, Junr., the son of William and Jane Carter. William Carter, Senr. willingly and voluntarily gives to his well beloved God son, the son of William and Jane Carter, a 100A tract of land where his father lived. Part of a parcel of land that formerly belonged to old Charles Sneed. Bounded by the Bever Dam, land that was formerly Giles Mathews, and corner tree near Griffins mill. Daughter Margaret has free liberty to work and tend on the same what she shall see fit for the term of sixteen years if she keeps unmarried, but when she marries in the term of the sixteen years to surrender which land to my grandson and his male heirs. But if he should die without a male heir lawfully begotten then it shall fall to my grandson John Carter, the son of Gyles and Mary Carter. Signed William Carter. Delivered in presence of John Lowen, Christor. Pritchett. Recorded 2 November 1733 T. Turner.

1A:274 - BOND - 2 November 1733 - Joseph Berry and Enoch Berry bound to Our Sovereign Lord the King his Heirs and Successors in the sum of 10,000 pounds of tobacco. Condition such that whereas Joseph Berry has obtained license to keep a ordinary at his now dwelling plantation, if therefore the said

Joseph Berry does as the law provides for and during the term of one whole year from the second day of November 1733, obligation to be void. (See 1A:236) Signed Joseph Berry, Enoch Berry. Recorded 2 November 1733 T. Turner.

1A:275 - ESTATE ACCOUNT - No Date Given - Account of the administration of Wm. Corbin's estate. Amounts paid to Mr. Turner, to plank for his coffin, to making coffin, to two gallons rum for funeral, to his mother for cash lent him, to John Corbin for looking after him and burying him. Recorded 4 January 1733 T. Turner.

1A:275 - DEED OF LEASE - 30 January 1734 - Maxfield Brown of the county of King George to Joseph Settle of same. After the first year, yearly rent of 530 pounds good merchantable tobacco in cask to lease 100A bounded by John Settle, Senr., Joseph Dodd, a branch called the mills branch, and John Sebastian. Lease is from the date hereof until one and twenty years. Joseph Settle is to plant 100 apple trees and to keep them in good repair under a close fence. He is not to fell nor to wast any timber belonging to the land. Signed Maxfield Brown, Joseph Settle. Delivered in presence of Std. Lightburn, Benj. Strother, Sibella Lightburn. Recorded 1 February 1733 T. Turner.

1A:276 - DEED OF GIFT - 26 May 1733 - Francis Wofendall of Hanover Parish, planter, to Elizabeth, daughter of said Francis Wofendall and wife of Saml. Kendall, of same. Francis Wofendall freely, clearly and absolutely gives 50A to the said Elizabeth. Land bounded by Giles Easther and main branch of Jingotague. If Elizabeth dies without heir, Saml. Kendall to have it during his natural life, then to return it to the giver and his heirs. Signed Francis Wofendall. Delivered in presence of St. Lightburn, Wm. Harrison. Memorandum - also gives one Neg. girl and her increase to daughter Elizabeth and her heirs. If no heir then Neg. and her increase returns to father and his heirs. Recorded 1 February 1733 T. Turner.

1A:276 - DEED OF LEASE - 1 January 1733 - Charles Carter, Esqr. of King George County to Joseph Hinson, planter, of same. Yearly rent of 500 pounds good tobacco to lease 190A tract surveyed by Mr. Thomas Hooper. About four miles above the falls of Rappahannock River and lying upon the river. The whole tract formerly divided into four lots. Lease is for and during the natural lives of the said Joseph Hinson, Ann his wife, and Margaret his daughter. Joseph Hinson agrees to pay quitrents each year, to build a good and suffficient dwelling house and a strong tobacco house, to plant an apple orchard and a peach orchard of 100 trees each, and not to waste or destroy the timber trees growing on the land. Signed Chs. Carter. Delivered in presence of Wm. Triplett, Alexr. Bell. Recorded 1 March 1733 T. Turner.

1A:277 - DEED OF LEASE - 27 February 1733 - William Thornton of Brunswick Parish, Gent., to Charles Carter of Urbanna in the county of Middlesex, Esqr. 5 shillings sterling for two lots or half acres in the town of Falmouth distinguished in the plat of the said town by the numbers 9 and 17. Lot number 9 is in breadth down King Street and in length up George Street. Lot number 17 is in length along Prince Street and in breadth down George Street. Signed Wm. Thornton. Delivered in presence of Benja. Robinson, Catesby Cocke. Recorded 1 March 1733 T. Turner.

1A:278 - DEED OF RELEASE - 28 February 1733 - William Thornton of Brunswick Parish, Gent., to Charles Carter of Urbanna in the county of Middlesex, Esqr. 30 pounds current money for two lots described in lease. Signed Wm. Thornton. Delivered in presence of Benja. Robinson, Catesby Cocke. Recorded 1 March 1733 T. Turner.

1A:279 - DEED OF SALE - 1 March 1733 - Robert Jones of Brunswick Parish in the county of Prince William, Gent., to John Woodbridge and William Robertson, the son of Ann Robertson an infant, both of the county of Richmond. 18 pounds current money of Virginia for 200A bounded by Richard Gill, Thomas Hord, and Colonel Ball. Taken out of a 2670A tract granted 11 February 1724. John Woodbridge is fulfilling one paragraph of the last will and testament of William Woodbridge wherein he did will and appoint the said John Woodbridge to purchase 200A near the falls of the Rappahannock and convey it to the said William Robertson and his heirs. Signed Robert Jones. Delivered in presence of Thomas Hill, John Coburn, Chas. Barret. Recorded 1 March 1733 T. Turner. Memorandum - quiet and peaceable possession delivered to Charles Lovelace in the behalf of the within William Robertson an infant. Delivered in presence of Brereton Jones, Clement Norman, Charles Lovelace.

1A:280 - POWER OF ATTORNEY - 24 February 1733 - Elizabeth Jones, wife of Robert Jones of Prince William County, appoints her trusty friend Thomas Turner her attorney to relinquish all her right of dower of or to 200A conveyed by deed 28 February 1733 to William Robertson an infant for a valuable consideration received of John Woodbridge by her husband Robert Jones. Signed Eliza. Jones. Delivered in presence of Charles Lovelace, Clement Norman, Brereton Jones. Recorded date not given T. Turner.

1A:281 - DEED OF LEASE - 4 April 1734 - John Corder of Hamilton Parish in the county of Prince William to William Remey of Hanover Parish, carpenter. 1500 pounds tobacco to lease 100A being that land that William Sarjant left to his God son William Wittelidge and now falls by heir at law to the within named John Corder. Signed John Cordill, Patience Cordill, Saml. Hackney. Delivered in presence of John Grant, Wm. Clater. Recorded 5 April 1734 T. Turner.

1A:281 - DEED OF RELEASE - 5 April 1734 - John Corder of Hamilton Parish in the county of Prince William to William Remey of Hanover Parish, carpenter. 1500 pounds tobacco for 100A described in lease. Bounded by line of William Carter near Mattock's path, Browns, John Chinn, and Thomas Randalph. Signed John Cordill, Patience Cordill, Samuel Hackney. Delivered in presence of John Grant, Wm. Clater. Recorded 5 April 1734 T. Turner.

1A:282 - POWER OF ATTORNEY - 5 April 1734 - Mary Hackney, wife of Samuel Hackney of Hambleton Parish in the county of Prince William, appoints Mr. Joseph Hudnall to acknowledge her right of dower and thirds at the Common Law of in to one hundred acres of land sold by her son-in-law John Cordill unto Wm. Remey. Signed Mary Hackney. Delivered in presence of John Cordill, Saml. Hackney. Recorded 5 April 1734 T. Turner.

1A:282 - DEED OF LEASE - 8 October 1733 - William Duff of Hanover Parish, planter, to John Rose of same, planter. Yearly rent of 500 pounds tobacco and the Quitrents to lease 100A. Bounded by the head of the spring branch where John Taylor formerly lived, line of William Hudson, and line of Capt. Benjamin Strothers. Lease is for and during the natural lives of John Rose and Frances Rose his now wife. Signed Wm. Duff. Delivered in presence of John Brown, Jno. Witherol, Wm. Sarjant. Recorded 3 May 1734 T. Turner.

1A:283 - INDENTURE - 28 February 1732/3 - Sarah Edge of Brunswick Parish doth voluntaryly and of her own free will and accord put place and bind her son John Edge, he being six years old the thirteenth day of July next ensuing, an apprentice or servant unto Peter Lowd his heirs Exrs. and Admrs. From the day of the date of these presents untill he shall arrive to the age of twenty-one years during all which term the sd. apprentice his sd. master faithfully shall serve. Signed Sarah Edge. Delivered in presence of Henry McKie, Joseph Armstrong, Mary Ovington. Recorded 3 May 1734 T. Turner.

1A:284 - ESTATE SCHEDULE - No Date Given - A schedule of the estate of John Eady a prisoner in the goal of Westmoreland County - 2 joynt plains, 1 plough plain, 3 mallets, 3 jack plains, 2 smoothing plains, 2 handsaws, 3 chiszells, 1 goudge, 1 rabbit plain, 4 hollow and round plains, 1 ogee plain, one and one-fourth round plain, 1 chalk roller, a rule and compass, 1 hammer and 4 plain stocks, 1 _ae plain, 1 sash plain, 1 felister, 1 leead plain, 1 plough plain, 1 Cornish plain, 2 saws, 1 dozen plain irons, 1 pr. of pinchers, 1 joyners hatchett, one-half doz. small chiszalls, 2 large carpenter chiszells, 1 fine goudge. Debts owed by John Rose, Thos. Osbourne, and Nicho. Minor. Signed John Edy. Recorded 5 April 1734 T. Turner.

1A:285 - DEED OF LEASE - 6 June 1734 - Thomas Thatcher of the county of

King George, planter, to Nicholas Smith of same. 5 shillings lawfull money to lease 250A formerly in the tenure of John Gilbert and now of Thomas Reeds. Part of 1000A formerly granted unto Sylvester Thatcher deceased, grandfather of the said Thomas Thatcher, by patents dated 6 October 1656 and 18 March 1660. Said premises were devised by the sd. Silvester Thatcher deceased father of the said Sylvester Thatcher and the heirs of his body by his last will and testament dated 18 July 1718 which sd. Sylvester Thatcher the son dying without issue, the said premises came to and vested in John Thatcher deceased and William Thatcher, two other sons of the said testator for their lives by virtue of the aforesd. will, and the sd. John Thatcher being dead the moiety or half part of the sd. premises hereby granted is thereby come to and vested in the sd. Thomas Thatcher who is now actually seized in fee simple in possession and is also seized of the reversion of the other moiety or half part of the sd. premises after the death of the sd. William Thatcher as heir at law of the sd. testator as aforesd. Signed Thomas Thatcher. Delivered in presence of Max Robinson, T. Turner, Harry Turner. Recorded 7 June 1734 T. Turner.

1A:286 - DEED OF RELEASE - 7 June 1734 - Thomas Thatcher of the county of King George and Catherine his wife to Nicholas Smith of same. 75 pounds lawfull money of Virginia for 250A described in lease. Signed Thomas Thatcher. Delivered in presence of Max Robinson, T. Turner, Harry Turner. Recorded 7 June 1734 T. Turner.

1A:288 - BOND - 7 June 1734 - Thomas Thatcher of the county of King George, planter, bound unto Nicholas Smith in the sum of 150 pounds. Condition such that if Thomas Thatcher shall keep all and every the agreements mentioned in one Indenture of Release bearing even date with these presents made between the bound Thomas Thatcher and Catherine his wife of the one part and Nicholas Smith of the other part, obligation to be void. Signed Thomas Thatcher. Delivered in presence of Max Robinson, T. Turner, Harry Turner. Recorded 7 June 1734 T. Turner.

1A:289 - DEED OF LEASE - 6 June 1734 - William Redman and Ann Redman his wife, the only daughter and sole heirs of Thomas Philpin, of King George County, planter, to Gowen Corbin of King and Queen County, Esqr. 5 shillings lawfull money of great Britain to lease 100A bounded between Omen Creek and Keys Swamp. Part of a dividend of land belonging to James Key and by him sold to Thomas Philpin, father of the aforesaid Ann Redman, by deed dated 6 December 1686. Signed William Redman, Ann Redman. Delivered in presence of Wm. Thornton, Jno. Gilbert. Recorded 7 June 1734 T. Turner.

1A:290 - DEED OF RELEASE - 7 June 1734 - William Redman and Ann Redman his wife, the only daughter and sole heirs of Thomas Philpin, of King

George County, planter, to Gowen Corbin of King and Queen County, Esqr. 40 pounds good lawfull money of Great Britain for 100A described in lease. Signed William Redman, Ann Redman. Delivered in presence of Wm. Thornton, John Gilbert. Recorded 7 June 1734 T. Turner.

1A:291 - DEED OF LEASE - 7 June 1734 - James Jones of Brunswick Parish, bricklayer, to Henry Jones of same, planter. Yearly rent of 1200 pounds tobacco and the Quitrents to lease 100A which William Lampton late of King George County deceased formerly purchased of one John Hopkins and Ann his wife and by his last will and testament bequeathed to his son Samuel Lampton and if he died before he arrived to the age of eighteen between his other three children (William Lampton, Ann Grigsby the wife of John Grigsby, and Joshua Lampton) which sd. Samuel Lampton died before he came to the age of eighteen the sd. William Lampton and Ann Grigsby by virtue of their fathers will became each of them respectfully seized of one-third part of the sd. land which sd. William Lampton, John Grigsby and Ann his wife have sold their thirds unto the above named James Jones. Partly in King George County and partly in Stafford County. Bounded by William Grigsby son of John Grigsby late of Stafford County deceased, by lands of Thomas Grigsby, and by Richard Rosser. Lease is for the natural lives of the sd. Henry Jones and Ann his wife or the longest liver of them or either of them. Leasee to plant 100 leathercoats and Ginitins apple trees, a good peach orchard, and thirty cherry trees. Signed Jas. Jones, Henry Jones. Delivered in presence of Enoch Berry, Charles Jones, Wm. Bowlin. Recorded 7 June 1734 T. Turner.

1A:293 - ESTATE ACCOUNT - No Date Given - Estate of William Miller deceased. Amounts paid to James Roberton, Neal McCormack, Bloomfield Long. A feather bed and furniture, one cow and calf were left legacies to Simon Miller. Account presented into court by John Miller, admr. of the estate of William Miller deceased. Recorded 7 June 1734 T. Turner.

1A:293 - DEED OF GIFT - 5 July 1734 - William Rowley, Senr. in consideration of the love good will and affection which he has and does bear towards his loving son William Rowley of King George County, gives unto sd. son William Rowley and his heirs the plantation and all the land joyning to it of that side of Grants Swamp whereon the said William Rowley, Senr. now lives which sd. land is part of 200A which his father John Rowley late of Stafford County deceased bequeathed to him. Signed Willm. Rowley. Delivered in presence of Jos. Crouch, John Grant. Recorded 5 July 1734 T. Turner.

1A:294 - DEED OF LAND - 5 July 1734 - Benjamin Rush and Amy his wife of Brunswick Parish to James Jones of same. 25 pounds current money of Virginia. Confirms unto James Jones all the said Amy's Right of Dower and thirds at the

Common Law of in and to all those two several plantations and pieces of land. 100A now in the tenure or occupation of Richd. Elkins and 150A now in the tenure or occupation of said Benjamin Rush being part of 1300A formerly granted unto Francis Hail and William Heabert 9 February 1663. The said 250A being sold unto James Jones by Joseph Elkins by lease and release dated 30 and 31 August 1732. Signed Benjamin Rush, Amy Rush. Delivered in presence of Richard Bryan, Will. Rowley, Francis Wofendall. Recorded 5 July 1734 T. Turner.

1A:295 - DEED OF LEASE - 4 July 1734 - Saint John Shropshire of Washington Parish in the county of Westmoreland, Gent., to Samuel Skinker of Hanover Parish, Gent. 5 shillings sterling to lease 124A bounded by Mr. Paul Micou and back line of John Simson's pattent. Part of a tract granted to John Simson deceased 6 June 1666 and by James Phillips late of the parish of St. Marys and county of Richmond deceased sold unto St. John Stropshire clerk of Washington Parish in Westmoreland County deceased, father to the above mentioned St. John Shropshire by indenture dated 3 May 1706. Signed St. John Shropshire. Delivered in presence of T. Lewis, Will. Turbervile, M. Battaley. Recorded 5 July 1734 T. Turner.

1A:296 - DEED OF RELEASE - 5 July 1734 - St. John Stropshire of Washington Parish in the county of Westmoreland, Gent., to Samuel Skinker of Hanover Parish, Gent. 35 pounds current money for 124A described in lease. Signed St. John Stropshire. Delivered in presence of T. Lewis, W. Turbervile, M. Battaley. Recorded 5 July 1734 T. Turner.

1A:298 - DEED OF LEASE - 2 July 1734 - Thomas Grimsley of Hanover Parish, planter, to Robert Rankins of same, planter. 5 shillings current money of Virginia to lease two tracts of land being the moyety or half part of 200A sold formerly by Adam Wofendall unto Thomas Grimsley, Senr. deceased, grandfather to the said Thomas Grimsley party to these presents, by deed dated 2 April 1676. One is a 60A tract bounded by land of the said Robert Rankins, of William Marshall, and of Jeremiah Strother. The other is a 38A tract adjoyning upon the land of William Marshall, of Frances Wofendall, and of William Hudson deceased. Signed Thomas Grimsley, Jane Grimsley. Delivered in presence of Isaac Arnold, Senr., Thomas Arnold, Mary Arnold. Recorded 5 July 1734 T. Turner.

1A:299 - DEED OF RELEASE - 3 July 1734 - Thomas Grimsley of Hanover Parish, planter, to Robert Rankins of same, planter. 5100 pounds good tobacco for two tracts of land described in lease. Signed Thomas Grimsley, Jane Grimsley. Delivered in presence of Isaac Arnold, Thomas Arnold, Mary Arnold. Recorded 5 July 1734 T. Turner.

1A:300 - BOND - 3 July 1734 - Thomas Grimsley of Hanover Parish bound unto Robert Rankins in the sum of 10,200 pounds tobacco. Condition such that if Thomas Grimsley faithfully and honestly keeps all agreements contained in deeds of lease and release dated 2 and 3 July 1734, obligation to be void. Signed Thomas Grimsley. Delivered in presence of Isaac Arnold, Senr., Thomas Arnold, Mary Arnold. Recorded 5 July 1734 T. Turner.

1A:301 - DEED OF LEASE - 29 July 1734 - Robert Jones of the county of Prince William, gent., to Catsby Cock of same, gent. 5 shillings sterling to lease 1470A bounded by Richard Gill, John Woodbridge, Beckwiths, Col. Carters, Turberviles, Hancock Lee, and Col. William Ball. Signed Robert Jones. Delivered in presence of Clement Norman, Will. Woodford, Edw. Barradall, John Grant. Recorded 2 August 1734 T. Turner.

1A:302 - DEED OF RELEASE - 30 July 1734 - Robert Jones of the county of Prince William, gent., to Catsby Cocke of same, gent. 188 pounds 16 shillings for 1470A described in lease. Signed Robert Jones. Delivered in presence of Clement Norman, Wm. Woodford, Edw. Barradall, John Grant. Recorded 2 August 1734 T. Turner.

1A:304 - BOND - 30 July 1734 - Robert Jones of the county of Prince William, gent., bound unto Catesby Cocke of same, gent., in the sum of 377 pounds 20 shillings. Condition such that if Robert Jones do well and truly keep all and singular agreements mentioned in certain deeds of lease and release dated 29 and 30 of this Instant July, obligation to be void. Signed Robert Jones. Delivered in presence of Clement Norman, Wm. Woodford, Edw. Barradall, John Grant. Recorded 2 August 1734 T. Turner.

1A:304 - DEED OF LEASE - 2 August 1734 - Samuel Skinker of Hanover Parish to Patrick Hamerick of Brunswick Parish. Patrick Hamerick to lease the tenement and tract of land whereon he now liveth. Bounded by John Popham, Benjamin Stribling, and the said Samuel Skinker. Lease is for and during the term of the natural lives of the sd. Patrick Hamerick and Margaret his wife or the longest liver of them. The first two years next ensuing he is to pay 692 pounds tobacco yearly and every year after to pay 800 pounds and cask. Signed Saml. Skinker, Patrick Hamrick. Delivered in presence of Jos. Strothers, Saml. Hearne. Recorded 2 August 1734 T. Turner.

1A:305 - DEED OF LEASE - 2 August 1734 - Wm. Thornton, Charles Carter, and Henry Fitzhugh the younger, Gentlemen Directors and Trustees for the Town of Falmouth to John Champe, Gent., of King George County. Whereas the said John Champe by a good deed of conveyance dated 4 October 1728 purchased Lot 28 in the town of Falmouth of John Warner of the county of

Stafford, but did not build a house within two years, the lot is revested in the Trustees and lyable to the purchase of any other person. No other person having moved for the sd. lott, the Trustees upon the petition of the sd. Champe (he the said Champe paying all charges) agreed to confirm unto him the sd. lot or half acre of land, if he pays the quitrents to the Proprietor and builds on the lott one framed house of brick, stone, or wood twenty foot square and nine foot pitch at least within two years after the date of this present deed. Signed Chs. Carter, Henry Fitzhugh, Junr. Delivered in presence of John Grant, Wm. Thornton, Junr. Recorded 2 August 1734 T. Turner.

1A:306 - DEED OF LEASE - 2 August 1734 - Wm. Thornton, Charles Carter and Henry Fitzhugh the younger, gentlemen Directors and Trustees for the Town of Falmouth to John Champe, gent., of King George County. Whereas John Champe by deed dated 1 October 1728 was possessed of two tenements of land containing one acre being within the town of Falmouth numbered 29 and 30 according to the platt thereof and the said John Champe not having built a house within two years of the said deed, the lotts are revested in the Trustees and lyable to the choice of purchase of any other person. No other person having moved for the said lotts, the Trustees upon the petition of the said Champe (he paying all the charges) agreed to confirm unto him the sd. two lotts if he pays the quitrents to the Proprietor and erects on each lot one framed house of brick, stone, or wood twenty foot square and nine foot pitched at least within two years. Signed Chas. Carter, Henry Fitzhugh, Junr. Delivered in presence of John Grant, Wm. Thornton, Junr. Recorded 2 August 1734 T. Turner.

1A:307 - DEED - 2 August 1734 - John Champe to Peter Daniell. 12 pounds current money for three lotts or one acre and half of land being within the Town of Falmouth in the county of King George numbered 28, 29, and 30 according to the platt thereof made and laid off by John Warner, surveyor of the sd. county of King George. Signed Jno. Champe. Delivered in presence of John Grant, Wm. Thornton, Junr. Recorded 2 August 1734 T. Turner.

1A:307 - DEED OF LEASE - 18 August 1734 - Thomas Hughs and Frances his wife of Hanover Parish to Maximilian Robinson of same. 5 shillings to lease 50A bounded by land of the sd. Robinson on the marsh side and land formerly owned by John Birkett deceased now in the possession of Daniel French. Signed Thom. Hughs, Frances Hughs. Delivered in presence of Clapham Richardson, Stephen Bowen, William Pannill. Recorded 1 November 1734 T. Turner.

1A:309 - DEED OF RELEASE - 19 August 1734 - Thomas Hughs and Frances his wife of Hanover Parish to Maximilian Robinson of same. 50 pounds current money for 50A described in lease. Part of a patent granted to Peter Mills for 400A which came to be the rights of Peter Mills his son who dying without issue it descended to Ann and Elizabeth his sisters. Elizabeth, the mother of the within mentioned Francis Hughs party to these presents, in her marriage with William Pannel had her part laid off by Charles Smith surveyor 12 April 1703 by agreement with those having a right to the other half which sd. land is where formerly Thomas Hughs lived at and the place where Southings ferry is kept. Signed Thos. Hughs, Frances Hughs. Delivered in presence of Clapham Richardson, Stephen Bowen, William Pannill. Recorded 1 November 1734 T. Turner.

1A:311 - DEED OF LEASE - 18 August 1734 - Thomas Hughs and Frances his wife of Hanover Parish to Clapham Richardson of same. 5 shillings to lease 150A bounded by land formerly John Birkits (now in the possession of Daniel French), the line of Col. William Robinson, and Jno. Payne's line. Signed Thos. Hughs, Frances Hughs. Delivered in presence of Max Robinson, William Pannill, Stephen Bowen. Recorded 1 November 1734 T. Turner.

1A:311 - DEED OF RELEASE - 19 August 1734 - Thomas Hughs and Frances his wife of Hanover Parish to Clapham Richardson of same. 100 pounds current money of Virginia for 150A described in lease. Part of a pattent granted to Peter Mills for 400A which came to be the right of Peter Mills his son who dying without issue it descended to Ann and Elizabeth his sisters. Elizabeth, mother of the within mentioned Frances Hughs party to these presents, in her marriage with Wm. Pannel had her part laid off by Charles Smith surveyor 12 April 1703 by agreement of those having a right to the other half. Signed Thomas Hughs, Frances Hughs. Delivered in presence of Max Robinson, William Pannill, Stephen Bowen. Recorded 1 November 1734 T. Turner.

1A:313 - DEED - 30 October 1734 - John Jett of Washington Parish in the county of Westmorland to Christopher Edrington of Hanover Parish. 25 pounds current money for 86A bounded by a branch of Thatchers Dam called the fork, land of Francis James, and a small branch which runeth out of the fork and near to the main road. Signed John Jett. Delivered in presence of Wm. Edwards, Wm. Edrington, Char. Hay. Gladis, wife of John Jett, acknowledged her free consent thereto. Recorded 1 November 1734 T. Turner.

1A:314 - DEED - 29 October 1734 - Maxfield Brown of Hanover Parish, planter, to Isaac Settle of same, planter. 3200 pounds tobacco for 100A whereon the sd. Isaace Settle now liveth. Bounded by John Settles, Senr., Joseph Settle, Joseph _____, Capt. Benja. Strothers. Signed Maxfield Brown. Delivered in presence of Joseph Settle, Std. Lightburn. Recorded 1 November 1734 T. Turner.

1A:316 - DEED OF LEASE - 23 December 1734 - Clapham Richardson of

Hanover Parish, planter, to Thomas Hughs of same, planter. 5 shillings to lease 150A bounded by land formerly John Birkets (now in the possession of Daniel French), line of Colo. William Robinson, and Jno. Payne's line. Signed Clapham Richardson. Delivered in presence of Max Robinson, Wm. Thornton, junr., Wm. Dekins. Recorded 3 January 1734 T. Turner.

1A:317 - DEED OF RELEASE - 24 December 1734 - Clapham Richardson of Hanover Parish, planter, to Thomas Hughs of same, planter. 100 pounds current money of Virginia for 150A described in lease. Signed Clapham Richardson. Delivered in presence of Max Robinson, Wm. Thornton, junr., William Deekins. Elizabeth, wife of Clapham Richardson, acknowledged her free consent thereto. Recorded 3 January 1734 T. Turner.

1A:319 - DEED OF LEASE - 24 August 1734 - Simon Tomison of the county of Spotsylvania, planter, to Thomas Monteith of King George County, merchant. 5 shillings lawfull current money to lease 180A. Signed Simon Tomison. Delivered in presence of Robert Duncan, Thos. Stanton, Junr., Jno. Mann. Recorded 3 January 1734 T. Turner.

1A:319 - DEED OF RELEASE - 26 August 1734 - Simon Tomison of the county of Spotsylvania, planter, to Thomas Monteith of the county of King George, merchant. 30 pounds current money for 180A which the sd. Simon Tomison his grandfather bought of Daniel McCarty. Signed Simon Tomison. Delivered in presence of Robert Duncan, Thos. Stanton, Junr., Jno. Mann. Recorded 3 January 1734 T. Turner.

1A:321 - BOND - 26 August 1734 - Simon Tomison of the county of Spotsylvania bound unto Thomas Monteith of the county of King George in the sum of 200 pounds sterling. Condition such that if Simon Tomison shall forever hereafter defend the said Thomas Monteith in the quiet possession of the sd. parcel of land from all persons claiming by, from or under him or in case of any molestation from any person claiming by any other title, repay the sd. Monteith the sum of thirty pounds and one pistole, obligation to be void. Signed Simon Tomison. Delivered in presence of Robert Duncan, Thos. Stanton, junr., Jno. Mann. Recorded 3 January 1734 T. Turner.

1A:321 - DEED - 7 February 1734 - William Thornton of Brunswick Parish, administrator of the estate of Thomas Benson late of the sd. parish deceased and guardian to the sd. Bensons children, Gent., to John Ambross of same, planter. The said William Thornton has bound three of the sd. Bensons female children (the profits of their estates not being sufficient to maintain them) to the sd. John Ambross to live and abide in the nature and quality of apprentices until each of them shall severally attain the age of eighteen years that is to say Mary Benson born 10 December 1725, Sarah and Ann Benson being twins born 7 October 1730 in all lawfull household employments but not to be obliged without their own consents to work in tobacco unless it be weed plants or to drop or plant and strip it but they may be obliged to tend corn, wheat, pease or any other vatables....or cotton, flax or hemp and the sd. John Ambross may have liberty to assign the sd. apprentices and their services to any other person provided it be with the consent of and approbation of the sd. Thornton and the Court. Signed Wm. Thornton, John Ambross. Delivered in presence of T. Turner, Harry Turner.

1A:322 - ESTATE APPRAISAL - 4 November 1734 - Estate of William Pitman - 2 baggs, 84 foot of plank, 1 pair men's shoes, 804 pounds tobacco, a remnant of Callicoo, Some tarr, one knife, and a grindstone. Appraisers Isaac Arnold, Joshua Farguson, Saml. Reeds. Recorded 7 February 1734. This additional inventory registered in the Inventory Book. No Signature of Clerk.

1A:322 - DEED OF LEASE - 5 March 1734 - Samuel Wharton of Hanover Parish to John Wrenn of same. 5 shillings sterling to lease 80A being the plantation that John Jones now dwells on. Bounded by Thomas Turner, the Gingoteague Run, Henry Long, and the main county road. Signed Saml. Wharton. Delivered in presence of Benja. Adie, James Strother, H. Turner. Recorded 7 March 1734 T. Turner.

1A:323 - DEED OF RELEASE - 5 March 1734 - Saml. Wharton of Hanover Parish to John Wrenn of same. 50 pounds sterling for 80A described in lease. Signed Saml. Wharton. Delivered in presence of Benja. Adie, James Strother, H. Turner. Recorded 7 March 1734 T. Turner.

1A:324 - DEED OF LEASE - 5 March 1734 - William Wood of St. Mark's Parish in the county of Orange, planter, to Rush Hudson of Hanover Parish, planter. 5 shillings sterling for two tracts of land. One 40A tract binding on Colo. Page, John Taylor and Rush Hudson. It is the land whereon Rush Hudson now dwells and whereon Henry Wood formerly lived, on the western side of Poyfresses Creek. A 100A tract whereon George Parsons now dwells and adjoined to the land of Rowland Thornton, John Willis, and Edward Dunnahoo. Formerly purchasesd by Henry Wood, father to the sd. William Wood, of John Hansford. Both tracts descended to the said William as heir at law to the said Henry. Signed William Wood. Delivered in presence of Benja. Adie, John Wrenn, George Parsons. Recorded 7 March 1734 T. Turner.

1A:325 - DEED OF RELEASE - 6 March 1734 - William Wood of St. Mark's Parish in the county of Orange, planter, to Rush Hudson of Hanover Parish, planter. 45 pounds current money for two tracts of land described in lease.

Signed William Wood. Delivered in presence of Benja. Adie, John Wrenn, George Parsons. Recorded 7 March 1734 T. Turner.

1A:327 - DEED OF LEASE - 25 December 1734 - James Jones of Brunswick Parish to Charles Jones of same. 700 pounds good tobacco and cask every year during the life of the sd. Charles Jones and also the life of Mary his wife for 50A that was layd out by Joseph Berry for the thirds of Auly Rush which is bounded by the land of Grace Stuart, Saml. Skinker, Gent., John Owens, and Edward Humpsted. The sd. Charles and Mary his wife agree to pay the Quitrents during their two lives, to plant 100 good apple trees within three years and to have them within a good fence, to make no wast of timber, and to suffer no person to trespass or encroach upon the land. Signed James Jones, Chas. Jones. Delivered in presence of Rowland Thornton, Jno. Naylor, Richd. Griffith. Recorded 7 March 1734 T. Turner.

1A:328 - DEED OF LEASE - 25 December 1734 - James Jones of Brunswick Parish, bricklayer, to William Anderson of Washington Parish in the county of Westmorland, joyner. 800 pounds tobacco to be paid in one cask every year during the life of the sd. William Anderson and also during the life of Ann his wife to lease 220A whereon the sd. William and Ann his wife now liveth. Part whereof lyeth in the county of King George and parish of Hanover and part whereof in the county of Wesmorland and parish of Washington. Bounded by lands of James Dishman, William Dowling, William Duff, the widdow Thomas, the widdow Berryman, James Cash, and John Heath. William Anderson and Ann his wife agree to plant 100 apple trees within three years and to keep a good fence around the orchard, to pay the quitrents during the term of their two lives, and to have liberty of timber as pine or poplar or any other that will suit shop work excepting such as will make board timber for the use of the plantation neither to suffer any board timber to lye rotting in the ground. The sd. Jones to lett the sd. Anderson have as many nails as will build a sixteen foot dwelling house planked above and below and to cause a dividing line between John Roach and the sd. Anderson to be done this year. Signed James Jones, Wm. Anderson. Delivered in presence of Rowland Thornton, Jno. Naylor, Richd. Griffith. Recorded 7 March 1734 T. Turner.

1A:329 - ARTICLES OF AGREEMENT - 7 March 1734 - Between John Champe of King George County and Thomas Hunter his servant, blacksmith. Thomas Hunter will learn one Negro man named Prince a slave belonging to the sd. John Champe the fine art of a Black Smith, or at least to make all manner of ploughs that's necessary for the country's use, narrow and broad hoes, grubing hoes, narrow axes and to learn the sd. Negro to temper all the above sd. work as a workman ought to do, and to shoe horses. Thomas Hunter doth hereby oblige himself to learn the said Negro compleat, to be approved of by any two sufficient blacksmiths such as the said John Champe and the sd. Hunter shall think fit to appoint to try if the sd. Negro be sufficiently learned. John Champe doth hereby agree and promise when the sd. Negro Prince shall be approved and compleat in all the above sd. work, Thoms. Hunter shall be free and clear from all service due. Thomas Hunter doth hereby agree to acquit John Champe from all freedom dues and that he will not sett up any shop nor work with any person whatsoever within twenty miles of the sd. John Champe. Signed John Champe, Thos. Hunter. Recorded 7 March 1734 T. Turner.

1A:329 - DEED OF LEASE - 11 January 1734 - William Thornton of Brunswick Parish, Gent., to John Hinshaw of same, house carpenter. To lease plantation whereon the said Hinshaw now lives for and during the term of the natural lives of Hinshaw and his present wife Ellinor Hinshaw, but not liberty to sell or assign the lease to any other person. Rent to be 930 pounds tobacco in one cask for two years, then to be clear of paying rent for one year. This method of paying two years and missing one to continue during the whole of the lease. Signed Wm. Thornton, John Hinshaw. Delivered in presence of Margaret Deakins, John Dermot, William Thornton, junr. Memorandum - John Hinshaw having delivered up the lease to Wm. Thornton, he assigns it unto James Hawkins and his wife Mary during their natural lives. Signed Wm. Thornton, James Hawkins. Recorded 4 April 1735 T. Turner.

1A:330 - DEED OF LEASE - 25 December 1734 - James Jones of Brunswick Parish, bricklayer, to William Fewell of same, carpenter. 700 pounds tobacco and cask to be paid yearly by the sd. William and Susanna his wife to lease 70A for their natural lives. Land bought of Joseph Ellkin and bounded by Grace Stuart, a new line made for Charles Jones, Edward Humstead, and Cashes ground. The sd. William and Susanna his wife agree to plant 100 apple trees and to keep them within a close fence, to pay the quitrents of the sd. land during their two lives, and to make no wast of timber. Signed Jas. Jones, Wm. Fewell. Delivered in presence of Peter Daniel, Abraham Kenyan, Charles Jones. Recorded 4 April 1735 T. Turner.

1A:331 - DEED OF LEASE - 5 December 1718 - Edward Leman of London linnen draper son and heir of Edward Leman late citizen and tallow chandler of London deceased to John Lomax of Essex County in Virginia, Gent. 21 pounds lawfull money of Great Britain to lease 400A lying in the freshes of Rappahannock River on the northside of same and a little above Taliaferro's Mount. Part of a patent of 5275A granted unto Thomas Chetwood and John Prosser, planters, 28 September 1667. The division thereof made by deed dated 26 July 1668. Cuthbert Potter bought land of the sd. Chetwood by deed 14 November 1668 and sold the 400A to Edward Leman 4 April 1688. Signed Edward Leman. Delivered in presence of Ann Turner, Sarah Turner, G.

Braxton, John Salter, William Moseley, Jere. Murdock. Lunsford Lomax presented into Court this deed from Edward Leman of London together with the receipt for the consideration money therein mentioned which was proved by the oath of Jeremiah Murdock, gent., Ann Turner, and Sarah Dick (late Sarah Turner). Recorded 4 April 1735 T. Turner.

1A:335 - DEED OF GIFT - 4 April 1735 - Elizabeth Day gives to Sarah Day her daughter one cow and calf, one feather bed and furniture, and fifteen pounds of new Pewter at her wedding day. Signed Elizabeth Day. Witness George Bush. Recorded 4 April 1735 T. Turner.

1A:336 - BOND - 26 December 1729 - Robert Richards of the county of King George bound unto John Savage of the county of Stafford (in the behalf of the daughters Anna and Elizabeth of Mr. Skrine deceased) in the sum of two hundred pounds sterling. Condition such that whereas Robert Richards by intermarrying with Margaret, widow of the above named William Skrine, hath taken the estate as appraised by Colo. Nicholas Smith admr. into his custody in which estate there is three negro children (Bristol, Billy, and Jefferey) born of a Negro wench called Nann. Now if the sd. Robert Richards his heirs Exctrs. or Admtors. do either upon the day of marriage or at the age of eighteen years deliver and pay unto the sd. Anna Skrine the aforesd. Negroes Bristol and Jefferey, if they or either of them do live, and likewise to the sd. Elizabeth Skrine at the age or day of marriage aforesd. the above mentioned negro Billy with the next child be it male or female the above sd. Negro Nanny is delivered of, if the sd. Negro child or others of them do live and likewise if either of the sd. children Anna or Elizabeth should happen to die before they arrive at the above sd. age or before the day of marriage then all the right to be invested in the survivor. Now if both die before the days aforesd. or on the contrary, if the sd. Robert Richards his heirs etc. doth justly and truly perform the aforesd. conditions and agreements, obligation to be void. Signed Robt. Richards. Delivered in presence of Margaret Richards, John Dermod. John Savage presented the above bond under the hand and seale of Robert Richards deceased which was proved by the oath of John Dermod and admitted to record. Recorded 2 May 1735 T. Turner.

1A:336 - KING"S ASSENT - At the Court of St. James the first day of November 1733. (List of Lords present) Whereas the Leiutenant Governor of his Majesty's Province of Virginia with the Council and Assembly of the said Province did in the year 1732 pass an Act Intitled An Act for sealing certain entail'd Lands, with the Appurtanances therein mentioned, in Thomas Turner in Fee Simple and for Settleing other land and Negroes of greater value to the same uses. And whereas the sd. Act together with a representation from the Lords Commissioners for trade and Plantations there upon have been referred to the Consideration of a Committee of the Lords of his Majesty's most honourable Privy Council for Plantation Affairs, the sd. Lords of the Committee did this day report their Opinion to his Majesty that the sd. Act was proper to be Approved. His Majesty in Council taking the same into consideration was graciously pleased to Declare his Approbation of the sd. Act and Pursuant to his Majesties royal Pleasure thereupon expresssed, the said Act is hereby Confirmed finally Enacted and ratified accordingly. Whereof the Governor, Leiutenant Governor, or Commander in Chief of his Majesties province of Virginia for the time being and all others whom it may concern are to take notice and govern themselves accordingly. Signed W. Sharpe. By the Governors Command Truly recorded in the Secretary's office in the Book of Proclamations. Test. Matt Kenipe. Thomas Turner presented the above assent into Court which on his motion was admitted to record. Recorded 2 May 1735 T. Turner.

1A:337 - DEED OF GIFT - 26 April 1735 - Catherine Plail of Hanover Parish to Richard Plail and John Plail her two sons of same. For the love and affection that she has for her two sons and for divers other good and valuable considerations, Catherine Plail gives her sons 100A to be divided between them. Richard to have the plantation and land next adjoining to make up the one half or fifty acres. Signed Catherine Plail. Delivered in presence of John Canaday, John Parsons, Thomas Reeds. By virtue of a power of attorney, William Robinson , Gent., acknowledged this deed of gift from Catherine to her two sons. Recorded 2 May 1735 T. Turner.

1A:338 - POWER OF ATTORNEY - 1 May 1735 - Catherine Plail of Hanover Parish appoints Colo. William Robinson her lawfull attorney to acknowledge a deed for land which she has made to her two sons. Signed Catherine Plaile. Delivered in presence of John Canaday, Thomas Reeds. Recorded 2 May 1735 T. Turner.

1A:339 - DEED OF LEASE - 25 March 1735 - Charles Carter, Esq., of King George County to Benjamin Robinson, Gent., of the county of Caroline. One pound of tobacco yearly to lease lott number 14 in the Town called Charles Town during the sd. Charles Carter's natural life. The sd. Benjamin Robinson will pay the quitrents of the sd. lot or half acre yearly and every year during the sd. term. Lott is part of greater tract of the sd. Carter's containing 333A, 50A being laid off for the town. Signed Chs. Carter. Delivered in presence of Saml. Poirier, W. Loney, Geo. Taylor. Memorandum that full possession of the lot had been given in June 1735 signed by Geo. Taylor, W. Loney, and Wm. Stevens. Recorded 6 June 1735 T. Turner.

1A:339 - DEED OF LEASE - 25 March 1735 - Charles Carter, Esq., of King George County to William Woodford, Gent., of the county of Caroline. One pound of tobacco yearly to lease lot number 12 in the Town called Charles Town during the sd. Charles Carter's natural life. William Woodford will pay the quitrents of the sd. lot or half acre yearly and every year during the sd. term. Lott is part of greater tract of the sd. Carter's containing 333A, 50A being laid off for the town. Signed Chs. Carter. Delivered in presence of Saml. Poirier, W. Loney, Geo. Taylor. Memorandum that full possession of the lot had been given in June 1735 signed by Geo. Taylor, W. Loney, and Wm. Stevens. Recorded 6 June 1735 T. Turner.

1A:340 - DEED OF LEASE - 25 March 1735 - Charles Carter, Esq., of King George County to John Taliaferro, Gent., of the county of Caroline. One pound of tobacco yearly to lease lot number 17 in the Town called Charles Town during the sd. Charles Carter's natural life. John Taliaferro will pay the quitrents of the sd. lot or half acre yearly and every year during the sd. term. Lott is part of greater tract of the sd. Carter's containing 333A, 50A being laid off for the town. Signed Chs. Carter. Delivered in presence of Saml. Poirier, W. Loney, Geo. Taylor. Memorandum that full possession of the lot had been given 5 June 1735 signed by Geo. Taylor, W. Loney, and Wm. Stevens. Recorded 6 June 1735 T. Turner.

1A:341 - DEED OF LEASE - 25 March 1735 - Charles Carter, Esq., of King George County to Matthias Job Banks of same. One pound of tobacco yearly to lease lot number 7 in the Town called Charles Town during the sd. Charles Carter's natural life. Matthias Job Banks will pay the quitrents of the sd. lot or half acre yearly and every year during the sd. term. Lott is part of greater tract of the sd. Carter's containing 333A, 50A being laid off for the town. Signed Chs. Carter. Delivered in presence of Mercer, Alexdr. Bell. Memorandum that full possession of the lot had been given 3 June 1735 signed by Geo. Taylor, W. Loney, and Wm. Stevens. Recorded 6 June 1735 T. Turner.

1A:342 - DEED OF LEASE - 5 June 1735 - William Duling of Hanover Parish, planter, to Thomas Turner of same, surgeon. 5 shillings sterling to lease 184A bounded by lands of Robert Peck, Sem Cox, and Peter Butler. Signed William Duling. Delivered in presence of Thos. Stribling, Wm. Thornton, junr., Harry Turner. Elizabeth, wife of William Duling, acknowledged the deed of lease. Recorded 3 October 1735 T. Turner.

1A:343 - DEED OF RELEASE - 6 June 1735 - William Duling of Hanover Parish, planter, to Thomas Turner of same, surgeon. 30 pounds current money for 184A described in lease. Signed William Duling. Delivered in presence of Thos. Stribling, Wm. Thornton, junr., Harry Turner. Elizabeth, wife of William Duling, acknowledged her free consent to the deed of release. Recorded 3 October 1735 T. Turner.

1A:345 - DEED OF LEASE - 2 July 1735 - Charles Dean of Hanover Parish, planter, to William Dean brother to the sd. Charles Dean of same, planter. 5 shillings current money of Virginia to lease 100A bounded by Colo. Nicholas Smith deceased. Part of a tract left to the sd. Charles Dean by his father John Dean. Signed Charles Deane. Delivered in presence of John Lowen, James Drake. Recorded 3 October 1735 T. Turner.

1A:346 - DEED OF RELEASE - 30 June 1735 - Charles Deane of Hanover Parish, planter, to William Deane brother to the sd. Charles Deane of same, planter. 4000 pounds tobacco for 100A described in lease. Signed Charles Deane. Delivered in presence of John Lowen, James Drake. Recorded 3 October 1735 T. Turner.

1A:347 - DEED OF GIFT - 1 June 1735 - John Corbin, Senior of Brunswick Parish for and in regard of the natural affection he bears to his loving son John Corbin, junr. gives the aforesd. John Corbin 50A of land bounded by Stephen Hansford and a branch of Lambs Creek. Signed John Corbin. Delivered in presence of John Grant, Sacheveral Norman, John Coburn. Recorded 3 October 1735 T. Turner.

1A:348 - DEED OF LAND - 1 August 1735 - John Corbin of Brunswick Parish, planter, to John Grant of same, planter. 2500 pounds tobacco and 10 shillings current money for 50A bounded by the mouth of a spring branch running near the line of Daniel Grant and by Stephen Hansford. Signed John Corbin. Delivered in presence of Bryant Chadwell, John Corbin, Junr., Willm. Reardon, David Bronaugh. Recorded 3 October 1735 T. Turner.

1A:349 - DIVISION OF ESTATE - 5 November 1735 - In obedience to an order of King George County Court dated 6 June 1735 two whose names are hereunto subscribed met at the house of Margaret Richards on 5 November 1735 and there have divided the estate of Robert Richards deceased according to his last will and testament. To Margaret Richards, widdow of Robert Richards, went Negroes Breeches, Sebe, Nanny, Jenny; Turner a boy of four years to serve; and various livestock and household goods (listed). To Frances Richards went Negroes Charles, Ben, Pegg, Sarah, and various livestock and household goods (listed). Margaret Richards was allotted the plantations of James Latham and Isaac Nichols with 238A being the one moiety of what lands Robert Richards deceased died possessed of. Frances Richards was allotted the plantations whereon Anthony Mefelin and Franklin Latham now live with 238A being the one moiety of what lands Robt. Richards deceased died possessed of. Three negroes, Bristoll, Coburn and Cano to be delivered to Anna Skrine and Elizabeth Skrine at their coming of full age or day of marriage. All the rest of the estate divided into two equal parts, valued at 145 pounds 17 shillings each going to Margaret Richards the widow and Frances Richards the only surviving child of Robert Richards. Signed John Champe, Jereh. Bronaugh, John Steward. Recorded 7 November 1735 T. Turner.

1A:350 - DIVISION OF ESTATE - 1 December 1735 - Persuant to an order of the sd. County Court bearing date 7 November 1735, the subscribers met at the house of Danl. McCarty, Gent., and divided the land, Negroes and stocks of cattle belonging to the estate of Nicholas Smith deceased and assigned one third thereof for the dower of Elizabeth, relict of the sd. Nicholas and now wife of the sd. Daniel as follows - the mansion house together with all the land adjoining thereto between Spicers Mill run perpetic run and Potomack River; one third of what profits shall or may arise of an 800A tract lying in Prince William County near the Marsh in full for the sd. Elizabeth's right of dower of all the lands belonging to the said Nicholas; twelve negroes Martin, Will, Phill, Boatswain, Anthony, Guiniver, Toby, Lewis, Daniel, George, David, and Ester; and 21 head of old cattle, seven yearlings, five sows, and five calves. Signed Max Robinson, Lunsford Lomax, T. Turner. Recorded 5 December 1735 T. Turner.

1A:351 - DEED OF GIFT - 5 December 1735 - Honour Richardson for and in consideration of the natural love and affection which she beareth unto her daughters and grandchildren gives her daughter Mary Hughs half of a 600A tract, which was given by her father John Barrow by his last will and testament dated 3 February 1684 unto his three sons Moses, Alexander, and Gonathan intail and for want of heirs of their bodies to his daughters Honour and Chisley and at the death of Chisley, the same is vested in the sd. Honour, and also 50A more of the sd. tract. After her decease, land to go to grand daughters Anne Hughs and Frances Hughs equally to be divided. For default of lawfully begotten heirs, land to go to the heirs of the sd. Mary Hughs lawfully begotten. All the remainder of the said tract she gives unto her daughter Elizabeth Yates. Signed Honour Richardson. Delivered in presence of Robt. Taylor, John Spencer, Geo. Payne. Secondly, she gives her grandchildren Anne Hughs and Frances Hughs one half of a tract called the black neck and all her moveable estate, cattle, hoggs, horses, and all other things belonging to her and the use of them to her daughter Mary Hughs during her life. Signed Honour Richardson. By virtue of a power of attorney, William Remey acknowledged the deed of gift. Recorded 5 December 1735 T. Turner.

1A:352 - POWER OF ATTORNEY - 5 December 1735 - Honour Richardson widow of Hanover Parish appoints William Remey to acknowledge her right and title to her land and tenements, cattle and other removeables in a Deed of Gift. Signed Honour Richardson. Delivered in presence of Robt. Taylor, Richard Golding, Thos. Wood. Recorded 5 December 1735 T. Turner.

1A:352 - DEED OF LEASE - 7 November 1735 - Benjamin Taylor of Orange County, planter, and Elinor his wife to John Coburn of King George County, planter. 5 shillings sterling to lease 150A bounded by a branch of Lambs Creek, the back line of the riverside pattent of John and George Mott, and land formerly belonging unto Peter Gallon. Part of a 400A tract out of a patent formerly granted to John and George Mott and by them given by Deed of Gift unto John Vickarys and by him unto his son Nathaniel Vickarys and by him sold unto Thomas Taylor, father of the sd. Benjamin Taylor, which sd. Thomas Taylor by his last will and testament dated 29 March 1712 devised the sd. 150A unto his three sons Thomas, Benjamin, and John Taylor of which three sons Benjamin Taylor is the only survivor. Signed Benjamin Taylor, Elinor Taylor. Delivered in presence of M. Battaley, Hen. McKie, Dav. Seale, John Corbin. Recorded 5 December 1735 T. Turner.

1A:353 - DEED OF RELEASE - 8 November 1735 - Benjamin Taylor of Orange County, planter, and Elinor his wife to John Coburn of King George County, planter. 30 pounds current money of Virginia for 150A described in lease. Signed Benjamin Taylor, Elinor Taylor. Delivered in presence of M. Battaley, Hen. McKie, David Seale, John Corbin. Recorded 5 December 1735 T. Turner.

2:1 - DEED OF LEASE - 10 May 1735 - _____ and Elinor his wife, Richard Elkins and Mary his wife, and Robert _____ and Ann his wife, Daughters and Coheirs of Robert Gallop late of the county of King George deceased, to George James of _____, planter. 5 shillings current money to lease 250A being on both sides of Deep Run issuing out of Rappahannock River about twelve miles above the falls. Bounded by Roger Abby. Granted unto Bryan Foley and Roger Gollop, father of the sd. Elinor, Mary, and Ann, by deed dated 27 February 1714/5. Signed James Brissee, Elinor Brissee, Richd. Elkins, Mary Elkins, Robt. Duncom, Ann Duncom. Delivered in presence of M. Battaley, Antho. Hayney, John Ambros. Recorded 6 February 1735 T. Turner.

2:3 - DEED OF RELEASE - 11 May 1735 - _____ and Elinor his wife, Richard Elkins and Mary his wife, and Robert _____ and Ann his wife, Daughters and Coheirs of Robert Gollop deceased, to George James of the county of Stafford, planter. 25 pounds current money of Virginia for 250A described in lease. Signed James Brissee, Ellinor Brissee, Richard Ellkins, Mary Ellkins, Robert Duncom, Ann Duncom. Delivered in presence of M. Battaley, Antho. Haynie, John Ambros. Recorded 6 February 1735 T. Turner.

2:6 - DEED OF DOWER - 11 May 1735 - John Owens of the county of King George, planter, and Elinor his wife, late widdow and relect of Robert Gollop deceased, to George James of the county of Stafford, planter. 5 pounds current money to quit claim the tract of land granted unto Bryan Foley and him the said Robert Gollop by deed dated 27 February 1714/5 whereof the sd. Elinor is by law intitled to her Dower which sd. tract upon the death of the sd. Robert Gollop came to and vested in his four daughters Mary, Ann, Elinor, and Phillis three of whom with James Brissee, Richard Ellkins and Robert Duncom their several husbands sold and conveyed their right, title and interest thereto to the sd. George James. Signed John Owens, Elinor Owens. Delivered in presence of James Lovell, M. Battaley, Antho. Haynie. Recorded 6 February 1735 T. Turner.

2:7 - ESTATE DIVISION - 16 December 1735 - Pursuant to an order of King George County Court dated the sixth day of December 1735 we whose names are hereunto subscribed being sworn before John Cham__, gent., have divided the estate of John Naylor deceased the sixteenth day of the same according to the purport of the sd. order as follows. To Ann Naylor the Widdow - Negro man Fanley, Negro woman Mary, white servant man, and various livestock, household goods, and tools (listed). For Hanah Naylor a Daughter - a Negro man Mingo, a Negro girl Winnie, a Negro girl Sukey and various livestock, household goods, and tools (listed). To Eliza. Naylor a Daughter - a Negro man Joe, a Negro woman Sary, a Negro boy Charles, and various livestock, household goods, and tools (listed). Signed Wm. Thornton, Robt. Doniphan, Stephen Hansford. John Champe certifies that the subscribers were sworn before him to make this division. Recorded 6 February 1735 T. Turner.

2:9 - DEED OF LEASE - 4 March 1735 - Mason French of the county of Westmorland, planter, and Catherine his wife to Farquhar Mathewson of the county of Stafford, Gent. 5 shillings sterling to lease 272A butting on the lands of Henry Fitzhugh, Esqr., Colo. William Thornton, Mr. Daniel French, and Mr. Hugh French. Signed Mason French, Cath. French. Delivered in presence of Anthony Thornton, William Dick, _____ Hooe. Recorded 5 March 1735 T. Turner.

2:10 - DEED OF RELEASE - 5 March 1735 - Mason French of the county of Westmorland, planter, and Catherine his wife to Farquhar Mathewson of the county of Stafford, Gent. 7180 pounds tobacco for 272A described in lease. Signed Mason French, Cath. French. Delivered in presence of Anthony Thornton, William Dick, Rice Hooe. Recorded 5 March 1735 T. Turner.

2:13 - INDENTURE - 2 December 1735 - Thomas Aims of King George County doth put himself apprentice to Isaac Johnson of same to learn his art trade or mistery of a Sadler during the full term of four years and a half next ensuing. Signed Thoms. Aims, Isaac Johnson. Delivered in presence of Thos. Gearing, Adcock Hobson. Recorded 5 March 1735 T. Turner.

2:13 - DEED OF LEASE - 22 March 1735 - Elizabeth Berryman, widdow of Westmorland County, and Willoughby Newton of same, Gent. to Benjamin Berryman of the county of King George, Gent. 5 shillings sterling to lease 750A that is part of a 1000A tract granted to Thomas Corley and John Noble 26 October 1666 between the great falls and the little falls. Thomas Corley conveyed the 1000A of land, which fell to him by survivorship, by deed dated 24 August 1685 to Alexander Swan and the sd. Alexander Swan conveyed 250A to William Smith by deed dated 30 May 1691. Alexander Swan conveyed the remainder of the 1000A to John Newton by deed dated 23 December 1695. Signed Eliza. Berryman, Willoughby Newton. Delivered in presence of Howson Kennet, Adam Crump, Willm. Taylor, Wm. Clark, John Smith, _____ Foote, James Berryman, Sarah Berryman. Recorded 2 April 1736 T. Turner.

2:15 - DEED OF RELEASE - 24 March 1735 - Elizabeth Berryman and Willoughby Newton to Benjamin Berryman of King George County. 8000 pounds good tobacco for 750A described in lease. Signed Eliza. Berryman, Willoughby Newton. Delivered in presence of Howsen Kennet, Adam Crump, Willm. Taylor, Willm. Clark, John Smith, George Foote, James Berryman, Sarah Berryman. Recorded 2 April 1736 T. Turner.

2:17 - DEED OF LEASE - 26 March 1736 - Scarlet Hancock of the county of Prince William, Gent., to John Tayloe of the county of Richmond, Esqr. 5 shillings good and lawfull money of Virginia to lease 337A lying in the parish of Brunswick. It is the land whereon John Gilbert and William Fickling now live and that was sold by Mr. John Fossaker to Colo. George Mason of Stafford County by deed dated 28 March 1692 and by the sd. Mason sold and conveyed unto Martin Scarlet by deed dated 1 May 1694 and by the said Martin Scarlet given and devised by his last will and testament bearing date 5 January 1705/6 unto William Smith son of Edward and Lettice Smith and in case of the said William's death before he attained twenty-one years of age, to the heirs of the aforesd. Littice Smith forever, who is the Scarlet Hancock partie to these presents. Bounded by Richard Shipway, Parson Waugh, and sunken land which divides the land hereby granted from John Fossicar. Signed Scarlet Hancock. Delivered in presence of Hugh Adie, Henry Elly, Wm. Williams, John Dennis. Recorded 2 April 1736 T. Turner.

2:18 - DEED OF RELEASE - 25 March 1736 - Scarlet Hancock of Prince William County, gent., to John Tayloe of the county of Richmond, Esqr. 150 pounds lawfull current money of Virginia for 337A described in lease. Signed Scarlet Hancock. Delivered in presence of Hugh Adie, Henry Elly, Wm. Williams, John Dennis. Ann, wife of Scarlet Hancock, acknowledged her free consent thereto which on the motion of John Champe, gent., in behalf of the sd. John Tayloe is admitted to record. Recorded 2 April 1736 T. Turner.

2:20 - DEED OF FEEOFMENT - 1 April 1736 - Samuel Prim of the county of King George, planter, and Elizabeth his wife and Martin Francis of same, planter, to George Fishpool of same, gent. 35 pounds current money of Virginia for 50A bounded by land of Edmund Barker, Elinor Whitridge, John Drake, William Doakins, William Tate. Part of land formerly in possession of Martin Fisher the Elder deceased who by his last will and testament dated 11 January 1699 gave all his lands to be equally divided between his son Martin Fisher and his daughter Elizabeth Kitchen, his son Martin to have his first choice and after the death of the sd. Martin Fisher the Elder the sd. land was by consent of the sd. Martin Fisher the younger and the sd. Elizabeth Kitchen equally divided between them and the premises hereby granted is part of the premises laid out and allotted by the division aforesd. for the part of the sd. Elizabeth Kitchen which sd. Elizabeth Kitchen by her deed in writing conveyed and made over unto her daughter the sd. Elizabeth Prim the fifty acres of land hereby granted. Signed Samuel Prim, Elizabeth Prim, Martin Francis. Delivered in presence of Wm. Brockenbrough, Wm. Deane, Thomas Highlander. Recorded 2 April 1736 T. Turner.

2:23 - DEED OF FEEOFMENT - 1 April 1736 - William Tate of the county of King George, planter, and Margaret his wife to George Fishpool of same, Gent. 35 pounds current money of Virginia for 50A bounded by land of Thomas Claytor, Senr., Thomas Claytor, Junr., Christopher Pritchett, and Samuel Prim. It is part of the land formerly in possession of Martin Fisher the Elder deceased whose will dated 11 January 1699 left it to his son Martin Fisher the younger and his daughter Elizabeth Kitchen. The said Elizabeth Kitchen by deed conveyed unto her daughter the sd. Margaret Taite the fifty acres of land hereby granted. (See preseding deed) Signed Wm. Tate, Margt. Taite. Delivered in presence of Wm. Brockenbrough, Wm. Deane, T. Highlander. Recorded 2 April 1736 T. Turner.

2:25 - DEED OF FEEOFMENT - 15 March 1735 - John Dodd, Junior of the county of King George and Ann his wife to Joseph Settle of same. 1400 pounds tobacco for 50A which his father John Dodd bought of John Brown and acknowledged in court to his son John Dodd and Ann his wife by deed of gift dated 1 August 1729. Bounded by Thomas White and the main swamp. Signed John Dodd, Isaac Settle. Recorded 2 April 1736 T. Turner.

2:27 - DEED OF LEASE - 29 April 1736 - William Settle of Hanover Parish, planter, to Richard Green of same, planter. 5 shillings current money of Virginia to lease 50A whereon William Settle now liveth. Part of a pattent of land granted unto William Baltrop, James Green, and Francis Lewis for 1050A. Bounded by the north side of the western main branch of Gengoteague Creek, land of William Duff, a small branch which divides it from land of Robert

Rankins, and land of Alford Head. Signed William Settle. Delivered in presence of Clapham Richardson, Thomas Arnold. Recorded 7 May 1736 T. Turner.

2:29 - DEED OF RELEASE - 30 April 1736 - William Settle of Hanover Parish, planter, to Richard Green of same, planter. 35 pounds current money of Virginia for 50A described in lease. Signed William Settle. Delivered in presence of Clapham Richardson, Thomas Arnold. Recorded 7 May 1736 T. Turner.

2:31 - BOND - 30 April 1736 - William Settle of Hanover Parish bound unto Richard Green of same in the sum of 70 pounds current money of Virginia. Condition such that if William Settle shall forever hereafter truly keep all agreements contained in deeds of lease and release dated 29 and 30 April 1736, obligation to be void. Signed William Settle. Delivered in presence of Clapham Richardson, Thomas Arnold. Recorded 7 May 1736 T. Turner.

2:32 - DEED - No Date Given - Margaret French, widdow of Daniel French late of this county deceased, humbly showeth that the said Daniel died testat but that she is not satisfied with the provision made for her by the sd. will it being as she conceives greatly to her prejudice, and therefore she hereby declares that she will not accept receive or take the legacies by the sd. will to her given and bequeathed or any part of them but doth hereby renounce all benefit and advantage which she may or might claim by the sd. will and therefore she prays that proper persons may be appointed to set apart her lawful part of all her sd. late husbands estate both real and personal. Signed Margaret French. Delivered in presence of Will. Jett, John Pratt. Recorded 4 June 1736 T. Turner.

2:32 - DEED OF LEASE - 2 June 1736 - James Brissee and Elinor his wife, Richard Elkins and Mary his wife, and Robert Duncom and Ann his wife, Daughters and Coheirs of Robert Gollop late of King George County, to George James of Stafford County, planter. 5 shillings current money of Virginia to lease 250A lying on both sides of Deep Run about twelve miles above the falls. Bounded by the west side of the sd. run about two miles and a half from the mouth thereof, land lately surveyed for Rodger Abbet, and by line on east side of sd. run. Granted to Bryan Foley and Robert Gollop father to the sd. Elinor, Mary, and Ann by deed dated 27 February 1714/5. Signed James Brissee, Elinor Brissee, Richd. Ellkins, Mary Ellkins, Robt. Duncom, Ann Duncom. Delivered in presence of M. Battaley, Alexr. Bell, James Strother. Recorded 4 June 1736 T. Turner.

2:34 - DEED OF RELEASE - 3 June 1736 - James Brissee and Elinor his wife, Richard Ellkins and Mary his wife, and Robert Duncom and Ann his wife, Daughters and Coheirs of Robert Gollop late of the county of King George, to George James of the county of Stafford, planter. 25 pounds current money of

Virginia for 250A described in lease. Signed James Brissee, Elinor Brissee, Richd. Ellkins, Mary Ellkins, Robt. Duncom, Ann Duncom. Delivered in presence of M. Battaley, Alexr. Bell, James Strother. Recorded 4 June 1736.

2:37 - DEED OF LEASE - 6 May 1736 - John Owen of Brunswick Parish, planter, and Elizabeth his wife, to Robert Hughs of same, planter, and Elizabeth his wife. 5 shillings sterling to lease 100A that is part of a pattent granted to the sd. John Owen 8 October 1694. Bounded by north side of county road, branch between William Owen and sd. plantation, corner with Capt. Skinker and Widdow Steward, James Jones, Edward Humstead, Rebecca Ellkins, and Richard Owen. The land which James Jones now holds was Hugh Wms. Signed John Owens. Delivered in presence of Robert Duncom, Henry Foley, John Fletcher. Then came John Owens and Elinor his wife and acknowledged this Deed of Lease to Robert Hughs and the sd. Elinor being solely examined acknowledged her free consent thereto which of the motion of Elizabeth Hughs, his wife, is admitted to record. Recorded 4 June 1736 T. Turner.

2:39 - DEED OF RELEASE - 7 May 1736 - John Owen of Brunswick Parish, planter, and Elinor his wife to Robert Hughs of same, planter, and Elizabeth his wife. 22 pounds current money for 100A described in lease. Signed John Owens, Elinor Owens. Delivered in presence of Robert Duncom, Henry Foley, John Fletcher. Recorded 4 June 1736 T. Turner.

2:41 - BOND - 6 May 1736 - John Owen of Brunswick Parish bound unto Robert Hughs in the sum of 44 pounds current money. Condition such that if John Owen shall truly fulfill all obligations mentioned in Indenture of Release bearing date with these presents, obligation to be void. Signed John Owen. Delivered in presence of Robert Duncom, Henry Foley, John Fletcher. Recorded 4 June 1736 T. Turner.

2:41 - POWER OF ATTORNEY - 30 January 1735 - John Becher of the City of Bristol appoints Samuel Skinker of Rappahannock River in Virginia in America his true and lawfull attorney to ask, demand and receive of and from the representatives of Charles Burgess late of Rappahannock River deceased or any other person or persons whatsoever whom it doth or may concern all and every debt and debts due sums of money merchandize and effects and all amounts of sales, amounts currant, notes, bills, bonds, warrants for confessing, judgments or other specialties and securitys for moneys whatsoever due or belonging to him. Signed John Becher. Delivered in presence of Griffith Smith, Henry Thomson. Recorded 2 July 1736 T. Turner.

2:42 - POWER OF ATTORNEY - 4 March 1735 - Charles Holt of the city of Bristol appoints Capt. Samuel Skinker, merchant in King George County in

Colony of Virginia, his true and lawfull attorney to ask, demand and receive of and from Richard Tutt, planter, all and every such sum or sums of money, goods, wares, merchandize as are due, owing or belonging to him. Signed Charles Holt. Delivered in presence of G. Smith, Geo. Lewis. Recorded 2 July 1736 T. Turner.

2:43 - POWER OF ATTORNEY - 30 June 1736 - George Davis of Goochland County appoints his friend Thomas Hughs to be his attorney and acknowledge a Deed of Sale of land with livery and seizen made to Daniel White the same day with these presents. Signed George Davis. Delivered in presence of Wil. Robinson, John White. Recorded 5 November 1736 T. Turner.

2:44 - DEED OF SALE - 30 June 1736 - George Davis and Patience his wife to Daniel White of King George County, Gent. 16 pounds current money of Virginia for 250A that is the land formerly sold to Nicholas Smith by Richard Jordan and Chisley his wife and now in the actual possession of the sd. Daniel White. The half part of a pattent granted to John Barrow 13 October 1657. Signed George Davis. Delivered in presence of Thomas Hughs, John Whit. Recorded 5 November 1736 T. Turner.

2:46 - ACCOUNTS - 1733 - Jeremiah Murdock, Gent., came into Court and made oath that the balance of 808 pounds tobacco is justly due from James Boddington to Messr. Scandrets of Bristol shown by accounts recorded. (Thomas Gough and Isaac Green are only persons mentioned in accounts.) Recorded 7 May 1736 T. Turner.

2:46 - ACCOUNTS - 1733 - Jeremiah Murdock, Gent., came into Court and made oath that the balance of 2667 pounds tobacco is justly due to him from James Boddington as shown by accounts recorded. (Wm. Kitchen and Capt. Benja. Strother are only persons mentioned in the accounts.) Recorded 7 May 1736 T. Turner.

2:47 - DEED OF LEASE - 3 November 1736 - George Underwood of Sittenbourn Parish to John Triplett of same and John Fox of Washington Parish in the county of Westmorland. 5 shillings sterling to lease all the reversion of a Pattent of Land granted to Willm. Underwood dated 10 September 1658. Signed George Underwood. Delivered in presence of Isaac Arnold, William Harvie, Original Brown. Recorded 5 November 1736 T. Turner.

2:48 - DEED OF RELEASE - 4 November 1736 - George Underwood of Hanover Parish to John Triplet of same and John Fox of Washington Parish in the county of Westmorland. 30 pounds current money of Virginia for tract of land described in lease. Signed George Underwood. Delivered in presence of

Isaac Arnold, William Harvey, Original Brown. Recorded 5 November 1736 T. Turner.

2:50 - DEED OF LEASE - 28 October 1736 - Edward Turbervile of the county of King George, planter, to John Champe of same, Gentleman. 5 shillings sterling to lease 150A lying in Brunswick Parish. Part of 400A given by John and George Mott deceased unto John Vickars also deceased and by him to his son Nathaniel Vickars and by him sold unto Thomas Taylor likewise deceased and by his son Benjamin Taylor sold unto the said Edward Turbervile. Bounded by a branch of Lambs Creek, the back line of the Elder Dividend formerly belonging unto the said Motts, line of Peter Gallon deceased, and line of Alexander Doniphan gentleman also deceased. Signed E. Turbervile. Delivered in presence of Geo. Gray, John Goodall, Sacheveral Norman. Recorded 5 November 1736 T. Turner.

2:51 - DEED OF RELEASE - 29 October 1736 - Edward Turbervile of the county of King George, planter, to John Champe of same, Gentleman. 2500 pounds tobacco for 150A described in lease. Signed E. Turbervile. Delivered in presence of Geo. Gray, John Goodall, Sacheveral Norman. Recorded 5 November 1736 T. Turner.

2:54 - DEED OF LEASE - 4 November 1736 - Edward Humstone of St. Paul's Parish in the county of Stafford, planter, to Thomas Grigsby of same, Gent. 5 shillings lawful money of England to lease 168A. All that tract of land which Thomas Gregg late of Stafford County by his last will and testament gave and bequeathed unto Edward Humstone and Lucy his wife and after their death fell unto the sd. Edward Humston the Younger being Heir at Law. Bounded by a branch of Poplar Swamp and land formerly Evan Williams'. Now in tenure and occupation of Robert Jones. Signed Edward Humston. Delivered in presence of Wm. Pickett, Hugh French, Joseph Berry. Sarah Hunston, wife of Edward, being solely examined acknowledged her free consent thereto. Recorded 5 November 1736 T. Turner.

2:55 - DEED OF RELEASE - 5 November 1736 - Edward Humston of St. Paul's Parish in the county of Stafford, planter, to Thomas Grigsby of same, Gent. 10,000 pounds tobacco for 168A described in lease. Signed Edward Humston. Delivered in presence of Wm. Pickett, Hugh French, Joseph Berry. Sarah Humston, wife of Edward, being solely examined acknowledged her free consent thereto. Recorded 5 November 1736 T. Turner.

2:59 - BOND - 5 November 1736 - Edward Humston of the parish of St. Paul's in the county of Stafford bound unto Thomas Grigsby of same in the sum of 200 pounds sterling. Condition such that as Edward Humston by certain deeds of lease and release confirmed unto the above named Thomas Grigsby one piece of land whereon Robert Jones now liveth containing 168A situate in the parish of Brunswick and county of King George, if the sd. Edward Humston shall forever defend the sd. land unto him the sd. Thomas Grigsby free from all manner of trouble, obligation to be void. Signed Edward Humston. Delivered in presence of Wm. Pickett, Hugh French, Joseph Berry. Recorded 5 November 1736 T. Turner.

2:59 - DEED OF LEASE - 3 November 1736 - Daniel Underwood of St. Mark's Parish in the county of Orange, planter, to Colo. John Taylor, Esqr. of the county of Richmond and company of the City of Bristol. 5 shillings good and lawfull money currency of Virginia to lease 70A lying in Hanover Parish near the Bristol Iron Works. Bounded by the line of the sd. company's land, the old field near the roadside, the said Underwood's cornfield, the land of Mary Tutt, land of William Tutt, and the Beverdam hills. Signed Daniel Underwood. Delivered in presence of Isaac Arnold, William Harvie, Original Brown. On the motion of John Triplett on behalf of sd. Taylor and Company, deed is admitted to record. Recorded 5 November 1736 T. Turner.

2:61 - DEED OF RELEASE - 4 November 1736 - Daniel Underwood of St. Mark's Parish in the county of Orange, planter, to Colo. John Taylor, Esqr. and Company of the City of Bristol. One seasoned Negro for 70A described in lease. Signed Daniel Underwood. Delivered in presence of Isaac Arnold, William Harvey, Original Brown. On the motion of John Triplett on behalf of the said Taylor and Company, deed was admitted to record. Recorded 5 November 1736 T. Turner.

2:63 - DEED OF LEASE - 4 June 1736 - Daniel White, Junior and Mary his wife of the county of King George to James Jones of Hanover Parish, bricklayer. 5 shillings sterling to lease 543A which is one undivided third of part of a 2100A tract granted to John Simpson by pattent dated 6 June 1666. Bounded by Corbins land by the Mill Road, Key's line, the back line of Simpsons pattent upon Thornton's land, Shropshire, Micou, Walter Anderson, and Lomax. Signed Daniel White, junr., Mary White. Delivered in presence of William Harrison, Daniel Grant, Isaac Arnold. Recorded 5 November 1736 T. Turner.

2:65 - DEED OF RELEASE - 5 June 1736 - Daniel White, Junior of the county of King George, planter, and Mary his wife to James Jones of same, bricklayer. 80 pounds sterling for 543A described in lease. Signed Daniel White, Junr., Mary White. Delivered in presence of William Harrison, Daniel Grant, Isaac Arnold. Recorded 5 November 1736 T. Turner.

2:69 - DEED OF SALE - 1 October 1736 - Stephen Hansford and Elizabeth his wife of Brunswick Parish, planter, to John Grant of same, planter. 30 pounds current money for 52A bounded by Jeremiah Bronaugh, Junr., Daniel Grant, and John Coburn. Signed Stephen Hansford, Elizabeth Hansford. Delivered in presence of Jerh. Bronaugh, Senr., David Bronaugh, Bryan Chadwell, Willm. Raredon. Recorded 5 November 1736 T. Turner.

2:71 - BOND - 1 October 1736 - Stephen Hansford of Brunswick Parish, planter, bound unto John Grant of same, planter, in the sum of 500 pounds sterling. Condition such that if Stephen Hansford keeps the covenants comprized in one Deed of Land bearing equal date with these presents, obligation to be void. Signed Stephen Hansford. Delivered in presence of Jereh. Bronaugh, Senr., David Bronaugh. Recorded 5 November 1736 T. Turner.

2:71 - DEED OF FEEOFMENT - 1 November 1736 - Metcalf Dickenson of Northfarnham Parish in the county of Richmond to Marmaduke Beckwith of the parish of Lunenburg in the county of Richmond. 20 pounds current money for 60A lying in Hanover Parish. Formerly purchased by Samuel Bowen late of the county of Richmond deceased of Francis Triplett of the same county deceased. Part of a greater tract formerly taken up by the said Francis Triplett. Bounded by Mr. James Scott, Joseph Minton, Samuel Nicholas, William Tiller, Capt. William Ball, and the land of the said Samuel Bowen. Signed Metcalf Dickenson. Delivered in presence of Tarpley Beckwith, Martha Sisson, John Hanes, Thomas Wilcox. Recorded 5 November 1736 T. Turner.

2:74 - DEED OF LEASE - 2 November 1736 - James Stephens of Hanover Parish and Mary Stephens his now wife to Samuel Wood of same, planter. 5 shillings current money of Virginia for two tracts. 50A whereon the said Samuel Wood now liveth bounded by land of Samuel Nichols deceased, Thomas King, and John Jett. 25A whereon Christian Wharton deceased did formerly live which land is divided from land of Thomas Wharton by a branch. Both tracts are in the forest near Tripletts old fields. Signed James Stephens, Mary Stephens. Delivered in presence of Isaac Arnold, Frans. Triplett, John Allan. Recorded 5 November 1736 T. Turner.

2:76 - DEED OF RELEASE - 3 November 1736 - James Stephens of Hanover Parish and Mary his wife to Samuel Wood of same, planter. 26 pounds current money of Virginia for two tracts described in lease. Signed James Stephens, Mary Stephens. Delivered in presence of Isaac Arnold, Francis Triplett, John Allan. Recorded 5 November 1736 T. Turner.

2:78 - BOND - 3 November 1736 - James Stephens of Hanover Parish bound unto Samuel Wood of same in the sum of 52 pounds current money of Virginia.

Condition such that whereas James Stephens and Mary his wife hath lawfully conveyed two tracts of land which are to contain 75A of land by deeds which bear date the second and third day of November 1736, if James Stephens shall keep all agreements made in the said deeds, obligation to be void. Signed James Stephens. Delivered in presence of Isaac Arnold, Francis Triplett, John Allan. Recorded 5 November 1736 T. Turner.

2:79 - DEED OF FEEOFMENT - 14 October 1736 - John Dodd, Junr. of the county of King George and Ann his wife to Joseph Settle of same. 1400 pounds tobacco for 50A which the said John Dodd's father John Dodd bought of John Brown and acknowledged in court to his son John Dodd and Ann his wife by Deed of Gift dated 1 August 1729. Bounded by Thomas White and the Main Swamp. Signed John Dodd, Ann Dodd. Delivered in presence of Benjamin Dodd, Statford Lightburn. Recorded 5 November 1736 T. Turner.

2:82 - DEED OF GIFT - 2 December 1736 - John Taylor of Hanover Parish for diverse good causes and valuable considerations but more especially for the natural love and affection that he has for his beloved daughter Martha Taylor as also for her maintaining him as long as he lives and paying and discharging all his just debts, gives grants assigns and conveys and makes over unto his daughter Martha Taylor and her heirs forever the whole tract of land whereon he now lives containing 100A together with all his stocks of horses, cattle, hoggs, and sheep with all his household furniture and all his personal estate. Signed John Taylor. Delivered in presence of Neal McCormick, John Willis, Saml. Green, Isaac Green. Recorded 4 February 1736 T. Turner.

2:83 - DEED OF LEASE - 3 February 1736 - James Skerlock and Sarah his wife of Hanover Parish to Robert Rankin of same, planter. 5 shillings current money of Virginia to lease 50A lying on the lower side of the Western main branch of Gengoteague. Bounded by a small spring branch which divides this land from the land of William Settle, and by the land of the sd. Rankins. Part of a pattent first granted unto William Baltrop, James Green, and Christopher Lewis for 1050A. Signed James Scurlock, Sarah Scurlock. Delivered in presence of Jos. Strother, William Settle. Sarah Settle, wife of William Settle, relinquished her right of dower. Recorded 4 February 1736 T. Turner.

2:85 - DEED OF RELEASE - 4 February 1736 - James Scurlock and Sarah his wife of Hanover Parish to Robert Rankins of same, planter. 25 pounds current money of Virginia for 50A described in lease. Signed James Scurlock, Sarah Scurlock. Delivered in presence of Jos. Strother, Wm. Settle. Sarah Settle, wife of William Settle, relinquished her right of dower. Recorded 4 February 1736 T. Turner.

2:87 - DEED OF LEASE - 3 January 1736 - Majr. William Woodford of Caroline County, Gent., to Thomas Catlett of same. 5 shillings lawfull money to lease 300A which is the lower moiety of a pattent of 600A granted to Mr. Charles Grimes dated 8 October 1657. Bounded by a place called Thicketty Point on the riverside and land of Joseph Berry. Signed Wm. Woodford. Delivered in presence of Benja. Robinson, Jno. Taliaferro, John Micou. Recorded 4 February 1736 T. Turner.

2:89 - DEED OF RELEASE - 4 January 1736 - Majr. William Woodford of Caroline County, Gent., to Thomas Catlett of same. 180 pounds sterling for 300A described in lease. Signed Wm. Woodford. Delivered in presence of Benja. Robinson, Jno. Taliaferro, John Micou. Recorded 4 February 1736 T. Turner.

2:92 - DEDIMUS COMMISSION - 3 March 1736 - Whereas Thomas Catlett, Gent., of Caroline County made application for a commission to take the acknowledgment and Privy Examination of Ann Woodford, wife of William Woodford, Gent. of Caroline County to a certain deed of land, Thomas Turner, Clerk of the King George County Court, commissions John Taliaferro, John Micou, William Taliaferro and Lawrence Battail or any two of them, being Justices for the County of Caroline, to take the acknowledgment and Privy Examination of the said Ann Woodford touching and concerning the premises and to Certifie the same to the Justices of the county of King George. On 19 March 1736/7 John Taliaferro and John Micou certified that Ann Woodford acknowledged her right of dower of certain Deeds of Land dated 3 and 4 February containing 300A lying in the county of King George. On the motion of Thomas Catlett, Gent., who returned them into Court, the commission with the Certificate of the Privy Examination were admitted to record. Recorded __ April 1737 T. Turner.

2:93 - DEED OF GIFT - 4 March 1736/7 - Maxfield Brown of Hanover Parish, planter, for diverse good causes and valuable considerations but more especially for the natural love and affection that he has for his beloved son Newman Brown, gives grants assigns conveys and makes over unto his said son Newman Brown 150A of land to be laid off to include the plantation whereon the said Maxfield Brown now dwells as also the plantation whereon the said Newman Brown now dwells. Signed Maxfield Brown. Delivered in presence of Harry Turner, Wm. Settle, James Scurlock. Recorded 4 March 1736 T. Turner.

2:94 - DEED OF GIFT - 4 March 1736/7 - Maxfield Brown of Hanover Parish, planter, for diverse good causes and considerations but more especially for the natural love and affection that he has for his beloved son George Brown, gives grants assigns conveys and makes over unto his said son George Brown that plantation whereon John Allen now lives together with 150A of land to be laid off convenient to the said plantation. Signed Maxfield Brown. Delivered in presence of Harry Turner, Wm. Settle, James Scurlock. Recorded 4 March 1736 T. Turner.

2:95 - DEED OF GIFT - 6 May 1737 - William Peck of Brunswick Parish, planter, for diverse good causes and considerations but more especially for the natural love and affection that he has for his son Robert Peck, gives grants assigns conveys and makes over unto his said son Robert Peck 100A of land to be laid off so as to include the plantation whereon he now dwells. Signed W. Peck. Delivered in presence of Harry Turner, Wm. Rowley, Junr. Recorded 6 May 1737 T. Turner.

2:96 - INDENTURE - 2 April 1737 - Elizabeth Seale of Hanover Parish binds her daughter Liza, being four years old last September, unto Mary Greecion of Hanover Parish with her the said Mary Greecion to live and abide as a servant until she shall arrive to the age of eighteen years. She the said Mary during the sd. service shall find and allow the sd. servant sufficient meat, drink, washing, lodging, and wearing apparel and likewise at all times do the best endeavorment to teach and keep her in the Principles of the Christian Religion by teaching her to say the Lords Prayer, the Creed, and the Ten Commandments and likewise the Church Catachism and one years learning and at the expiration of her service to give her such dues as are allowed by law. Signed Elizabeth Seale, Mary Greecion. Delivered in presence of B. Adie, Susanna Alford. Recorded 6 May 1737 T. Turner.

2:97 - DEED OF FEEOFMENT - 6 April 1737 - Ann Edmonds of the county of King George, widow, to George Fishpool of same, Gent. 20 pounds sterling for 2A contiguous to the land and plantation whereon the said Ann Edmonds now liveth. Beginning at the Crabb Landing between Bray's Church and Bray's warehouses and from the said landing a straight course to the Main Road and down the road 'till it meets the upper side of the upper warehouse and by the side thereof a straight course to the Rappahannock River and along sd. river to the Crabb Landing. Signed Ann Edmonds. Delivered in presence of Jas. Jones, William Walker, Alexander Carson. Recorded 6 May 1737 T. Turner.

2:100 - INDENTURE - 10 March 1736/7 - Elizabeth Robinson of Hanover Parish binds her son Francis an apprentice and servant to Bourn Price of Hanover Parish 'till he be of the full age of twenty-one during all which time the said Bourn Price binds himself to provide and give the sd. servant good and sufficient meat drink washing lodging and cloths and at least two years schooling and at the determination of the said time the sd. Price further agrees to give the said servant a new suit of Druggat Cloths with one fine hatt shoes

stockings and three good Dowlass or Garlick Holland shirts with two silk
handkerchiefs. Signed Elizabeth Robinson, Bourn Price. Delivered in presence
of Taylor Chapman, William Stone, Jere. Murdock. Recorded 6 May 1737 T.
Turner.

2:101 - INDENTURE - 6 May 1737 - William Thornton of Brunswick Parish
administrator of Thomas Benson, late of said parish deceased, and guardian
appointed by the Court to the said Benson's children, binds William Benson an
orphan son of the before mentioned Thomas (the profits of whose estate not
being sufficient to maintain him) an apprentice to William Clark of Brunswick
Parish to live and abide with him until he shall arrive to the age of twenty-one
years, he being born the thirtyeth day of June one thousand seven hundred
twenty and eight to learn the Trade and Mistery of a Taylor and likewise as soon
as may be to learn him to write and read as the law directs and not to command
or compel his said apprentice to work among Tobacco without his own free
consent.....and at the expiration to give him besides his common wearing
apparel, one good new suit of Druggatt with hatt, neckcloth, shirt, stockings, and
shoes suitable and likewise a sett of good working tools, that is to say goose
shears, two thimbles, and one hundred of sorted needles. Signed Wm. Thornton,
Wm. Clark. Delivered in presence of Antho. Hayney, David Bronaugh.
Recorded 6 May 1737 T. Turner.

2:102 - DEED OF LEASE - 6 May 1737 - William Flowers of King George
County to John Simpson of same. Yearly rent of 550 pounds tobacco and 3
shillings sterling to lease 140A during the term of the natural lives of the
aforesd. John Simpson and Mary Simpson his wife or the longest liver of them.
Land is bounded by the white oak branch, a line of Colo. Fitzhugh, and a line of
Abraham Kenyon. Signed William Flowers. Delivered in presence of Simon
Tomison, Barbery Tomison, Antho. Hayney. Recorded 6 May 1737 T. Turner.

2:104 - DEED OF LEASE - 4 May 1737 - William Letman and Frances his wife
of Hanover Parish, planter, to Margaret Vivion of same. 5 shillings current
money to lease 300A being the plantation tract and parcel of land late in
possession of Samuel Bowen and bought by the said Samuel Bowen of Francis
Triplet by deed dated 17 April 1677. Signed William Littman, Frances Littman.
Delivered in presence of Antho. Hayney, B. Adie, David Bronaugh. Recorded 6
May 1737 T. Turner.

2:106 - DEED OF RELEASE - 5 May 1737 - William Letman and Frances his
wife of Hanover Parish, planter, to Margaret Vivion of same. 35 pounds current
money of Virginia for 300A taken up by Francis Triplett and by him sold by
deed dated 17 April 1677 unto Samuel Bowen father to the sd. Frances. Signed
William Littman, Frances Littman. Delivered in presence of Antho. Haynie, B.

Adie, David Bronaugh. Recorded 6 May 1737 T. Turner.

2:109 - DEED OF LEASE - 4 May 1737 - Mary Bowing of Hanover Parish, spinster, to Margaret Vivion of same. 5 shillings current money of Virginia to lease 300A late in the possession of Samuel Bowing and bought by the said Samuel of Francis Triplett by deed dated 17 April 1677. Signed Mary Bowing. Delivered in presence of Antho. Haynie, B. Adie, David Bronaugh. On the motion of Thomas Vivion, Gent., on behalf of the sd. Margaret, this lease was admitted to record. Recorded 6 May 1737 T. Turner.

2:111 - DEED OF RELEASE - 5 May 1737 - Mary Bowing of Hanover Parish, spinster, to Margaret Vivion of same. 35 pounds current money of Virginia for 300A taken up by Francis Triplett and by him sold by deed dated 17 April 1677 unto Samuel Bowin father to the said Mary. Signed Mary Bowing. Delivered in presence of Antho. Haynie, B. Adie, David Bronaugh. On the motion of Thomas Vivion, Gent., on behalf of the sd. Margaret, this release was admitted to record. Recorded 6 May 1737 T. Turner.

2:114 - DEED OF LEASE - 6 May 1737 - Thomas Charles of Lancaster County to Francis Triplett of Hanover Parish. 5 shillings current money of Virginia to lease 105A. It is the moiety or half part of 210A of land sold by Robert Finch unto Frances Velden and the said Thomas Charles by deeds of lease and release dated 17 and 18 May 1727. Bounded by land of Francis James. Part of the old field which is called and known by the name of Tripletts old Field and is divided by the Main or County Road from the land of Francis Velldon where the sd. road crosses the old Field and joyning upon the head branches of Thatchers Dam. Signed Thomas Charles. Delivered in presence of William Wofendall, Clapham Richardson. Recorded 6 May 1737 T. Turner.

2:216 - DEED OF RELEASE - 6 May 1737 - Thomas Charles of Lancaster County to Francis Triplett of Hanover Parish. 20 pounds current money of Virginia for 105A described in lease. Signed Thomas Charles. Delivered in presence of William Wofendall, Clapham Richardson. The said Thomas Charles and Betty his now wife shall and will at any court upon the request of the sd. Francis Triplett acknowledge personally or by Power of Attorney these presents to the end the same may be recorded. Recorded 6 May 1737 T. Turner.

2:118 - SCHEDULE OF ESTATE - 6 May 1737 - Two old Beds and bedsteads bord and hide, one flock Bed and one Feather bed, two Potts and hooks, three chairs, two Pales and one half bushel and one bucket, one old box and one old chest, one small table, one spinning wheel, two Pewter Dishes, two basons, Four Pieces of year then wear, one frying pan and ladle, one old horse, saddle and bridle, one box iron, a looking glass, a horse coller and traces, a meal sifter, one meal bagg, eight shoats, a flesh fork. A just and true schedule of the Estate of Richard Hornbuckle. Signed Richd. Hornbuckle. Recorded 6 May 1737 T. Turner.

2:119 - DEED OF LEASE - 2 June 1737 - Eliner Whitredg of Hanover Parish, daughter of John Whitredg, to Thomas Highlander of same, planter. 5 shillings sterling to lease 200A. One hundred acres of which is now in the possession of the above named Thomas Highlander the right and inheritance of John Whitredg deceased; the other hundred acres being in the possession of William Remey formerly the right and inheritance of Wm. Whitredg deceased given him by his God Father William Sarjant. Bounded by Edmond Barker, John Cook, George Fishpool, and John Drake. Signed Elliner Whitredg. Delivered in presence of William Deakins, Marten Frances, John Beddo. Recorded 3 June 1737 T. Turner.

2:121 - INDENTURE - 3 June 1737 - Elizabeth Seale of Hanover Parish binds Charles Seale her son of the age of seven years to William Tutt, carpenter of same, to learn the trade of carpenter and to serve the sd. William until he arrive to the age of twenty-one years faithfully. William Tutt agrees to allow the sd. Charles Seale all necessary cloths, meat, drink, washing, and lodging during the said term and likewise to give unto him sufficient learning and at the expiration of his time of servitude shall give unto him one suit of Druggat cloths and one set of carpenter's tools. Signed William Tutt, Eliza. Seale. Delivered in presence of Samuel Reids, Robert Elliston. Recorded 3 June 1737 T. Turner.

2:122 - DEED OF BARGAIN - 15 January 1736 - Isaac Johnson of Hanover Parish in consideration of a debt due by him to William Duff of same amounting to 3104 pounds of tobacco and two pounds six shillings and five pence does bargain, sell, assign and set over to him the said William Duff - three feather bedds, three sheets, three blankets, three ruggs, three cows and calves, two mares, nine hoggs, three iron potts, twelve flagg bottom chairs, four Pewter dishes, eighteen plates, all the crop of tobacco now in the house, one cupboard, three chests, three bedsteds, and two pair pot hooks. Signed Isaac Johnson. Delivered in presence of Alexr. Howard, Willm. Sarjant. Recorded 4 June 1737 T. Turner.

2:123 - DEED OF BARGAIN AND SALE - 31 May 1737 - John Willis of Hanover Parish to William Robinson of same. 70 pounds current money of Virginia for 161A. John Willis deceased, grandfather of the said John Willis party to these presents, was in his lifetime seized in Fee of 261A granted unto him by patent dated 21 October 1669 and by assignment indorsed on the back of the said Letters Pattent 26 April 1701 did give and grant unto his son William Willis 161A by the name of all the remaining of the within Pattent of Land except 100A formerly given to his eldest son John. The said William Willis is dead and the said 161A are descended to the said John Willis party to these presents the eldest son and heir of the Body of the said William Willis. An inquisition was taken before Benjamin Berryman, Gent., Sherif of the county of King George 11 March last past to enquire of the value of the 161A in order to dock the intail of the same and it is found the value is sixty pounds and no more and that the said 161A are a separate parcel and not parcel or contiguous to other intailed lands in the possession and seizen of the said John Willis (sd. inquisition now remaining in the secretary's office of this Colony). Signed John Willis. Delivered in presence of Wm. Mackay, Harry Turner. Recorded 4 June 1737 T. Turner.

2:126 - DEED OF LEASE - 1 June 1737 - John Willis of Hanover Parish, planter, and William Robinson of same, Gentleman, to Joseph Strother and Maximilian Robinson, Gentlemen Churchwardens of Hanover Parish. 5 shillings current money to lease 261A formerly granted unto John Willis, grandfather of the sd. John Willis party to these presents, 21 October 1669. 100A part whereof were given by John Willis the grandfather to his son John Willis deceased in Feetail 10 December 1694. By the death of John Willis the son without issue, the 100A reverted and came to the sd. John Willis party to these presents as heir at law of the sd. John Willis the grandfather. The residue of the sd. premises were given by the sd. John Willis the grandfather to his son William, father of the sd. John Willis to these presents, now deceased in Fee Tail by assignment endorsed on the back of the Letters Patent 26 April 1701 and by the death of the said William Willis are descended to the said John Willis party to these presents as his eldest son and heir. Signed John Willis, Wil. Robinson. Delivered in presence of Wm. Mackay, Harry Turner. Recorded 4 June 1737 T. Turner.

2:128 - DEED OF RELEASE - 2 June 1737 - John Willis of Hanover Parish, planter, and William Robinson of same, Gentleman, to Joseph Strother and Maximilian Robinson Gentlemen Churchwardens of Hanover Parish. The Vestry of the said Parish have contracted for the absolute purchase of the 261A in order to assign and set apart the same for a Glebe for the use of the Minister of the said Parish and his successors forever. The said John Willis and Elizabeth his wife and the said William Robinson in consideration of 120 pounds current money do release and confirm unto the churchwardens the 261A described in lease. Signed John Willis, Elizabeth Willis, Wil. Robinson. Delivered in presence of Wm. Mackay, Harry Turner. Recorded 4 June 1737 T. Turner.

2:133 - BOND - 2 June 1737 - John Willis of Hanover Parish, planter, bound unto Joseph Strother and Maximilian Robinson of same in the sum of 240 pounds current money of Virginia. Condition such that if John Willis shall truly keep all agreements particularly mentioned in one deed of Release bearing even date with these presents made between the above bound John Willis and Elizabeth his wife and William Robinson, Gentn., of the one part and the above named Joseph Strother and Maximilian Robinson of the other part, obligation to be void. Signed John Willis. Delivered in presence of Wm. Mackay, Harry Turner. Recorded 4 June 1737 T. Turner.

2:134 - BOND - 1 July 1737 - John Edwards, John Champe, and Thomas Turner bound to their Sovereign Lord the King his Heirs and Successors in the sum of 1000 pounds sterling money of England. Condition such that whereas the above bounded John Edwards, Gent., is appointed Sherif of this county, if the said John Edwards do when therein required render to the auditor and receiver general a particular perfect and true account of all his Majestys Dues arising in the said county and also due payment make of all other public dues and fees put into his hands to collect to the several persons to whom the same shall be due and payable and true performance make of all matters and things relating to his sd. office during his continuance therein, obligation to be void. Signed John Edwards, John Champe, T. Turner. Delivered in presence of Harry Turner. Recorded 1 July 1737 T. Turner.

2:135 - MORTGAGE - 4 June 1737 - Thomas Williams, Junr. of King George County, planter, in consideration of 25 pounds 8 shillings 10 pence and half penny current money do sell unto Samuel Skinker two Negro women slaves named Nann and Kate. If the aforesaid Thomas Williams, Junr. shall truly pay or cause to be paid unto the aforesd. Samuel Skinker the above mentioned sum at or upon the first day of June next ensuing, then this present writing to be void. Signed Thomas Williams. Delivered in presence of Wm. Strother, Wm. Duling. On the motion of Joseph Strother, Gent., on behalf of the sd. Samuel, this mortgage was admitted to record. Recorded 5 August 1737 T. Turner.

2:136 - INDENTURE - 12 January 1736 - Benjamin Miller of the county of King George, planter, binds himself apprentice to William Tutt of same, carpenter, to serve the term of five years from the date hereof to work at the trade of a carpenter and also to help to tend corn. William Tutt obliges himself to instruct the said Benjamin Miller in the Trade and Mistery of a carpenter and to provide him with sufficient clothing, meat, drink, washing and lodging and at the expiration thereof to give him one Kersey coat, Druggatt waiscoat and britches, Dowlass shirt and Ozenbrigs shirt, one felt hatt, one pair shoes and stockings, one broad axe, handsaw, and carpenter's adz. No Signatures. Recorded 2 September 1737 T. Turner.

2:137 - POWER OF ATTORNEY - 2 June 1737 - Edward Turbervile authorizes Capt. Joseph Berry his attorney to relinquish all the right of dower and thirds at the common law which he has in a certain plantation and tract of land by virtue of his marriage with Sarah the late Widdow and Relect of William Willis her former husband deceased and now sold and lawfully conveyed by her son John Willis to the Churchwardens of the Parish of Hanover by Deed of Release bearing equal date with these presents. Signed E. Turbervile. Delivered in presence of Thomas Catlett, Wm. Bartlett, Archd. McPherson. Recorded 2 September 1737 T. Turner.

2:138 - RECEIPT - 2 August 1737 - Received of John Owens 44 pounds 4 shillings being by computation my wife's proportion of her father Robert Gollop and her uncle Henry Gollop's Estates and do discharge the said Owen of the same. Signed Thomas Monteith, Phillis Monteith. Test: John Shilcott. Recorded 2 September 1737 T. Turner.

2:138 - RECEIPT - 14 December 1732 - Received of John Owen and Eliner his wife full and ample satisfaction for all we can ask, crave, or demand of the Estates of Robert and Henry Gollop our deceased Father and Uncle and do discharge the sd. John and Elinor his wife of the same and all other demands on any account whatsoever. Signed James Brissee, Eliner Brissee. Test: Thomas Monteith, Mary Reynolds. Recorded 2 September 1737 T. Turner.

2:139 - RECEIPT - 18 September 1733 - Having settled and adjusted all accounts betwixt me and John Owen I do hereby acknowledge myself to have received my part of my father Robert Gollop's Estate as likewise full satisfaction for all I can ask, crave, or demand of the Estate of my uncle Henry Gollop. Signed Robert Duncomb. Test: Thomas Monteith. Recorded 2 September 1737 T. Turner.

2:139 - DEED OF FEEOFMENT - 2 September 1737 - William Remy of Hanover Parish, carpenter, and Barbary his wife to John Dodd of same, planter. 2490 pounds tobacco for 50A commonly called by the name of Wolfpitt Neck. Bounded by John Dodd's spring branch, John Quisenbury, Ireland Swamp, and Edmond Barker. Part of the land taken up by John Weir who conveyed the same unto James Trent and David Howseman and by the last will and testament of James Trent left to his daughter Ann Trent and bought by Nicholas Hawkins of John James husband to the said Ann Trent and by Nicholas Hawkins sold unto Thomas Davis and by him sold unto the within named William Remy. Signed William Remy. Delivered in presence of John Drake, Edmd. Barker, John Quisenbury. Recorded 2 September 1737 T. Turner.

2:142 - BOND - 2 September 1737 - George Fishpool of Hanover Parish, Gent., bound unto John Dodd of same in the sum of forty pounds current money of Virginia. Condition such that if George Fishpool doth not interrupt, trouble or molest the above said John Dodd concerning the 50A of land that the within deed specifies, obligation to be void. Signed Geo. Fishpool. Delivered in presence of William Remey, William Claytor. No Recorded Date or Signature of Clerk.

2:142 - DEED OF LEASE - 2 March 1736 - John Willis of Hanover parish, planter, to Isaac Pitman of same, planter. 5 shillings good and lawfull money to lease 60A. Bounded by Archdell Combs deceased and near the road which leads from Major Jeremiah Murdocks to the Bristol Iron Works, the sd. Isaac Pitman, Ralph Wormley, Esqr. deceased, land formerly belonging to Thomas James, and a small branch that heads in the cornfield of the sd. John Willis. Signed John Willis. Delivered in presence of Thomas Dickeson, Richd. Hornbuckle. Recorded 7 October 1737 T. Turner.

2:144 - DEED OF RELEASE - 3 March 1736 - John Willis of Hanover Parish, planter, to Isaac Pitman of same, planter. 50 pounds current money of Virginia for 60A described in lease. Signed John Willis, Isaac Arnold. Delivered in presence of Thomas Dickeson, Richd. Hornbuckle. Elizabeth Willis, the wife of John Willis, relinquished her right of dower and thirds at the common law to 50A of the sd. 60A conveyed in said release. Recorded 7 October 1737 T. Turner.

2:147 - BOND - 3 March 1736 - John Willis of Hanover Parish bound unto Isaac Pitman of same in the sum of 100 pounds current money of Virginia. Condition such that if John Willis shall honestly fulfill all agreements contained in one deed of lease and one deed of release which bear dates the 2 and 3 March 1736 between the above bounden John Willis and the above named Isaac Pitman, obligation to be void. Signed John Willis. Delivered in presence of Isaac Arnold, Thomas Dickeson, Richd. Hornbuckle. Recorded 7 October 1737 T. Turner.

2:148 - DEED OF LEASE - 1 September 1737 - James Stevens and Mary his wife of Sittenburn Parish to Robert Vaulx of Washington Parish in the county of Westmoreland. 5 shillings lawful money of Great Britain to lease 125A where one Thomas Wharton formerly did or now lives. Bounded by Thomas Ammon, Christopher Ederington, Bristol Iron Works, Thomas King, and Nichols. Signed James Stevens, Mary Stevens. Delivered in presence of James Hore, Francis Jett, Francis James. Recorded 7 October 1737 T. Turner.

2:149 - DEED OF RELEASE - 2 September 1737 - James Stevens and Mary his wife of Sittenburn Parish to Robert Vaulx of Washington Parish in the county of Westmoreland. 19 pounds current money of Virginia for 125A described in lease. Signed James Stevens, Mary Stevens. Delivered in presence of James Hore, Francis Jett, Francis James. Recorded 7 October 1737 T. Turner.

2:151 - BOND - James Stevens of Sittenburn Parish bound unto Robert Vaulx of Washington Parish in the county of Westmoreland in the sum of 100 pounds current money of Virginia. Condition such that if James Stevens does well and truly keep all agreements mentioned in the deeds of lease and release bearing even date with these presents from one J. Stevens to Robert Vaulx for 125A, obligation to be void. Signed James Stevens. Delivered in presence of James Hore, Francis Jett, Francis James. Recorded 7 October 1737 T. Turner.

2:152 - INDENTURE - 4 November 1737 - Peter McDaniel of Brunswick Parish of his own accord doth put place and bind himself an apprentice or servant unto William Welch to serve him during the term of five years next ensuing. At the expiration of the sd. term the sd. William Welch to give him a young mare and a decent suit of apparel from head to foot besides his wearing cloths. Signed Peter McDaniel. Delivered in presence of T. Lewis, Neal McCormack. Recorded 4 November 1737 T. Turner.

2:153 - INDENTURE - 4 November 1737 - Peter McDaniel binds himself an apprentice or servant unto William Welch to serve him during a term of five years next ensuing. (Same as preceding indenture) Signed Willm. Welch. Delivered in presence of T. Lewis, Neal McCormack. Recorded 4 November 1737 T. Turner.

2:154 - BOND - 4 November 1737 - John Edwards and John Champe, Gent., bound to Our Sovereign Lord the King his Heirs and Successors in the sum of 38,258 pounds of tobacco. Condition such that whereas John Edwards hath the collection of the said county put into his hands amounting to 19,129 pounds of tobacco, if the said John Edwards doth faithfully collect and duly pay the same to the respective creditors as also all such clerks and secretarys fees to the respective officers to whom the same be due and payable according to law, obligation to be void. Signed John Edwards, John Champe. Delivered in presence of Harry Turner. Recorded 4 November 1737 T. Turner.

2:155 - RECEIPT - 14 April 1735 - Received of Ann Pitman the Widdow and administrator of William Pitman deceased late of King George County in full of all and each of our parts of the said William Pitman his estate belonging to every of us the subscribers his sons and daughters and do own and acknowledge to be therewith fully contented satisfied and paid. Signed Robert Taliaferro, Isaac Pittman, Thomas Pittman, Moses Pitman. Delivered in presence of Isaac Arnold, Senr., Joshua Farguson, Senr. Recorded 6 January 1737 T. Turner.

2:155 - DEED OF LEASE - 24 January 1737 - Isaac Arnold, Senr. of Hanover Parish to Alexander Adear of same. Yearly rent of 500 pounds good tobacco to lease 50A whereon the said Alexander hath now possession and hath begun to clear ground. Lease is for and during the term of the natural lives of the said Alexander Adare, his now wife Elinor, and their son Thomas Adare. Bounded by the fork of a small branch of Gengoteague Creek, land formerly granted to Prosser and Chetwood, John Berry deceased, Thomas Arnold, Senr. deceased, Isaac Arnold, Junr., and a small run of water on the road side which leads from William Duffs to King George Courthouse. Part of a pattent of land for 226A granted unto John Doyle, late of the county of Richmond deceased, 23 January 1716. The said Alexander and Elinor shall within the space of three years plant fifty apple trees and one hundred peach trees and the same kept under a good fence. The said Isaac Arnold, Senr. doth hereby oblige himself to build upon the sd. land one dwelling house twenty foot in length and twelve foot in breadth and an inside chimney to be completed and finished by Christmas next. Signed Alexander Adear, Isaac Arnold, Senr. Delivered in presence of John Wren, John Hellier, Mary Hellier. Recorded 3 February 1737 T. Turner.

2:157 - BOND - 24 January 1737 - Alexander Adear of Hanover Parish bound unto Isaac Arnold, Senr. in the sum of 40 pounds current money of Virginia. Condition such that in case the sd. Alexander and Elinor his wife and Thomas his sd. son party to these presents shall at all times hereafter during their and every of their several lives well truly faithfully and honestly observe all agreements contained in the said lease and also pay the said annual rent, obligation to be void. Signed Alexander Adare. Delivered in presence of John Hellier, John Wren, Mary Hellier. Recorded 3 February 1737 T. Turner.

2:158 - INDENTURE - 1 October 1737 - Alexander Sutter of the county of King George doth put and place himself apprentice unto the said Robert Hughs of same him to serve after the manner of an apprentice for and during and untill the full end and term of three years next ensuing. Robert Hughs will teach and instruct his sd. apprentice in all the arts of a Taylor and at the expiration of the said term of three years, he shall give his said apprentice a set of Taylor's Tools and a suit of common apparel. Signed Robert Hughs, Alexander Sutter. Delivered in presence of Joshua Farguson, John Coburn. Recorded 3 February 1737 T. Turner.

2:159 - DEED OF LEASE - 3 February 1737 - Henry Fitzhugh, Esqr. of Stafford County to Richard Curtis of King George County. Yearly rent of 500 pounds tobacco to be made upon the said plantation and four hens, capons, or pullets to lease 100A whereon the said Curtis now lives. Lease is for and during the term and space of the natural lives of the sd. Richard Curtis, Sarah Curtis his wife, and George Curtis his son or the longest liver of them. Bounded by the north side of the main branch of Muddy Creek, William Pain, and Daniel McFarlain. The sd. Richard Curtis to pay the Quitrents for the said land. Signed Henry Fitzhugh, Junr., Richd. Curtis. Delivered in presence of Farqr. Matheson,

John Grant. Recorded 3 February 1737 T. Turner.

2:161 - DEED OF LEASE - 14 January 1737 - Henry Fitzhugh of Stafford County, Esqr., to Stephen Boing of King George County, planter. Yearly rent of 500 pounds tobacco to be made upon the said plantation and four hens, capons, or pullets to lease 100A. Lease is for and during the term of the natural lives of the said Stephen Boing and Mathew and John Boing brothers to the said Stephen. Bounded by William Pain, John Pain, John Smith, and Peter Jett. The sd. Stephen Boing is to pay the Quitrents of the land and within three years to plant an orchard to contain at least fifty apple trees. Signed Henry Fitzhugh, Junr. Delivered in presence of George Lee, Geo. Fraser. Recorded 3 February 1737 T. Turner.

2:163 - DEED OF LEASE - 14 January 1737 - Henry Fitzhugh of Stafford County, Esqr., to Peter Jett of King George County, planter. Yearly rent of 500 pounds tobacco to be made upon the said plantation and four hens, capons, or pullets to lease 100A. Lease is for and during the term of the natural lives of the said Peter Jett, and Rebecca his wife, and Francis his son. Bounded upon Charles Webster, William Pain, and the Glebe line. The said Peter Jett to pay the Quitrents of the land and within three years plant an orchard to contain at least fifty apple trees. Signed Henry Fitzhugh, Junr. Delivered in presence of George Lee, Geo. Fraser. Recorded 3 February 1737 T. Turner.

2:165 - DEED OF LEASE - 3 February 1737 - Henry Fitzhugh, Esqr., of Stafford County to George Jones of King George County. Yearly rent of 500 pounds tobacco to be made on the said plantation and two hens, capons, or pullets to lease 100A whereon the said George Jones now lives. Lease is for and during the term and space of the natural lives of the said George Jones, Ann his wife, and George his son or the longest liver of them. Bounded by the brink of the main branch of Muddy Creek and running along up the sd. branch to a wolf pitt. The said George Jones to pay the Quitrents of the land. Signed Henry Fitzhugh, Junr., George Jones. Delivered in presence of Farqr. Matheson, John Grant. Recorded 3 February 1737 T. Turner.

2:166 - DEED OF LEASE - 3 February 1737 - Henry Fitzhugh, Esqr., of Stafford County to William Pain of King George County. Yearly rent of 500 pounds tobacco to be made upon the said plantation and four hens, capons, or pullets to lease 100A lying on the north side of the Main Branch of Muddy Creek. It is the plantation whereon the said William Pain now lives. Lease is for and during the term and space of the natural lives of the said William Pain, Mary Pain his wife, and John Pain his son or the longest liver of them. Bounded by Richard Curtis, John Jett, Peter Jett, and Stephen Bowen. The said William Pain is to pay the Quitrents of the land. Signed Henry Fitzhugh, Junr., William

Pain. Delivered in presence of John Grant, Farqr. Matheson. Recorded 3 February 1737 T. Turner.

2:168 - DEED OF LEASE - 3 February 1737 - Henry Fitzhugh of Stafford County, Esqr., to John Pain of King George County, planter. Yearly rent of 500 pounds tobacco to be made upon the said plantation and four hens, capons, or pullets to lease 100A whereon the said John Pain now lives. Part of a patent joying upon the lines of Colson, Charles Webster, and John Smith. Lease is for and during the term of the natural lives of the said John Pain, Ann Pain his wife, and George Pain his son or the longest liver of them. The said John Pain is to pay the Quitrents of the land and within three years plant an orchard to contain at least fifty apple trees. Signed Henry Fitzhugh, Junr., John Pain. Delivered in presence of Farqr. Matheson, John Grant. Recorded 3 February 1737 T. Turner.

2:170 - DEED OF LEASE - 3 January 1737 - Peter Newport and Elizabeth his wife of Hanover Parish to Robert Rankins of same, planter. 5 shillings current money of Virginia to lease two tracts. One 50A tract adjoyning to the land whereon the said Robert Rankins now lives and left to the said Elizabeth by the last will and testament of James Butler her father. One 30A tract adjoyning to the same left to the said Elizabeth by the last will and testament of Richard Butler her uncle. Both parcels are part of a tract containing 1050A granted to William Baltrop, James Green, and Francis Lewis. Signed Peter Newport, Eliza. Newport. Delivered in presence of Samuel Reeds, Joseph Tutt, Willm. Duff, Junr. Recorded 3 February 1737 T. Turner.

2:171 - DEED OF RELEASE - 3 January 1737 - Peter Newport and Elizabeth his wife of Hanover Parish to Robert Rankins of same, planter. 20 pounds current money of Virginia for two tracts described in lease. Signed Peter Newport, Elizabeth Newport. Delivered in presence of Samuel Reeds, Joseph Tutt, William Duff, Junr. Recorded 3 February 1737 T. Turner.

2:174 - DEED OF LEASE - 27 February 1737 - Ellin Shippy of Brunswick Parish, widdow, to John Corbin of same, planter. 5 shillings sterling to lease 160A whereon the said Corbin now lives. Whereas Richard Shippy formerly husband to the said Ellin together with the said Ellin did in the year 1692 sell the same unto the said John Corbin but the said Ellin was not at court personally to be privately examined as the law requires she still retains a good right in Fee simple to the said land. Signed Ellen Shippy. Delivered in presence of William Thornton, John Grant, Daniel Grant, Bryan Chadwell. Recorded 3 February 1737 T. Turner.

2:176 - DEED OF RELEASE - 28 February 1737 - Ellen Shippy of Brunswick Parish, widdow, to John Corbin of same, planter. 3500 pounds tobacco heretofore paid to Ellen Shippy and her sd. husband Richard Shippy as likewise 30 shillings now in her hand for 160A described in lease. Signed Ellen Shippy. Delivered in presence of William Thornton, John Grant, Daniel Grant, Bryan Chadwell. Recorded 3 March 1737 T. Turner.

2:178 - DEED OF LEASE - 1 March 1737 - John Fox of Washington Parish in the county of Westmoreland to Francis Jeames of same. 5 shillings to lease 105A. Bounded by Christopher Edderington, John Jeames, and the main road. Signed John Fox. Delivered in presence of John Nunn, Elizab. Finch. Recorded 3 March 1737 T. Turner.

2:180 - DEED OF RELEASE - 2 March 1737 - John Fox of Washington Parish in the county of Westmoreland to Francis Jeames of same. 15 pounds current money of Virginia for 105A described in lease. Signed John Fox. Delivered in presence of John Nunn, Eliza. Finch. Mary Fox, wife of John Fox, relinquished her right of dower. Recorded 3 March 1737 T. Turner.

2:182 - DEED OF GIFT - 27 February 1737 - Sarah Hammet of Hanover Parish gives and makes over to her loving daughter Agnes Hammet after her decease all her household goods and stock and all that she is possessed with. Signed Sarah Hammet. Delivered in presence of William Marshall, John Marshall. Recorded 3 March 1737 T. Turner.

2:182 - DEED OF SALE - 13 March 1737/8 - An inventory of all the Goods and Chattles belonging to Thomas Apperson and by him made over unto Elizabeth Lomax, Gentlewoman, and for the satisfaction of one thousand and four pounds of Tobacco for Rent due to the said Elizabeth Lomax in manner and form following - Three feather Beds two Ruggs and four Blankets three Bedsteads, one high one and two low ones, eight Flag chairs two small Tables and one Spinning Wheel and bench one dark black horse with a star in his Forehead and branded on the near buttock with a C one Dozen of Plates and 3 dishes and 4 Basons hold one Gallon each and one of a Pottle two old hunting Saddles Seven Cows and one Small Bull and one Calf four hoggs and ten piggs two small Iron potts one large one and one brass Kettle two Water Pails and two piggens and one washing tubb one spice mortar and pestle and one box Iron and Heaters two pair pot hooks two Mares and Colts one small Heifer. Signed Thomas Apperson. Delivered in presence of Willm. Longmire, James Scurlock. Recorded 7 April 1738 T. Turner.

2:183 - DEED OF LEASE - 18 October 1737 - Francis Strother and Elizabeth his wife of Brunswick Parish to Samuel Moon of Hanover Parish. 5 shillings sterling to lease 200A lying on the Rappahannock River and adjoyning to the lands of John Tayloe, Esqr., and Benjamin Palmer. Part of a Pattent for 15,654A

granted to John and George Mott 17 October 1670 which said 200A of land
descended to the said Elizabeth, she being the only daughter and Heir at Law to
Richard Fossaker deceased. Signed Francis Strother, Elizabeth Strother.
Delivered in presence of Jno. Gilbert, Samuel Reeds, Sarah Gilbert. Recorded 7
April 1738 T. Turner.

2:185 - DEED OF RELEASE - 19 October 1737 - Francis Strother and
Elizabeth his wife of Brunswick Parish to Samuel Moon of Hanover Parish. 220
pounds current money of Virginia for 200A described in lease. Signed Francis
Strother, Elizabeth Strother. Delivered in presence of Jno. Gilbert, Samuel Reed,
Sarah Gilbert. Recorded 7 April 1738 T. Turner.

2:188 - DEED OF LEASE - 2 March 1737 - John Corbin of Brunswick Parish,
planter, to John Grant of same, planter. 5 shillings sterling to lease 160A
whereon John Corbin now liveth except a quantity of the same formerly given
by the said John Corbin to his son John Corbin, Junr. for 50A 3 October 1735,
the residue being 110A more or less. Part of a Patent granted to John and
George Mott. Bounded by a certain corner tree to Haberd. Signed John Corbin.
Delivered in presence of Wm. Thornton, Daniel Grant, John Hobby, Bryan
Chadwell. Recorded 7 April 1738 T. Turner.

2:190 - DEED OF RELEASE - 3 March 1737 - John Corbin of Brunswick
Parish, planter, to John Grant of same, planter. 6500 pounds tobacco and 10
shillings current money and 3000 nails for 110A described in lease. Signed John
Corbin. Delivered in presence of Wm. Thornton, Daniel Grant, John Hobby.
Presented into court by the said Grant and proved by the Oaths of Wm.
Thornton, Daniel Grant, and Bryant Chadwell and admitted to record. Recorded
7 April 1738 T. Turner.

2:194 - BOND - 3 March 1737 - John Corbin of Brunswick Parish, planter,
bound unto John Grant of same, planter, in the sum of 200 pounds sterling
money of Great Britain. Condition such that if John Corbin shall always and at
all times hereafter warrant and for ever defend the said land and premises, 110A
granted by certain deed of release bearing equal date with these presents, unto
him the said John Grant free from all manner of incumbrance whatsoever,
obligation to be void. Signed John Corbin. Delivered in presence of Wm.
Thornton, Daniel Grant, Jno. Hobby, Bryant Chadwell. Recorded 7 April 1738
T. Turner.

2:195 - DEED OF LEASE - 13 February 1737 - John Elliott of Washington
Parish in the county of Westmoreland, Gentleman, to Daniel McCarty of same,
Gentn. 5 shillings to lease two tracts. One 100A tract lying in Hanover Parish
formerly in the possession of Martin Fisher being part of 300A of land formerly

purchased by the said Martin Fisher's father of one William Jinnings. One 30A tract lying in Hanover Parish formerly purchased by the said Martin Fisher's father of one William Payne. The inheritance of which parcels of land by several mesne conveyances in the law came to one David Dickey. The said David Dickey by deeds dated 30 and 31 December 1719 conveyed the same to Humphrey Quessensbury deceased who in his last will and testament bequeathed it to his son Thomas Quessenbury who conveyed it unto John Finch of Westmoreland County by deeds dated 12 and 13 September 1728, and by the said John Finch ordered in his last will and testament dated 25 December 1735 to be sold by John Elliott his Executor. Signed John Elliott. Delivered in presence of Denis McCarty, R. Vaulx. Recorded 5 May 1738 T. Turner.

2:197 - DEED OF RELEASE - 14 February 1737 - John Elliott of Washington Parish in Westmoreland County, Gent., to Daniel McCarty of same, Gent. 50 pounds current money of Virginia for two tracts of land described in lease. Signed Jno. Elliott. Delivered in presence of Dennis McCarty, R. Vaulx. Recorded 5 May 1738 T. Turner.

2:199 - BOND - 14 February 1737 - John Elliott of Washington Parish in the county of Westmoreland, Gent., bound unto Daniel McCarty of same in the sum of 100 pounds sterling. Condition such that if John Elliott shall truly keep all the agreements particularly mentioned in a certain indenture of release bearing even date with these presents between the said John Elliott and Daniel McCarty, obligation to be void. Signed John Elliott. Delivered in presence of Denis McCarty, R. Vaulx. Recorded 5 May 1738 T. Turner.

2:200 - DEED OF GIFT - 7 May 1738 - John Corbin, Senior of Brunswick Parish in regard of the natural affection he bears to his well beloved son John Corbin, Junr. gives him 50A lying in Brunswick Parish bounded by Stephen Hansford, John Grant, a ridge beside the Rowling Road betwixt the Potomack and Rappahannock, a branch of Lambs Creek, and the North East Run being the run which runs from Richard Bryan into Lambs Creek. Signed John Corbin, Senr. Delivered in presence of John Coburn, Sacheveral Norman, Bridget Coburn. Recorded 5 May 1738 T. Turner.

2:201 - DEED OF LEASE - 1 January 1737 - Charles Carter, Esqr., of King George County to John Pattason, planter, of same. Yearly rent of 630 pounds good sound merchantable tobacco to be made on the said land to lease 200A made up of two tracts. One 195A tract is part of a greater tract of Carter's lying upon the Rappahannock River about four miles above the falls containing 782A and formerly divided into four tenements. This 195A is in the lower part near the river bounded by Thomas Hooper and the river. One 5A tract adjoyns to the aforesaid 195A and lyes in the upper lott of the greater tract. Lease is for and during the lives of the said John Pattason, Ann his wife, and Thomas Fletcher, Junr. It is further agreed that in case of the demise of either of the Partys named, for the consideration of 600 pounds of good tobacco in cask another life may be added to this lease in place of the deceased. John Pattason shall pay the Quitrents of the said 200A yearly and he is to plant an apple orchard of one hundred trees and a peach orchard of like quantity under a good fence. Signed Chs. Carter. Delivered in presence of Willm. Triplett, Alexr. Bell. Recorded 5 May 1738 T. Turner.

2:203 - ESTATE SETTLEMENT - 30 March 1738 - Settlement of Thomas King's Estate - one Negro man named Peter, one Grey Mare, one Feather Bed and Furniture Bedstead hide and cord, one Looking Glass, one Old Grey Mare, two Cows and Calves, one Stear, one-fourth pound shooe thread, one old Chest, one-half pound Brown thread, three and one-half pounds picked cotton, two sheep, three raw hides, one old side saddle, three pounds wool, one Coller and Hames from Traces, one Spinning Wheel, one spice Mortar and Pestle, one Iron pot Rack, two Frying Panns, one Furrow Plough, one Cullender, one Kirb Bridle, one Pail, one Piggen, six Hoggs, ten Geese, seventy-five and one-half pounds Pot Iron, five pounds good Pewter, eight pounds old Pewter, one Cow and Yearling, one Howcake Baker, one Ladle, eight Glazed Panns, one Butter Pott, one old Bed, and old Rugg. (Shows wife's Right of Dower to the Real Estate of Thomas King deceased and a child's part, but does not name them.) This account settled according to an Order of King George Court Bearing date the 3 March 1737 by us the subscribers - Thomas Vivion, Jere. Murdock, Thomas Monroe. This account presented into Court by Elizabeth King. Recorded 7 July 1738 T. Turner.

2:205 - DEED OF LEASE - 7 July 1738 - Francis Stone of Hanover Parish to William Stone and Mary his wife of same. To lease 70A lying upon the branches of Porrage Pott Swamp joyning on the land of Anthony Carnaby, Slatt, and John Payne. Lease is for and during the natural life of William Stone and Mary his wife or the longest liver of them two with this express proviso - that neither the said William Stone or Mary his now wife shall have liberty to lease rent lett out or put a Quarter on the said plantation and if either of them does, this lease to be void. William Stone and Mary his wife agree within seven years to plant one hundred good apple trees under a good and lawfull fence and to pay the yearly Quitrents of the said land. Signed Francis Stone, Willm. Stone. Delivered in presence of Thomas Ammon, Willm. Thatcher, Robt. Brooking. Recorded 7 July 1738 T. Turner.

2:206 - DEED OF LEASE - 2 August 1738 - Thomas Stanton of St. Mark's Parish in the county of Orange, planter, to John Piper of Washington Parish in the county of Westmoreland, planter. 5 shillings current money of Virginia to lease 236A lying on Eastward side of Deep Run. Bounded by tract granted unto Mr. Andrew Jackson, and the said Deep Run. Signed Thomas Stanton. Delivered in presence of Harry Turner, Robt. Elliston, Richd. Bryan, Antho. Haynie, George Tankersley, Geo. Fishpool. Recorded 1 September 1738 T. Turner.

2:208 - DEED OF RELEASE - 3 August 1738 - Thomas Stanton and Sarah his wife of St. Mark's Parish in the county of Orange to John Piper of Washington Parish in the county of Westmoreland, planter. 55 pounds current money for 236A described in lease. Signed Thomas Stanton, Sarah Stanton. Delivered in presence of Harry Turner, Robt. Elliston, Richd. Bryan, Antho. Haynie, Geo. Tankersley, Geo. Fishpool. Recorded 1 September 1738 T. Turner.

2:211 - BOND - 3 August 1738 - Thomas Stanton of St. Mark's Parish in the county of Orange, planter, bound unto John Piper of Washington Parish in the county of Westmoreland for 110 pounds current money of Virginia. Condition such that if Thomas Stanton shall truly keep all agreements particularly mentioned and expressed in one Indenture of Release bearing even date with these presents between Thomas Stanton and Sarah his wife and John Piper, obligation to be void. Signed Thomas Stanton. Delivered in presence of Harry Turner, Robt. Elliston, Richd. Bryan, Antho. Haynie, Geo. Tankersley, Geo. Fishpool. Recorded 1 September 1738 T. Turner.

2:212 - DEED OF FEEOFMENT - 29 August 1738 - George Fishpool of Hanover Parish to Phillip Pead of same. 25 Pistoles money of Virginia for 100A bounded by the land of Thomas Highlander, John Drake, Gyles Carter, William Deacons, land which formerly belonged to Christopher Pritchet, land of Thomas Claytor, Senr. and Junr., and land of John Cook. Part of the land formerly in possession of Martin Fisher the Elder deceased who on 11 January 1699 bequeathed all his land to be equally divided between his son Martin Fisher and his daughter Elizabeth Kitchen. The premises hereby granted is part of the premises layed out and allotted for the portion of the said Elizabeth Kitchen who conveyed and made over to her daughters Elizabeth Prim and Margaret Taite the 100A hereby granted. Signed Geo. Fishpool. Delivered in presence of Thomas Highlander, Edmond Barker, Ambrose Smithers. Recorded 1 September 1738 T. Turner.

2:215 - BOND - 29 August 1738 - George Fishpool of Hanover Parish bound unto Philip Pead of same in the sum of 50 Pistoles lawfull money of Virginia. Condition such that if George Fishpool shall truly keep all agreements contained in a certain Indenture of Bargain and Sale bearing date with these presents between the said George Fishpool and Philip Pead, obligation to be void. Signed George Fishpool. Delivered in presence of Thos. Highlander, Edmd. Barker.

Recorded 1 September 1738 T. Turner.

2:216 - SETTLEMENT OF ESTATE - 28 July 1738 - The Estate of Willm. Grant, Junr. deceased - monies paid to Elizabeth Grant and Mary Grant orphans, Margt. White, Elliner Carter, Humphry Quisenbury, William Remey for a coffin, Henry Drake, Capt. Daniel McCarty, Capt. Daniel White, James Drake, John Brantran, Charles Deane, Edward Barradall, Majr. Champe, Doctr. Fishpool, and Archd. Douglass. Pursuant to the Courts Appointment we whose names are hereunto subscribed do find the Balance due in Favour of the Orphans in the hands of John Grant the twenty fourth of March last was 26 pounds 18 shillings and 3 pence. Wm. Thornton, John Champe. Recorded 1 September 1738 Turner.

2:220 - DEED OF LEASE - 2 November 1738 - John Grant of the county of Stafford, Gentleman, and Margaret his wife Executors of the Last Will and Testament of William Strother late of King George County deceased to Augustine Washington of the county of Prince William, Gent. 5 shillings to lease 280A where the said William Strother lately dwelt in Brunswick Parish. Premises were formerly purchased by the said William Strother in his life time in three several parcels of Alice Cale, widdow, Thomas Harwood, and John Hartshorn. Signed John Grant, Margt. Grant. Delivered in presence of William Thornton, junr., Thomas Turner, junr., Anthony Haynie. Recorded 3 November 1738 T. Turner.

2:222 - DEED OF RELEASE - 3 November 1738 - John Grant of the county of Stafford, Gent., and Margaret his wife Executors of the Last Will and Testament of William Strother late of the county of King George, Gent., deceased to Augustin Washington of the county of Prince William, Gent. 317 pounds for 280A described in lease. Whereas the said William Strother in his last will and testament dated 20 November 1732 did declare that his lands in Prince William and King George Countys be sold to the highest bidder by his Executor his loving wife Margaret, if she should think convenient, John Grant and Margaret his wife Excutrix have exposed to sale the premises and the said Augustine Washington was the highest bidder. Signed John Grant, Margt. Grant. Delivered in presence of William Thornton, junr., Thomas Turner, junr., Antho. Haynie. Recorded 3 November 1738 T. Turner.

2:225 - INDENTURE - 2 November 1738 - George Reaves of Brunswick Parish doth freely and voluntarily put, place, and bind himself an apprentice and sevant to John Booth of same, weaver, and Hannah his wife to learn the Art and Mistery of a weaver and with them abide during the term of two years next ensuing. Signed Geo. Reeaves, Jno. Booth. Delivered in presence of Alexander Simpson, Henry McKie. Recorded 3 November 1738 T. Turner.

2:226 - DEED OF GIFT - __ December 1738 - Richard Tankersley, Senr. of St. Mary's Parish in the county of Caroline, planter, together with Margaret his now wife for the good will and affection they bear to Thomas Peatross and Martha his now wife make a free gift unto the said Thomas Peatross and Martha his now wife of all that parcel of land containing 100A for and during the term of their natural lives and after their decease to Rachel Peatross, daughter of Thomas and Martha Peatross. Joyning upon the land of William Wharton and Benjamin Dodd, and lying upon Gingoteague Run. Land is in the possession of John Williard, a tenant to Edward Marshall his wife having her thirds in the land. Signed Richard Tankersley, Margt. Tankersley. Delivered in presence of Joseph Berry, Robt. Ray, Jacob Fose. Recorded 2 February 1738 T. Turner.

2:228 - DEED OF SALE - 2 February 1738/9 - Samuel Simms of Hanover Parish, planter, to William Duff, Senr. of same. In consideration of a debt due by Simms to Duff for rent and other considerations amounting unto 1244 pounds of tobacco, Simms assigns and setts over unto William Duff what tobacco and corn he now has on his plantation, one Feather Bed, one Rugg, one Blanket, three Iron Potts, one Frying Pan, one Iron Ladle, one pair Flesh Forks, a pair of Firetongs, two sows and four pigs, and one Chestnut couler'd mare with a white strip in her face branded on the near Buttock with RO. Signed Saml. Simms. Delivered in presence of Ann Dennis, William Sarjant. Recorded 2 Feb. 1738 T. Turner.

2:229 - INDENTURE - 17 January 1739 - Sarah Quisenbury of Richmond County doth bind and put her son Humphry Quisenbury apprentice to John Quisenbury of King George County until he arrives to the age of twenty-one years, he the said Humphry being six years old the sixteenth day of June next. Signed Sarah Quisenbury, John Quisenbury. Delivered in presence of Cha. Deane, John Beddo. Recorded 2 February 1738 T. Turner.

2:230 - INDENTURE - 2 February 1738/9 - John Cofton, late of the county of Caroline, doth bind himself apprentice to William Clark, Taylor, of the county of King George to serve for the full term of five years. William Clark obliges himself to instruct the said apprentice in the Art and Mistery of the trade of a Taylor and at the expiration of the said term to give the said John Cofton a suit of Kirsey, two shirts, one pair of Hose, a pair of shoes, a felt hatt, a handkerchief and a set of tools. Signed John Cofton, Wm. Clark. Delivered in presence of Benja. Berryman, Gibson Berryman. Recorded 2 February 1738 T. Turner.

2:231 - DEED OF FEEOFMENT - 22 November 1738 - Lawrence Downton of Washington Parish and county of Westmoreland, planter, to William Dodgin of Hanover Parish. 20 pounds current money of Virginia for 100A bequeathed to the said Lawrence Downton by his father Nicholas Downton. Bounded by

Maxfield Brown, Majr. Wright, and John Brown. Signed Law. Downton. Delivered in presence of Newman Brown, George Brown, Robt. Montgomery. Recorded 2 February 1738 T. Turner.

2:233 - BOND - 30 November 1738 - Lawrence Downton of Westmorland County bound unto William Dodgin of King George County in the sum of 40 pounds current money of Virginia. Condition such that if the said Downton or anyone shall at any time for ever hereafter molest or disturb the said William Dodgin from having peaceable and quiet possession of a tract of land sold to the said William Dodgin by the said Lawrence Downton by Deed of Feeofment bearing date of 22 November 1738 being 100A it shall and is agreed by both partys that the above obligation to be in full force, otherwise to be void. Signed Lawrence Downton. Delivered in presence of Newman Brown, George Brown, Robert Montgomery. Recorded 2 February 1738 T. Turner.

2:234 - DEED OF SALE - 25 January 1738 - William Remey of Hanover Parish, planter, to Henry Drake of same. 3000 pounds tobacco and 12 pounds 10 shillings current money for two tracts of land. One 50A tract bounded by William Carter's orchard, John Dodd's spring branch, and Joseph Carpenter. One 100A tract being that land that William Sarjant left to his Godson William Witteredge and bounded by the line of William Carter's near Mattox Park, Brown's, Roe's, John Chin's and Thomas Randolf's. Signed William Remey. Delivered in presence of John Beddo, William Clator, Clapham Drake. Barbary Remey, wife of William Remey, relinquished her Right of Dower. Recorded 2 February 1738 T. Turner.

2:237 - PLAT OF LAND DIVISION - 5 October 1738 - Surveyed for Edmond Donoho and John Green 105 Acres of Land and divided between them by a line mutually agreed on between themselves - beginning at a white oak on a branch of Portrages Creek and running east then northwest near a tobacco house in an old field then south to the head of a branch by Mr. Rowland Thornton's plantation, then down the said branch to an ash stump in the said branch then east then north then east to Crows Swamp then down the said swamp to a corner in the swamp then west near Neal McCormack's tract to the said Portrages Creek then along the said creek the several courses to the beginning. Surveyed by Joseph Berry. Recorded 3 February 1738 T. Turner.

2:238 - BOND - 3 February 1738 - John Edwards and Lunsford Lomax, Gentn., bound to Our Sovereign Lord the King his Heirs and Successors in the sum of 16,306 pounds of tobacco. Condition such that whereas the above bounden John Edwards hath the collection of the sd. County put into his hands amounting to 8,153 pounds of tobacco, now if the sd. John Edwards doth faithfully collect and duly pay the same to the respective creditors also all such clerks and secretarys fees as shall be put into the hands of the said John Edwards to collect and pay the said fees to the respective officers to whom the same be due and payable according to law, obligation to be void. Signed Jno. Edwards, Lunsford Lomax. Recorded 3 February 1738 T. Turner.

2:239 - DEED OF LEASE - 2 March 1738 - Henry Fitzhugh of the county of Stafford, Esqr., to James Jones of the county of King George, bricklayer. Yearly rent of twelve pounds current money of Virginia to lease 50A where the said James Jones now dwells. Formerly holden by Walter Anderson, Ordinary Keeper, by virtue of a lease from the said Henry Fitzhugh and being the land on which King George Court House now stands. Bounded by James Micou, Elizabeth Lomax, and Robert Benson. Lease is for and during the natural lives of the said James Jones, Hester Jones his wife, and Joseph Jones his son or the longest liver of them. Signed Henry Fitzhugh. Delivered in presence of W. Jordan, Wm. MacKay, William Allison. Recorded 2 March 1738 T. Turner.

2:241 - DEED OF LEASE - 31 January 1738/9 - William Wharton of Hanover Parish to John Wren of same. 5 shillings sterling to lease 26A bounded by the Ferry Road, the main branch of Gengoteague, and the Old Road. Signed Wm. Wharton. Delivered in presence of Thos. Bartlett, Geo. Tankersley, John Thornley. Recorded 2 March 1738/9 T. Turner.

2:242 - DEED OF RELEASE - 31 January 1738/9 - William Wharton of Hanover Parish to John Wren of same. 50 pounds sterling for 26A described in lease. Signed Wm. Wharton. Delivered in presence of Thos. Bartlett, Geo. Tankersley, John Thornley. Recorded 2 March 1738 T. Turner.

2:245 - DEED OF LEASE - 28 November 1738 - Henry Long of Hanover Parish, planter, to Francis Baltrop late of the Province of Maryland. 5 shillings good and current money of Virginia to lease 200A whereon the said Henry Long now liveth and inhabiteth. Formerly given by Henry Long, Senr. to his son Henry Long, Junr. party to these presents by deed dated 2 April 1716. Bounded on the east by land formerly belonging to Samuel Wharton, Senr. deceased, on the south side by the County Road which leads from Gengoteague Bridge to Strother's Church, and on the west side by Mr. Thomas Turner and Isaac Arnold, Senr. and joyning upon the land of Thomas Arnold, Isaac Arnold, Junr. and Mrs. Mary Thornley. Signed Henry Long, Ann Long. Delivered in presence of Wm. Wharton, John Wren, Thos. Bartlett. Recorded 2 March 1738 T. Turner.

2:247 - DEED OF RELEASE - 29 November 1738 - Henry Long of Hanover Parish, planter, to Francis Baltrop late of the Province of Maryland. 110 pounds good and current money of Virginia for 200A described in lease. Signed Henry Long, Ann Long. Delivered in presence of Wm. Wharton, John Wren, Thos.

Bartlett. Recorded 2 March 1738/9 T. Turner.

2:249 - BOND - 29 November 1738 - Henry Long of Hanover Parish bound unto Francis Baltrop late of the Province of Maryland in the sum of 220 pounds good and current money of Virginia. Condition such that whereas the above bounden Henry Long hath lawfully conveyed unto the said Francis Baltrop a certain tract of land lying in the parish of Hanover joyning on the upper side of the land of Samuel Wharton and on the North side of the County Road which leads from Gengoteague Bridge to Strother's Church and upon the land of Mr. Thomas Turner and several others containing in the whole two hundred acres of land as in one deed of lease and one deed of release dated the 28 and 29 November 1738, if the said Henry Long his heirs and every one of them shall when thereto requested by the sd. Francis Baltrop acknowledge the said Deeds in the open Court of King George County and also faithfully observe all agreements contained in the said Deeds, obligation to be void. Signed Henry Long. Delivered in presence of John Wren, Wm. Wharton, Thos. Bartlett. Recorded 2 March 1738 T. Turner.

2:251 - DEED OF LEASE - No Date Given - John Champe, Gent., and Jane his wife of the county of King George to James Jones of same, bricklayer. 5 shillings lawfull money of England to lease a parcel of land which was formerly the dwelling plantation of the said Jones. It lyes in Brunswick Parish and is bounded by South East end of a bridge called North Bridge, the Main Road, Poplar Swamp, Mathews back line which was surveyed by John Savage, and a run which has its fountain from a spring on the land where Richard Ellkins, Senr. deceased formerly lived. Part of 2000A formerly granted unto Lt. Col. Saml. Mathews 7 September 1654 by Richard Bennit, Esqr. Signed John Champe, Jane Champe. Delivered in presence of David Seale, Peter Nugent, John Taliaferro. Recorded 2 March 1738 T. Turner.

2:253 - DEED OF RELEASE - No Date Given - John Champe, Gent., and Jane his wife of Brunswick Parish to James Jones of Hanover Parish, bricklayer. 70 pounds sterling for a parcel of land described in lease. Signed John Champe, Jane Champe. Delivered in presence of David Seale, Peter Nugent, John Taliaferro. Recorded 2 March 1738 T. Turner.

2:256 - DEED OF LEASE - 2 April 1739 - Thomas Williams of Brunswick Parish, planter, to Francis Thornton of same, Gent. 5 shillings to lease two tracts. One 100A tract formerly purchased by the sd. Thomas Williams of Robert Harrison and Elizabeth his wife by deed dated 14 March 1705. One 30A tract purchased by the said Thomas Williams of James Kay by deeds dated 24 and 25 February 1717. Signed Thomas Williams. Delivered in presence of William Thornton, junr., Antho. Haynie, Josiah Farguson. Recorded 6 April

1739 T. Turner.

2:258 - DEED OF RELEASE - 3 April 1739 - Thomas Williams and Bathias his wife of Brunswick Parish to Francis Thornton of same. 60 pounds sterling and 5000 nails for two tracts of land described in lease. Signed Thomas Williams, Bathias Williams. Delivered in presence of William Thornton, junr., Antho. Haynie, Josiah Farguson. Recorded 6 April 1739 T. Turner.

2:261 - POWER OF ATTORNEY - 15 September 1738 - Henry Sarjeant of Lancaster in the County of Lancaster and Kingdom of Great Britain, Mariner, appoints Thomas Nicholson of Whitehaven in the county of Cumberland and said Kingdom of Great Britain, Mariner, and William Duff in the Province of Virginia, Gentleman, his true and lawful attorneys jointly and severally for him and in his name to sell all that tract of land containing 1000A lying in the county of Spotsylvania and the sd. Province of Virginia and now in the tenure possession and occupation of him the said William Duff. Signed Henry Sarjeant. Delivered in presence of William Brockelbank, Edward Dixon, Abraham Benn, Samuel Donaldson. Recorded 4 May 1739 T. Turner.

2:263 - INDENTURE - 11 May 1739 - Elliner Adare of Hanover Parish binds her eldest son John Adare an apprentice or servant unto Joseph Tutt of the same, ships carpenter, untill he the said John shall arrive to the age of twenty-one years the sd. John Adare being seventeen years old the eleventh of January last. The sd. Joseph Tutt agrees to instruct the said John Adare in the Art and Mistery of a ship carpenter so far as to make him capable of building a good flatt after the usual and best manner that will carry thirty Hogsheads of Tobacco and to build any other boat of a smaller size and to cork the same and the said John not to be imployed any part of the said time in making or tending tobacco. At the time of freedom the said master to give and deliver to him the said John a full and new suit of apparel and one new saddle and bridle and if in case the said Joseph Tutt should dye before the said John his indentured time is expired, then the said John to be free. Signed Elliner Adare. Delivered in presence of Isaac Arnold, Thomas Williams, John Willis. Recorded 1 June 1739 T. Turner.

2:265 - INDENTURE - 11 May 1739 - Elliner Adare of Hanover Parish binds her son Thomas Adare an apprentice or servant unto the said Joseph Tutt untill the said Thomas Adare shall arrive to the age of twenty-one years the said Thomas Adare being eight years old the eleventh of July next ensuing. The said Joseph Tutt will instruct the said Thomas Adare as soon as he shall be able to learn the Art and Mistery of a ship carpenter. At the time of his freedom said master to deliver to him the sd. Thomas Adare one full and new suit of apparel and if in case the said Joseph Tutt should dye before the said Thomas his indentured time is expired, then the said Thomas Adare to be free. Signed

Elliner Adare. Delivered in presence of Isaac Arnold, Thom. Williams, John
Willis. Recorded 1 June 1739 T. Turner.

2:266 - DEED OF FEEOFMENT - 5 July 1739 - John Berry of Brunswick
Parish, planter, to Henry Berry of same, planter. 10,000 pounds good tobacco
for 250A whereon the said Henry Berry now lives. Formerly belonged to Henry
Berry deceased, father of the said John Berry and Henry Berry and devised to
the said John Berry by the last will and testament of the said Henry Berry dated
9 October 1695. Bounded by the Huckelberry Swamp, land formerly belonging
to William Berry deceased now in the possession of William Wheeler and
Christopher Rodgers, the Tansatt Branch, and line of the land formerly
belonging to James Kay now belonging to Capt. Samuel Skinker. Signed John
Berry. Delivered in presence of William Wheler, Enoch Berry, Joseph Berry.
Recorded 5 July 1739 T. Turner.

2:269 - DEED OF LEASE - 9 January 1738 - William Thornton of the county
of King George to Anthony Strother of same. Yearly rent of 930 pounds good
tobacco for the first and second year and the third year rent free and so to
continue his method of paying to lease 225A on the Rappahannock River about
two miles below the falls. Lease is for time that Anthony Strother and
Behethalan his wife shall think fit to live and abide thereon provided that they
do not at any time hereafter presume to work clear cutdown or tend any land or
ground that hath not been heretofore cleared and tended nor presume to cut
down any wood or timber except such as shall be necessary and directly for the
use of the said tenement. If the said William Thorton shall think fit at any time
to sell the said land, he may do it without any incumbrance of this lease except
to pay Anthony or Behethalan the just value of their improvements in houses on
the said tenement. Signed Will. Thornton, Antho. Strother. Delivered in
presence of Jeas Mackie, Benja. Strother, Margaret Strother. Recorded 7
September 1739 T. Turner.

2:272 - DEED OF LEASE - 1 December 1738 - Roswell Neale of St. Mary's
County of the Province of Maryland, Gent., to Augustine Washington, Gent.
Yearly rent of four pounds Virginia currency and the Quitrents to lease 300A
near the falls of the Rappahannock River adjoyning to the land of the said
Augustine Washington and Henry Fitzhugh, Esqr. Formerly in the occupation of
Margaret Strother, Widdow of Mr. William Strother late of King George County
deceased. Lease is for and during the natural life of him the said Roswell Neale.
Signed Roswell Neale. Delivered in presence of Robt. Osborn, ___ Thompson,
Wm. Wroe, Benjamin Weeks, Thos. Spillman. Recorded 7 September 1739 T.
Turner.

2:273 - DEED OF LEASE - 4 September 1739 - John Grimsley of St. Mary's

Parish in the county of Caroline to Benjamin Strother of Hanover Parish. 5 shillings sterling to lease one moiety or half of a tract of land lying in Hanover Parish left unto him by his father John Grimsley deceased by his will dated 27 January 1725. Signed John Grimsley. Delivered in presence of John Hamilton, Benja. Strother, M. Battaley. Recorded 7 September 1739 T. Turner.

2:275 - DEED OF RELEASE - 5 September 1739 - John Grimsley of St. Mary's Parish in the county of Caroline to Benjamin Strother of Hanover Parish. 15 pounds current money of Virginia for 50A described in lease. Signed John Grimsley. Delivered in presence of Jno. Hamilton, Benja. Strother, M. Battaley. Recorded 7 September 1739 T. Turner.

2:277 - DEED OF LEASE - 14 May 1739 - Benjamin Berryman, Gent. of King George County to John Berryman, minor. 5 shillings sterling to lease 200A that is part of a 750A tract conveyed by deeds dated 22 and 24 March 1735 from Elizabeth Berryman and Willoughby Newton, both of the county of Westmoreland, to the said Benjamin Berryman. Land is also part of 400A formerly escheated from Samuel Dudley, Jacob Daniel, and John Farmer by Benja. Berryman, Gent. deceased of Westmoreland County. Signed Benjamin Berryman. Delivered in presence of Anthony Thornton, Mason French, David Jones. Recorded 7 September 1739 T. Turner.

2:278 - DEED OF RELEASE - 14 May 1739 - Benjamin Berryman of King George County, Gent., to John Berryman, minor, of the county of Westmoreland. 1000 pounds tobacco for 200A described in lease. Part of 400A formerly escheated from Samuel Dudley, Jacob Daniel, and John Farmer by Benjamin Berryman, Gent. deceased of Westmoreland County, who bequeathed it to his son John Berryman above mentioned and the other moiety to his son Benjamin Berryman above mentioned. Signed Benjamin Berryman. Delivered in presence of Anthony Thornton, Mason French, David Jones. Recorded 7 September 1739 T. Turner.

2:280 - DEED OF LEASE - 1 June 1739 - William Owens of the county of Westmoreland, planter, and Jane his wife to Robert Hughs of Brunswick Parish, taylor. 5 shillings sterling to lease 100A abutting upon Richard Owen, Major John Fitzhugh deceased, Capt. Samuel Skinker, and the sd. Robert Hughs. It is a moiety given to William and Richard Owens by Deed of Gift from John Owen dated 2 March 1724. Signed William Owens. Delivered in presence of Alexr. Smeter, William Owens, John Swillavan. Recorded 2 November 1739 T. Turner.

2:282 - DEED OF RELEASE - 2 June 1739 - William Owen of the county of Westmoreland, planter, and Jane his wife to Robert Hughs of Brunswick Parish, taylor. 4000 pounds tobacco for 100A described in lease. Signed William Owens. Delivered in presence of Alexr. Smeter, William Owens, John Swillavan, Joshua Owens. Recorded 2 November 1739 T. Turner.

2:284 - BOND - 2 June 1739 - William Owen of Westmoreland County, planter, bound unto Robert Hughs of King George County, taylor, in the sum of 8000 pounds of tobacco. Condition such that if William Owens shall truly keep all agreements mentioned in certain Deeds of Lease and Release made between the above bound William Owen and Robert Hughs, obligation to be void. Signed William Owens. Delivered in presence of Alexr. Smeter, William Owens, John Swillavan, Joshua Owens. Recorded 2 November 1739 T. Turner.

2:285 - DEED OF LEASE - 2 November 1739 - Christopher Hinson of Washington Parish in the county of Westmoreland, planter, to Nicholas Quisenbury of same, planter. 5 shillings lawfull money of Great Britain to lease 88A whereon Elizabeth Peirce now lives. Bounded by said Nicholas Quisenbury, Anthony Carnaby, the County Road, and the Holly Branch. Land was formerly conveyed by one George Ervin to Alexander Hinson deceased father of the said Christopher Hinson. Signed Christopher Hinson. Delivered in presence of Humphry Quisenbury, George Quisenbury, William Quisenbury. Recorded 2 November 1739 T. Turner.

2:286 - DEED OF RELEASE - 1 November 1739 - Christopher Hinson of Washington Parish in the county of Westmoreland, planter, to Nicholas Quisenbury of same, planter. 4500 pounds tobacco for 88A described in lease. Signed Christopher Hinson. Delivered in presence of Humphry Quesenbury, George Quesenbury, William Quesenbury. Recorded 2 November 1739 T. Turner.

2:289 - BOND - 2 November 1739 - Christopher Hinson of Washington Parish and county of Westmoreland bound unto Nicholas Quisenbury of same in the sum of sixty pounds sterling. Condition such that if Christopher Hinson shall truly keep all agreements mentioned in certain Deeds of Lease and Release bearing even and equal date with these presents made between the above bounden Christopher Hinson and the above named Nicholas Quisenbury for 88A of land lying in the county of King George, obligation to be void. Signed Christopher Hinson. Delivered in presence of Humphry Quesenbury, George Quesenbury, William Quesenbury. Recorded 2 November 1739 T. Turner.

2:290 - DEED OF LEASE - 3 October 1739 - Mason French, Junr. of Prince William County to John Jett of the county of King George. 5 shillings current money to lease 200A whereon the said John Jett now lives lying on the branches of Muddy Creek. Bounded by Henry Fitzhugh, Esqr., Farqr. Mathewson,

Samuel Strother, and the Glebe land of Brunswick Parish. Signed Mason
French. Delivered in presence of Antho. Strother, James Hackley, Samuel
Reeds. Recorded 7 December 1739 T. Turner.

2:292 - DEED OF RELEASE - 4 October 1739 - Mason French, Junr. of the
county of Prince William to John Jett of the county of King George. One Negro
and 15 pounds current money for 200A described in lease. Signed Mason
French. Delivered in presence of Antho. Strother, James Hackley, Samuel
Reeds. Recorded 7 December 1739 T. Turner.

2:294 - DEED OF LEASE - 4 March 1739 - William Thornton of Brunswick
Parish, Gent., to Elias Sharp of same, planter. Yearly rent of 830 pounds
tobacco, except in the year 1740, to lease 100A lying on the Rappahannock
River. Part of the land the said Thornton formerly bought of George Proctor.
Bounded by Jeremiah Bronaugh the younger, the Main Road, Doctor William
Stevenson, and the river. Lease is for and during the natural lives of Elias Sharp
and Margaret his wife, or the longest liver, provided they make this said land
their residence and place of abidence during their said natural lives. Signed Wm.
Thornton, Elias Sharp. Delivered in presence of John Steward, Jno. Hobby,
David Bronaugh. Recorded 7 March 1739 T. Turner.

2:295 - DEED OF LEASE - 7 March 1739 - James Jones of the county of King
George, Undertaker in Architecture, to William Marquis of same, planter.
Yearly rent of 630 pounds tobacco in one cask and the Quitrents to lease 100A
where Richard Ellkins, Senr. formerly lived. Bounded by lines of Richard
Ellkins, John Owens, Catesby Cocke, Thomas Grigsby, and other lands of the
aforesd. Jones. Lease is for and during the natural lives of the said William
Marquis and Elizabeth his wife, or the longest liver of them. Within three years
they are to plant an orchard of one hundred apple trees, peach trees, and cherry
trees and to keep a good fence around the orchard. Signed Jas. Jones, William
Marquis. Delivered in presence of Rowland Thornton, Franis. Thornton, Thos.
Vivion. The within named William Marquis to live one year rent free in
consideration whereof he is to make either a twenty foot dwelling house or a
thirty foot tobacco house. Recorded 7 March 1739 T. Turner.

2:297 - DEED OF LEASE - 7 March 1739/40 - James Jones of the county of
King George, Undertaker in Architecture, to William Owens of the county of
Westmoreland, planter. Yearly rent of 850 pounds good tobacco in one cask to
lease 220A where the sd. William Owen now dwells. Part in King George
County and part in Westmoreland County. Bounded by James Dishman,
William Dowling, William Duff, the Widdow Thomas, the Widdow Berryman,
James Cash, and John Roach. Lease is for and during the natural lives of
William Owen and Jane Owen his wife, or the longest liver of the two. Within

three years, the said William Owen is to plant an orchard consisting of an hundred good winter appletrees with peach trees and cherry trees and to keep a good fence around it. Signed James Jones, Willm. Owen. Delivered in presence of Wm. Edwards, Richd. Bryan, Thos. Monroe. Recorded 7 March 1739 T. Turner.

2:299 - DEED OF SALE - 7 March 1739 - William Spencer of Prince William County, Gent., to Richard Barnes of the county of Richmond, Gent. 30 pounds sterling for the following slaves - George, Harry, Ann, Jenny, Tom, Forrester, George, and a boy which boy and Jenny, Tom, Forrester, and George are the children of the sd. Ann which three first mentioned slaves by the marriage of Penelope Manley with Francis Spencer, Gent., father to the said William Spencer, became the proper slaves of the said father and after his death the right and property therein descended to the said William Spencer. A former sale thereof made to the said Richard Barnes on or about 27 September last past and sealed and delivered in the presence of Thomas Brooke and Abraham Barnes of St. Mary's County in the Province of Maryland. Signed William Spencer. Delivered in presence of Hump. Pope, John Hazel, Geo. Deavenport. Recorded 7 March 1739 T. Turner.

2:300 - DEPOSITION - Various Dates - King George County - Robert English aged about thirty-seven years saith that he was well acquainted with Rodger Day and that he often heard him acknowledge Patrick Hamrick to be his cousin and shipmate and further saith that Rodger Day once told him if Patrick Hamrick woud go up where he lived he would give him land for his lifetime and assist him in building he having no other relations in this country and further saith not. Signed Robert English. Sworn before John Champe 3 September 1739. Prince William County - Thomas Hart aged about fifty years saith that he was well acquainted with Roger Day and that he often heard him say and acknowledge Patrick Hamrick to be his cousin and further saith that Roger Day often told him that they were brother and sisters children. Signed Thomas Hart. Sworn before Antho. Seale 5 September 1739. Edward Graham of Prince William County aged about sixty years being first sworn saith that he well knew Roger Day and that he many times heard the aforesd. Day say that Patrick Hamrick and he was Brother and sisters children and always acknowledged Hamrick to be his cousen and further saith not. Signed Edward Graham. Sworn before John Champe 3 January 1739. The Depositions were presented into court by John Mercer, Gent., Attorney for Patrick Hamrick and on his motion were admitted to record. Recorded 7 March 1739 T. Turner.

2:301 - DEED OF LEASE - 3 March 1739 - William Flowers of Brunswick Parish, planter, to William Simpson of Overwharton Parish in the county of Stafford, planter. 5 shillings sterling for 100A bounded by the White Oak

Branch, Colo. Fitzhugh, and Kenyon (formerly Elzy's). Signed Willm. Flowers. Delivered in presence of Thos. Vivion, Peter Daniel, Harry Turner. Recorded 6 June 1740 T. Turner.

2:302 - DEED OF RELEASE - 4 March 1739 - William Flowers of Brunswick Parish, planter, to William Simpson of Overwharton Parish in the county of Stafford, planter. 6500 pounds tobacco for 100A described in lease. Signed William Flowers. Delivered in presence of Thos. Vivion, Peter Daniel, Harry Turner. Recorded 6 June 1740 T. Turner.

2:304 - DEED OF LEASE - 1 July 1740 - William Thatcher of the county of King George to Thomas Vivion of same. 5 shillings lawful money to lease 200A upon the branches of Underwood's Beaverdam. Bounded by Triplett's line, a branch of the Beaverdam Swamp which divides this land from the Bristol Company, and Mrs. Tutt. Part of a tract of land belonging to Capt. William Underwood who bequeathed it to the said William Thatcher party to these presents. Signed William Thatcher. Delivered in presence of Peter Daniel, Bourn Price, James Daniel. Recorded 1 August 1740 T. Turner.

2:305 - DEED OF RELEASE - 1 July 1740 - William Thatcher of the county of King George to Thomas Vivion of same. 95 pounds current money of Virginia for 200A described in lease. Signed William Thatcher. Delivered in presence of Peter Daniel, Bourn Price, James Daniel. Recorded 1 August 1740 T. Turner.

2:307 - DEED OF LEASE - 31 July 1740 - John Piper of the county of Westmoreland, planter, to Joshua Farguson of the county of King George, planter. 5 shillings lawful money to lease 15A lying in Hanover Parish. Bounded by the northside of a branch of Poultereges Creek, back line of the land of the sd. Joshua Farguson, the Glebe land whereon the Reverend Mr. William Mackay now liveth, and Major Jere. Murdock. Signed John Piper. Delivered in presence of William Plunkett, John Farguson, Junr., James Scurlock. Recorded 1 August 1740 T. Turner.

2:308 - DEED OF RELEASE - 1 August 1740 - John Piper of the county of Westmoreland, planter, to Joshua Farguson of the county of King George, planter. 6 pounds 10 shillings lawful money and two acres of land lying on the north side of a branch of Poultereges Creek (being a corner of the land of the said Farguson) for 15A described in lease. Part of two patents, one granted to the said Piper's grandfather by Sir William Berkeley in 1662 and the other granted to the said John Piper by the Hon. Lord Thomas Fairfax in 1737. Signed John Piper. Delivered in presence of Willm. Plunkett, John Farguson, Junr., James Scurlock. Recorded 1 August 1740 T. Turner.

2:310 - DEED OF RELEASE - 1 August 1740 - William Pannel of the county of Caroline, planter, to Henry Fitzhugh of the county of Stafford, Esquire. 70 pounds for 150A lying in Hanover Parish according to a survey thereof lately made by one Joseph Berry. Part of a 2100A tract formerly granted to John Simpson 16 June 1666. Signed Wm. Pannel. Delivered in presence of Jno. Grant, Jas. Jones. Recorded 1 August 1740 T. Turner.

2:312 - DEED - 1 August 1740 - Mary Edrington of Westmoreland County, widdow, to William Rowley, Junr. of Brunswick Parish. 12 pounds current money for cornmill and half acre of land appertaining to the said mill on the Dogue Run. The said half acre of land and half of the said mill is now in the possession of the aforesaid Mary Edrington and the other half in the possession of William Rowley, Senr. and commonly known by the name of Rowley's Mill. Signed Mary Edrington. Delivered in presence of Robt. Lovell, Jno. Edwards. Recorded 1 August 1740 T. Turner.

2:313 - DEED - 1 August 1740 - Joseph Strother, Gent., Sheriff of the county of King George to Joseph Settle of same, planter. 2400 pounds tobacco for 50A formerly in the Seizen of George Green lying between the lines of the land of Maxfield Brown, Isaac Settle, and William Marshall. Sold by the sheriff according to writ issued by the court of the county of Stafford to pay debts owed by John Sebastian to James Pead of the county of Stafford. Signed Joseph Strother. Delivered in presence of John Minor, Nicho. Strother. Recorded 1 August 1740 T. Turner.

2:315 - DEPOSITION - 21 April 1740 - William Rowley, Senr. aged about seventy years saith that he knew a white oak standing on the North side of a hill which was always reputed Richard Rosser's corner which tree is now rotten and gone and further saith not. Sworn to before John Champe. Signed Will. Rowley. On 21 April 1740 Wm. Rowley put up a locust post in the spot where the above mentioned corner tree formerly stood. Delivered in presence of John Champe, Benja. McCarty, Robt. Smith, Howard Todd, Willm. Kelly, Jon. Jackson. Sarah Rosser produced this Deposition of William Rowley, Senr. into Court and on her motion the same was admitted to record. Recorded 6 June 1740 T. Turner.

2:315 - DEED OF LEASE - 26 July 1740 - Alford Head of Hamilton Parish in the county of Prince William, planter, to Harry Turner of Hanover Parish. 5 shillings current money of Virginia to lease 100A adjoining to the lands of William Peck, Robert Harrison, Grace Berry, Richard Green, William Duff, and corners on the land whereon William Jameson now dwells belonging to Thomas Turner. Formerly purchased of Robert Peck by William Head the Elder and on his decease descended to William Head the Younger who was Heir at Law and eldest son of the said William Head the Elder. On the decease of the said

William Head the Younger the same became vested in the aforesaid Alford Head party to these presents who was the eldest son and Heir at Law to the said William Head the Younger. Signed Alford Head. Delivered in presence of Henry Churchman, Thomas Turner, Junr., Willm. Marshall. Recorded 1 August 1740 T. Turner.

2:317 - DEED OF RELEASE - 27 July 1740 - Alford Head of Hamilton Parish in the county of Prince William, planter, to Harry Turner of Hanover Parish. 4000 pounds crop tobacco for 100A described in lease. Signed Alford Head. Delivered in presence of Henry Churchman, Thomas Turner, Junr., William Marshall. Recorded 1 August 1740 T. Turner.

2:319 - DEED OF LEASE - 3 October 1738 - Daniel McCarty of Washington Parish in the county of Westmoreland, Gent., to John Pope of Copley Parish in the county of Westmoreland, planter. 5 shillings lawfull money to lease 150A whereon Christopher Prichet now dwells binding on the land of Rawliegh Chin, Giles Carter, John Bartlett, and Lawrence Butler. Sold and conveyed by the said Christopher Prichet unto Daniel McCarty by deeds dated 29 and 30 September 1738. Signed Danl. McCarty. Delivered in presence of Jno. Elliott, Lawr. Butler, junr., James Carter, Jos. Butler. Recorded 3 October 1740 T. Turner.

2:320 - DEED OF RELEASE - 4 October 1738 - Daniel McCarty of Washington Parish in the county of Westmoreland, Gent., to John Pope of Copely Parish in the county of Westmoreland, planter. 40 pounds current money of Virginia for 150A described in lease. Signed Danl. McCarty. Delivered in presence of Jno. Elliott, Lawr. Butler, Junr., James Carter, Jos. Butler. Recorded 3 October 1740 T. Turner.

2:321 - BOND - 28 October 1738 - Daniel McCarty of Washington Parish in the county of Westmoreland, Gent., bound unto John Pope of Coupley Parish in the county of Westmoreland in the sum of 40 pounds current money of Virginia. Condition such that if Daniel McCarty shall truly keep all agreements mentioned in certain Indenture of Release bearing even date with these presents between the said Daniel McCarty and the sd. John Pope, obligation to be void. Signed Danl. McCarty. Delivered in presence of Jno. Elliott, Lawr. Butler, Junr., James Carter, Jos. Butler. Recorded 3 October 1740 T. Turner.

2:322 - DEED OF LEASE - 5 November 1740 - Mary Tutt of the county of King George to Francis Triplett of same, planter. 5 shillings sterling to lease 150A bounded by a corner tree of Daniel Underwood, old mill path formerly belonging to Richard Tutt, the head of Wolf Pit Branch, land now in the possession of John Fox, and Beaver Dam. Signed Mary Tutt. Delivered in presence of Thos. Robinson, John Triplett, Joseph Tutt. Recorded 7 November

1740 T. Turner.

2:323 - DEED OF RELEASE - 6 November 1740 - Mary Tutt of the county of
King George to Francis Triplett of same, planter. 90 pounds current money of
Virginia for 150A described in lease. Signed Mary Tutt. Delivered in presence
of Thos. Robinson, John Triplett, Joseph Tutt. Recorded 7 November 1740 T.
Turner.

2:326 - DEED OF LEASE - 7 November 1740 - Thomas Gough of
Overwharton Parish in the county of Stafford to Moses Pitman of Hanover
Parish. 60 pounds current money of Virginia for 60A bounded by Conway and
John Anderson. Signed Thomas Gough, Sarah Gough. Delivered in presence of
Josiah Farguson, John Willis, John Minor, junr. Recorded 7 November 1740 T.
Turner.

2:327 - DEED OF RELEASE - 7 November 1740 - Thomas Gough of
Overwharton Parish in the county of Stafford to Moses Pitman of Hanover
Parish. 60 pounds current money of Virginia for 60A described in lease. Signed
Thomas Gough, Sarah Gough. Delivered in presence of Josiah Farguson, John
Willis, Junr., John Minor, junr. Recorded 7 November 1740 T. Turner.

2:328 - DEED - 2 September 1740 - Peter Daniel of the county of Stafford to
James Crap of the county of King George. 12 pounds current money of Virginia
for three lotts within the Town of Falmouth numbered 28, 29, and 30 according
to the plat thereof laid off by John Warner, Surveyor, or one and a half acre.
William Thornton, Charles Carter, and Henry Fitzhugh the Younger, Gentn.
Directors of the Town of Falmouth by deed dated 2 August 1734 sold these lotts
to John Champe who by a deed dated the same day and year conveyed the lotts
to Peter Daniel. Signed Peter Daniel. Delivered in presence of Josiah Farguson,
John Willis, John Willis, Junr. Recorded 7 November 1740 T. Turner.

2:329 - DEED OF FEEOFMENT - 7 November 1740 - John Piper of the county
of Westmoreland, planter, and Mary his wife to Mary Fishpool of same,
widdow. 32 pounds 5 shillings currency for all that parcel of land in Hanover
Parish being the same premises lately recovered in the General Court of this
colony by William Thrustout, Lessee of the said John Piper, against Elias Yeats
by Judgment dated 22 October last past. Signed John Piper, Mary Piper.
Delivered in presence of Will. Jett, Geo. Davenport, Cha. Deane. This deed on
the motion of William Brockenbrough on behalf of the sd. Fishpool was
admitted to record. Recorded 7 November 1740 T. Turner.

2:331 - DEED - 4 December 1740 - Hugh Milligan of St. Paul's Parish and
Stafford County, planter, to Benjamin Stribling of King George County, planter.

Hugh Milligan confirms unto Benjamin Stribling his full Right Interest and property of his Lands and Tenements in Stafford County as also two Negroes Tom and Jack together with Sixteen head of Cattle and Thirty head of Hogs and all Household Furniture Chests of Goods with what tobacco and corn is now on the sd. Milligan's Plantation and all other estate whatever. The sd. Benjamin Stribling doth hereby promise and agree to find the sd. Hugh Milligan a sufficient Living equal to his circumstance during the sd. Milligan's Life and at his death a Christian Burial and also to pay what Debts the sd. Milligan at this time Justly Owes. Signed Hugh Milligan. Delivered in presence of John Champe, Samuel Reids, David Anderson, John Coburn. Recorded 5 December 1740 T. Turner.

2:332 - DEED OF LEASE - 2 April 1741 - Richard Green of Hanover Parish, planter, to Harry Turner of same. 5 shillings current money of Virginia to lease 50A lying in Hanover Parish. Part of a patent of land granted unto William Balthrop, James Green, and Francis Lewis for 1050A. Bounded by the Northside of the Western Main Branch of Gingoteague Creek, William Duff, Robert Rankins, and land of the sd. Harry Turner. Signed Richard Green. Delivered in presence of Arthur Spicer, Nicho. Strother. Recorded 3 April 1741 T. Turner.

2:333 - DEED OF RELEASE - 3 April 1741 - Richard Green of Hanover Parish, planter, to Harry Turner of same. 28 pounds current money for 50A described in lease. Signed Richard Green. Delivered in presence of Arthur Spicer, Nicho. Strother. Recorded 3 April 1741 T. Turner.

2:336 - DEED OF SALE - 3 April 1741 - William Gates of the county of King George for consideration of a debt due from him to Adam Reid amounting to thirteen pounds current money of Virginia makes over unto the sd. Adam Reid two Beds and furniture, one Bay Mare and Colt, two Sows, Thirteen Pigs and Six Shoats, 3 Iron Pots, one Dozn. Pewter Plates and Six Pewter Dishes. Signed William Gates. Delivered in presence of T. Turner, Frans. Thornton. Recorded 3 April 1741 T. Turner.

2:337 - DEED OF LEASE - 30 April 1741 - John Jett of the county of Westmoreland to William Jett of the county of King George. 5 shillings lawfull money to lease 170A binding on the North West Side of a Swamp called Fork Swamp now known by the name of the Head Swamp of Monroes Dam. Now in the Possession of William Edwards and Mary Edrington which land was formerly the Estate of William Jett deceased and by the sd. William Jett's last Will and Testament dated 27 May 1695 bequeathed to Peter Jett deceased and the Heirs of his body lawfully begotten and for want of such Heirs to the Surviving Brothers whereby it became the proper Estate of John Jett who is party to these presents. Signed John Jett. Delivered in presence of Thos. Vivion, Cha. Dean, Thos. Ammon. Recorded 1 May 1741 T. Turner.

2:338 - DEED OF RELEASE - 1 May 1741 - John Jett of the county of Westmoreland to William Jett of the county of King George. 10 pounds current money of Virginia for 170A described in lease. Signed John Jett. Delivered in presence of Thos. Vivion, Cha. Deane, Thos. Ammon. Recorded 1 May 1741 T. Turner.

2:341 - DEED OF LEASE - 26 March 1741 - William Wharton of Washington Parish in the county of Westmoreland, planter, to Harry Turner of Hanover Parish. 5 shillings current money of Virginia to lease 50A adjoining the land of Robert Johnson, Thomas Peatross, John Wren, and Thomas Turner. Signed William Wharton. Delivered in presence of T. Turner, William Longmire, Thomas Apperson. Recorded 1 May 1741 T. Turner.

2:342 - DEED OF RELEASE - 27 March 1741 - William Wharton of Washington Parish in the county of Westmoreland, planter, to Harry Turner of Hanover Parish. 25 pounds current money for 50A described in lease. Signed William Wharton. Delivered in presence of T. Turner, William Longmire, Thomas Apperson. Recorded 1 May 1741 T. Turner.

2:345 - DEED OF LEASE - 3 April 1741 - Farquhar Mathewson of St. Paul's Parish in the county of Hanover to Anthony Haynie of Brunswick Parish. 5 shillings sterling to lease 272A butting on the lands of Henry Fitzhugh, Esqr., Colo. William Thornton, Mr. Danl. French, and Mr. Hugh French. Part of boundary is an Hickory formerly called Scotts upper corner. Signed Farquhar Mathewson. Delivered in presence of Harry Turner, Nic. Strother. Recorded 1 May 1741 T. Turner.

2:346 - DEED OF RELEASE - 4 April 1741 - Farquhar Mathewson of St. Paul's Parish in the county of Hanover to Anthony Haynie of Brunswick Parish. 35 poundss current money for 272A described in lease. Signed Farquhar Mathewson. Delivered in presence of Harry Turner, Nic. Strother. Recorded 1 May 1741 T. Turner.

2:349 - DEED OF LEASE - 20 January 1740 - James Grant of King George County, planter, to Thomas Monteith of same, merchant. 5 shillings lawfull current money of Virginia to lease 100A which the said James Grant bought of Jonathan Clerk. Bounded by Colson's land and land formerly belonging to Peter Gallon. Part of 400A formerly given by John and George Motts unto John Vickars. Signed James Grant. Delivered in presence of Stephen Hansford, John Coburn, Thomas Ficklin. Recorded 5 June 1741 T. Turner.

2:350 - DEED OF RELEASE - 21 January 1740 - James Grant of King George County, planter, to Thomas Monteith of same, merchant. 30 pounds 10 shillings and one Pistole current lawfull money of Virginia for 100A described in lease. Signed James Grant. Delivered in presence of Stephen Hensford, John Coburn, Thomas Ficklin. Recorded 5 June 1741 T. Turner.

2:352 - BOND - 21 January 1740 - James Grant of King George County, planter, bound unto Thomas Monteith of same, merchant, in the sum of 200 pounds sterling. Condition such that if James Grant keeps all agreements specified in a certain Lease and Release dated the 20 and 21 January 1740 made between the above bounden James Grant and the said Thomas Monteith, obligation to be void. Signed James Grant. Delivered in presence of Stephen Hansford, John Coburn, Thomas Ficklin. Recorded 5 June 1741 T. Turner.

2:353 - DEED OF FEEOFMENT - 5 June 1741 - Edward Phegin of Hambleton's Parish in the county of Prince William to Samuel Moon of Hanover Parish. 25 pounds sterling for 150A bounded by Maxfield Brown, George Green, Francis Thornton, Thomas Hews, and William Combs. Signed Edward Pheagin. Delivered in presence of Fras. Strother, Senr., Stafford Lightburn, George Riding. Recorded 5 June 1741 T. Turner.

2:355 - DEED OF LEASE - 29 July 1740 - Henry Fitzhugh of the county of Stafford, Esqr., to Saml. Walker of the county of King George, planter. Yearly rent of 500 pounds tobacco made upon the said land and four hens, capons, or pullets to lease 105A bounded by the Main Branch and Chinn's line. Lease is for and during the natural lives of the said Samuel Walker, Anne Walker his wife, and William Walker his son, or the life of the longest liver of them. Samuel Walker is to pay the Quitrents and within three years plant fifty apple trees. Signed Henry Fitzhugh. Delivered in presence of William Allison, Thomas Leigh, Danl. Neale. Recorded 5 June 1741 T. Turner.

2:358 - DEED OF LEASE - 1 June 1741 - Marmaduke Beckwith of Lunenburgin Parish in the county of Richmond to Jonathan Sydenham of Hanover Parish. 5 shillings current money to lease 60A formerly purchased by Samuel Bowen of Francis Triplett. Part of a Great Tract taken up by the said Triplett. Said land was sold by William Litman and Frances his wife to one Thomas Dickerson who dying without a will the land descended to his son Metcalfe Dickerson who sold the same to the said Beckwith. Bounded on the lines of William Ball, James Scott, Joseph Minton, Samuel Nichols, and William Tiller. Signed Marmaduke Beckwith. Delivered in presence of T. Turner, W. Jordan. Recorded 5 June 1741 T. Turner.

2:359 - DEED OF RELEASE - 2 June 1741 - Marmaduke Beckwith of

Lunemberg Parish in the county of Richmond to Jonathan Sydenham of Hanover Parish. 55 pounds current money of Virginia for 60A described in lease. Signed Marmaduke Beckwith. Delivered in presence of T. Turner, W. Jordan. Recorded 5 June 1741 T. Turner.

2:361 - BOND - 2 June 1741 - Marmaduke Beckwith of Lunemburg Parish in the county of Richmond bound unto Jonathan Sydenham of the county of King George in the sum of 110 pounds current money. Condition such that if Marmaduke Beckwith shall truly keep all agreements mentioned in one indenture bearing even date with these presents made between Marmaduke Beckwith and Jonathan Sydenham, obligation to be void. Signed Marmaduke Beckwith. Delivered in presence of T. Turner, W. Jordan. Recorded 5 June 1741 T. Turner.

2:362 - DEED OF LEASE - 16 April 1741 - Hancock Lee of King George County, Gent., to William Pickett of Spotsylvania County, planter. Yearly rent of four pounds current money of Virginia to lease 150A lying in Hanover Parish. Part of a large tract belonging to the said Hancock Lee and to be laid off to the said Wm. Picket's liking. All necessary timber may be gotten of that part of the land on that side of the road next to Major George Turbervile. Lease is for and during the natural lives of the said William Picket, Elizabeth his wife, and John his son. Signed Hancock Lee. Delivered in presence of James Hewitt, T. Jameson, Richd. McGraw. Recorded 4 July 1741 T. Turner.

2:364 - DEED OF LEASE - 30 April 1741 - Sherwood Grimsley of Saint Mary's Parish in the county of Caroline to Benjamin Strother of Hanover Parish. 5 shillings sterling to lease one moiety or half of a tract of land left unto the said Sherwood Grimsley by his father John Grimsley deceased by his Last Will and Testament dated 27 January 1725. Signed Sherwood Grimsley. Delivered in presence of Joseph Strother, John Minor, Junr., John Grant. Recorded 3 July 1741 T. Turner.

2:365 - DEED OF RELEASE - 1 May 1741 - Sherwood Grimsley of Saint Mary's Parish in the county of Caroline to Benjamin Strother of Hanover Parish. 15 pounds current money of Virginia for 50A described in lease whereon the said Sherwood Grimsley's father John Grimsley deceased formerly lived. Signed Sherwood Grimsley. Delivered in presence of Joseph Strother, John Minor, junr., Jno. Grant. Recorded 3 July 1741 T. Turner.

2:366 - DEED OF LEASE - 1 July 1741 - John Champe, Junr. of Brunswick Parish, Gentleman, to John Tool of same, planter, and Mary his wife. Yearly rent of 600 pounds of tobacco to lease 50A bounded by John Carree, the North Swamp, the Honourable John Taylor, Esqr., and the said John Champe. Lease is for and during and unto the full end and term of the natural lives of the said John Tool and Mary his wife. Signed John Champe. No Signature of Witnesses. Recorded 3 July 1741 T. Turner.

2:368 - DEED OF LEASE - 5 August 1741 - John Popham and Elizabeth his wife of King William Parish in the county of Goochland, Gentleman, to John Steward of Brunswick Parish, planter. 5 shillings sterling to lease 126A bounded by John Price, the head of the Westernmost Branch of Kay's Swamp, Benjamin Stribling, Hales Road, and Charles Steward. Signed John Popham, Elizabeth Popham. Delivered in presence of W. Battersly, Hen. Mckie, Jno. Hobby, Harry Turner, Jno. Grant, Jno. Edwards, Edmd. Pendleton. Recorded 4 September 1741 T. Turner.

2:370 - DEED OF RELEASE - 6 August 1741 - John Popham and Elizabeth his wife of King William Parish in the county of Goochland, Gentleman, to John Steward of Brunswick Parish, planter. 60 pounds for 126A described in lease. Part of 2186A patent granted to James Kay by Colonel Thomas Lee agent for the proprietors 13 June 1715, 500A being waste or surpluss land. The other 1686A being formerly granted to Colonel Gerrard Fowlke and Mr. Richard Haibord by patent bearing date of 23 March 1664. Sold by the said Haibord (he being the survivor) to James Kay grandfather to the present James Kay to whom this land descends by inheritance. Signed John Popham, Elizabeth Popham. Delivered in presence of W. Batterly, Hen. McKie, Jno. Hobby, Harry Turner, Jno. Grant, Edmd. Pendleton, Jno. Edwards. Recorded 4 September 1741 T. Turner.

2:373 - BOND - 6 August 1741 - John Popham of King William Parish in the county of Goochland, Gent., bound unto John Steward of Brunswick Parish in the sum of 120 pounds current money of Virginia. Condition such that if John Popham truly keeps all agreements specified in certain Deeds of Lease and Release bearing equal date with these presents between the bounden John Popham and the said John Steward, obligation to be void. Signed John Popham. Delivered in presence of W. Battersly, Hen. McKie, John Hobby, John Edwards, Harry Turner, John Grant, Edmd. Pendleton. Recorded 4 September 1741 T. Turner.

2:374 - DEED OF LEASE - 2 June 1741 - Samuel Kendall of Washington Parish in the county of Westmoreland, planter, to Jeremiah Murdock of Hanover Parish, Gent. 5 shillings current money of Virginia to lease 50A that is part of 105A patented by Thomas Kendall as by his deed from William Fitzhugh andd George Brent agents for the proprietors dated 19 March 1696/7. Said 50A was sold by the said Thomas Kendall to his son William Kendall by deeds dated 2 and 4 March 1716. And by the said William Kendall the same land was sold unto the said Samuel Kendall party to these presents by deeds dated 28 and 29 November 1721. Bounded by Portrages Creek and land of Isaac Pitman formerly John Greens. Signed Samuel Kendall. Delivered in presence of T. Jameson, Harry Turner, Josiah Farguson. Recorded 4 September 1741 T. Turner.

2:376 - DEED OF RELEASE - 3 June 1741 - Samuel Kendall and Sarah his wife of Washington Parish in the county of Westmoreland, planter, to Jeremiah Murdock of Hanover Parish. 100 pounds current money of Virginia for 50A described in lease. Signed Samuel Kendall, Sarah Kendall. Delivered in presence of T. Jameson, Harry Turner, Josiah Farguson. Recorded 4 September 1741 T. Turner.

2:379 - BOND - 3 June 1741 - Samuel Kendall of the county of Westmoreland, planter, bound unto Jeremiah Murdock of the county of King George in the sum of 500 pounds current money of Virginia. Condition such that if the bounden Samuel Kendall shall keep all agreements mentioned in one Indenture of Release bearing even date with these presents made between the bounden Samuel Kendall and Sarah his wife and the above named Jeremiah Murdock, obligation to be void. Signed Samuel Kendall. Delivered in presence of T. Jameson, Harry Turner. Josiah Farguson. Recorded 4 September 1741 T. Turner.

2:380 - DEED OF LEASE - 28 September 1741 - Charles Carter, Esqr. of King George County to John Humphrys, Junr. of same, planter. Yearly rent of 530 pounds of good sound tobacco produce of ye said plantation to lease 151A that is part of a Greater Tract of ye said Carters known by the name of Stanstead Tract lying upon Clayburns Run. Bounded by road as leads from Falmouth to John Humphreys, Senr. and the West most line of Wilkinson's Pattent. Lease is for and during the natural lives of John Humphreys, Margt., and Jams. Humphrey his son. They are also to pay the Quitrents, to build one dwelling house twenty feet long and sixteen feet wide with an inside chimney, to build one tobacco house twenty feet long and twenty feet wide, and to plant an orchard of 100 apple trees and 100 peach trees and to keep the same well trim'd and fenced. Signed Charles Carter, John Humphrey. Delivered in presence of Hancock Lee, Henry Machen. Recorded 2 October 1741 T. Turner.

2:382 - DEED OF RELEASE - 10 June 1741 - Francis Strother and Elizabeth his wife of St. Mark's Parish in the county of Orange to Samuel Moon of Hanover Parish. 220 pounds current money of Virginia for 200A lying on the Rappahannock River and adjoining the land of John Tayloe, Esqr., and of Benjamin Palmer. Part of 15,654A patent granted to John and George Mott 17 October 1670 which said 200A descended to the said Elizabeth she being the only daughter and Heir at Law to Richard Fossaker deceased. Signed Francis Strother, Elizabeth Strother. Delivered in presence of David Robinson, Nic. Strother, Wm. Thatcher, Jno. Gilbert. Recorded 2 October 1741 T. Turner.

2:385 - DEED OF FEEOFMENT - 3 February 1741 - James Crap of the county of King George, Gent., to Robert Sheddin of same, merchant. 41 pounds 10 shillings current money for a lot or half acre distinguished by the number 28 as by a plat thereof of the Town of Falmouth made by John Warner, Surveyor. Conveyed unto the said James Crap along with lots 29 and 30 by Peter Daniel by deed dated 2 September 1740. The said Peter Daniel bought them of John Champe who by deed dated 2 August 1734 bought the said lots of William Thornton, Charles Carter, and Henry Fitzhugh Gentlemen and Trustees for the Town of Falmouth. Signed James Crap. Delivered in presence of Anthony Strother, John Grant, Sam. Earles, T. Jameson, James Hewitt. A memorandum was signed by John Grant, R. Rogers, Sam Earles, James Hewitt. Recorded 5 March 1741 Harry Turner.

2:388 - BOND - 3 February 1741 - James Crap bound unto Robert Sheddin of the Town of Falmouth, merchant, in the sum of 100 pounds current money of Virginia. Condition such that if James Crap shall at the County Court to be held at King George County in the month of March next appear and acknowledge the said deed to the said Robert Sheddin according to the true intent and meaning thereof and also that Margery the wife of the said James Crap shall relinquish all her Right and Title of Dower, obligation to be void. Signed James Crap. Delivered in presence of Anthony Strother, John Grant, Sam Earles. Recorded 5 March 1741 Harry Turner.

2:389 - DEED OF LEASE - 2 December 1741 - Newman Brown of Hanover Parish, planter, to William Marshall of same, planter. 5 shillings current money of Virginia to lease 100A whereon the said William Marshall now dwells and adjoined to the land of Mr. William Randolph. Given by Francis Slaughter by Deed of Gift dated 11 July 1711 unto Ann Hudson who is mother of Martha Brown wife of Newman Brown. Signed Newman Brown. Delivered in presence of J. Mercer, Jona. Sydenham, John Champe, Harry Turner. Recorded 2 April 1742 T. Turner.

2:390 - DEED OF RELEASE - 3 December 1741 - Newman Brown and Martha his wife of Hanover Parish to William Marshall of same, planter. 4000 pounds tobacco for 100A described in lease. Signed Newman Brown. Delivered in presence of J. Mercer, Jon. Sydenham, John Champe, Harry Turner. Recorded 2 April 1742 T. Turner.

2:393 - DEED OF LEASE - 27 January 1741 - Daniel Grant and Mary his wife of Brunswick Parish to James Scurlock of Hanover Parish. 5 shillings current money of Great Britain to lease 110A that is part in King George County, part in Westmoreland County and part in Stafford County. First granted to Thomas Harvey as by deed dated 20 July 1697 for 220A and by other conveyances became the land of William Pannel deceased, father to the said Mary Grant, who bequeathed it to be equally divided between his two daughters Catharine and Mary. Bounded by Henry Berry and Robert Peck, Hayles Path, George King, John Pearce, the Beaver Damm of Jordan's Bridge and Thomas Porter. Signed Daniel Grant, Mary Grant. Delivered in presence of Wm. Waller, Wm. Sergeant, Nic. Strother. Recorded 2 April 1742 T. Turner.

2:395 - DEED OF RELEASE - 28 January 1741 - Daniel Grant and Mary his wife of Brunswick Parish to James Scurlock of Hanover Parish. 30 pounds current money of Virginia for 110A described in lease. Signed Daniel Grant, Mary Grant. Delivered in presence of Wm. Waller, Wm. Sejant, Nic Strother. Recorded 2 April 1742 T. Turner.

2:397 - BOND - 28 January 1741 - Daniel Grant of Brunswick Parish, planter, bound unto James Scurlock of Hannover Parish in the sum of 60 pounds current money. Condition is such that if Daniel Grant doe truly execute, perform and keep all and every clause, title, covenant, and condition mentioned in one Indenture of Release bearing equal date with these presents made by the said Daniel Grant unto the said James Scurlock of 110A being one moiety of land formerly granted to one Thomas Harvey and by several other conveyances became William Pannels which he left to be divided between his two daughters Catharine and Mary, obligation to be void. Signed Daniel Grant. Delivered in presence of Wm. Waller, Wm. Serjeant, Nic. Strother. Recorded 2 April 1742 T. Turner.

2:398 - DEED OF LEASE - 1 April 1742 - William James of St. George Parish in the county of Spotsylvania, planter, to Jeremiah Murdock of Hanover Parish, Gent. 5 shillings current money of Virginia to lease 20A. Bequeathed by the Last Will and Testament of John Willis the Elder dated 7 June 1715 to Thomas James and Mary his wife during their natural lives and after their decease to descend to David James son of the said Thomas James which on the death of the said David James the same land became vested in the said William James party to these presents who was the next brother and Heir at Law to the sd. David James deceased. Bounded by Isaac Arnold, Wormley's line now the said Jeremiah Murdocks, Isaac Pitman, and John Willis. Signed William James. Delivered in presence of M. Battaley, Jas. Strother, Harry Turner, Jos. Strother. Recorded 2 April 1742 T. Turner.

2:399 - DEED OF RELEASE - 2 April 1742 - William James of St. George

Parish in the county of Spotsylvania, planter, to Jeremiah Murdock of Hanover Parish, Gent. 12 pounds current money of Virginia for 20A described in lease. Signed William James. Delivered in presence of M. Battaley, Jas. Strother, Harry Turner, Jos. Strother. Recorded 2 April 1742 T. Turner.

2:402 - BOND - 2 April 1742 - William James of the county of Spotsylvania bound unto Jeremiah Murdock of the county of King George in the sum of 25 pounds current money of Virginia. Condition such that if William James shall keep all agreements particularly mentioned in one Indenture of Release bearing even date with these presents made between the above bound William James and the above named Jeremiah Murdock, obligation to be void. Signed William James. Delivered in presence of M. Battaley, Jas. Strother, Harry Turner, Jos. Strother. Recorded 2 April 1742 T. Turner.

2:403 - DEED OF LEASE - 5 November 1741 - John Gollothan and Mary Sandford both of Washington Parish in the county of Westmoreland, planters, to Giles Carter, Senr. of Hanover Parish, planter. 2 shillings 6 pence current money of Virginia to lease 130A bounded on the lands of Thomas Claytor, Philip Peads, William Deakins, and the sd. Giles Carter. Part of a tract of land formerly patented by Mr. John Lord who conveyed it to one Martin Fisher who sold the same to Nathaniel Hall and John Motley who sold the same to Thomas Pritchet father to Christopher Pritchet, Junr. who sold the same to Martin Gollothan father to the said John Gollothan. Signed John Gollorthun, Mary Sandford. Delivered in presence of Thomas Highlander, John Bartlett, John Saull. Recorded 2 April 1742 T. Turner.

2:405 - DEED OF RELEASE - 6 November 1741 - John Gollothan and Mary Sandford both of Washington Parish in the county of Westmoreland, planters, to Giles Carter, Senr. of Hanover Parish, planter. 5000 pounds tobacco and a Guinea for 130A described in lease. Signed John Gollothan, Mary Sandford. Delivered in presence of Thomas Highlander, John Bartlett, John Saull. Recorded 2 April 1742 T. Turner.

2:407 - BOND - 6 November 1741 - John Gollothan and Mary Sandford both of Washington Parish in the county of Westmoreland, planters, bound to Giles Carter of Hanover Parish, planter, in the sum of 10,000 pounds of good tobacco. Condition such that if John Gollothan and Mary Sandford shall truly keep all agreements contained in certain Indentures of Bargain and Sale by way of Lease and Release made between the said John Gollothan and Mary Sandford and the above named Giles Carter, obligation to be void. Signed John Gollothan, Mary Sandford. Delivered in presence of Thos. Highlander, John Bartlett, John Saull. Recorded 2 April 1742 T. Turner.

2:408 - DEED OF GIFT - 2 April 1742 - William Wheeler of Brunswick Parish for Divers good Causes and Considerations but Especially for the Love and Affection he bears to his Daughter in Law Elizabeth Strother gives unto the said Elizabeth Strother one Negro Girl Named Rose to her and her heirs for Ever. Signed William Wheeler. Delivered in presence of Jas. Strother, Nic. Strother. Recorded 2 April 1742 T. Turner.

2:408 - DEED OF LEASE - 29 March 1742 - John Triplett of Washington Parish in the county of Westmoreland to Darby Tool of Hanover Parish. 5 shillings current money of Virginia to lease 140A lying in Hanover Parish. Part of a Patent of Land granted unto William Underwood, Senr. late of King George County deceased. Bounded by the Bryery Bottom on the lower side of the road which leads from the Bristol Iron Works to the Ridge Road which divides King George County from Westmoreland County, land of the said John Triplett, a Deep Bottom which leads unto Underwoods beaver Dam, Mr. Thomas Vivion, and John Canady. Signed John Triplett. Delivered in presence of Isaac Arnold, Henry Care, Thomas Underwood. Recorded 2 April 1742 T. Turner.

2:410 - DEED OF RELEASE - 30 March 1742 - John Triplett of Washington Parish in Westmoreland County to Darby Tool of Hanover Parish. 70 pounds current money of Virginia for 140A described in lease. Signed John Triplett. Delivered in presence of Isaac Arnold, Henry Care, Thos. Underwood. Recorded 2 April 1742 T. Turner.

2:412 - BOND - 30 March 1742 - John Fox of Hanover Parish bound unto Darby Tool of same in the sum of 140 pounds current money of Virginia. Condiditon such that whereas John Triplett of Westmoreland County hath bargained and sold unto Darby Tool 140A in King George County....the above bounden John Fox for Value Received in seventy pounds current money of Virginia paid by the said Darby Tool the receipt whereof the said John Fox doth thereby acknowledge, the said John Fox doth promise the sd. Darby Tool to defend the aforesd. bargained and sold land with an especiall warranty that if in case the said 140A or any part thereof shall be taken away that the said John Fox to deliver unto Darby Tool ten shillings for every acre of land so lost, if the said John Fox shall truly keep that promise, obligation to be void. Signed John Fox. Delivered in presence of Isaac Arnold, Henry Care, Thos. Underwood. Recorded 2 April 1742 T. Turner.

2:413 - BOND - 3 April 1742 - James Strother and Benjamin Strother bound unto Our Sovereign Lord the King his Heirs and Successors in the sum of 17,000 pounds of tobacco. Condition such that whereas the above bounden James Strother hath the Collection of the sd. County put into his hands amounting to 8,500 pounds of tobacco, now if the said James Strother doth faithfully collect and duly pay the same to the Respective Creditors as also all such Clerks and Secretarys' fees as shall be put in to the hands of the said James Strother to collect and pay the said fees to the respective officers to whome the same be due and payable according to Law then this obligation to be void. Signed Jas. Strother, Benj. Strother. Recorded 3 April 1742 T. Turner.

2:414 - DEED OF LEASE - 1 April 1742 - Francis Baltrop of Hanover Parish to John Wren of same. 5 shillings sterling to lease 17A bounded by lines of the sd. John Wren and the Main Road. Signed Francis Baltrop, Ann Baltrop. Delivered in presence of Harry Turner, John Moor. Recorded 7 May 1742 T. Turner.

2:415 - DEED OF RELEASE - 2 April 1742 - Francis Baltrop and Ann his wife of Hanover Parish to John Wren of same. 9 pounds 12 shillings for 17A described in lease. Signed Francis Baltrop, Ann Baltrop. Delivered in presence of Harry Turner, John Moor. Recorded 7 May 1742 T. Turner.

2:417 - DEED OF BARGAIN AND SALE - 7 May 1742 - Francis Baltrop and Ann his wife of the county of King George to Harry Turner of same. 40 pounds current money of Virginia for 72A bounded by the south side of a branch of Gengoteague Creek, by the spring of Isaac Arnold the Elder, the Main Branch of Gingoteague, and by the corner of the sd. Baltrops land and the land of Isaac Arnold the Younger. Signed Francis Baltrop, Ann Baltrop. Delivered in presence of John Wren, Geo. Tankersley. Recorded 7 May 1742 T. Turner.

2:420 - DEED OF GIFT - 7 April 1742 - John Doggin of Hanover Parish makes over all his personal estate unto John Nichols, planter, of the same parish. Signed John Doggin. Delivered in presence of Bourne Price, James Triplett. Recorded 4 June 1742 T. Turner.

2:420 - DEED OF GIFT - 21 June 1742 - John Dogens of the county of King George for divers good causes and considerations and for keeping his daughter Mildred Dogens till she arrive to the age of eighteen hereunto moving grants and confirms unto Ann Dogens all and singular his goods and chattels household and all other his substance whatsoever. To have and to hold from henceforth to her own proper use and uses thereof and therewith to do order and dispose at her will and pleasure. Signed John Dogens. Delivered in presence of John Deddo, Richard Haily. Recorded 2 July 1742 T. Turner.

2:421 - DEED OF LEASE - 6 May 1742 - John Triplett of Washington Parish in the county of Westmoreland and Francis Triplett of Hanover Parish to John Canady of Hanover Parish. 5 shillings current money of Virginia to lease 121A. Part of a greater tract devised to the said John Triplett and Francis Triplett by their father William Triplett by his last will and testament dated 3 September

1738. Signed John Triplett, Francis Triplett. Delivered in presence of Cha. Ewell, William Ballendine. Recorded 6 August 1742 Harry Turner.

2:423 - DEED OF RELEASE - 7 May 1742 - John Triplett of Washington Parish in the county of Westmoreland and Francis Triplett of Hanover Parish to John Canady of Hanover Parish. 44 pounds current money of Virginia for 121A described in lease. Signed John Triplett, Francis Triplett. Delivered in presence of Cha. Ewell, William Ballendine. Recorded 6 August 1742 Harry Turner.

2:425 - BOND - 7 May 1742 - John Triplett of the county of Westmoreland and Francis Triplett of the county of King George bound unto John Canady of the county of King George in the sum of 88 pounds current money of Virginia. Condition such that if John Triplett and Francis Triplett shall truly keep all agreements mentioned in one Indenture of Release bearing date with these presents between them and the above named John Canady, obligation to be void. Signed John Triplett, Francis Triplett. Delivered in presence of Cha. Ewell, William Ballendine. Recorded 6 August 1742 Harry Turner.

2:426 - DEED - 10 May 1742 - James Crap of the county of King George, planter, to John Bogle and John Baird of Glasgow, merchants. 28 pounds 14 shillings current money for one lott or half acre numbered 30 in the town of Falmouth. Paid by Andrew Ross attorney and agent for the said John Bogle and John Baird. James Crap bought the lot of Peter Daniel who was sold lots 28, 29, and 30 by the Trustees of the Town of Falmouth. Signed James Crap. Delivered in presence of James Strother, John Grant, Robt. Shedden, James Hewitt, Sam. Earle. Recorded 6 August 1742 Harry Turner.

2:428 - MORTGAGE - 23 February 1741 - Thomas Lanphier of the county of Stafford for and in consideration of the sum of 19 pounds 1 shilling and 2 pence current money of Virginia does bargain, sell, and confirm unto Thomas Turner of the aforesd. county his Heirs and Assigns one Servant Man named David Harding, one Sorrel Horse, fifteen Pewter Dishes, thirty-one Pewter Plates and his stock of Hogs to his and their own Proper Use and behoof for Ever. Signed Thos. Lanphier. Delivered in presence of Saml. Skinker, Harry Turner, Antho. Haynie, Thomas Turner, Junr. Recorded 6 August 1742 Harry Turner.

2:429 - DEED OF FEEOFMENT - 12 March 1741 - Lyonel Lyde, Esqr., Jere. Innis, Thomas Longman, Edward Cooper, Samuel Jacob, Samuel Dyke in or near the City of Bristol and John Tayloe, Esqr. in Richmond County in the Colony of Virginia and other Partners, some of whom are dead, to Ralph Falkner and Edward Neal in the Province of Maryland and John Triplett, Charles Ewell, and Nathaniel Chapman of the Colony of Virginia in Partnership. 225 pounds sterling for 440A formerly bought by the Iron Mine Company of

Bristol situate on the Rappahannock River. Sundry parcels of land bought of Richard Tutt, John Underwood, Benjamin Johnson, and Daniel Underwood. On which said lands the copartners aforesd. have standing and erected One Iron Furnace, a Grist Mill, Coal House, Stables and Divers other Houses, buildings and improvements. Signed John Tayloe for self and company. Delivered in presence of James Rallings, Owen Campbell, Thomas Due, Thomas Harper, William Ballendine. Recorded 6 August 1742 Harry Turner.

2:432 - DEED OF SALE - 5 June 1742 - Lundford Lomax of the county of Caroline, Gentleman, to Charles Carter of the county of King George, Esquire. 300 pounds sterling for 400A lying in the freshes of the Rappahannock River on the North Side thereof with bounds beginning by the river side a little above Talliaferro's Mount. Conveyed to Edward Lemman, tallow chandler of London, by Cuthbert Potter of Middlesex County by deed 10 April 1680 with proviso that if the said Cuthbert Potter his Executors or Administrators should pay the said Edward Lemman 115 pounds 9 shillings sterling within seven years, indenture should be void. Since during the term of seven years mentioned Cuthbert Potter had not paid the said amount, Edward Lemman, Linnen Draper of London and son and heir of the said Edward Lemman tallow chandler, conveyed the same to John Lomax of Essex County in Virginia, Gentleman father of the said Lunsford Lomax by deed dated 5 December 1718. Part of a patent for 5,275A granted to Thomas Chetwood and John Rosser by patent dated 28 September 1667. Signed Lunsford Lomax. Delivered in presence of Henry Fitzhugh, T. Turner, Fras. Thornton, Peter Hedgman, Wm. Waller. Recorded 6 August 1742 Harry Turner.

2:434 - DEED OF LEASE - 5 August 1742 - Lewis Griffie, cooper, of Baltimore County in the Province of Maryland to John Kemp of same. 5 pounds sterling money of Great Britain to lease 414A once in the possession of Lewis Griffie the Elder, father to the aforesaid Lewis Griffie. Bounded by Clayburn's Swamp and the Great Tract of John Waugh Clerk. Signed Lewis Griffie. Delivered in presence of John Bryan, Henry Berry, Joel Berry. Recorded 6 August 1742 Harry Turner.

2:436 - DEED OF RELEASE - 6 August 1742 - Lewis Griffie, cooper, of Baltimore County in the Province of Maryland to John Kemp of same. 85 pounds current money of Virginia for 414A described in lease. Signed Lewis Griffie. Delivered in presence of John Bryan, Henry Berry, Joel Berry. Recorded 6 August 1742 Harry Turner.

2:438 - DEED OF LEASE - 2 September 1742 - William Thornton, Gent., and Francis his wife of the county of King George to Anthony Strother of same, Gent. 5 shillings sterling to lease 235A whereon the said Anthony Strother now lives and lying below the mouth of Clayburn Run. Purchased by the sd. Wm. Thornton as follows - 35A next to the run between the River and the Main Road of Charles and Alice Cale by deed dated 2 March 1723 and 200A of Thomas Stone in the Province of Maryland by deed dated 2 March 1721. All part of a 2000A tract granted to John Catlett, Gent., by patent dated 2 June 1666 which by sundry main conveyances became vested in the said Charles and Alice Cale and the sd. Thomas Stone. Signed William Thornton, Francis Thornton. Delivered in presence of John Champe, Charles Deane, George Morton. Recorded 3 September 1742 Harry Turner.

2:439 - DEED OF RELEASE - 3 September 1742 - William Thornton, Gent., and Francis his wife of the county of King George to Anthony Strother of same, Gent. 150 pounds sterling for 235A described in lease. Signed Wm. Thornton, Frances Thornton. Delivered in presence of John Champe, Cha. Deane, George Morton. Recorded 6 September 1742 Harry Turner.

2:441 - DEED OF LEASE - 30 September 1742 - George and Daniel Underwood of the county of Orange and John Fox of the county of King George to John Triplett of the county of King George. 5 shillings to lease 200A beginning at the fork of the Rappahannock Iron Mine Company's Waggon Road. Bounded by Reedy Swamp, the sd. Company's lands, lands of Francis Triplett and John Triplett, and the Cross Roads. Part of a patent granted to Capt. William Underwood and by several conveyances and devices became the possession of the sd. George and Daniel Underwood and John Fox. Signed Geo. Underwood, Daniel Underwood. Delivered in presence of John Thornley, Henry Drake, Wm. Longmire. Recorded 1 October 1742 Harry Turner.

2:442 - DEED OF RELEASE - 1 October 1742 - George and Daniel Underwood of the county of Orange and John Fox of the county of King George to John Triplett of the county of King George. 130 pounds current money for 200A described in lease. Signed Geo. Underwood, Daniel Underwood. Delivered in presence of John Thornley, Henry Drake, William Longmire. Elizabeth, wife of George Underwood, acknowledged her free consent thereto. Recorded 1 October 1742 Harry Turner.

2:444 - DEED OF SALE - 3 June 1742 - John Tayloe of the county of Richmond, Esquire, to Harry Turner of the county of King George. 15 pounds current money of Virginia for one lott or half acre numbered 13 being in the Town of Falmouth. Said lott was conveyed by the Directors and Trustees of the Town of Falmouth to John Williams by deed dated 1 October 1728 and by the said John Williams conveyed unto Lyonel Lyde, Esqr., John Lewis, and William Williams of the City of Bristol and John Tayloe of the county of Richmond in the Colony of Virginia, Esqr. by deeds dated 19 and 20 November 1729. Signed

John Tayloe. Delivered in presence of Ch. Carter, Wm. Waller, Catesby Cocke, William Walker, T. Turner. Recorded 5 November 1742 Harry Turner.

2:446 - DEED OF SALE - 3 June 1742 - John Tayloe of the county of Richmond, Esqr., to Thomas Turner the Younger of the county of King George. 10 pounds current money of Virginia for one lott or half acre numbered 19 being in the Town of Falmouth. Said lott was conveyed by the Directors and Trustees of the Town of Falmouth to John Williams by deed dated 1 October 1728 and by the said John Williams conveyed to Lyonel Lyde, Esqr., John Lewis, and William Williams of the City of Bristol and John Tayloe of the county of Richmond in the Colony of Virginia by deeds dated 19 and 20 November 1729. Signed John Tayloe. Delivered in presence of Ch. Carter, Wm. Waller, Catesby Cocke, William Walker, T. Turner. Recorded 5 November 1742 Harry Turner.

2:448 - INDENTURE - 30 September 1742 - William Bryant of Hanover Parish for and in consideration of the sum of 8 pounds 10 shillings current money to him in hand paid by James Scurlock of Hanover Parish doth bind himself as a Servant unto the sd. James Scurlock for and during the term of five years. Signed William Bryant. Delivered in presence of William Settle, William Serjant. Recorded 1 October 1742 Harry Turner.

2:449 - INDENTURE - 30 September 1742 - Between James Scurlock of Hanover Parish of the one part and William Bryant of same. The sd. William Bryant doth bind himself as a servant unto the said James Scurlock. And the said James Scurlock for himself, his Heirs, Exrs., Admrs., and Assigsns Do Covenant and Agree with him the said William Bryant to Provide and find for him at their Own Proper Cost and Charge Sufficient Dyett Washing and Lodging and Apparel During the Continuance of the Term of five Years and at the Expiration of the said Term Discharge him the said William Bryant from his servitude. Signed James Scurlock. Delivered in presence of William Settle, William Serjant. Recorded 1 October 1742 Harry Turner.

2:450 - MARRIAGE SETTLEMENT - 15 February 1741 - Abraham Kenyon of Brunswick Parish, planter, to John Carter of St. George Parish in the county of Spotsylvania, planter. Whereas a marriage is intended between the said John Carter and Sarah Kenyon Daughter of the said Abraham Kenyon and Whereas by the Last Will and Testament of Francis Waddington Deceased Dated 24 January 1723 the said Sarah hath a right to Divers Slaves now in the hand and possession of her said Father Abraham Kenyon Also the Right of the said Slaves Exclusive of the said Will is Vested in Elizabeth her Mother now the Wife of the said Abraham Nevertheless as well for the Advancement of the said John and Sarah in the World as for Settling Peace in the Premises and to prevent any dispute or Difference that may at any time hereafter arise Concerning the Right of the said Slaves or any of them it is hereby Mutually Covenanted and Agreed on Between the Partys to these Presents That the said Abraham Kenyon on the day of Marriage between the said John Carter and Sarah Kenyon or at any other timee afterwards when required Shall Peaceably and Quietly surrender and Deliver up to the said John Carter the four Slaves Jack, Jenny, Pat, and Ned. Upon receipt of the four slaves, John and Sarah shall and will acquit Release and for Ever Discharge the said Abraham Kenyon of all property claim either of them may have in any other Part of the said Abraham Kenyon's Estate. Signed Abraham Kenyon, John Carter. Delivered in presence of John Kenyon, Micajah Poole. Recorded 5 November 1742 Harry Turner.

2:451 - BOND - 15 February 1741 - John Carter of St. George Parish in the county of Spotsylvania bound unto Abraham Kenyon of Brunswick Parish in the sum of 500 pounds sterling. Condition such that if John Carter shall truly fulfill all agreements made between above mentioned Abraham Kenyon and the above bounden John Carter bearing equal date with these presents, obligation to be void. Signed John Carter. Delivered John Carter. Delivered in presence of John Kenyon, Micajah Poole. Recorded 5 November 1742 Harry Turner.

2:452 - DEED OF FEEOFMENT - 4 June 1741 - Daniel White of Hanover Parish, Gent., and Ann his wife to Jonathan Sydenham of same, merchant. 15 pounds current money for 3A that is part of 30A sold to Nicholas Smith, Gent., and by him conveyed to Ann White now wife of the said Daniel by deed dated 30 October 1722. Bounded by Clapham Richardson and the Upper End of Brocks ground. Signed Daniel White, Anne White. Delivered in presence of John Payne, George Keesee, William Thatcher, William Walker, Will. Jett. Memorandum - William Robinson, Gentlem., received this livery and seizen for and in behalf of Jonathan Sydenham. Signed John Payne, George Keesee, William Thatcher, Will. Jett, James Jones, William Walker. Recorded 5 November 1742 Harry Turner.

2:454 - DEDIMUS COMMISSION - 7 September 1741 - Whereas Jonathan Sydenham, merchant, hath made application for a commission to take the acknowledgment and Privy Examination of Ann White wife of Daniel White to certain deeds for land, Thomas Turner Clerk of the County Court impowers William Robinson and Maximilion Robinson being Justices for the County of King George to take the acknowledgment and Privy Examination of the said Ann White. The commissioners examined Ann White privately and certify her free acknowledgment 31 May 1742. Recorded 5 November 1742 Harry Turner.

2:455 - DEED OF LEASE - 1 July 1742 - William Newton of Brunswick Parish to John Thomas of Washington Parish in the county of Westmoreland. Yearly rent of 600 pounds tobacco and the Quitrents to lease 150A lying in Brunswick Parish. Part of a 1000A tract belonging to the said William Newton. Located on the North Side of the Little Falls Run and to extend between the said run and the line of Colol. William Ball. Lease is for and during the natural lives of the said John Thomas, Susannah his now wife, and Benjamin Thomas his son or the longest liver of them. The said John Thomas will at his own proper cost and charge build one dwelling house sixteen feet long and twelve feet wide, one milk house eight foot square, and one tobacco house thirty-two feet long and twenty foot wide, and plant 100 apple trees and twenty cherry trees. Signed William Newton. Delivered in presence of Winkfield Shropshire, William Edwards. Recorded 5 November 1742 Harry Turner.

2:457 - DEED - 3 December 1742 - Samuel Dingle of the county of King George, taylor, and Lucy his wife to the Honble. John Custis of the City of Williamsburg, Esqr. 10 shillings for 50A near the head of Queen's Creek in Bruton Parish in the county of York. John Davis, the former husband of the said Lucy Dingle, lately died seized of an undivided moiety devised to the said John Davis and Lewis Davis by their father Wm. Davis deceased intail and now in the actual possession of the said John Custis. Signed Samuel Dingle, Lucy Dingle. Delivered in presence of James Jones, Edward Hoyle, Samuel Hoyle. Recorded 3 December 1742 Harry Turner.

2:458 - DEED OF LEASE - 1 August 1741 - William Stevenson of London, merchant, to George Morton of Hanover Parish, Gent. 5 shillings sterling to lease 200A lying upon the North Side of Rappahannock River. It is the same which was sold unto the said Stevenson by the Executors of John Dinwiddie by deeds dated 1 and 2 April 1731. Signed William Stevenson. Delivered in presence of William Thornton, junr., Elias Perryman, John Wilcox, James Scott, Aldred Deyman, Joseph Woolcombe, William Furness. Recorded 4 March 1742 Harry Turner.

2:460 - DEED OF RELEASE - 2 August 1741 - William Stevenson of London, merchant, to George Morton of Hanover Parish, Gent. 205 pounds sterling for 200A described in lease. Signed William Stevenson. Delivered in presence of William Thornton, junr., Elias Perryman, John Wilcox, James Scott, Aldred Deyman, Joseph Woolcombe, William Furness. Recorded 4 March 1742 Harry Turner.

2:462 - BOND - 2 August 1741 - William Stevenson of London, merchant, bound unto George Morton of Hanover Parish in the sum of 500 pounds sterling. Condition such that if the above bound William Stevenson duly fulfills the Several Engagements he has Entered into by deeds of Lease and Release and Particularly if the said Stevenson shall Execute such further Customary Deeds as shall be presented unto him at all times hereafter on the Behalf of the sd. George Morton for the full Securing to the said George Morton his Heirs and Assigns for Ever an Entire Right unto the said Tract of Land, obligation to be void. Signed William Stevenson. Delivered in presence of William Thornton, junr., Elias Perryman, John Wilcox, James Scott, Aldred Deyman, Joseph Woolcombe, William Furness. Recorded 4 March 1742 Harry Turner.

2:463 - DEED OF LEASE - 11 April 1743 - Weedon Arnold of Washington Parish in the county of Westmoreland, planter, to Harry Turner of Hanover Parish. 5 shillings sterling to lease two tracts of land. One 100A tract whereon Isaac Arnold, Junr. now lives and was conveyed by Isaac Arnold, Senr. to James Arnold, father to the said Weedon Arnold party to these presents, by deeds dated 24 and 25 February 1719. One 50A tract adjoyning to the aforesd. tract being purchased by Thomas Arnold of Adam Wofendall by deed dated 1 March 1694/5 which said land was by the sd. Thomas Arnold bequeathed to the said James Arnold to whom the said Weedon Arnold is the eldest son and Heir at Law. Signed Weedon Arnold. Delivered in presence of Thos. Turner, Junr., William Rankins, John Rankins. Recorded 6 May 1743 Harry Turner.

2:464 - DEED OF RELEASE - 12 April 1743 - Weedon Arnold of Washington Parish in the county of Westmoreland, planter, to Harry Turner of Hanover Parish. 30 pounds current money of Virginia for two tracts of land described in lease. Signed Weedon Arnold. Delivered in presence of Thomas Turner, Junr., William Rankins, John Rankins, T. Turner. Recorded 6 May 1743 Harry Turner.

2:466 - LETTER OF CREDIT - 29 May 1742 - Captain John Butler, You must Sail with the first fair Wind to Spithead and there wait Convoy with the same Proceed to Gibralter and Port Mahon According to your Charter Party Exactly Protesting Either for Want of Convoys or Otherways in Case of Need Hoping however that you'll have no Occasion for it When Discharged Port Mahon You are to Proceed to Virginia to Comply with your Charter Party from thence home Again taking Care also to make regular protest in Case of Need should you during this Voyage meet with any Misfortunes or Want Necessarys for the Ship your draughts on me Shall be duly Honoured as Frugality and Dispatch will Chiefly tend to Mine and the Rest of Your Owners Interest, I do most Earnestly Recommend you the Same So Wishing you Health and a good Voyage I remain Your Friend and Owner. Signed Libert Dorrien. This Letter of Credit from Libert Dorrien to John Butler was presented into Court and admitted to record. Recorded 6 May 1743 Harry Turner.

2:467 - DEED OF GIFT - 5 May 1743 - Robert Johnson of Hanover Parish for the good will and affection which he bears towards his loving son William Johnson freely, clearly, and absolutely gives unto the sd. William Johnson all the tract of land whereon the said Robert Johnson now lives (after his decease) with all houses, out houses, buildings and edifices whatsoever belonging to the said tract of land. He gives unto his youngest son John Johnson the sum of twenty pounds current money of Virginia (upon the father's decease) or otherwise to let him the said John Johnson have the aforesd. land upon the non payment of the sum of the aforesd. twenty pounds. The land joyns upon the mill of Colol. Thos. Turner and to the land of William Furlong and is a parcel of land bought of Samuel Wharton, being by estimation 88A. If the said Robert Johnson dies before his son John is of age, his son William Johnson is to take care of him until he is of age to receive his twenty pounds current money of Virginia. P.S. if William Johnson dyes without Heir that then the Land falls to John Johnson. Signed Robert Johnson. Delivered in presence of Robert Johnson, Junr., Eliza. Jones, Stafford Lightburn. Recorded 6 May 1743 Harry Turner.

2:468 - INDENTURE - 4 May 1743 - John Dancer of Hanover Parish for and in consideration of the maintenance of a Male Child that Amey Sickle a Servant to James Donaldson of Washington Parish in the county of Westmoreland swore before one of his Majesties Justices of the Peace for the sd. county of Westmoreland was begotten by him the sd. John Dancer and Owen Campbell of Hanover Parish became his security to the Church Wardens of Washington Parish to save the Parish harmless from any charge that should come to the Parish by reason of the said child which child was born 1 April last and sent to the house of the sd. Owen Campbell. The sd. John Dancer doth bind himself as a servant to the sd. Owen Campbell and his assigns for and during the term of four years from the first day of April last past. Owen Campbell agrees to provide for John Dancer during the term above mentioned sufficient diet, washing, lodging, and apparel and likewise to provide for and maintain the sd. child during the space and term of three years. If the child should happen to die before the end of the sd. three years the sd. Owen Campbell will pay unto the sd. John Dancer twenty shillings for every year that the child shall not live to compleat the sd. term of three years. Signed Owen Campbell, John Dancer. Delivered in presence of Robert Miller, William Sarjant. Recorded 6 May 1743 Harry Turner.

2:469 - BOND - 3 October 1741 - James Strother, John Champe, and Benjamin Strother bound unto Our Sovereign Lord the King and his Heirs and Successors in the penal sum of 1000 pounds sterling. Condidition such that whereas the above bound James Strother is this day sworn in Sheriff for the county of King George, if he renders to the auditor and Receiver General of his Majesty's Revenues a particular perfect and true account of all his Majesty's rents and dues arising within the said county and also due payment make of all other public dues and fees put into his hands to collect within the said county and unto the several persons to whom the same shall be due and payable and true performance to make of all matters and things relating to his office during his continuance therein, obligation to be void. Signed James Strother, John Champe, Benj. Strother. Delivered in presence of Harry Turner. Recorded 3 June 1743 Harry Turner.

2:470 - DEED OF LEASE - 30 March 1743 - James Jones of King George County, planter, and Hannah his wife to Thomas Monteith of same, merchant. 5 shillings lawfull current money of Virginia to lease 150A lying on the East Side of Deep Run. Part of 400A granted the said Jones by patent dated 28 September 1724. Signed James Jones, Hannah Jones. Delivered in presence of Daniel Grant, James Fletcher, Jno. Hobby. Recorded 3 June 1743 Harry Turner.

2:472 - DEED OF RELEASE - 31 March 1743 - James Jones of King George County, planter, and Hannah his wife to Thomas Monteith of same, merchant. 20 pounds 12 shillings lawfull current money of Virginia for 150A described in lease. Signed James Jones, Hannah Jones. Delivered in presence of Daniel Grant, James Fletcher, Jno. Hobby. Recorded 3 June 1743 Harry Turner.

2:474 - BOND - 31 March 1743 - James Jones of King George County, planter, and Hannah his wife bound unto Thomas Monteith of same, merchant, in the sum of 300 pounds sterling. Condition such that if James Jones and Hannah his wife truly keep all agreements in a certain Lease and Release bearing equal date with these presents made between the above James Jones and Hannah his wife of the one part and the sd. Thomas Monteith of the other part, obligation to be void. Signed James Jones, Hannah Jones. Delivered in presence of Daniel Grant, James Fletcher, Jno. Hobby. Recorded 3 June 1743 Harry Turner.

2:475 - DEDIMUS COMMISSION - 15 July 1743 - Whereas Thomas Monteith has made application for a commission to take the acknowledgment and Privy Examination of Hannah Jones, wife of James Jones, to certain deeds of land, Harry Turner Clerk of the County Court impowers Charles Carter, Benjamin Berryman, John Champe and Richard Bryan, Gent. or any two being Justices for the said county of King George to take acknowledgment and Privy Examination of the said Hannah Jones. John Champe and Richard Bryan examined Hannah Jones privately and apart from her husband James Jones and the said Hannah Jones freely and willingly of her own accord and without any compulsion of her sd. husband relinquished unto the sd. Thomas Monteith all her Right of Dower 23 August 1743. Recorded 2 September 1743 Harry Turner.

2:476 - DEED OF LEASE - 30 May 1743 - Francis Wofendall of Hanover Parish, planter, to Thomas Turner of same, Gent. 5 shillings current money to lease 100A commonly called Rich Bottom lying on the branch of Gengoteague Creek. Conveyed by John Underwood and Elizabeth his wife unto the said

Francis Wofendall by deeds dated 28 and 29 June 1719. Land is part of a patent for 550A granted unto Francis Slaughter 10 September 1662 and by the sd. Slaughter bequeathed to the sd. John and Elizabeth Underwood. Signed Francis Wofendall. Delivered in presence of John Wren, John Thornley, Francis Strother, Harry Turner. Recorded 3 June 1743 Harry Turner.

2:477 - DEED OF RELEASE - 31 May 1743 - Francis Wofendall of Hanover Parish, planter, to Thomas Turner of same, Gentleman. 10 pounds sterling for 100A described in lease. Signed Francis Wofendall. Delivered in presence of John Wren, John Thornley, Francis Strother, Harry Turner. Recorded 3 June 1743 Harry Turner.

2:479 - DEED - 9 May 1743 - Thomas Turner, Daniel McCarty, and Max. Robinson Gentlemen Directors and Trustees for Leeds Town in King George County to William Jordan, Gentleman, of the county of Richmond. 33 pounds current money of Virginia for two half acres or lotts in Leeds Town numbered 21 and 22 on Frederick Street as per a platt and survey made by Mr. Robert Brooke 28 November 1742. William Jordan his Heirs and Assigns to build on the said lott one house of brick, stone or wood well framed of the dimensions of twenty foot square and nine foot pitched at the least within two years, otherwise deed is void. Signed T. Turner, Danl. McCarty, Max Robinson. Delivered in presence of Jonath. Sydenham, Harry Turner, Arthur Spicer, Jas. Jones, Jos. Morton, Wm. Brokenbrough. Recorded 1 July 1743 Harry Turner.

2:480 - BOND - 2 September 1743 - Jonathan Sydenham, John Champe, and William Jordan bound unto our Sovereign Lord the King his Heirs and Successors in the sum of 1000 pounds sterling. Condition such that whereas the above bounden Jonathan Sydenham is this day sworn Sheriff for the county of King George, if he do render to the auditor and Receiver General of his Majesties Revenues a Particular Perfect and True Account of all his Majesties Rents and Dues arising within the said county and also due payment make of all other Public dues and fees put into his hand to collect within the sd. county unto the several persons to whom the same shall be due and payable and true performance make of all matters and things relating to his office during his continuance therein, obligation to be void. Signed John. Sydenham, John Champe, Wm. Jordan. Recorded 2 September 1743 Harry Turner.

2:481 - DEED OF LEASE - 8 August 1743 - Benjamin Miller of St. Ann's Parish in the county of Essex to Thomas Turner of Hanover Parish. 5 shillings current money to lease 40A bequeathed by William Miller father of the said Benjamin Miller which sd. land lies within the tract of land whereon the sd. Thomas Turner now dwells. Signed Benjamin Miller. Delivered in presence of Harry Turner, Richd. Hooe, Ann Lloyd, William Coppin, John Farrill. Recorded

2 September 1743 Harry Turner.

2:482 - DEED OF RELEASE - 9 August 1743 - Benjamin Miller of St. Ann's Parish in the county of Essex to Thomas Turner of Hanover Parish. 30 pounds current money of Virginia for 40A described in lease. Signed Benjamin Miller. Delivered in presence of Harry Turner, Richd. Hooe, Ann Lloyd, William Coppin, John Farrel. Recorded 2 September 1743 Harry Turner.

2:484 - DEED OF LEASE - 1 September 1743 - Chithester Chin of Hanover Parish and Agatha his wife to Benjamin Weeks of Washington Parish in the county of Westmoreland. 5 shillings sterling to lease 435A lying in Richmond and King George Countys. Devised unto the sd. Chithester Chin by the last will and testament of his father Rawleigh Chin late of Lancaster County deceased. Signed Chithester Chinn, Agatha Chinn. Delivered in presence of Rob. Vaulx, Wm. Longmire, Thos. Pratt. Recorded 2 September 1743 Harry Turner.

2:485 - DEED OF RELEASE - 2 September 1743 - Chithester Chinn of Hanover Parish and Agatha his wife to Benjamin Weeks of Washington Parish in Westmoreland County. 180 pounds current money of Virginia for 435A described in lease. 268A being part of a tract of land containing 1585A first granted unto William Serjeant and Joan Clerk by patent dated 26 September 1678 and sold to the said Rawleigh Chinn by one Stanley Gower by deed dated 4 May 1720. The remaining 167A is another part of the sd. 1585A aforementioned sold by one Edward Bryan to the sd. Rawleigh Chinn father to the sd. Chichester Chinn by deed dated 10 June 1720. Signed Chichester Chinn, Agatha Chinn. Delivered in presence of Rob. Vaulx, Wm. Longmire, Thos. Pratt. Recorded 2 September 1743 Harry Turner.

2:488 - BOND - 2 September 1743 - Chichester Chinn and Agatha (husband and wife) of Hanover Parish bound unto Benjamin Weeks of Washington Parish in the county of Westmoreland in the sum of 500 pounds sterling. Condition such that if the above bound Chichester Chinn and Agatha his wife shall truly keep all agreements mentioned in the aforesaid Indenture of Release, obligation to be void. Signed Chichester Chinn, Agatha Chinn. Delivered in presence of Robt. Vaulx, Wm. Longmire, Thos. Pratt. Recorded 2 September 1743 Harry Turner.

2:489 - DEDIMUS COMMISSION - 9 March 1742 - Whereas Robert Sheddin has made application for a commission to take the acknowledgment and Privy Examination of Margary Crap wife of James Crap to a certain deed of land for a lott in Falmouth Town numbered 28, Harry Turner Clerk of the County Court impowers John Champ, Benjamin Berryman and Richard Bryan Gentlemen or any two to take the acknowledgment and Privy Examination of the said Margery Crap. Benja. Berryman and Richd. Bryan examined Margary Crap and she consented to the conveying of the said lott 28 May 1743. Recorded 2 September 1743 Harry Turner.

2:490 - DEDIMUS COMMISSION - 9 March 1742 - Whereas Andrew Ross agent for John Bogle and John Bair, merchants in Glasgow, has made application for a commission to take the acknowledgment and Privy Examination of Margery Crap wife of James Crap to a certain deed of land for a lott in Falmouth Town numbered 30, Harry Turner Clerk of the County Court impowers John Champe, Benjamin Berryman and Richard Bryan Gentlemen or any two to take the acknowledgment and Privy Examination of Margery Crap. Benjamin Berryman and Richard Bryan examined Margery Crap and she consented to the conveying of the said lott 28 May 1743. Recorded 2 September 1743 Harry Turner.

2:490 - DEED - 24 June 1743 - Frances Thornton of the county of King George, widow and relict of William Thornton, to William Thornton of same, only son and heir of the said William Thornton deceased. The said Frances Thornton clearly and absolutely and for ever quit claims unto the said William Thornton all and all manner of Dower and right and title of dower whatsoever which she hath in all and every the plantation, messuages, lands, tenements and herediments which were of the said William Thornton deceased lying in the Counties of King George, Prince William or elsewhere within the colony of Virginia. Frances Thornton also doth quit claim unto the said William Thornton all legacies, gifts, bequests, slaves, personal estate, and demands what soever bequeathed to her by the last will and testament of the said William Thornton deceased dated 3 November last past. William Thornton doth agree to permit the said Frances Thornton to peaceably and quietly during the term of her natural life to occupy, possess and enjoy the mansion house with the garden thereunto and all the household goods and furniture used in the mansion house at the time of the death of William Thornton. William Thornton shall at his own cost provide in a handsome and plentiful manner good and sufficient provisions of all kinds for the maintenance and support of her house keeping. He will also pay her yearly sixteen pounds sterling or the value thereof in goods of her own choice and the further sum of five pounds together with the yearly wages of a servant woman if she should think fit to hire one. The said William Thornton shall pay unto the said Frances Thornton 200 pounds current money of Virginia together with interest for the same at the rate of five pounds per centum per annum until the principal sum shall be fully paid. Signed Frances Thornton, William Thornton. Delivered in presence of Ann Robertson, Ignatius West, John Hobby, Fran. Thornton. Recorded 2 September 1743 Harry Turner.

2:493 - DEED OF LEASE - 10 June 1743 - James Jones of Hanover Parish, bricklayer, to James Cash of Washington Parish in the county of Westmoreland, planter. 5 shillings current money of Virginia to lease 220A whereon William Owen now dwells. Part in King George County and part in Westmoreland County. Bounded by Edward Roach, Samuel Dishman, the head of a valley near the road that goes from Pecks to John Thomas, land formerly belonging to Sem Cox, Hale's Road, the west side of a fine Cool Spring Run that runs into Upper Machotick Creek, and William Cash. Signed James Jones. Delivered in presence of Harry Turner, Joseph Berry, John Wren. Recorded 2 September 1743 Harry Turner.

2:494 - DEED OF RELEASE - 11 June 1743 - James Jones and Hester his wife of Hanover Parish, bricklayer, to James Cash of Washington Parish in the county of Westmoreland, planter. 83 pounds current money of Virginia for 220A described in lease. Signed Jas. Jones, Hester Jones. Delivered in presence of Harry Turner, Joseph Berry, John Wren. Recorded 2 September 1743 Harry Turner.

2:497 - DEED OF LEASE - 2 August 1743 - Bridgett Coburn relict of John Coburn of Brunswick Parish, widow, to John Champe of same, Gentleman. 5 shillings sterling to lease 150A bounded by a branch of Lambs Creek, the backside line of the river side patent of John and George Mott, and land formerly belonging to Peter Gallon. Part of 400A out of a patent formerly granted to John and George Mott and by them given by deed of gift unto John Dickary and by him bequeathed unto his son Nathaniel Dickary and by him sold unto Thomas Taylor who by his last will dated 29 March 1712 devised the said 150A of land unto his three sons Thomas, Benjamin, and John Taylor of which the aforesaid Benjamin Taylor is the only survivor and the Heir at Law who sold the land to John Coburn and Bridgett his wife by deeds dated 7 and 8 November 1735. Signed Bridgett Coburn. Delivered in presence of John Taliaferro, Jr., David Seale, Cheviralls Norman. Recorded 2 September 1743 Harry Turner.

2:499 - DEED OF RELEASE - 3 August 1743 - Bridgett Coburn relict of John Coburn of Brunswick Parish, widow, to John Champe of same, Gentleman. 30 pounds current money of Virginia for 150A described in lease. Signed Bridgett Coburn. Delivered in presence of John Talliaferro, Junr., David Seale, Cheveralls Norman. Recorded 2 September 1743 Harry Turner.

2:501 - DEED OF RELEASE - 27 August 1743 - Daniel White of Hanover Parish, Gentn., and Ann his wife to Jonathan Sydenham of same, merchant. 15 pounds current money for 3A that is part of 30A sold to Nicholas Smith, Gent., and by him conveyed to Ann White now wife of Daniel White by deed dated 30 October 1722. Bounded by Clapham Richardson and the upper end of Brocks ground. Signed Daniel White, Ann White. Delivered in presence of Thos. Vivion, Agathy White, M. Robinson. Recorded 2 September 1742 Harry Turner.

2:503 - DEDIMUS COMMISSION - 27 May 1743 - Whereas Jonathan Sydenham, Gent., hath made application for a commission to take acknowledgment and Privy Examination of Ann White wife of Daniel White, Harry Turner Clerk of the County Court impowers Max. Robinson, Thomas Vivion, and Charles Ewell or any two being Justices for the said county of King George to take the acknowledgment and Privy Examination of the said Ann White. Thomas Vivion and M. Robinson examined Ann White and she freely consented to the sale of the land made by Daniel White her husband to Jonathan Sydenham. Recorded 2 September 1743 Harry Turner.

2:504 - DEED OF LEASE - 29 July 1743 - Mary Brock, Ann Edmonds, and George White of the county of King George to Margaret French of same. 5 shillings lawfull money to lease one half of all that parcel of land containing by estimation 853A lying upon the north side of Rappahannock River in Hanover Parish. Bounded by branch of the sd. River, corner tree of Tobias Smith's land now in the possession of Ann Edmonds, a branch of Purpetock Creek, and Thomas Hopkins deceased. Taken up by Mr. John Burkett and Mr. David Stern by pattent dated 26 September 1678 which said patent including a certain pattent of 400A formerly taken up by William Mills and repattented by Peter Mills his son 20 February 1662 and the said Peter Mills died without legal disposition it became the estate of Ann and Elizabeth daughters of the said William Mills and the said John Birket marrying Ann the coheir of the said Wm. Mills and she died without legal disposition one half of the said land became the proper estate of the said Mary Brock, Ann Edmonds and George White who are partys to these presents. Signed Mary Brock, Ann Edmonds, George White. Delivered in presence of Thos. Vivion, Will. Jett, Thos. Pratt. Recorded 2 September 1743 Harry Turner.

2:506 - DEED OF RELEASE - 30 July 1743 - Mary Brock, Ann Edmonds, and George White of the county of King George to Margaret French of same. 10 pounds current money of Virginia for one half of an 853A tract described in lease. Signed Mary Brock, Ann Edmonds, George White. Delivered in presence of Thos. Vivion, Will. Jett, Thos. Pratt. Recorded 2 September 1743 Harry Turner.

2:508 - INDENTURE - 5 October 1743 - Ann Crouch of Hanover Parish doth bind her son Joseph Crouch being twelve years old the twelfth day of September last past unto John Hellier of same an apprentice until he shall come to the age of twenty-one for to learn the Cooper's Trade. John Hellier doth agree that if he should die before the sd. Joseph's time is expired, that the sd. Joseph is to be free. Signed John Hellier. Recorded 7 October 1743 Harry Turner.

2:509 - INDENTURE - 5 October 1743 - Ann Crouch of Hanover Parish binds her son Joseph Crouch unto John Hellier of same an apprentice until he shall come to the age of twenty-one for to learn the Cooper's Trade, during which term of time the sd. Joseph his sd. master John Hellier faithfully shall serve and at the expiration of his time the said John Hellier doth promise and agree to and with the sd. Ann Crouch to give her son Joseph a full set of Coopers Tools and a full suit of Druggett. Signed Ann Crouch. Recorded 7 October 1743 Harry Turner.

2:510 - POWER OF ATTORNEY - 2 November 1742 - William Bodle of Whitehaven in the county of Cumberland, merchant, appoints his loving son in law Christopher Chamney of Whitehaven his true and lawfull attorney to ask demand sue for recover and receive of and from the executors of the last will and testament of Rodham Kennar of St. Mary's Parish in Caroline County all such legacys, sum and sums of money as shall or may appear to be given and bequeathed to him. Signed William Bodle. Delivered in presence of Edward Dixon, Thomas Taylor. Recorded 7 October 1743 Harry Turner.

2:511 - DEED OF LEASE - 6 October 1743 - Mary Tutt widow of Spotsilvania County to John Fox of Hanover Parish. 5 shillings sterling to lease two parcels of land containing 220A. Both part of a pattent originally grant to Capt. Willm. Underwood late of Richmond County. One part was bequeathed by the sd. Underwood unto the sd. Mary Tutt and bounded by a deep valley, the Spring Branch, and Underwoods Beaver dam. The other part was bequeathed by the sd. Underwood to his daughter Sarah who together with her husband John Gilbert sold the same to the said Mary Tutt and is bounded by the lands of John and Francis Triplett, and John Plunkett. Signed Mary Tutt. Delivered in presence of John Gilbert, Josiah Farguson, Edward Simm. Recorded 7 October 1743 Harry Turner.

2:512 - DEED OF RELEASE - 7 October 1743 - Mary Tutt widow of Spotsylvania County to John Fox of Hanover Parish. 85 pounds current money of Virginia for two parcels of land containing 220A described in lease. Signed Mary Tutt. Delivered in presence of John Gilbert, Josiah Farguson, Edward Sim. Recorded 7 October 1743 Harry Turner.

2:514 - DEED - 17 September 1743 - Thomas Turner, Harry Turner, and Maximilian Robinson, Gentlemen Directors and Trustees for Leeds Town in King George County to Daniel McCarty, Gentleman of the county of Westmoreland. 19 pounds 10 shillings current money of Virginia for two half acres or lotts in the Town of Leeds numbered 1 and 7 as by a plot and survey made by Mr. Robert Brooke on 28 November 1742. Daniel McCarty shall build on the sd. lott one house of brick, stone or wood of the dimensions of twenty foot square and nine foot pitched at the least within two years (and place the same according to the rule and direction of the said Directors), otherwise this deed to be void and the lott to be revested in the Trustees to be by them sold again by auction to the highest bidder. Signed T. Turner, Harry Turner, Max Robinson. Delivered in presence of W. Jordan, Rob. Vaulx, Richd. Kelsick. Recorded 4 November 1743 Harry Turner.

2:515 - DEED - 1 November 1743 - Thomas Turner and Harry Turner Gentlemen Directors and Trustees for Leeds Town in King George County to James Jones of the county of King George. 10 pounds current money of Virginia for one half acre lott in the sd. Town of Leeds numbered 13 as by a plott and survey made by Mr. Robert Brooke 28 November 1742. James Jones shall build on the said lott one house of brick, stone or wood of the dimensions of twenty foot square and nine foot pitched at least within two years (and place the same according to the rule and direction of the said Directors), otherwise this deed to be void and the lott to be revested in the Trustees to be by them sold again by auction to the highest bidder. Signed T. Turner, Harry Turner. Delivered in presence of John Champe, John Moore. Recorded 4 November 1743 Harry Turner.

2:516 - DEED - 1 November 1743 - Thomas Turner and Harry Turner Gentlemen Directors and Trustees for Leeds Town in King George County to James Jones of the county of King George. 28 pounds current money of Virginia for one half acre or lott in the sd. Town of Leeds numbered 18 as by a plott and survey made by Mr. Robert Brooke 28 November 1742. James Jones shall build on the said lott one house of brick, stone, or wood of the dimensions of twenty foot square and nine foot pitched at the least (and place the same according to the direction of the sd. Directors), otherwise this deed to be void and the lott to be revested in the sd. Trustees to be by them sold again by auction to the highest bidder. Signed T. Turner, Harry Turner. Delivered in presence of John Champe, John Moore. Recorded 4 November 1743 Harry Turner.

2:517 - DEED - 17 September 1743 - Thomas Turner and Harry Turner Gentlemen Directors and Trustees for Leeds Town in King George County to Jonathan Sydenham of same county. 4 pounds 15 shillings current money of Virginia for one half acre or lott in Leeds Town numbered 24 as per a plott and survey made by Robert Brooke, Gentleman, 28 November 1742. Jonathan Sydenham shall build on the said lott one house of brick, stone, or wood well framed of the dimensions of twenty foot square and nine foot pitched at the least within two years (and place the same according to the rule and direction of the sd. Directors), otherwise this deed to be void and the lott to be revested in the said Trustees to be by them sold again to the highest bidder. Signed T. Turner, Harry Turner. Delivered in presence of Danl. McCarty, Jos. Morton, W. Jordan.

Recorded 4 November 1743 Harry Turner.

2:518 - DEED - 17 September 1743 - Thomas Turner and Harry Turner Gentlemen Directors and Trustees of Leeds Town in King George County to Jonathan Sydenham, Gent., of same. 32 pounds 10 shillings current money of Virginia for one half acre of lott in Leeds Town numbered 39 as per a plot and survey made by Robert Brooke, Gent., 28 November 1742. Jonathan Sydenham shall build on the said lott one house of the dimensions of twenty foot square and nine foot pitched at least within two years (and place the same according to the rule and direction of the said Directors), otherwise the deed to be void and the lott to be revested in the sd. Trustees to be by them sold again by auction to the highest bidder. Signed T. Turner, Harry Turner. Delivered in presence of Danl. McCarty, Jos. Morton, W. Jordan. Recorded 4 November 1743 Harry Turner.

2:519 - DEED - 17 September 1743 - Thomas Turner and Harry Turner Gentlemen Directors and Trustees of Leeds Town in King George County to Joseph Morton of the Town of Leeds. 20 pounds 15 shillings current money of Virginia for two half acres or lotts in Leeds Town numbered 25 and 26 as per a plat and survey made by Robert Brooke 28 November 1742. Joseph Morton shall build on each of the said lotts one house of brick, stone, or wood well framed of the dimensions twenty foot square and nine foot pitched within two years (and place the same according to the rule and direction of the said Directors), otherwise this deed to be void and the lotts to be revested in the said Trustees to be by them sold again at auction to the highest bidder. Signed T. Turner, Harry Turner. Delivered in presence of Danl. McCarty, Jona. Sydenham, W. Jordan. Recorded 4 November 1743 Harry Turner.

2:529 - DEED - 17 September 1743 - Thomas Turner, Daniel McCarty, and Harry Turner Gentlemen Directors and Trustees for Leeds Town in King George County to Robert Vaulx, Gentleman, of the county of Westmoreland. 11 pounds 10 shillings current money of Virginia for one half acre or lott in Leeds Town numbered 14 as per a plott and survey made by Mr. Robert Brooke 28 November 1742. Robert Vaulx shall build on said lott one house within two years, otherwise this deed to be void and the lott to be revested in the said Trustees. Signed T. Turner, Danl. McCarty, Harry Turner. Delivered in presence of Richard Barnes, Jon. Sydenham, Richard Kelsick. Recorded 4 November 1743 Harry Turner.

2:521 - DEED OF LEASE - 3 November 1743 - Henry Head of St. George Parish in the county of Spotsylvania and Frances his wife to Benjamin Strother of Hanover Parish, Gent. 5 shillings sterling to lease 48A bounded by Gingoteague branch, corner to William and John Pitman, corner to orphans of

William Brown deceased, William Marshall, and John Easter. Said tract of land granted to Doctor Alexander Spence deceased father to the above mentioned Francis Head. Signed Henry Head, Frances Head. Delivered in presence of John Allen, Henry Berry, Junr., Joseph Dodd. Recorded 4 November 1743 Harry Turner.

2:523 - DEED OF RELEASE - 4 November 1743 - Henry Head of St. George Parish in the county of Spotsylvania and Francis his wife to Benjamin Strother of Hanover Parish. 24 pounds current money of Virginia for 48A described in lease. Signed Henry Head, Frances Head. Delivered in presence of John Allen, Henry Berry, Junr., Joseph Dodd. Recorded 4 November 1743 Harry Turner.

2:526 - BOND - 4 November 1743 - Henry Head of St. George Parish in the county of Spotsylvania, planter, bound unto Benjamin Strother of Hanover Parish in the sum of 100 pounds sterling. Condition such that if the bounden Henry Head shall truly keep Benjamin Strother forever in the quiet and peaceable possession and enjoyment of forty-eight acres mentioned in one Deed of Release bearing equal date with these presents and from any right, title, interest, property claim and demand of him the said Henry Head and Frances his wife, Robert Dearing and Elizabeth his wife, John Sorril and Sarah his wife, and William Hutcheson and Ruth his wife, obligation to be void. Signed Henry Head. Delivered in presence of John Allen, Henry Berry, Junr., Joseph Dodd. Recorded 4 November 1743 Harry Turner.

2:527 - DEED OF SALE - 27 May 1743 - William Owens of the county of King George sells unto James Jones his landlord sundry goods and chattles for 1211 and a half pounds of tobacco which he owes the sd. James Jones - one cow and calf, one steer of three years old, one old grey horse, two old feather beds and sheets, blankets, bolsters, bedcords and bedsteads belonging to them, three iron potts, four pewter dishes, two basons, ten pewter plates, one chest with several pieces of cloathing in it and seven head of hogs. Signed William Owens. Delivered in presence of James Cannon, Joshua Lampton, Jane Angeir. Recorded 4 November 1743 Harry Turner.

2:527 - DEED - 26 November 1743 - Maximilian Robinson and Harry Turner Gentlemen Directors and Trustees for Leeds Town in King George County to Thomas Turner of the same county. 32 pounds current money of Virginia for one half acre or lott in the said Town of Leeds numbered 23 as per a plott and survey made by Mr. Robert Brooke 28 November 1742. Thomas Turner shall build on the said lott one house within two years, otherwise this deed to be void and the lott to be revested in the sd. Trustees. Signed Max. Robinson, Harry Turner. Delivered in presence of Jos. Morton, Henry Drake, Nicho. Smith. Recorded 2 December 1743 Harry Turner.

2:528 - DEED - 26 November 1743 - Thomas Turner and Harry Turner Gentlemen Directors and Trustees for Leeds Town in King George County to Arthur Spicer, Gent., of same county. 20 pounds 10 shillings current money of Virginia for one half acre or lott in the said Town of Leeds numbered 32 as per a plott and survey made by Mr. Robert Brooke 28 November 1742. Arthur Spicer shall build on the said lott one house within two years, otherwise this deed to be void and the lott to be revested in the sd. Trustees. Signed T. Turner, Harry Turner. Delivered in presence of John Champe, Richard Bryan. Recorded 2 December 1743 Harry Turner.

2:529 - DEED - 26 November 1743 - Thomas Turner and Harry Turner Gentlemen Directors and Trustees for Leeds Town in King George County to William Brokenbrough, Gent., of the county of Richmond. 41 pounds current money of Virginia for one half acre or lott in Leeds Town numbered 33 as per a plott and survey made by Mr. Robert Brooke 28 November 1742. William Brokenbrough shall build on the said lott one house within two years, otherwise this deed to be void and the lott to be revested in the sd. Trustees. Signed T. Turner, Harry Turner. Delivered in presence of John Champe, Richard Bryan. Recorded 2 December 1743 Harry Turner.

2:530 - DEED OF LEASE - 4 January 1743 - Thomas Turner of the county of King George, Gentleman, to William Jordan of the county of Richmond, Gentleman. 5 shillings current money for one lott or half acre within the Town of Leeds numbered 23 together with all houses, outhouses, woods and underwoods, trees, waters, and water courses. Signed T. Turner. Delivered in presence of Nicho. Smith, Harry Turner, Josiah Farguson. Recorded 6 January 1743 Harry Turner.

2:531 - DEED OF RELEASE - 5 January 1743 - Thomas Turner of the county of King George, Gentleman, to William Jordan of the county of Richmond, Gentleman. 32 pounds current money of Virginia for one lott or half acre described in lease. Signed T. Turner. Delivered in presence of Nicho. Smith, Harry Turner, Josiah Farguson. Recorded 6 January 1743 Harry Turner.

2:533 - DEED OF LEASE - 3 February 1743 - James Jones of Hanover Parish to Peter Newgent of Brunswick Parish, planter, and Martha his wife. Yearly rent of 800 pounds good tobacco and cask to lease 100A bounded by Richard Ellkin, Matthews line, a branch down to the North Bridge, the Main Road, Poplar Swamp, and John Owens. Lease is for and during and unto the full end and term of the natural lives of Peter Newgent and Martha his wife. They are to plant 100 good winter apple trees and 100 peach trees in three years and keep them enclosed with a good fence and to pay the Quitrents of the said 100A. Signed James Jones. Delivered in presence of Josa. Lampton, John Henshaw, Lewis

Markham. Recorded 3 February 1743 Harry Turner.

2:535 - DEED OF SALE - 13 December 1743 - Thomas Thatcher of the county of King George, planter, to Thomas Vivion of same, Gentleman. 45 pounds 11 shillings current money for 100A. Whereas William Underwood, grandfather of the said Thomas, by his last Will and Testament dated 19 July 1717 and proved in the Richmond County Court 7 August 1717 devised unto his grandsons John and William Thatcher 200A of land, equally divided between them, lying between the land of William Triplett and Mary Tutt, and the sd. John Thatcher after the death of the sd. William Underwood departed this life before he attained lawful age and without issue, thereupon the sd. William sold the sd. land devised to him and the sd. John unto the said Thomas Vivion. But the sd. Thomas Thatcher, being Elder brother of the sd. John and William, brought his Ejectment against the sd. Thomas Vivion and by the judgment of the County Court of King George 5 November 1742 recovered the land aforesd. Signed Thomas Thatcher. Delivered in presence of John Wharton, Bourn Price, Thomas Plaile. Recorded 6 January 1743 Harry Turner.

2:537 - POWER OF ATTORNEY - 20 October 1743 - Lyonel Lyde of the City of Bristol, Esqr., and William Williams of the parish of St. Philip and Jacob in the county of Gloucester, Gentlemen, have each of them appointed John Tayloe the Younger, merchant, their true and lawfull attorney to make, execute and deliver to any person or persons such conveyance, bargain and sale of the Fee Simple and Inheritance of any Lands, Tenements, and Hereditaments to them the said Lyonel Lyde and William Williams and also to John Tayloe the Elder, Esqr., belonging as shall be thought necessary and requisite to be done and performed and to do or cause to be done any other matter or thing in and about the Sale and Disposal of such Lands, Tenements, and Hereditaments. Signed Lyonel Lyde, William Williams. Delivered in presence of Henry Churchman, Matthew Davis. Recorded 3 February 1743 Harry Turner.

2:538 - DEED OF GIFT - 30 December 1743 - Margaret Harper of the county of King George for divers causes and considerations, but more especially for the natural affection she bears to her grand daughter Mary Jean Als. Harper, gives grants and devises unto her one Negro boy called Jemmy, a young black horse branded with M with her new woman's saddle and bridle, a good feather bed and bolster with two pair cotton sheets, one pr. blankets and one rug all to be good, two new pewter dishes and half a dozn. Pewter plates unused, which said articles she hereby gives to have and to hold to her the sd. Mary Harper Als. Jean and to her Heirs for ever. Signed Margt. Harper. Delivered in presence of Cha. Ewell, Joshua Farguson, Samuel Reeds. Recorded 6 January 1743 Harry Turner.

2:538 - DEED OF LEASE - 2 February 1743 - William Flowers of Hanover Parish, planter, to James Hewett of same, planter. 5 shillings sterling to lease 150A whereon the same William Flowers doth now, or lately did live. The greatest part lying in Brunswick Parish, a small part extending into Overwharton Parish in Stafford County. Signed William Flowers. Delivered in presence of Richard Bryan, John Moore, Frans. Thornton. Recorded 3 February 1743 Harry Turner.

2:540 - DEED OF RELEASE - 3 February 1743 - William Flowers of Hanover Parish, planter, and Mary his wife to James Hewett of same, planter. 130 pounds current money of Virginia for 250A described in lease. 100A sold to the said William Flowers by John Jones the younger deceasesd by deeds dated 6 and 7 June 1728. Said one hundred acres bounded by line that was formerly line of Simon Thomas, land that formerly belonged to William Elzey, land bought by Thomas Elzey deceased of John Waugh Clerk deceased, and the dividing line of two hundred acres devised by the aforesd. Thomas Elzey to his son Thomas Elzey. 150A is part of two hundred and fifty acres sold by Thomas Barby of Stafford County, planter, to the said William Flowers by deed dated 14 October 1730 and adjoins the above mentioned one hundred acres. Bounded by line dividing this from two hundred more acres sold by John Waugh Clerk to one David Evans. One hundred acres of this two hundred and fifty acre tract was sold by the said William Flowers to William Simpson. Signed William Flowers, Mary Flowers. Delivered in presence of Richard Bryan, John Moore, Fras. Thornton. Recorded 3 February 1743 Harry Turner.

2:544 - BOND - 24 January 1743 - James Grant and Catharine Grant of Brunswick Parish bound unto James Hewett of same in the sum of 100 pounds current money of Virginia. Condition such that whereas the sd. Catharine wife to the sd. Grant and relict to John Jones deceased has some pretensions of right to a certain tract of land for life given by the sd. Jones' will to his son John Jones by him sold to William Flowers and by the sd. Flowers sold to the sd. James Hewett and whereas the sd. Grant and Catharine his wife being unwilling to engage themselves in a doubtful lawsuit do therefore for and in consideration of the sum of twenty shillings current money to the sd. Catharine paid by the sd. Hewett do oblige themselves to make the sd. Hewett a good and valued title as by council learned in the law shall be thought requisite at anytime that the sd. Hewett shall require, then this obligation to be void. Signed James Grant, Catharine Grant. Delivered in presence of Nicholass Strother, James Jones, James Strother, Anth. Haynie. Memorandum - The subscribers testify that they heard Catharine Grant mother to John Jones that sold his land to William Flowers say that her son was twenty-one years old and upwards near twenty-two years of age at the time of sale to William Flowers. Signed Nicho. Strother, James Strother, Antho. Haynie. Recorded 4 January 1744 Harry Turner.

INDEX

DISKINS, John, 52; Mr., 32
DISMAN, John, 125
DIXON, Edward, 193, 228
DOAKINS, William, 162
DODD, Ann, 162, 169; Benjamin, 169, 189; John, 38, 86, 93, 162, 169, 177, 190; Joseph, 86, 141, 231
DODGIN, William, 189, 190
DOGENS, Ann, 213; John, 213; Mildred, 213
DOGGIN, John, 213
DONALDSON, James, 221; Samuel, 193
DONAPHAN, Mott, 108; Robert, 108
DONDALL, Thomas, 123
DONIPHAN, Alexander, 12, 20, 94, 166; Mary, 26, 110, 111; Mot, 12; Mott, 94, 117; Robert, 12, 13, 15, 25, 26, 43, 51, 52, 77, 78, 94, 110, 111, 117, 132, 160
DONIPHON, Ellinor, 20; Robert, 19, 20
DONOHO, Edmond, 190
DONOLY, Mary, 76
DORELL, Sampson, 41
DORIEN, Libert, 220
DOUGINS, John, 38
DOUGLASS, Archibald, 188
DOWLING, William, 152, 197
DOWNING, Ann, 62; George, 27, 28, 62; Joseph, 62
DOWNMAN, Travors, 16
DOWNTON, Lawrence, 132, 189, 190; Nicholas, 38, 133, 189
DOYLE, John, 125, 126, 130, 136, 180
DRAKE, Clapham, 190; Henry, 188, 190, 216, 231; James, 157, 188; John, 105, 162, 174, 177, 187
DUCHINNIA, Samuel, 98
DUDLEY, Samuel, 71, 195

DUE, Thomas, 215
DUFF, William, 34, 35, 43, 44, 112, 126, 127, 143, 152, 162, 174, 180, 182, 189, 193, 197, 200, 203
DULING, Elizabeth, 156; William, 156, 176
DUNCAN, Robert, 53, 150; Thomas, 52, 53
DUNCANS, James, 85
DUNCOM, Ann, 159, 163, 164; Robert, 159, 160, 163, 164
DUNCOMB, Robert, 177
DUNFEE, Eleanor, 21
DUNKIN, John, 106
DUNNAHOO, Edward, 151
DUNNOHO, Edmund, 10
DYKE, Samuel, 8, 214

-E-

EADY, John, 143
EAGLESTON, John, 2
EARLE, Samuel, 214
EARLES, Sam, 209; Samuel, 105, 209
EASTER, John, 231
EASTHER, Giles, 141
EDDERINGTON, Christopher, 183
EDERINGTON, Christopher, 178
EDGAR, William, 103
EDGE, John, 143; Sarah, 143
EDMONDS, Ann, 171, 227; Anne, 1; Cor., 7; Cornelius, 1, 2, 25
EDRINGTON, Christopher, 149; Mary, 200, 203; William, 149; Xtroph., 63; Xtropher., 64
EDWARDS, John, 176, 179, 190, 191, 200, 207; William, 149, 198, 203, 219
EDY, John, 52, 96, 133
ELIZABETH MC CARTY, Anthony, 158; Boatswain, 158; Daniel, 158; David, 158; Ester, 158; George, 158; Guiniver, 158; Lewis, 158;